BOOKS

Business Statistics

FIFTH EDITION

Douglas Downing, Ph.D.
School of Business and Economics
Seattle Pacific University

Jeffrey Clark, Ph.D.
Mathematics Department
Elon University

BARRON'S

All inquiries should be addressed to:
Barron's Educational Series, Inc.
250 Wireless Boulevard
Hauppauge, NY 11788
www.barronseduc.com

Library of Congress Catalog Card No. 2009035939

ISBN-13: 978-0-7641-4239-0
ISBN-10: 0-7641-4239-9

Library of Congress Cataloging-in-Publication Data
Downing, Douglas.
    Business statistics / Douglas Downing, Jeffrey Clark.
    —5th ed.
        p.   cm.—(Business review books)
    ISBN-13: 978-0-7641-4239-0
    ISBN-10: 0-7641-4239-9
    1. Commercial statistics.   2. Statistics.   I. Clark, Jeff,
    1961–   II. Title.
    HF1017.D65   2010
    519.5—dc22   2009035939

CONTENTS

PREFACE

In this book you will learn how to apply statistical methods for analyzing data. Chapter 1 lists some of the ways in which statistical methods serve as valuable tools for business decision makers. We will cover many statistical techniques with examples of calculations and interpretations.

It takes practice to learn statistics. Each chapter starts with a list of key terms, with definitions, that you will learn in that chapter. The book contains discussion questions and exercises at the ends of the chapters. The discussion questions cause you to think about the concepts you have just learned, and they expand your understanding of the applications of those concepts. The exercises give you practice in performing statistical calculations. The answers for the discussion questions and the exercises are also included at the ends of the chapters; complete solutions for the computational problems are included where appropriate. In some other cases all formulas necessary to work the problems are given. Where there are several problems of the same type, complete or sample calculations are shown for the first problem.

Several Greek letters and other symbols are used frequently in statistics. You may check the List of Symbols section to become familiar with these. You can learn the meanings of the new terms introduced in this book and set in boldface type by checking the Glossary in Appendix 1.

You will quickly realize that you will need to use a computer to perform your calculations. If you will be regularly working with statistics, you should obtain and learn to work a computer statistics program. Appendix 2 discusses some of the essential features of calculations, computer statistics programs, and the spreadsheet Microsoft Excel.

Appendix 3 contains frequently used statistical tables for the normal, chi-square, t, and F distributions.

While doing statistical calculations, be sure you are aware of the effect of rounding. For example, even a simple fraction such as 1/3 cannot be expressed exactly as a decimal fraction with a finite number of digits. Therefore, we will frequently use decimal approximations to the quantities that we calculate in this book. So, for example, if you see an expression such as "1/3 = .333," be warned that this is a short form of the complete statement which would be ".333 is a decimal approximation of the fraction 1/3, rounded to three decimal places." In this case, the first nonincluded digit is less than .5, so we simply drop it. However, if the first nonincluded digit is greater than or equal to .5, then we need to increase the previous digit by 1. For example, 2/3 rounded to three decimal places is .667.

In the fifth edition, we have added many new questions and examples.

You may find more information on the book's web page at *myhome.spu. edu/ddowning/bstat.html.*

The web page includes links to data sources, and it also includes practice exercises. In the later chapters of the book, the practice exercises require extensive use of the computer. We have spared you the need to type the data into your computer by making the practice data available on the web page. You can copy the data off the Web, paste it into your spreadsheet, and then work on the calculations. Portions of this book have been published in our other book, *E-Z Statistics*, which contains a more complete treatment of the mathematical development of statistics.

Douglas Downing
Jeffrey Clark

LIST OF SYMBOLS AND ABBREVIATIONS

POPULATIONS AND SAMPLES

Σ (capital sigma) summation

for example: ΣX_i or $\sum_{i=1}^{n} X_i$

N number of items in a population

n number of items in a sample

i, j used as subscripts

for example: X_i or X_{ij}

μ (mu) population mean

$\bar{x}$ sample average (in general, a bar over a quantity signifies average)

σ (lower case sigma) population standard deviation

σ^2 population variance

$$\sigma^2 = \frac{\sum_{i=1}^{n}(X_i - \bar{x})^2}{n}$$

s^2 sample variance, version 2

$$s^2 = \frac{\sum_{i=1}^{n}(X_i - \bar{x})^2}{n-1}$$

f_i (frequency); number of items in category i

PROBABILITY

$\Pr(A)$ probability that event A will occur

$\Pr(A \mid B)$ conditional probability that event A will occur, given that event B has occurred

$N(A)$ number of outcomes in event A

s	total number of possible outcomes
A^c	A complement; consists of all outcomes that are not in event A
$!$	factorial
	for example: $6! = 6 \times 5 \times 4 \times 3 \times 2 \times 1 = 720$
$\binom{n}{j}$	number of combinations of n things taken j at a time;

$$\binom{n}{j} = \frac{n!}{j!(n-j)!}$$

$_nC_j$	same as $\binom{n}{j}$
$_nP_j$	number of permutations of n things taken j at a time;

$$_nP_j = \frac{n!}{(n-j)!}$$

RANDOM VARIABLES

capital letters, such as X, Y, and Z, are used to represent random variables

$f(a)$	probability function for a random variable; for discrete random variables $f(a) = \Pr(X = a)$
$F(a)$	cumulative distribution function for a random variable; $F(a) = \Pr(X \leq a)$
$E(X)$	expectation (expected value) of X
μ	mean (same as expectation)
$\mathrm{Var}(X)$	variance of X
σ^2	variance
$\mathrm{Cov}(X, Y)$	covariance of X and Y
λ	(lambda) used as parameter for Poisson distribution
n	number of trials for binomial distribution
p	probability of success for binomial distribution
Z	represents standard normal random variable (mean 0, variance 1)
$\Phi(z)$	cumulative distribution function for standard normal random variable; $\Phi(z) = \Pr(Z < z)$
χ^2	chi-square distribution
t	t distribution
F	F distribution

STATISTICAL ESTIMATION

a hat over a symbol indicates that this quantity is being used as an estimator for an unknown population parameter
for example: $\hat{b}$

ANALYSIS OF VARIANCE AND REGRESSION

a	vertical intercept of simple regression line
b	slope of simple regression line
$b_1, \ldots, b_{m-1}$	estimated multiple regression coefficients
b_m	estimated multiple regression constant term
$B_1, \ldots, B_{m-1}$	true multiple regression coefficients
B_m	true multiple regression constant term
COLSS	column sum of squares
e	base of the natural logarithm function
e	elasticity
e	error term in regression model
ERSS	error sum of squares
MSE	mean square error
r	correlation coefficient
r^2	coefficient of determination for simple linear regression
R^2	coefficient of multiple determination
RGRSS	regression sum of squares
ROWSS	row sum of squares
$s(b_i)$	standard error of coefficient b_i
SE_{line}	squared error about the line
SE_{av}	squared error about the average
TSS	total sum of squares
TRSS	treatment sum of squares
x	independent variable(s) in regression
y	dependent variable in regression

BUSINESS DATA

BLS	Bureau of Labor Statistics
CPI	consumer price index

GDP   gross domestic product
NNP   net national product

MATHEMATICAL SYMBOLS

{ }	braces; indicate set membership
∪	union
∩	intersection
∅	empty set
π	3.14159 . . .
e	2.71828 . . .
log	logarithm; if $a^n = x$ then $\log_a x = n$
| |	absolute value
$\sqrt{}$	square root
>	greater than
≥	greater than or equal
<	less than
≤	less than or equal

HYPOTHESIS TESTING

H_o	null hypothesis
H_a	alternative hypothesis
Type I error	rejecting the null hypothesis when it is really true
Type II error	accepting the null hypothesis when it is really false
α	probability of Type I error
β	probability of Type II error

1

WHY STATISTICS?

USING STATISTICAL TECHNIQUES IN BUSINESS

Why, you may be wondering, should a business manager study statistics? In this book you will learn many powerful statistical techniques. You will learn how to extract meaningful information from piles of raw data, how to make inferences about the nature of a population based on observations of a sample taken from that population, how to predict the rates of occurrences of random events, and how to understand and interpret statistical calculations performed by others.

There are times when statistics seem to take on an almost magical quality. How can pollsters make reasonably accurate predictions of the presidential vote when they ask only a sample of a few thousand voters out of the total voting population of 130 million? How can television rating services estimate the total audience for a show based on a small sample of selected households? In this book we will learn why these methods work.

Many people think of statistics as a boring and difficult subject. Admittedly some parts of statistics are quite difficult, but there are other parts that are concise and elegant. Part of the reason why statistics has a reputation for difficulty dates from the time prior to computers when statisticians were forced to perform laborious calculations by hand. Now it is possible to have a computer do most of the tedious work, leaving you much freer to understand the meaning of what is going on. Early in your statistics career you should learn how to use a computer spreadsheet or statistics package or a calculator with built-in statistics operations.

Even though you'll use the computer to do calculations, be sure you know how to do the calculations yourself. Don't think of the computer as a magic box performing unfathomably mysterious feats.

TWO MEANINGS OF THE WORD *STATISTICS*

The word **statistics** has two different (but related) meanings. In the most common usage, *statistics* means "a collection of numerical data." For example, you may look at the statistics that summarize the performance of a football team's season, the statistics that list the number of births and deaths in a city, or the statistics that describe the characteristics of a new building. There are also important national business statistics that you should become aware of, such as the gross domestic product (GDP) and the consumer price index (CPI).

The word *statistics* also refers to the branch of mathematics that deals with the analysis of statistical data. In Chapter 2 we will study **descriptive statistics**, which is the process of obtaining meaningful information from sets of numbers that are often too large to deal with directly. You are undoubtedly already familiar with some aspects of descriptive statistics, such as how to calculate the average of a set of numbers. In most of the rest of the book we will be studying **inferential statistics**, which is the process of using observations from a sample to estimate the properties of a larger population.

YOU SHOULD REMEMBER

1. Powerful statistical techniques, with calculators and appropriate computer programs assisting with the calculations, are valuable tools in business.

2. The word *statistics* has two meanings: (1) a body of numerical data, and (2) a branch of mathematics, encompassing descriptive statistics and inferential statistics, which deals with the analysis of statistical data.

POPULATIONS AND SAMPLES

The term **population** refers to all of the people or things in the group you are interested in. A **sample** is a group of items chosen from the population. Examples include the following:

- population: the 31 flavors of ice cream at a 31-flavor ice cream store
  sample: the five flavors that you have tested in order to determine whether this store sells good ice cream

- population: all voters in the United States
  sample: the 3,000 people who are interviewed as part of an opinion poll

- population: all people in the United States with television sets
  sample: the people who are surveyed by the Nielson television rating service

- population: all people in the United States
  sample: the people from 50,000 households interviewed in the Census Bureau's monthly Current Population Survey

You may wonder why you should study samples instead of populations. If you happen to choose a sample that is very unrepresentative of the corresponding population, you will make very inaccurate predictions when you try to estimate the characteristics of the population based on that sample. You could avoid that danger by studying the entire population instead. However, there are several reasons why samples are studied instead of populations. The most important reason is the excessive cost and/or difficulty of studying the entire population. Any business decision maker is faced with the problem of limited resources. It would not be a wise use of resources to undertake the expense of studying the entire population if predictions based on a sample are almost as accurate. (The key question you are probably asking is, How do we know that a sample is likely to represent the population accurately? That will be one of the most important questions that we will answer in this book.) The U.S. government is subject to the same types of limitations. It would be very costly for the government to calculate the monthly unemployment index by actually counting the total number of unemployed people. Instead, the unemployment figure is calculated from the Current Population Survey, which is a monthly sample. There are times, though, when the entire population is investigated. Every four years the presidential preferences of the complete voting population are checked in an election, and every 10 years a census of the total population is conducted.

There are other reasons why samples are studied instead of populations. In some cases the process of investigating an item destroys it. For example, suppose you are trying to measure the amount of stress that a particular type of post can withstand before it breaks. Obviously you cannot investigate the entire population of posts because then you would have no unbroken posts left. There are also times when you cannot obtain access to the entire population. Sometimes it can be more accurate to deal with data from a sample rather than from a population. For example, if you are conducting a survey that requires the use of trained interviewers, you have a much better chance of obtaining accurate results if you need only to train enough interviewers to conduct a few thousand interviews instead of a few million.

YOU SHOULD REMEMBER

1. Because it is expensive, difficult, and sometimes impractical to survey an entire population, a sample is usually selected for study.

2. To avoid inaccurate predictions, it is essential that the sample be representative of the population from which it is chosen.

APPLYING STATISTICS IN BUSINESS

Here are some examples of business applications of statistics:

- A firm preparing to introduce a new product needs to estimate the preferences of the consumers in the relevant market. It can often do this by conducting a marketing survey based on interviews with some randomly selected households. The results of the survey can then be used to estimate the preferences of the entire population.

- Statistical techniques are needed to disentangle the separate effects of several different factors. For example, the demand for ice cream in a community can be expected to depend on the price of ice cream, the level of average income, the number of children in the community, and the average temperature. If you have observations of all the different factors involved, you can use regression analysis to determine which factors have the most important effects.

- An auditor has the job of checking the books of a company to make sure that they accurately reflect the financial condition of the company. The auditor will need to check through piles of original documents such as sales slips, purchase orders, and requisitions. It would require massive amounts of work to check every single original document; instead, the auditor can check a randomly selected sample of documents and make inferences about the entire population of documents based on that sample.

- Before a new drug is marketed, it is necessary to perform extensive experiments to make sure the drug is safe and effective. Some people need to be given the drug to test it, but you won't know if the drug makes a difference unless you have another group so you can compare. The best way to test a drug is to take two groups that are as much alike as possible, give the drug to one of the groups but not to the other, and then see whether the results for the two groups are different. The group that is given the drug is called the experimental group (or treatment group), and the other group is called the control group. Statistical analysis is necessary to determine whether any observed differences really were caused by the drug or could have been caused by other factors.

- If you are receiving a large shipment of goods from a supplier, you will want to make sure that the goods meet the quality standards agreed upon. It would be very expensive to perform a quality control check on every single item, but once again statistical techniques come to the rescue by allowing you to make inferences about the quality of the entire lot by checking a randomly selected sample of items chosen from the lot.

- Financial investments involve risk. Statistical analysis allows you to estimate the risk and expected return from an investment portfolio, and how changing the composition of a portfolio can affect the risk and return.

- Insurance actuaries need to study statistics to estimate the probabilities of various events and to analyze the risk for the insurance company.

- Advertising rates for television and radio stations are based on ratings, which are determined by statistical samples.

- When analyzing natural phenomena, such as weather or wildlife populations, you usually have to work with a sample because it is impractical to observe the entire population.

RELATIONSHIP BETWEEN PROBABILITY AND STATISTICS

In order to understand statistical inference it is necessary to understand several concepts in **probability**. Probability and statistics are very closely related because they ask opposite types of questions. In probability, we know how a process works and we want to predict what the outcomes of that process will be. In statistics, we don't know how a process works but we can observe the outcomes of the process. We want to use the information about the outcomes to learn about the nature of the process.

We will develop the ideas of probability by concentrating on familiar random processes: flipping a coin, tossing dice, and drawing cards from well-shuffled decks. Learning how the principles of probability apply to situations where you know how the process works will help you to understand how statistical inference can be used to learn about the nature of an unknown process. For example, suppose you have 40 blue marbles and 60 red marbles in a jar and you draw 10 randomly selected marbles out of the jar. By using probability theory you can calculate the probability that exactly 6 of the 10 selected marbles will be red. Now suppose that before an election you ask 1,000 randomly selected people the name of their favorite presidential candidate. You cannot calculate the probability that 60 percent of the people in the sample will agree with your preference because you don't know the presidential preferences of all the people in the population. However, by using statistical inference you can estimate the presidential preferences of the population based on the presidential preferences of the people in your sample.

Two types of problems might make the sample unrepresentative. First, there might be a systematic error or bias. For example, if you conduct your survey on the Internet, then you will systematically be more likely to include people that use the Internet rather than people who don't. Since those people may have different views than the population at large, your sample may be unrepresentative. However, if your sample is chosen by a process that is truly random, so that each member of the population is equally likely to be included in the sample, then you are guaranteed that your sample contains no systematic bias. Even with a random sample, though, the possibility exists that your sample may be unrepresentative because you had bad luck with your sample selection. If your sample is large enough, this probability is relatively small. By studying probability in this book, we will be able to develop a precise formula indicating how likely it is that your random sample will be representative of the population.

These examples are only a small sample drawn from the total population of ways that statistical tools can be useful in business.

YOU SHOULD REMEMBER

1. Examples of business applications of statistical techniques include the use of samples to estimate the preferences or infer the quality of an entire population, and the use of regression analysis to distinguish the separate effects of several factors.

2. Knowledge of probability concepts helps us to predict the outcome of a process.

KNOW THE CONCEPTS

DO YOU KNOW THE BASICS?

Test your understanding of Chapter 1 by answering the following questions:

1. Why do statisticians investigate samples instead of populations?
2. How can you tell whether a particular sample will accurately represent the population?

For questions 3–7, imagine that you are conducting a medical experiment for which you will divide your subjects into two groups: an experimental group and a control group.

3. Why should you try to have the groups as much alike as possible?
4. Should the people know which group they are in?
5. What is the best system for assigning people to the two groups?
6. Why shouldn't you test only the treatment group, and not have a control group?
7. Is it ethical to withhold the medicine from the control group?
8. One hundred customers at a shopping mall are interviewed to determine whether they would purchase a television at a given price. Is the group of 100 customers a sample or a population?
9. A factory ships 500 coffee tables per week, and ten are inspected each week for quality control. Is the set of 500 tables a sample or a population?
10. The salaries at a given company are summarized in a chart. Is the collection of salaries for the company a sample or a population?
11. Why should a sample be selected randomly?
12. What is the best way to reduce the chance that bad luck will make your sample unrepresentative?

TERMS FOR STUDY

control group	probability
descriptive statistics	sample
experimental group	statistics
inferential statistics	treatment group
population	

ANSWERS

KNOW THE CONCEPTS

1. The main reason for using samples is that it would be too expensive to survey entire populations.
2. There is no way to know *for sure* whether the sample accurately represents the population unless you conduct a census of the entire population. However, the methods of inferential statistics can be used to estimate the likelihood that the sample is representative of the population.
3. Suppose the two groups are very different to start with. Then, if you observe different experimental results for the two groups, you cannot be sure that these differences are due to the treatment you are investigating.

4. No. People may react differently if they know which group they are in.

5. Ideally the people should be divided into the two groups completely at random.

6. If you only observe the treatment group, you cannot tell if the medicine actually made a difference.

7. You could argue that it would be unethical if you knew the medicine worked, but the reason you are conducting the test is because you're not yet sure that the medicine does work.

8. The group of 100 customers is a subset of all potential customers for the television, and is a sample.

9. The set of 500 tables consists of all the tables being produced and not just the ones being inspected. It is a population.

10. The collection of salaries represents the entire company and forms a population.

11. Random selection ensures that there is no systematic problem (bias) with the sample.

12. Choose a larger sample. However, you have to compare the benefit of the larger sample with its cost.

2
DESCRIPTIVE STATISTICS

KEY TERMS

frequency histogram a bar diagram that illustrates how many observations fall within each category

interquartile range when data are sorted and split into four lists, the interquartile range is the range of the middle two fourths (same as **IQR**)

mean the value that is equal to the sum of a list of numbers divided by the number of numbers (same as **average**); written as μ for a population and $\bar{x}$ for a sample

median if a list of numbers has an odd number of items, then the median is the middle number (when the list is arranged in order); if the list has an even number of items, then the median is the average of the two numbers closest to the middle

mode the value or values that occur most frequently in a list of numbers

range the difference between the largest and the smallest numbers in a list

standard deviation the square root of the variance; written as σ for a population and s for a sample

variance a measure of dispersion for a list of numbers; written as σ^2 for a population and s^2 for a sample

MEASURES OF CENTRAL TENDENCY: MEAN, MEDIAN, AND MODE

If you've just been given a large pile of numbers, you have little or no hope of understanding them unless you can figure out some way to summarize them. For example, suppose you are managing a pizza parlor and you are keeping track of your daily sales figures for several different types of pizza.

Suppose you have observed the following values for daily sales of pepperoni pizzas during a 9-day period:

$$40, 56, 38, 38, 63, 59, 51, 50, 46$$

• MEAN

A list of numbers like this is called **raw data**. One useful thing to do would be to calculate the **average** of all of the numbers. To calculate the average we just add up all the numbers and divide by the number of numbers. The average is also called the **mean**. The average in the pepperoni example can be calculated like this:

$$\frac{40 + 56 + 38 + 38 + 63 + 59 + 51 + 50 + 46}{9} = \frac{441}{9}$$
$$= 49.0$$

Therefore, on average, you have sold 49 pepperoni pizzas per day.

We can derive a general formula for the average. Suppose we have n numbers. We'll call them $x_1, x_2, x_3, \ldots, x_n$. The little numbers next to and slightly below the x's are called **subscripts**. We'll use the symbol $\bar{x}$ (x with a bar written over it) to stand for the sample average. Then we can write this formula:

$$\bar{x} = \frac{x_1 + x_2 + x_3 + \cdots + x_n}{n}$$

(The population average is written as μ.)

The average is an example of a **statistic**. A statistic is a single number that is used to summarize the properties of a larger group of numbers. We will talk about some other important statistics later.

We can save some writing by using **summation notation**. In summation notation we use the Greek capital letter sigma: Σ. The expression Σx means "add up all the values of x." The average can be written as $\bar{x} = (\Sigma x)/n$. Sometimes the summation symbol is written like this:

$$\sum_{i=1}^{n} x_i$$

to indicate that we start with $i = 1$ and keep going until $i = n$.

• MEDIAN

Another useful statistic is the **median**. The median is the halfway point of the data, that is, half of the numbers are above it and half are below. To compute the median, we must put the list of numbers in order. Here, in descending order, is the list for our pepperoni pizza example:

1. 63	6. 46
2. 59	7. 40
3. 56	8. 38
4. 51	9. 38
5. 50	

For this list the median value is 50. Four values are greater than 50, and four values are below 50. (If you have a long list, it helps to have a computer put the numbers in order. Note that you also could put the list in ascending order.)

When there is an odd number of items in the list, it is easy to find the single number that is exactly in the middle. What if we have a list with an even number of items? Suppose we have the following eight observations for daily mushroom pizza sales:

1. 53	5. 47
2. 52	6. 46
3. 49	7. 44
4. 48	8. 41

We have already placed the values in order, but this time we cannot find a single number that is exactly in the middle. Instead, the median is equal to the number halfway between the two numbers closest to the middle. In this case the two numbers closest to the middle are 47 and 48 (the fourth and fifth values), so the median is halfway between 47 and 48, or 47.5. You may also think of the median as being equal to the average of the two middle numbers: $47.5 = (47 + 48)/2$.

Like the average, the median is a measure of what is called the **central tendency** of the distribution. In other words, the mean or median often gives you a good idea about the size of the number you are likely to get if you select one value from the list at random. There are times when the median gives a better measure of the central tendency of a list than does the mean. For example, suppose that these figures represent sales of bacon/pineapple pizza for a 9 day period:

$$36, 35, 37, 29, 39, 36, 340, 35, 36$$

Note that one day a large busload of bacon/pineapple pizza lovers arrived at your pizza place, so bacon/pineapple pizza sales were much larger than usual that day. If we calculate the average for this list we get:

$$\frac{623}{9} = 69.22$$

However, we can see that none of the actual values is very close to 69.22. We can put the list in order:

1. 340	6. 36
2. 39	7. 35
3. 37	8. 35
4. 36	9. 29
5. 36	

and then determine that the median is 36. We can see that in this case the value of the median gives us a much better idea of what our sales are actually likely to be on a given day. The median can be very helpful when working with sets of numbers that have a few large values. For example, if you are in a room with 30 other people and Bill Gates walks in, the average wealth of the people in the room increases by millions of dollars. This is misleading since you and the others that were in the room to start with haven't become any richer. On the other hand, your median income will not change or change only a little if one more person walks in, however wealthy (s)he may be, since the median depends only on the middle value of the incomes.

In general, when a list contains one extreme value (either far above or far below the other numbers in the list), the average will not be very representative of most of the numbers in the list. In that case the median is a better measure of the central tendency. However, the average is often easier to calculate, so it is more often used. When a distribution of numbers is reasonably symmetric without an extremely high or low value, then the values of the median and the mean will usually be close together.

• *MODE*

Another interesting statistic is the **mode**. The mode is the value that occurs most frequently. If there is more than one value that occurs the greatest number of times, all such values are called *modes*. For the pepperoni sales the value of the mode is 38, because the number 38 occurs twice in the list while none of the other numbers occurs more than once. For the bacon/pineapple sales the mode is 36, which occurs three times. There is no mode for the mushroom pizza sales since no values occur more than once. Many distributions that arise in practice are reasonably symmetric with most of the values concentrated near the middle, in which case the mean, median, and mode are all close together. However, a distribution can have more than one mode. A distribution with two modes is called a **bimodal** distribution.

YOU SHOULD REMEMBER

1. Summation notation: the Greek capital letter sigma, Σ, means "add up the values."

example: $\displaystyle\sum_{i=1}^{n} x_i = x_1 + x_2 + \cdots + x_n$

2. Measures of central tendency:

mean (average) $= \bar{x} = \dfrac{x_1 + x_2 + \cdots + x_n}{n} = \displaystyle\sum_{i=1}^{n} \dfrac{x_i}{n}$

median: when a list is arranged in order, the value such that as many numbers in the list are above it as below it

mode: the value in a list that occurs most frequently

MEASURES OF DISPERSION: VARIANCE AND STANDARD DEVIATION

It would be very helpful if we had a way of measuring the unpredictability of the daily sales figures. We will use the term **dispersion** or **spread** to refer to the degree to which a group of numbers are scattered away from their average. If you sold a total of exactly 200 pizzas every single day, there would be no spread to the figures. On the other hand, if you sold 400 pizzas half the time and zero pizzas the other half the time, the average would still be the same but the degree of dispersion would be much greater. One way to measure the dispersion is simply to take the difference between the highest value and the lowest value. This quantity is called the **range**. For pepperoni sales the range is $63 - 38 = 25$, and for bacon/pineapple sales the range is $340 - 29 = 311$. The range gives you an idea of the spread between the highest value and the lowest value, but it is not really a very good measure of the spread of the entire distribution. The range does not convey any information about any item in the list except the highest and lowest values. Here are two lists that have the same range:

List a	List b
500	500
250	490
250	480
250	20
250	10
0	0

but it is clear that the overall spread of list b is much greater than the spread of list a.

One problem with the range is that it will be greatly affected by the presence of very large or very small values. One way to solve that problem is to ignore the bottom and top quarters of the data and calculate the range of the remaining values. This quantity is called the **interquartile range** (or IQR). To calculate the IQR:

1. Put the list in order:

2. Find the value such that 3/4 of the other values are at or below it. (This value is called the *third quartile* or *75th percentile*.)

3. Find the value such that 1/4 of the other values are below it. (This value is called the *first quartile* or *25th percentile*.)
4. Take the difference between these two values.

One of the really nice things about IQR is that it doesn't change much if you add a really large or really small value to your data set. It pays attention only to the middle 2/4 of the data.

YOU SHOULD REMEMBER

1. The distribution of the numbers in a list can be characterized by calculating **quartiles** and **percentiles**:

   quartiles: The first quartile is the number in the list such that one-fourth of the items in the list are below it; the third quartile is the number in the list such that three-fourths of the items in the list are below it.

   percentiles: The pth percentile in a list is the number such that p percent of the numbers are below it.

2. range: the largest value minus the smallest value

   interquartile range: the value of the third quartile (75th percentile) minus the value of the first quartile (25th percentile)

We still need a measure of dispersion that takes into account all of the numbers in the list. Consider the pepperoni sales figures, which have a mean of 49. One way to measure how spread out the sales figures are is to see if the numbers cluster around 49 or are far away from it.

We will define the **deviation** to be how far away the measurement is from the mean. (We will compute that by subtracting the mean from each measurement.) If they are all close to the mean, then the sales figures are all close

Pepperoni Sales	Mean	Deviation
40	49	−9
56	49	7
38	49	−11
38	49	−11
63	49	14
59	49	10
51	49	2
50	49	1
46	49	−3

to each other; on the other hand, if many are far away from the mean, then they are far away from each other as well.

You can tell when a sales figure is above the mean, as with 56; the deviation (7) is positive. When the sales figure is below the mean, as with 38, the deviation (−11) is negative. When the sales figure is exactly at the mean, as with 49, the deviation is 0.

Now that we have the deviations, we want to combine them in some way to have a single number that measures the dispersion.

We could try averaging the deviations, but if you try that, the average is 0. This isn't just a coincidence; with a little bit of algebra you can show that the average of the deviations will always be 0. A measurement that is always 0 isn't very helpful.

A different approach turns out to have many nice properties. Instead of averaging the deviations themselves, we will average the squares of the deviations. (Remember that the square of a number is that number multiplied by itself.) Squares can never be negative, so we will never have any cancellation between positive and negative numbers when taking the average.

Pepperoni Sales	Mean	Deviation	Squared Deviation
40	49	−9	81
56	49	7	49
38	49	−11	121
38	49	−11	121
63	49	14	196
59	49	10	100
51	49	2	4
50	49	1	1
46	49	−3	9
		Sum =	682

and the average of the squared deviations is 75.7778.

• VARIANCE

The average of the squared deviations is called the **population variance** and is written as σ^2 (σ is the Greek lowercase letter sigma). If you are ever so fortunate as to have all of the population data available to you, then the population variance is a good way to measure how spread out it is. In general, the formula for population variance is written:

$$\sigma^2 = \frac{(x_1 - \mu)^2 + (x_2 - \mu)^2 + (x_3 - \mu)^2 + \ldots + (x_n - \mu)^2}{n} = \frac{\Sigma(x_i - \mu)^2}{n}$$

The population variance can also be calculated from this formula:

$$\sigma^2 = \overline{x}^2 - (\overline{x})^2$$

where $\overline{x^2}$ is the average value of x^2, and $(\overline{x})^2$ is the square of the average value of x. This saves a bit of calculation because you only do one subtraction at the end. For the pepperoni example,

Pepperoni	Sales	Sales^2
	40	1,600
	56	3,136
	38	1,444
	38	1,444
	63	3,969
	59	3,481
	51	2,601
	50	2,500
	46	2,116
Sum:	441	22,291
Average:	$\overline{x} = 49$	$\overline{x^2} = 2{,}476.7778$

Then the variance is $\overline{x^2} - (\overline{x})^2 = 2{,}476.7778 - 49^2 = 75.7778$, which is the same as we found earlier.

Unfortunately, much of the time you will have sample data, instead of population data. These will be measurements taken from a population whose mean you don't know exactly, but which you can approximate by taking the mean of your sample (assuming that your sample was chosen randomly). When we use the sample mean $\overline{x}$ instead of the population mean μ to calculate the variance, we compute it just a little bit differently. Instead of dividing by how many numbers in the sample, you divide by one less, n − 1. For our pepperoni sales, the sample variance is $682/(9 - 1) = 682/8 = 85.25$.

We'll use s^2 to stand for the sample variance (as opposed to σ^2 for the population variance). In general the formula for the sample variance is

$$s^2 = \frac{(x_1 - \overline{x})^2 + (x_2 - \overline{x})^2 + (x_3 - \overline{x})^2 + \ldots + (x_n - \overline{x})^2}{n - 1}$$

$$= \frac{\Sigma(x_i - \overline{x})^2}{n - 1}$$

$$= \left(\overline{x^2} - (\overline{x})^2\right)\left(\frac{n}{n - 1}\right)$$

• *STANDARD DEVIATION*

We use σ^2 to stand for population variance and s^2 to stand for sample variance, which might make you think that they are the square of something. And you're right.

One problem with interpreting the meaning of the variance is the units. If your data is measured in numbers of pizzas, then your variance will be measured in units of pizzas squared. (We're not sure what pizzas squared look like, although Sicilian pizza comes close.)

If you want your units to match the ones you started with, it is best to take the square root of the variance to find the **standard deviation**. To find the population standard deviation σ:

$$\sigma = \sqrt{\frac{(x_1 - \mu)^2 + (x_2 - \mu)^2 + (x_3 - \mu)^2 + \cdots + (x_n - \mu)^2}{n}}$$

$$= \sqrt{\frac{\Sigma(x_i - \mu)^2}{n}}$$

$$= \sqrt{\overline{x^2} - (\overline{x})^2}$$

(Recall μ is the population mean.)

To find the sample standard deviation s:

$$s = \sqrt{\frac{(x_1 - \overline{x})^2 + (x_2 - \overline{x})^2 + (x_3 - \overline{x})^2 + \cdots + (x_n - \overline{x})^2}{n - 1}}$$

$$= \sqrt{\frac{\Sigma(x_i - \overline{x})^2}{n - 1}}$$

$$= \sqrt{(\overline{x^2} - (\overline{x})^2)\left(\frac{n}{n - 1}\right)}$$

(Recall $\overline{x}$ is the sample average.)

For the pepperoni sales, the sample standard deviation $s = \sqrt{85.25} = 9.233$.

How can you tell if the value of the standard deviation is large or small? Sometimes it helps to compare the size of the standard deviation to the size of the average. The **coefficient of variation** is defined as this ratio:

$$\text{coefficient of variation} = \frac{\text{standard deviation}}{\text{average}}$$

For our pepperoni sales, this works out to be 9.233/49 = 0.188 = 18.8 percent.

One advantage of the coefficient of variation is that its value does not depend on the units you are using. However, the coefficient of variation should only be calculated for quantities that are never negative.

Descriptive statistics are easy to calculate in Excel. First, you'll have to type your numbers into the spreadsheet. Alternatively, if your data is already in another file or on the Internet, you can copy and paste the data into Excel. Use the "Data Text to Columns" command to split the data into separate columns if necessary.

Excel contains many built-in statistical functions. You will probably remember some of them, so you can type those into your spreadsheet when you

YOU SHOULD REMEMBER

1. If you have a list of N numbers $(x_1, x_2, x_3, \ldots, x_N)$ that represent an entire population:

population variance:

$$\sigma^2 = \frac{(x_1 - \mu)^2 + (x_2 - \mu)^2 + (x_3 - \mu)^2 + \ldots + (x_N - \mu)^2}{N}$$

$$= \frac{\Sigma(x_i - \mu)^2}{N}$$

$$= \overline{x^2} - (\overline{x})^2$$

population standard deviation:

$$\sigma = \sqrt{\frac{(x_1 - \mu)^2 + (x_2 - \mu)^2 + (x_3 - \mu)^2 + \ldots + (x_N - \mu)^2}{N}}$$

$$= \sqrt{\frac{\Sigma(x_i - \mu)^2}{N}}$$

$$= \sqrt{\overline{x^2} - (\overline{x})^2}$$

2. If you have a list of n numbers $(x_1, x_2, x_3, \ldots, x_n)$ that represent a sample:

sample variance:

$$s^2 = \frac{(x_1 - \overline{x})^2 + (x_2 - \overline{x})^2 + (x_3 - \overline{x})^2 + \ldots + (x_n - \overline{x})^2}{n - 1}$$

$$= \frac{\Sigma(x_i - \overline{x})^2}{n - 1}$$

$$= \left(\overline{x^2} - (\overline{x})^2 \right) \left(\frac{n}{n - 1} \right)$$

sample standard deviation:

$$s = \sqrt{\frac{(x_1 - \overline{x})^2 + (x_2 - \overline{x})^2 + (x_3 - \overline{x})^2 + \ldots + (x_n - \overline{x})^2}{n - 1}}$$

$$= \sqrt{\frac{\Sigma(x_i - \overline{x})^2}{n - 1}}$$

$$= \sqrt{\overline{x^2} - (\overline{x})^2} \sqrt{\left(\frac{n}{n - 1} \right)}$$

need them. However, you don't have to remember the exact form of each function, because Excel includes a way for you to look up any function. Click on the "f_x" symbol, which stands for "insert function." A dialog box will appear containing a list of all the functions. You can also type in a description of what you want to do, and Excel will look up the function for you. (A list of some Excel statistical functions is in Appendix 2). After you've selected a function, another dialog box will appear with a description of how that function works and how to enter the arguments (the values that will be used by that function). You can enter a range of values either by typing the cell coordinates (such as A2:A6) or by using the mouse to highlight the range you want.

Here are the basic descriptive statistics for the pepperoni pizza example. The data values are in cells B2 to B10. The Excel functions are in cells B11 to B18. Cells A11 to A18 contain labels, and cells C11 to C18 list the functions that appear in the adjacent cells. In reality you would not need to include the formula list in column C, but it is included here so you can see which functions have been typed into which cells. (Remember that when you look at a cell in a spreadsheet, you will see the result of the formula entered there rather than the formula itself. However, if you click on a cell, then the function contained in that cell will appear in the display line at the top of the screen.)

	A	B	C	D	E
1		Sales			
2		40			
3		56			
4		38			
5		38			
6		63			
7		59			
8		51			
9		50			
10		46			
11	average (mean):	49.0	← AVERAGE(B2:B10)		
12	median:	50	← MEDIAN(B2:B10)		
13	mode:	38	← MODE(B2:B10)		
14	range:	25	← MAX(B2:B10) − MIN(B2:B10)		
15	variance (population)	75.778	← VARP(B2:B10)		
16	variance (sample)	85.25	← VAR(B2:B10)		
17	standard deviation (population)	8.705	← STDEVP(B2:B10)		
18	standard deviation (sample)	9.233	← STDEV(B2:B10)		

In reality you would not calculate both the population and sample versions of the variance and standard deviation, as we have done here. You need to determine whether your data is a population or a sample and then use the appropriate version. We have shown both here to illustrate how they can both be calculated in Excel.

FREQUENCY HISTOGRAMS

Matters become more complicated if we are given a longer list of numbers. For example, suppose we are managing a marching band and need to order uniforms. We need to know the heights (in inches) of the members:

$$67, 65, 68, 67, 67, 64, 69, 66, 66, 66,$$
$$68, 71, 67, 67, 70, 65, 65, 66, 70, 64,$$
$$67, 68, 66, 68, 64, 65, 67, 66, 69, 68,$$
$$65, 69, 68, 67, 68, 67, 67, 67, 66, 66$$

Keeping track of the entire list is cumbersome. It would help to summarize the list by counting the number of people at each height and making a table like this:

Height	Frequency
64	3
65	5
66	8
67	11
68	7
69	3
70	2
71	1

The number of people at each height is called the frequency of occurrence of that height, so this table is called a **frequency table**. Notice that we get a much clearer picture of the nature of the distribution of heights from the frequency table than we do from the original list. We can obtain a still clearer view by drawing a picture of the frequency table (called a **frequency his-**

togram, see Figure 2-1). The height of each bar is the number of people who have the indicated height.

We can use the information from the frequency table to calculate the average. We can calculate the total of all the heights like this:

$$64 + 64 + 64 +$$
$$65 + 65 + 65 + 65 + 65 +$$
$$66 + 66 + 66 + 66 + 66 + 66 + 66 + 66 +$$
$$67 + 67 + 67 + 67 + 67 + 67 + 67 + 67 + 67 + 67 + 67 +$$
$$68 + 68 + 68 + 68 + 68 + 68 + 68 +$$
$$69 + 69 + 69 +$$
$$70 + 70 +$$
$$71$$
$$= 2,676$$

As you look at all those numbers, you can quickly see an easier way: all we need to do is multiply each height value times its frequency of occurrence, and then add up all of these products. Here is how it works:

Figure 2–1

Height	Frequency	Height × Frequency
64	3	192
65	5	325
66	8	528
67	11	737
68	7	476
69	3	207
70	2	140
71	1	71
total:		2,676

Since the total of all the heights is 2,676, and there are 40 people, we can calculate that the average height is 66.9.

In general, suppose we have a list of numbers containing m different values (call them $x_1, x_2, \ldots, x_m$). We'll let f_1 stand for the frequency of occurrence of the value x_1. For example, in the list above, x_1 is 64 and f_1 is 3. In general, we will use f_i to represent the frequency of occurrence for the value x_i. Let n be the total number of observations, which is equal to

$$n = f_1 + f_2 + f_3 + \cdots + f_m$$

Then the average can be calculated from the following formula:

$$\text{average} = \frac{f_1 x_1 + f_2 x_2 + f_3 x_3 + \cdots + f_m x_m}{n}$$

$$= \frac{\sum_{i=1}^{m} f_i x_i}{n}$$

We can also calculate the median from the frequency table data. Since there are 40 people altogether, the median height is halfway between the heights of the 20th person and the 21st person. From the frequency table we can see that 27 people have heights less than or equal to 67, and 24 people have heights greater than or equal to 67. Therefore, both the 20th person and the 21st person must have heights of 67, which is the median.

We know that 50 percent of the people in the band have heights of 67 or less. Suppose we also wish to know what percent of the heights are 65 or less. From the frequency table we can calculate that 8 people are in that category, so $8/40 = 20$ percent of the band members have heights of 65 or less. This calculation is an example of the more general concept of *percentiles*. We can calculate many different percentiles for a set of numbers. For example, the 25th percentile is the number such that 25 percent of the items in the list are at or below it; the 60th percentile is the number such that 60 percent of the items in the list are below it; and so on.

Percentiles are commonly used when you want to compare yourself to the rest of the population. For example, growth charts for children are often shown as percentiles. If your child's height at a certain age is at the 60th percentile, then you know that the child is taller than 60 percent of the other children of that age. Results for standardized test scores are often given as percentiles. If your score is at the 65th percentile, then your score is higher than the scores of 65 percent of the people taking the test.

We can calculate the variance of the band members' heights using the frequency information from one of these formulas:

$$\text{Var}(x) = \frac{\sum_{i=1}^{m} f_i (x_i - \bar{x})^2}{n}$$

$$= \frac{\sum_{i=1}^{m} f_i x_i^2}{n} - \left(\frac{\sum_{i=1}^{m} f_i x_i}{n} \right)^2$$

(Since we have information for all members of the band, our data comes from a population.)

In our case we have a variance of 2.69 and a standard deviation of 1.64.

GROUPED DATA

Here's our next problem: we need to analyze the adjusted gross income figures for all year 2006 U.S. tax returns. Obviously, we do not want to see a list of all 138,394,756 different values for gross income. Instead, we would like to have the information in frequency table form. We would like the data presented to us as a frequency table that groups the data according to broad categories. We can call data in that form **grouped data**.

If you do have a list of all of the data values, you can use Excel to calculate the frequency distribution.

1. Create a column in your spreadsheet containing a list of the maximum value in each class in order (these values are called the **class limits**).

2. At the top of the next column enter the formula

= FREQUENCY(*data, bins*)

where *data* is the range containing your data and *bins* is the range containing your class limits. Press control, shift, and enter simultaneously (because you are entering a range of cells all at once).

3. The result will be an array in a single cell. To see the value in a range of cells, select that cell and extend to a range containing one more cell than the number of bins, press F2, then press CONTROL, SHIFT, and

ENTER together. The resulting frequencies start with the number of entries below the lowest class limit and end with the number of entries above the largest class limit.

Fortunately, for the income tax data, the IRS provides the information in frequency table form. Here is the table for 2006:

Adjusted Gross Income Year 2006	Number of Returns	Midpoint (thousands)
No adjusted gross income	2,675,594	0.0
$1 under $5,000	11,633,370	2.5
$5,000 under $10,000	11,786,747	7.5
$10,000 under $15,000	11,711,680	12.5
$15,000 under $20,000	10,937,694	17.5
$20,000 under $25,000	9,912,261	22.5
$25,000 under $30,000	8,749,761	27.5
$30,000 under $40,000	14,151,824	35.0
$40,000 under $50,000	10,687,193	45.0
$50,000 under $75,000	18,854,917	62.5
$75,000 under $100,000	11,140,408	87.5
$100,000 under $200,000	12,088,423	150.0
$200,000 under $500,000	3,121,485	350.0
$500,000 under $1,000,000	589,306	750.0
$1,000,000 under $1,500,000	150,431	1250.0
$1,500,000 under $2,000,000	64,007	1750.0
$2,000,000 under $5,000,000	98,724	3500.0
$5,000,000 under $10,000,000	24,975	7500.0
$10,000,000 or more	15,956	—
Total returns	138,394,756	

Source: *www.irs.gov/taxstats/indtaxstats/*

We'll calculate the average value for adjusted gross income. We used this formula to calculate the average height of the band members:

$$\overline{x} = \frac{\sum_{i=1}^{m} f_i x_i}{n}$$

However, there are some complications now that we have the data grouped by classes rather than individual values. For example, the table tells us that 9,912,261 families have incomes between $20,000 and $25,000. However, the table doesn't tell us about the exact distribution within this range. All 9,912,261 might have incomes of $20,001, or they might all have incomes of $24,999. Both of these possibilities, though, seem unlikely. We will guess that the incomes of the 9,912,261 families are probably spread uniformly over the interval from \$20,000 to \$25,000. Therefore, we can assume that if we considered all 9,912,261 people in this class, their average income is \$22,500 (halfway between the two boundaries of the interval). The two end points of an interval are the class limits, and the point halfway between them is called the **class mark.** To simplify the calculations, we'll measure income in units of thousands, so the class marks will be 0, 2.5, 7.5, 12.5, and so on (rather than 0, 2,500, 7,500, 12,500 and so on).

If we let f_i represent the number of observations in class i and x_i represent the class mark for class i, then we can calculate the average $\bar{x}$ from this formula:

$$\bar{x} = \frac{f_1 x_1 + f_2 x_2 + \cdots + f_m x_m}{n}$$

$$= \frac{\sum_{i=1}^{m} f_i x_i}{n}$$

We will run into a problem with this method when we come to the last class because there is no upper limit to this class. Therefore, we can't use the midpoint. This type of class is called an **open-ended class**. Open-ended classes may occur at either the top or the bottom of grouped data, and they cause problems for calculating some statistics, including the average. In this case we are bailed out by the IRS because it reports that the average income of those in the top category is \$28.358 million.

Income ($ thousands)	Frequency	Class Mark	Product	Cumulative Frequency	Cumulative Fraction
none	2,675,594	0.0	0	2,675,594	0.0193
0–5	11,633,370	2.5	29,083,425	14,308,964	0.1034
5–10	11,786,747	7.5	88,400,603	26,095,711	0.1886
10–15	11,711,680	12.5	146,396,000	37,807,391	0.2732
15–20	10,937,694	17.5	191,409,645	48,745,085	0.3522
20–25	9,912,261	22.5	223,025,873	58,657,346	0.4238
25–30	8,749,761	27.5	240,618,428	67,407,107	0.4871
30–40	14,151,824	35.0	495,313,840	81,558,931	0.5893
40–50	10,687,193	45.0	480,923,685	92,246,124	0.6665
50–75	18,854,917	62.5	1,178,432,313	111,101,041	0.8028
75–100	11,140,408	87.5	974,785,700	122,241,449	0.8833
100–200	12,088,423	150.0	1,813,263,450	134,329,872	0.9706
200–500	3,121,485	350.0	1,092,519,750	137,451,357	0.9932
500–1,000	589,306	750.0	441,979,500	138,040,663	0.9974
1,000–1,500	150,431	1250.0	188,038,750	138,191,094	0.9985
1,500–2,000	64,007	1750.0	112,012,250	138,255,101	0.9990
2,000–5,000	98,724	3500.0	345,534,000	138,353,825	0.9997
5,000–10,000	24,975	7500.0	187,312,500	138,378,800	0.9999
10,000+	15,956	28358.0	452,480,248	138,394,756	1.0000
Sum	138,394,756.0		8,681,529,958		

We can now calculate the average income by multiplying each frequency amount by its class mark and then dividing the sum of those products by the total number of returns:

$$= \frac{8,681,529,958}{138,394,756} = 62.730 \text{ thousand}$$

(The result overstates the true value because the average for each class tends to be less than the midpoint of the class, particularly for the higher classes.)

We can also calculate the median adjusted gross income. Since there are 138,394,756 total returns, we must find one return such that $138,394,756/2 = 69,197,378$ have lower incomes and 69,197,378 have higher incomes.

In the previous table, we calculated the cumulative frequency (the total number of returns with income at or below a given class) and the cumulative fraction (the fraction of the returns at or below a given class).

By adding $2,675,594 + 11,633,370$, we find that 14,308,964 taxpayers, or 10.3 percent of the total have incomes less than $5,000. Clearly the median income must be much greater than $5,000. By looking down the cumulative fraction column, we find that 48.7 percent have incomes below $30,000, and that 58.9 percent have incomes below $40,000.

This information does not tell us exactly where the median income is, but it does provide a very important clue. We know that the median income must be above $30,000 and below $40,000, since that is the first class where the cumulative fraction exceeds 0.5. We can narrow our search for the median income to the 14,151,824 households with incomes in the $30,000 to $40,000 class. We will assume that the 14,151,824 households in this class are distributed evenly in the class. Since 69,197,378 households in the total population have incomes less than the median income, we can calculate as follows:

$$
\begin{array}{rl}
69,197,378 & \text{households have incomes less than the median} \\
-\ 67,407,107 & \text{households have incomes less than \$30,000} \\
\hline
1,790,271 & \text{households above \$30,000 but less than the median}
\end{array}
$$

Therefore, $1,790,271/14,151,824 = 12.65$ percent of the people in the $30,000 to $40,000 class have incomes below the median. Since we assumed that income in that class is evenly distributed, the median income must be

$$\$30 + 0.1265 \times 10 = \$31.265 \text{ thousands}$$

Here is the general formula for calculating the median once the median class has been identified (assuming that the values within the median class are uniformly distributed):

$$\text{median} = x_L + \frac{(N/2 - n_L)w}{n_m}$$

where x_L is the lower class limit of the median class (30 in our example), N is the total number of items in the population (example: 138,394,756),

n_L is the total number of items *below* the median class (example: 67,407,107), n_m is the number of items *in* the median class (example: 14,151,824), w is the width of the median class (example: $40 - 30 = 10$).

Note that when the number of items in the list is large, we don't really need to worry about whether there is an odd or even number of items. Also note that the open-ended class poses no problem for calculating the median.

• *THE HISTOGRAM*

It would be helpful to create a graph illustrating the income distribution. We might draw a bar diagram such as the one in Figure 2-2. However, this diagram is misleading. It illustrates a big jump in frequency when you move from the 25–30 category to the 30–40 category, but the reason for the jump is because the category is wider. To correctly illustrate the distribution, we need to draw a diagram where the width of each bar represents the width of the category. Also, if the width of a category is double the preceding category, we need to divide the height of the bar in half to compensate. The resulting diagram, called a **histogram**, is designed so that the area of each bar is proportional to the number of items in that category. Figure 2-3 shows the histogram for the income data. The height of each bar equals the frequency for that category divided by the width of the category. This means the absolute height of each bar is less important than the relative height, so no vertical scale is given. If the total area of all the bars is set as 1, then the area of a particular bar or group of bars gives the fraction of taxpayers whose income falls in that category. Since the number of taxpayers with income over $200,000 is relatively small, the bars above that level are very small. Figure 2-4 provides a close-up view of the histogram for categories below $100,000.

The histogram is created as a scatter graph in Excel. Here are the first few rows of the data to create the scatter graph.

0	0
0	2,326.674
5,000	2,326.674
5,000	0
5,000	2,357.349
10,000	2,357.349
10,000	0
10,000	2,342.336
15,000	2,342.336
15,000	0
15,000	2,187.539
20,000	2,187.539
20,000	0

The numbers in the first column (0, 5,000, 10,000, and so on) are the upper limits of the classes, and the numbers in the second column are the heights

Figure 2-2

Figure 2–3. Income Distribution Histogram

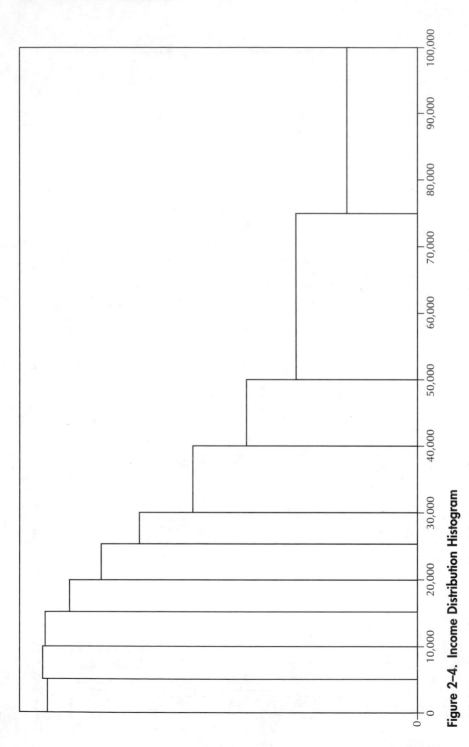

Figure 2–4. Income Distribution Histogram

of the bars. The first number (2,326.675) is calculated by dividing the frequency of the first nonzero category (11,633,370) by the width of the category (5,000). The numbers are arranged this way so that when Excel draws a scatter graph with lines it will trace out the histogram.

Here are some histograms for different shapes of distributions. See Figures 2–5(a) to (d).

Unimodal Symmetric

Figure 2–5(a)

Skewed Left

Figure 2–5(b)

Skewed Right

Figure 2–5(c)

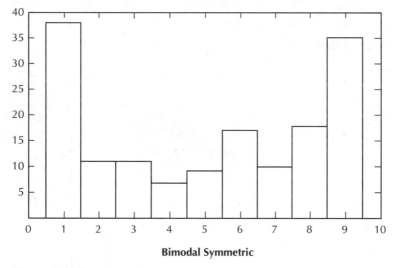

Bimodal Symmetric

Figure 2–5(d)

• OTHER GRAPHS

There are four more types of graphs that we will mention here. Suppose we were given the following grouped data for the daily withdrawals at a bank:

Withdrawal	Frequency
500–600	12
600–700	36
700–800	63
800–900	81
900–1,000	77
1,000–1,100	42
1,100–1,200	24

We can plot this information on a histogram (see Figure 2–6).

Figure 2–6

THE FREQUENCY POLYGON

The same information can be shown on a diagram called a **frequency polygon**. Instead of using a bar to represent each class, we place a dot above the class midpoint. Then the dots are connected with line segments (see Figure 2–7).

Figure 2–7. Frequency Polygon

THE OGIVE

It also can be useful to calculate the cumulative frequencies. The cumulative frequency for each class is the total number of observations in that class or in a lower class.

Withdrawal	Frequency	Cumulative Frequency
500–600	12	12
600–700	36	48
700–800	63	111
800–900	81	192
900–1,000	77	269
1,000–1,100	42	311
1,100–1,200	24	335

A graph of the cumulative frequencies is called an **ogive** (see Figure 2–8).

THE PIE CHART

If we would like to see how a total quantity is divided into different categories, the best type of diagram to draw is a **pie chart**. Each category is

Figure 2–8. Ogive

represented by a wedge in the pie. The angular size of each wedge is proportional to the fraction of the total that belongs to that category.

Here is a table showing U.S. government spending by category in the
president's proposed budget for fiscal year 2010. Figure 2–9 illustrates the
pie chart.

Category	Amount ($ billion)	Fraction
Defense	707	0.197
Other discretionary	687	0.191
Social Security	696	0.194
Medicare	452	0.126
Medicaid	290	0.081
Other mandatory	612	0.170
Net interest	136	0.038
Disaster costs	11	0.003
Total:	3,591	1

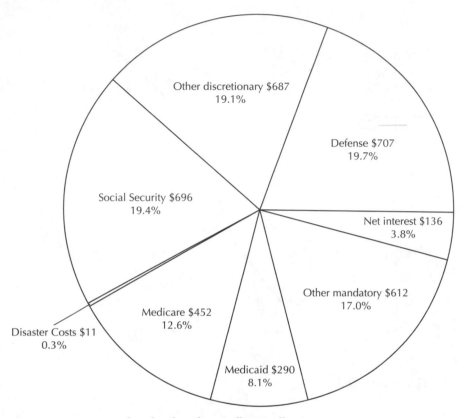

Figure 2–9. Proposed Federal Budget (Billion Dollars)

The purpose of a pie chart is to illustrate what fraction of the total a particular category represents. You can tell at a glance whether a particular category represents a fraction that is closer to a quarter or a third or half of the total. However, a bar chart would be better if you need to indicate the relative size of the items compared to each other.

You should never use special effects such as an exploded pie chart (which pulls some slices away from the circle) or a three-dimensional effect that tilts the pie chart so it is not a circle. These effects distort the view of the data.

You also should be careful with using color. It probably is best to make the slices all the same color and represent them with their outline (unless color is used to illustrate an additional aspect of the data). Too much extraneous color can distract from the data.

A good rule to remember: Just because your software makes it possible to create a special visual effect does not mean that it is necessarily wise to do so.

Creating graphs by hand is a lot of work. Fortunately, computer programs are now available with a wide variety of graphics capabilities; these will be discussed later.

STEM-AND-LEAF PLOT

A clever way of drawing a picture to describe the distribution of some numbers in a sample is to use the numbers themselves. The following process, invented by John Tukey, is called a stem-and-leaf plot. As always, it's easier to describe if we work with an example.

GIVEN We have the following 40 scores (out of 100) on a standardized mathematics test:

78 59 86 94 43 56 78 84 57 89 96 68 67 65 75 73 67 87 84 45 56 94 87 56 85 76 86 79 78 77 59 76 68 49 86 87 83 94 85 96

DESIRED We want a simple way of describing the distribution of the data, giving some sense of the range and median.

SOLUTION Notice that the data all have two digits. The first digit ranges from 4 to 9; if we were to group the data, a natural way of doing so would be into 40s, 50s, and so on. We'll do that in a picture:

```
4 |
5 |
6 |
7 |
8 |
9 |
```

Instead of counting up the number of data in the 40s, 50s, and so on, we'll put the second digit for each data point in the appropriate row. For example, using the first five data points, our picture would look like:

```
4 | 3
5 | 9
6 |
7 | 8
8 | 6
9 | 4
```

If we finish off the first row of 20 data points, our picture would look like:

```
4 | 35
5 | 967
6 | 8757
7 | 8853
8 | 64974
9 | 46
```

We can quickly finish off the second row of data, and our complete picture looks like:

```
4 | 359
5 | 967669
6 | 87578
7 | 885369876
8 | 649747566735
9 | 46446
```

What we've done is akin to making a frequency count using tick marks, but using the last digits of the data as the tick marks. We can easily count up the number of data points in each row of our picture:

```
(3)    4 | 359
(6)    5 | 967669
(5)    6 | 87578
(9)    7 | 885369876
(12)   8 | 649747566735
(5)    9 | 46446
```

Now we have a sense for the distribution (note the peak in the 80s) and the range (lowest is 43, highest is 96), and we can quickly find the median. Since there are 40 data points, the median lies between the 20th and 21st ordered data points. We haven't completely ordered the data points, but since there are $3 + 6 + 5 = 14$ data points in the first three rows, we know that the median is between the 6th and 7th largest number in the 70s row, i.e., between 78 and 78; i.e., the median for the data is 78.

A **stem-and-leaf plot** is a frequency chart constructed for two- or three-digit sample points using the last digit as a counter for the frequency class corresponding to the beginning digits. Typically stem-and-leaf plots are drawn with the stem (the beginning digits) listed vertically and the last digits (forming the leaves) listed horizontally. Often, the length of each leaf is recorded to the left of the stem.

The strength of the stem-and-leaf plot lies in its ability to give you the information quickly and easily, without having to perform calculations: a sample of 100 data points can be analyzed by hand in only a couple of minutes.

If more than two or three digits are present in the values of the data points, you would probably want to round them off before proceeding.

It may happen that the stem-and-leaf plot as described above groups the data into too small a number of leaves:

GIVEN   The following 30 measurements in inches are the heights of the students in a statistics class:

68 62 64 65 67 59 68 63 63 72 71 62 65 65 58 65 66 67 63
68 63 65 65 67 69 65 71 70 68 67

DESIRED   We want a way of describing the distribution, indicating the range and median.

SOLUTION   This set of data has been rounded to two digits. The first digit for each data point is a 5, 6, or 7. A three-leafed stem-and-leaf plot for this data set looks like:

(2)   5 | 98
(24)   6 | 824578332555673835579587
(4)   7 | 2110

which tells us about the peak in the 60s but otherwise doesn't help us to get a sense for the distribution. Instead of grouping all of the 60s together, we can split the leaves up into early 50s (50–54), late 50s (55–59), early 60s (60–64), late 60s (65–69), early 70s (70–74), and late 70s (75–79):

(2)   5 | 98
(7)   6 | 2433233
(17)   6 | 85785556785579587
(4)   7 | 2110

(Note that because the students in the class are neither very short nor very tall, the first and last rows are not affected.) We can see that the peak in heights lies in the upper 60s, the range is from 58 to 72, and the median (which lies between the 15th and 16th ordered data points) lies between the 6th and 7th largest data points in the third row, i.e., between 65 and 65; i.e., the median is 65.

* * * *

Note to Chapter 2: In some books the term "average" is used as a generic term for measures of central tendency; in this sense it includes the mean, median, and mode. However, in everyday usage the term "average" is always used as a synonym for "mean."

The mean discussed in this chapter is also sometimes called the "arithmetic mean" to distinguish it from a quantity called the "geometric mean." The geometric mean of two numbers is the square root of their product.

For example, if an investment increases because of compound interest from $100 today to $121 two years from today, its value one year from today is the geometric mean $\sqrt{100 \times 121} = \$110$.

YOU SHOULD REMEMBER

1. For very large lists it would be too cumbersome to keep track of the entire list. The data can be summarized by defining categories and then counting the number of data points in each category (called the *frequency*). If we have *m* groups, and we let f_i be the frequency for group *i*, then we can approximate the mean with this formula:

$$\text{mean} = \frac{\sum_{i=1}^{m} f_i x_i}{\sum_{i=1}^{m} f_i} = \frac{\sum_{i=1}^{m} f_i x_i}{n}$$

where $n = \sum_{i=1}^{m} f_i$ is the total number of data items, and x_i is the midpoint for class *i*.

2. It is also very informative to represent data in graphical form. For grouped data the distribution can be displayed on a frequency diagram, using bars of different heights to represent the frequencies. Other types of diagrams are *frequency polygons* (formed by placing a dot at the midpoint of each category at a height proportional to the number of items in that category), *ogives* (graphs of the cumulative frequency distribution), *pie charts* (where each category is represented by a wedge-shaped sector of a circle whose size depends on the proportion of items in that category), and *stem-and-leaf plots* (where the last digit of a number is plotted on a frequency chart for the beginning digits).

CORRELATION AND SCATTER GRAPHS

Sometimes one quantity has an effect on another quantity. We can illustrate this relationship with a scatter graph, which measures one quantity along the horizontal axis and the other quantity along the vertical axis.

Suppose we have observed ice cream consumption on four different days, and find that consumption increases when the temperature rises:

Day	Temperature	Ice Cream Cones Sold
Monday	60	5
Tuesday	70	25
Wednesday	80	45
Thursday	90	65

Figure 2-10 illustrates this relationship. Each dot represents the observations of the two variables for one day. We could draw a straight line that

Figure 2–10

passes through each of the dots, indicating a strong relationship. (Actually, we would never assume that such a relationship exists if we only have four observations. In order to reliably estimate the relationship we would need many more observations. Chapter 16 on Simple Regression goes into this in more detail. However, in order to introduce the concept it helps to work with an example with a small number of observations.)

The *correlation* (represented by *r*) indicates the nature of the relationship. If all of the dots lie along a straight line, and that line is upward sloping, then the value of the correlation is 1. This means that an increase in one of the variables is associated with an increase in the other variable.

The value of the correlation is always between −1 and 1:

$$-1 \leq r \leq 1$$

If the dots lie along a straight line with a negative slope, then the correlation is −1. This means that an increase in one variable is associated with a decrease in the other variable. For example, suppose we have observations of temperature and coat sales:

Day	Temperature	Coats Sold
Monday	60	24
Tuesday	70	16
Wednesday	80	8
Thursday	90	0

Figure 2-11 illustrates this relationship with a scatter graph.

Here are some observations of temperature and toothpaste sales in four different cities.

City	Temperature	Toothpaste Tubes Sold
River City	70	30
Elm City	70	50
Lake City	80	30
Maple City	80	50

Figure 2-12 shows the scatter graph. You could not draw a straight line connecting these dots, indicating that there is no tendency for toothpaste sales to be related to temperature. Another way of putting it: knowledge of the

Figure 2–11

Figure 2–12

temperature would be no help in predicting the value of toothpaste sales (although it would be a big help in predicting ice cream or coat sales). The correlation in this case is 0. If the dots form a pattern similar to a box on the scatter graph, the correlation will be zero.

To calculate the correlation between two variables x and y, set up a table with columns for x, y, x^2, y^2, and xy. Then calculate the average of each of these quantities, and use this formula for the correlation r:

$$r = \frac{\overline{xy} - \overline{x} \times \overline{y}}{\sqrt{(\overline{x^2} - \overline{x}^2)(\overline{x^2} - \overline{x}^2)}}$$

The formula can also be written:

$$r = \frac{\overline{xy} - \overline{x} \times \overline{y}}{\sigma_x \sigma_y}$$

where $\sigma_x = \sqrt{\overline{x^2} - \overline{x}^2}$, the population standard deviation of x, and $\sigma_y = \sqrt{\overline{y^2} - \overline{y}^2}$, the population standard deviation of y.

Here is the calculation for the ice cream example:

	x	y	x^2	y^2	xy
	60	5	3,600	25	300
	70	25	4,900	625	1,750
	80	45	6,400	2,025	3,600
	90	65	8,100	4,225	5,850
Sum:	300	140	23,000	6,900	11,500
Average:	$\overline{x} = 75$	$\overline{y} = 35$	$\overline{x^2} = 5,750$	$\overline{y^2} = 1,725$	$\overline{xy} = 2,875$

$$\text{correlation} = r = \frac{2,875 - 75 \times 35}{\sqrt{(5,750 - 75^2)(1,725 - 35^2)}} = \frac{250}{\sqrt{125 \times 500}} = 1$$

Here is the calculation for the coat example:

	x	y	x^2	y^2	xy
	60	24	3,600	576	1,440
	70	16	4,900	256	1,120
	80	8	6,400	64	640
	90	0	8,100	0	0
Sum:	300	48	23,000	896	3,200
Average:	$\overline{x} = 75$	$\overline{y} = 12$	$\overline{x^2} = 5,750$	$\overline{y^2} = 224$	$\overline{xy} = 800$

$$\text{correlation} = r = \frac{800 - 75 \times 12}{\sqrt{(5,750 - 75^2)(224 - 12^2)}} = \frac{-100}{\sqrt{125 \times 80}} = -1$$

Here is the calculation for the toothpaste example:

x	y	x^2	y^2	xy
70	30	4,900	900	2,100
70	50	4,900	2,500	3,500
80	30	6,400	900	2,400
80	50	6,400	2,500	4,000
Sum: 300	160	22,600	6,800	12,000
Average: $\bar{x} = 75$	$\bar{y} = 40$	$\overline{x^2} = 5,650$	$\overline{y^2} = 1,700$	$\overline{xy} = 3,000$

$$\text{correlation} = r = \frac{3,000 - 75 \times 40}{\sqrt{(5,650 - 75^2)(1,700 - 40^2)}} = \frac{0}{\sqrt{25 \times 100}} = 0$$

Figure 2-13 shows how sales of tacos are affected by temperature. There is a slight tendency for higher temperatures to lead to an increase in taco sales, but people also buy tacos in cities with lower temperatures. We find that the correlation in this case is 0.5596. When there is some relationship, but not a close one, the correlation will be roughly halfway between 0 and 1.

City	Temperature x	Tacos y	x^2	y^2	xy
River City	50	10	2,500	100	500
Elm City	60	35	3,600	1,225	2,100
Lake City	70	12	4,900	144	840
Maple City	80	40	6,400	1,600	3,200
Sum:	260	97	17,400	3,069	6,640
Average:	$\bar{x} = 65$	$\bar{y} = 24.25$	$\overline{x^2} = 4,350$	$\overline{y^2} = 767.25$	$\overline{xy} = 1,660$

$$\text{correlation} = r = \frac{1,660 - 65 \times 24.2500}{\sqrt{(4,350 - 65^2)(767.25 - 24.25^2)}} = \frac{83.75}{\sqrt{125 \times 179.1875}} = 0.5596$$

The Excel function CORREL(range1, range2) calculates the correlation for the values contained in the two indicated ranges. (Be sure both ranges have the same number of items, and be sure that each item in one range is in the same position as the corresponding observation in the other range.)

Figure 2-13

Here are three more examples. You would expect that there is some connection between height and weight, but not a perfect correlation. Figure 2-14 illustrates the scatter diagram comparing height and weight for American League baseball players in 2009. Each dot represents one person. You can see a general upward trend: greater weight is associated with greater height, but if you try to draw a line through the dots, you would miss a lot of points. The correlation is 0.557.

Figure 2-15 illustrates the relation between population and the number of representatives for each of the 50 U.S. states. You can see that a line could be drawn that would almost connect each dot. There is a good reason for this: the number of representatives is determined by the population in a state. There are two reasons why the connection is not exact: (1) the number of representatives must be rounded to a whole number, and each state has at least one representative; and (2) the population shown is the 2008 estimate, which is different from the 2000 census population used to allocate representatives. The correlation is 0.997, which is very close to 1.

Figure 2-16 illustrates the relation between 2008 population and area for the 50 U.S. states. The diagram indicates there is little relationship between the two (there is no tendency for more people to live in states with more area). The correlation is 0.124.

YOU SHOULD REMEMBER

1. A scatter diagram illustrates the relationship between two quantities. Each dot represents one person, place, time, or other item and shows the values of the two variables for that item.

2. The correlation is a quantity between −1 and 1 that indicates the nature of the relationship between the two quantities. A value of 1 indicates there is a positively sloped straight line that will pass through each dot on the scatter diagram, indicating a larger value of one variable is associated with a larger value for the other variable. A value of −1 indicates there is a negatively sloped line that passes through all the dots. A value of 0 indicates there is no linear relationship between the quantities.

Some graphs are easy to create in Excel. Highlight the data. On the "Insert" tab, select the type of graph, and choose the options you want.

Figure 2–14

Figure 2–15

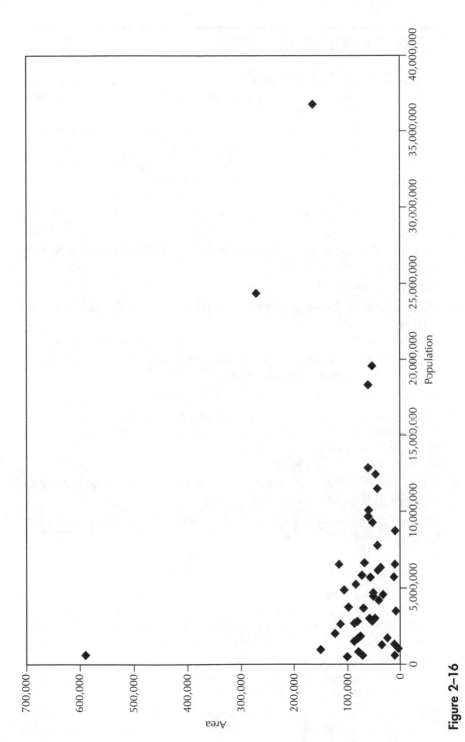

Figure 2–16

KNOW THE CONCEPTS

DO YOU KNOW THE BASICS?

Test your understanding of Chapter 2 by answering the following questions:

1. When does the median work better than the mean as a measure of the typical value in a group?

2. Suppose you conduct a survey in which people indicate how much they like quiche (using a scale of 1 to 10). If half the people love quiche and the other half detest quiche, what will the frequency distribution look like? What will be the best measure of central tendency for this distribution?

3. Why do you need to know the variance of your daily sales figures if you are managing a firm?

4. Why are open-ended classes sometimes used?

5. Do open-ended classes pose problems for calculating the mean? For calculating the median?

6. If there were a sudden arrival of a group of very tall people in your population, what would happen to the frequency diagram for height? To the mean? To the median? To the variance?

7. When is a pie chart better than a bar diagram?

8. Suppose you are a clothing manufacturer. You do not design garments for extremely tall or extremely short people. If you would like your range of products to appeal to half of the population, what measure of population heights do you most need to know?

9. If the standard deviation of a list is zero, what must be true about the numbers in the list?

10. What is the difference in the formula for calculating the variance of a population and the variance of a sample?

11. Which type of diagram would best illustrate the market share for different companies that make a particular product?

12. If you wish to illustrate whether a particular stock moves up and down at the same time as the market average, or whether it moves independently of the market average, or whether it moves opposite the market average, which type of diagram should you use? What numerical measure would you use?

13. What measure could you use to indicate whether your sales will be affected by a downturn in the national economy?

14. Which would be a better measure of average CEO pay: the average pay of the top 20 most highly paid CEOs or the average pay of the top 10,000?

TERMS FOR STUDY

average
bimodal
central tendency
class limits
class mark
coefficient of variation
dispersion
frequency diagram
frequency polygon
frequency table
grouped data
histogram
interquartile range
mean
median
mode
normal distribution
ogive

open-ended class
percentile
pie chart
population standard deviation
population variance
quartile
range
raw data
sample standard deviation
sample variance
skewed
standard deviation
statistic
subscript
summation notation
tail
variance

PRACTICAL APPLICATION

COMPUTATIONAL PROBLEMS

For each list of numbers calculate the mean, median, range, interquartile range, and the sample standard deviation.

1. 68	53	55	63	80
51	62	79	65	50
60	74			

2. 227	231	204	210	203
211	235	232	222	222
239	203	236	231	234
232				

3. 22	22	21	28	25
23	24	21	22	25

4. 168	172	169	171	168
160	163	167	166	164
170	172	165	175	170
170	171			

5. 108	100	102	113	98
101	98	106	100	114
102	102	114	106	106
97	103	103		

6. Find the coefficient of variation for Exercises 1–5.

For each exercise below you are given a frequency table. Calculate the mean, median, and population standard deviation.

7.

	Frequency		Frequency
0–1,000	12	6,000–7,000	48
1,000–2,000	15	7,000–8,000	40
2,000–3,000	19	8,000–9,000	30
3,000–4,000	22	9,000–10,000	16
4,000–5,000	30	10,000–11,000	4
5,000–6,000	56	11,000–12,000	2

8.

	Frequency		Frequency
0–10	122	80–90	180
10–20	180	90–100	175
20–30	256	100–110	143
30–40	350	110–120	120
40–50	311	120–130	106
50–60	278	130–140	99
60–70	250	140–150	97
70–80	211	150–160	75

9.

	Frequency		Frequency
0–100	69	600–700	250
100–200	133	700–800	219
200–300	174	800–900	170
300–400	211	900–1,000	136
400–500	255	1,000–1,100	68
500–600	288		

10.

	Frequency		Frequency
0–500	34	5,500–6,000	78
500–1,000	62	6,000–6,500	83
1,000–1,500	75	6,500–7,000	96
1,500–2,000	98	7,000–7,500	119
2,000–2,500	160	7,500–8,000	140
2,500–3,000	125	8,000–8,500	156
3,000–3,500	119	8,500–9,000	130
3,500–4,000	96	9,000–9,500	111
4,000–4,500	84	9,500–10,000	95
4,500–5,000	76	10,000–10,500	84
5,000–5,500	71		

11. Go to *frodo.elon.edu/bstat5/index.html* and download the Excel file containing the ages of customers surveyed at two stores. Plot frequency histograms for both sets of data and compare and contrast the results.

12. Go to *myhome.spu.edu/ddowning/bstat.html* and find a list of national economic measures. Paste the data into Excel and calculate the requested statistics.

ANSWERS

KNOW THE CONCEPTS

1. The median is better when there are a few very large or very small values in the population.

2. This type of distribution is called a *bimodal distribution*; the frequency diagram resembles a two-humped camel. Neither the mean nor the median provides a good indicator of the typical value. In other words, there is no "best measure."

3. If the sales figures have a relatively small variance, it will be easier to make plans for your business. If the variance is large, you must develop a way to cope with this uncertainty. For example, you may be able to let your inventory level fluctuate. You must determine the consequences of the two types of problems that can occur with erratic sales: (a) some days there will be unsold merchandise remaining; (b) other days you may run out of merchandise. The decisions you make will depend on the relative seriousness of these two types of problems.

4. It is not always possible to obtain precise data for the extremely high or low values in a distribution.

5. Open-ended classes make it difficult to calculate the mean, but they pose no problem for calculating the median.

6. The bars at the upper end of the frequency diagram for height will become larger; the mean will be increased significantly; the median will also increase, but probably not as much as the mean; and the variance will become larger.

7. A pie chart provides a clearer picture than a bar diagram of the fraction of items in each category.

8. It would be most helpful to know the interquartile range, since half of the values are contained between the third quartile and the first quartile.

9. They are all the same.

10. The formula for population has n in the denominator; the variance for a sample has $n - 1$ in the denominator.

11. A pie chart would indicate what share of the market each firm has. A bar chart would be a good indicator if you wish to see how the shares compare to each other.

12. A scatter diagram. The correlation coefficient will be close to 1 if the stock moves with the market; it will be close to 0 if the stock moves independently of the market; and it will be close to −1 if it moves opposite the market.

13. Calculate the correlation of sales with a measure of the overall economy, such as national income. If there is a positive correlation, the national downturn will hurt your business. If there is a negative correlation, it would indicate that your product is one that people turn to more during hard times.

14. It depends on what you are trying to measure. The average of the top 10,000 is a more representative group of all CEOs, but it would include a large number of companies of very different sizes. The average of the top 20 would give you a good measure of some very large companies, but this average isn't very representative of companies in general.

PRACTICAL APPLICATION

Here are the formulas and definitions you need for doing Exercises 1–10:

$$\text{mean} = \frac{x_1 + x_2 + \cdots + x_n}{n} = \frac{\sum_{i=1}^{n} x_i}{n}$$

median: the value such that half the numbers in a list are at or above it and half are at or below it.

range: the largest value minus the smallest value

sample standard deviation,

$$s = \sqrt{\left(\frac{n}{n-1}\right)(\overline{x^2} - \overline{x}^2)}$$

Complete calculations are shown below for Exercise 1 and Exercise 7. The same methods are used for Exercises 2–5 and 8–10 respectively.

1. Total = 68 + 53 + 55 + 63 + 80 + 51 + 62 + 79
         + 65 + 50 + 60 + 74 = 760
   Mean = 760/12 = 63.333   Median = (62 + 63)/2 = 62.5
   Range = 80 − 50 = 30
   $\overline{x^2}$ = $(68^2 + 53^2 + 55^2 + 63^2 + 80^2 + 51^2 + 62^2 + 79^2$
         $+ 65^2 + 50^2 + 60^2 + 74^2)/12 = 4{,}109.5$
   $s = 10.360$

2. Total: 3,572

    Mean = 223.25   Median = (227 + 231)/2 = 229

    Range = 239 − 203 = 36

    x^2 = 49,995

    s = 12.835

3. Mean = 23.300   Median = 22.5   Range = 7

    s = 2.214

4. Mean = 168.294   Median = 169   Range = 15

    s = 3.788

5. Mean = 104.056   Median = 102.5   Range = 17

    s = 5.341

6. Coefficient of variance = 16.4% (Exercise 1)

    = 5.7% (Exercise 2)

    = 9.5% (Exercise 3)

    = 2.3% (Exercise 4)

    = 5.1% (Exercise 5)

7. Total in population = 12 + 15 + 19 + 22 + 30 + 56

    + 48 + 40 + 30 + 16 + 4 + 2

    = 294

    Total of all items = 500 × 12 + 1,500 × 15 + 2,500 × 19

    + 3,500 × 22 + 4,500 × 30

    + 5,500 × 56 + 6,500 × 48

    + 7,500 × 40 + 8,500 × 30

    + 9,500 × 16 + 10,500 × 4

    + 11,500 × 2

    = 1,680,000

    Mean = 1,680,000/294 = 5,714.2857

    Median = 5,000 + (294/2 − 98) × 1,000/56 = 5,875

    x^2 = (500^2 × 12 + 1,500^2 × 15 + 2,500^2 × 19 + 3,500^2 × 22

    + 4,500^2 × 30 + 5,500^2 × 56 + 6,500^2 × 48

    + 7,500^2 × 40 + 8,500^2 × 30 + 9,500^2 × 16

    + 10,500^2 × 4 + 11,500^2 × 2)/294

    = 38,508,503

    Variance = 38,508,503 − 5,714.2857^2 = 5,855,442

    Standard deviation = 2,419.8

8. Mean = 66.5   Median = 59.3

    Standard deviation = 39.6

9. Mean = 550   Median = 550.2

    Standard deviation = 257

10. Mean = 5,575   Median = 5,794.9

    Standard deviation = 2,914.2

11. The first store has a slightly greater spread of ages and is bimodal; the second store has a single peak with customers in their early forties.

3

INTRODUCTION TO PROBABILITY AND HYPOTHESIS TESTING

We will investigate the act of coin tossing as an introduction to probability. Admittedly there are few occasions where a business decision depends on the outcome of a coin toss, but study of the probabilities associated with coin tosses provides valuable practice for some more difficult concepts we will encounter later on.

COIN TOSSING

If you flip a coin, the result will be either a head or a tail. However, it is practically impossible to predict correctly which outcome will occur. You could, in theory, calculate the path of the coin by using the laws of mechanics, if you knew the initial force that was applied to it and the other forces acting on it, and thus determine which side would be up when the coin comes to a stop. This would be very hard, though, so for practical purposes a coin toss is a good example of a random event: there is no accurate way to predict what the result will be.

If you toss a coin more than once, though, you can make some interesting predictions about what will happen. This is a general feature of random events, and it is one of the foundations of probability: you can't say what will happen in one occurrence, but if you watch the same thing happen many times you will be able to predict some patterns. For example, if you throw a dart at a phone book and try to guess the height of the person whose name is hit by the dart, you will probably be wrong. If you select 100 people at random and try to guess their average height, you will be much more likely to get it right.

If you flip a coin twice, there are four possibilities for the result: head-head, head-tail, tail-head, and tail-tail. (After this, H will be used for head and T for tail.) There are two possibilities for the first flip, and for each possible result of the first flip there are two possibilities for the second flip.

Now, if you need to know whether you will see no head, one head or two heads in the two flips, you can make a prediction. Assuming that the coin is a fair one, not biased toward head or tail, each of the four possible outcomes (HH, HT, TH, TT) is equally likely. You will see two heads if outcome 1 (HH) occurs, and you will see no head if outcome 4 (TT) occurs. Therefore, you have just as much chance of seeing no head as you do of seeing two heads. However, you will see exactly one head if either outcome 2 (HT) or outcome 3 (TH) occurs. Hence your best bet is to guess that one head will appear on the two flips. Of course, you still have a 50 percent chance of being wrong, but you have a much better chance of being right than if you had guessed no head or two heads.

You probably could have figured this much out for yourself without knowing anything about probability theory. Now use the same ideas to figure out how many heads are likely to appear if you toss a coin any number of times. Intuitively you will guess that if you toss a coin 92 times, the number of heads that show up will probably be about 46. At the opening of the play "Rosencrantz and Guildenstern Are Dead," Guildenstern tosses 92 heads in a row, thereby losing a lot of money to Rosencrantz. Intuitively, you know that this is extremely unlikely to occur.

· COMPUTING PROBABILITIES

In general, if you tossed a coin n times, n being a large number, you would expect that the number of heads would be close to $n/2$ and that you would be unlikely to get n heads in a row. First, let us consider the case of flipping the coin three times. There are eight possible outcomes:

HHH, HHT, HTH, HTT, THH, THT, TTH, TTT

This is the first step in computing a probability: find out how many possible outcomes there are. Then find out how many of those outcomes lead to the event that you are interested in. The **probability** of that event occurring is equal to the number of ways of getting that event divided by the total number of possible outcomes. For example:

Event You're Interested In	Outcomes That Lead to That Event	Number of Outcomes	Probability of Event
No head	TTT	1	1/8
One head	HTT, THT, TTH	3	3/8
Two heads	HHT, HTH, THH	3	3/8
Three heads	HHH	1	1/8

If you are forced to guess how many heads will appear on three flips, you should guess either one or two. You clearly shouldn't guess none or three.

We can follow the same method if we need to make a prediction about the results of four flips: list all the outcomes, and then count how many outcomes have no head, how many outcomes have one head, and so on. This method would get a bit tedious, though, and it would be very difficult if we tried it for a large number of flips. What is needed is a way to count the outcomes without having to list them all. That concept is one of the important ideas in probability.

First, we need to count all the possible outcomes from four flips. There are two possibilities for the first toss, then for each of those possibilities there are two for the second toss, then for each of these combinations there are two possibilities for the third toss, and so on. Altogether, there will be $2 \times 2 \times 2 \times 2 = 2^4 = 16$ possible outcomes. You should be able to convince yourself that, if you flip a coin n times, there will be 2^n possible outcomes. Now you can see why the listing method doesn't work. If you flip a coin 10 times, there will be $2^{10} = 1,024$ possible outcomes.

Next, we need to count how many outcomes have zero head, how many have one head, and so on, up to how many have four heads. The case of zero head is easy, since there is only one outcome (TTTT) that has zero head. To calculate the number of possibilities with one head, we need to figure out how many different ways we can write one H and three T's. Since there are four possible places for the H, there are four possibilities: HTTT, THTT, TTHT, TTTH. Now we need to figure out how many ways we can write two H's and two T's. There are four possible places to put the first H (call it H1):

$$H1 \underline{\ }\ \underline{\ }\ \underline{\ },\ \underline{\ }\ H1 \underline{\ }\ \underline{\ },\ \underline{\ }\ \underline{\ }\ H1 \underline{\ },\ \underline{\ }\ \underline{\ }\ \underline{\ }\ H1$$

For each of these possibilities there are three places to put the second H (call it H2):

H1 H2 __ __,   H1 __ H2 __,   H1 __ __ H2,
H2 H1 __ __,   __ H1 H2 __,   __ H1 __ H2,
H2 __ H1 __,   __ H2 H1 __,   __ __ H1 H2,
H2 __ __ H1,   __ H2 __ H1,   __ __ H2 H1

(Note that we have to worry only about where to put the H's, since once we've done that it will be obvious where to put the T's.) There are 12 of these possible ways to arrange the H's. However, it doesn't make any difference which is H1 and which is H2; __ H1 H2 __ is the same as __ H2 H1 __. We must divide by 2 to avoid double-counting these duplications. That means there are six possible ways to get two heads:

HHTT, HTHT, HTTH, THHT, THTH, TTHH

Therefore, the results for four flips are as follows:

Number of Heads (h)	Number of Outcomes with h Heads	Probability That h Heads Will Occur
0	1	$1/16 = .0625$
1	4	$4/16 = .2500$
2	6	$6/16 = .3750$
3	4	$4/16 = .2500$
4	1	$1/16 = .0625$

(You should note that these probabilities are symmetric—that is, the probability that you will get h heads is exactly the same as the probability that you will get h tails.)

Now we need to figure out a general formula for the number of outcomes that have h heads in n tosses. In principle it is the same as what we did before: we need to figure out how many ways we can write h capital H's on n blanks. There are n possibilities for the first H that we write, then $n - 1$ places left for the second, $n - 2$ places left for the third, and so on. Altogether, there will be

$$n \times (n - 1) \times (n - 2) \times (n - 3) \times \cdots \times (n - h + 1)$$

ways of writing down all the H's. Then we must divide by

$$h \times (h - 1) \times (h - 2) \times (h - 3) \times \cdots \times 3 \times 2 \times 1$$

to eliminate the duplications caused by the different orderings. Therefore, if we flip a coin n times, the number of possible outcomes that have exactly h heads will be

$$\frac{n \times (n-1) \times (n-2) \times (n-3) \times \cdots \times (n-b+1)}{b \times (b-1) \times (b-2) \times \cdots \times 3 \times 2 \times 1}$$

• USING FACTORIALS

The quantity $b \times (b-1) \times (b-2) \times (b-3) \times \cdots \times 3 \times 2 \times 1$ is interesting. It turns out that there are many times in probability theory when we need to calculate the product of all the numbers from 1 up to another particular number. This quantity is called the **factorial** of the number, and it is symbolized by an exclamation mark (!). For example:

$$3! = 3 \times 2 \times 1 = 6, \qquad 4! = 4 \times 3 \times 2 \times 1 = 24,$$

$$10! = 10 \times 9 \times 8 \times 7 \times 6 \times 5 \times 4 \times 3 \times 2 \times 1 = 3,628,800,$$

$$69! = 1.71 \times 10^{98}$$

As you can see, factorials become very big very fast. It should be obvious that $1! = 1$. There are also some formulas where we may need to find $n!$ for $n = 0$. These formulas work only if $0!$ has the value of 1, so we will make that definition.

Now we can use the factorial notation in the denominator to simplify the formula for the number of combinations with b heads:

$$\frac{n \times (n-1) \times (n-2) \times (n-3) \times \cdots \times (n-b+1)}{b!}$$

We can also write the numerator in a shorter fashion using the factorial function. We multiply and divide the numerator by $(n-b)!$:

$$n \times (n-1) \times (n-2) \times \cdots \times (n-b+1)$$

$$= \frac{n \times (n-1) \times (n-2) \times \cdots \times (n-b+1) \times (n-b)!}{(n-b)!}$$

$$= \frac{n \times (n-1) \times (n-2) \times \cdots \times 3 \times 2 \times 1}{(n-b)!}$$

$$= \frac{n!}{(n-b)!}$$

Therefore, we can write our formula in a very compact form:

$$\frac{n!}{b!(n-b)!}$$

(We will see this formula again in Chapter 4.)

What all this means is that we are now willing to predict that, if we flip a coin n times, the probability that we will get h heads is

$$\left[\frac{n!}{h!(n-h)!}\right]2^{-n}$$

Let's make sure that this formula works for $n = 5$ (in this case 2^{-n} is 1/32):

Table 3-1

h	Number of Combinations with h Heads		Probability of h Heads
0	$\frac{5!}{0!5!} = 1$	TTTTT	1/32 = .031
1	$\frac{5!}{1!4!} = 5$	HTTTT, THTTT, TTHTT, TTTHT, TTTTH	5/32 = .156
2	$\frac{5!}{2!3!} = 10$	HHTTT, HTHTT, HTTHT, HTTTH, THHTT, THTHT, THTTH, TTHHT, TTHTH, TTTHH	10/32 = .313
3	$\frac{5!}{3!2!} = 10$	TTHHH, THTHH, THHTH, THHHT, HTTHH, HTHTH, HTHHT, HHTTH, HHTHT, HHHTT	10/32 = .313
4	$\frac{5!}{4!1!} = 5$	HHHHT, HHHTH, HHTHH, HTHHH, THHHH	5/32 = .156
5	$\frac{5!}{0!5!} = 1$	HHHHH	1/32 = .031

We can also use the formula to see that the chance of getting 92 heads in a row is 2.019×10^{-28}. Keep that in mind if you decide to try to break Rosencrantz and Guildenstern's record.

The Excel function BINOMDIST will calculate these probabilities. See Chapter 7.

YOU SHOULD REMEMBER

1. The study of coin tossing provides a good introduction to probability because we can easily understand the process that is occurring.

2. To find the probability that h heads will appear if we toss a coin n times, we first need to calculate the number of possible outcomes (2^n). Then we need to calculate the number of possible ways of tossing h heads:

$$\frac{n!}{h!(n-h)!}$$

3. The exclamation point represents a function called the *factorial function*, which is the product of all the whole numbers from 1 up to the number:

$$n! = n \times (n-1) \times (n-2) \times (n-3) \times \cdots \times (3) \times (2) \times (1)$$

Therefore, the probability of tossing h heads if we toss a fair coin n times is

$$\frac{\dfrac{n!}{h!(n-h)!}}{2^n}$$

HYPOTHESIS TESTING

During all of these calculations we have assumed that the coin was a fair coin—that is, during any particular flip there was a 50 percent chance of flipping a head and a 50 percent chance of flipping a tail. Now we will consider an even more perplexing problem: How can we tell whether the coin is really fair? You will especially need to know the answer to this question if you are considering playing a coin-flipping game with an unkempt-looking stranger in a strange town. To put it formally, if we let p stand for the probability that the coin will come up heads, how do we know that $p = 1/2$?

In our coin example we should first, of course, make an obvious check. If the coin has two heads, then $p = 1$; if it has two tails, then $p = 0$. Once we've done that, though, it is very difficult to tell just by looking at the coin whether it is fair. Intuitively, we can't think of any reason why it might be more likely to come up "heads" rather than "tails" (or vice versa), but it might be unbalanced in such a way as to make one outcome more likely than the other. If we flip the coin once, we won't have a clue as to whether it is fair.

However, if we flip the coin many times, we will start getting some information that we can use to estimate how fair it is.

• *THE NULL HYPOTHESIS AND THE ALTERNATIVE HYPOTHESIS*

Problems of this sort are called **hypothesis testing** problems. First we decide on the hypothesis we want to test. In this case our hypothesis is that $p = 1/2$. The hypothesis that is to be tested is often called the **null hypothesis**. The only other possibility is that the null hypothesis is wrong. The hypothesis that says, "The null hypothesis is wrong" is called the **alternative hypothesis**. In our case the alternative hypothesis is that the coin is not fair ($p \neq 1/2$). We know that either the null hypothesis or the alternative hypothesis must be true, since they are the only two possibilities. The question is: Do we accept the null hypothesis and say that the coin is fair, or do we reject the null hypothesis and say that the coin is unfair?

It is clear intuitively that we should flip the coin many times; let n be the number of flips. Then, if the number of heads that appears is close to $n/2$, we should accept the hypothesis that the coin is fair. If the number of heads is very far from $n/2$, we should reject the hypothesis that the coin is fair. The big question is: How far away from $n/2$ can it be before we say the coin is unfair?

Therefore, our test procedure will work like this. We will pick a number c. If the number of heads (h) is between ($n/2 - c$) and ($n/2 + c$), we will accept the null hypothesis and say that the coin is fair; otherwise we will say that the coin is not fair. We can call the region from ($n/2 - c$) to ($n/2 + c$) the **zone of acceptance**. If h is not in the zone of acceptance, we will be very critical of the hypothesis and will reject it. Therefore, the zone for which the hypothesis will be rejected is called the **rejection region** or **critical region**. (See Figure 3–1.)

The main problem now is: How far away from $n/2$ can we let the number of heads get before we say that the coin is unfair—that is, how big should we make c?

Figure 3–1. Number of heads in *n* flips

• *AVOIDING TYPE I AND TYPE II ERRORS*

We would like to make the right judgment about our null hypothesis. There are two ways we can be right: we can accept the hypothesis when it is true, or we can reject it when it is false. However, that means that there are also two ways we can be wrong: we might reject the hypothesis when it is really

Table 3-2

	Accept Hypothesis	Reject Hypothesis
Hypothesis is true	right	Type I error (we want to avoid this)
Hypothesis is false	Type II error	right

true, or we might accept the hypothesis when it is really false. The first kind of mistake is called a **Type I error**, and the second kind of mistake is called a **Type II error**. We will find out how to predict the chances of a Type I error. However, predicting the chances of a Type II error is much harder. That is because there is only one way the null hypothesis can be true, but there are many ways that it can be false.

Table 3–2 shows the possibilities.

If we choose a large value for c, we will have a wide zone of acceptance and we will be more likely to accept the hypothesis than we would with a small value of c. That means that there is less chance of committing a Type I error—that is, we're not likely to reject the hypothesis if it is really true. However, if we make the zone of acceptance large, we are increasing the risk that we will accept the hypothesis even if it is really false, thereby committing a Type II error.

The other strategy is to choose a narrow zone of acceptance. If we do that, it is unlikely that we will commit a Type II error (we're not likely to accept the hypothesis if it is really false) but we stand a much greater chance of committing a Type I error (rejecting the hypothesis when it is really true). Obviously there is an inherent trade-off involved in hypothesis testing. We usually can't devise a single test procedure that will minimize the chances of committing both types of error.

Often we will be more worried about the possibility of incorrectly rejecting the hypothesis, so we will be more careful about avoiding Type I errors. If we're going to have the courage to tell the unkempt stranger that we think his coin is unfair, then we want to make almost certain that we're right. (Otherwise he might get nasty.) In scientific work, if we decide to accept the hypothesis, we're likely to keep on searching for more evidence to see whether we can make a convincing case for it. If, on the other hand, we decide to reject the hypothesis, that means we're really convinced that the hypothesis is false, so we can stop.

What is often done in statistics is to set an upper limit to the probability of committing a Type I error. Usually this limit is set at either 10 percent, 5 percent, or 1 percent, depending on how hard we want to make it to reject the null hypothesis. At first it can be confusing to remember the difference between Type I and Type II errors. Just remember that our number one priority is to avoid errors of Type I, which we do by making certain that we don't reject the hypothesis unless we're pretty sure it's wrong. We'll decide on a 10 percent test. The probability that h will equal a particular value k is

$$\frac{n!}{k!\,(n-k)!} \times 2^{-n}$$

Now, we need to figure out how wide to make the zone of acceptance. Let's suppose that the coin is fair. Once we make that assumption, we know exactly what the probabilities are, using the principles we developed earlier in the chapter. If n is the number of flips and h is the number of heads, that means we want to make sure there is only a 10 percent chance that our test procedure will say the coin is unfair when it is really fair.

Suppose that $n = 20$. Then we can make a table of the probabilities that $h = 0$, $h = 1$, $h = 2$, and so on (See Table 3–3). These probabilities are shown in Figure 3–2.

Table 3-3. Results of Tossing a Coin 20 Times

Number of Heads	Probability				
0	.000001				
1	.000019				
2	.000181				
3	.001087				
4	.004621				
5	.014786				
6	.036964				
7	.073929				
8	.120134				
9	.160179				
10	.176197	8 to 12:			
11	.160179	.7368	7 to 13:		
12	.120134		.8847	6 to 14:	
13	.073929			.9586	5 to 15:
14	.036964				.9882
15	.014786				
16	.004621				
17	.001087				
18	.000181				
19	.000019				
20	.000001				

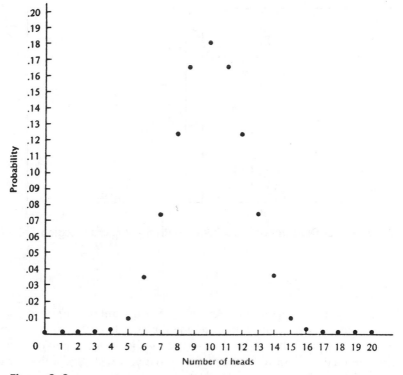

Figure 3–2

We want to choose our zone of acceptance so that there is roughly a 90 percent chance that h will land in the zone and only a 10 percent chance that h will land outside the zone. If we add up the probabilities for $h = 7$, $h = 8$, $h = 9$, $h = 10$, $h = 11$, $h = 12$, and $h = 13$, we find that if the coin is fair there is a .8847 probability that h will have one of these seven values. Therefore, we'll design our test like this: We will flip the coin 20 times and count the number of heads (h). If h is between 7 and 13, we will accept the hypothesis and say that the coin is fair. If h is less than or equal to 6, or if h is greater than or equal to 14, we will say that the coin is unfair.

In this way we can ensure that the probability of erroneously rejecting the hypothesis (Type I error) is only about 12 percent. For example, suppose that there are 5 heads out of the 20 flips. Then we can say with a fair degree of confidence that the coin is not fair. We cannot say this with absolute certainty, because there is a 1.48 percent chance that only 5 heads will turn up in 20 flips of a fair coin. Therefore there still is a possibility that we might commit a Type I error by saying that the hypothesis is false when it is really true. However, we have made sure that the probability of this happening is less than 12 percent.

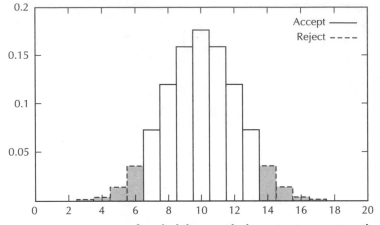

Figure 3–3. Bar Diagram of Probabilities with the Rejection Region Shaded

Of course, you can be still more cautious if you want to. Suppose you are very worried about erroneously rejecting the fair-coin hypothesis, so you want to make sure that the chance of that happening is about 4 percent. In that case you can change your test procedure so that you will accept the fair-coin hypothesis if *h* is between 6 and 14. With this procedure, you are even more sure that you won't say that the coin is unfair when it is really fair. However, by widening the zone of acceptance you are increasing the chances of committing a Type II error—that is, saying that the coin is fair when it is really unfair. There is no way to calculate the probability of a Type II error, since you don't know the probabilities for the different numbers of heads if the coin is unfair. Therefore, even after you've decided to accept the hypothesis, you're not sure that the coin is really fair. For example, suppose the probability of heads is .51. Then you are very likely to accept the fair-coin hypothesis even though the coin is not fair. The only way to improve on this situation is to increase the number of flips.

In this section, we started with how big a chance we are willing to take on a Type I error. We then worked backward to find a zone of acceptance that tells us how many heads we can flip and still believe that the coin is fair. Another technique is to take your data (the number of heads flipped) and find the chance of getting such a result if the null hypothesis is true (the coin is fair). This chance is called a *p* value. For example, if the *p* value is 0.005, then you would reject the null hypothesis if you were willing to live with a 0.005 chance of a Type I error or if you were willing to live with any larger value for the chance of a Type I error. A smaller *p* value gives you more confidence that rejecting the null hypothesis is the right decision.

We'll talk more about hypothesis testing and *p* values in Chapter 13.

YOU SHOULD REMEMBER

1. Many common statistical problems are *hypothesis testing* problems. The hypothesis that is being tested is called the *null hypothesis,* and the hypothesis that says, "The null hypothesis is wrong," is called the *alternative hypothesis.*

2. In general, it is not possible to prove that the null hypothesis is true or false. After some observations have been collected, however, it is possible to use statistical analysis to determine whether the null hypothesis should be accepted or rejected.

3. There are two possible types of errors:

   Type I error: saying that the null hypothesis is *false* when it is really *true*

   Type II error: saying that the null hypothesis is *true* when it is really *false*

   It is a common procedure to design the test so that the chance of committing a Type I error is less than a specified amount (often 5 percent).

4. The *p* value is the probability of getting the observed result, or one even more unfavorable to the null hypothesis, if the null hypothesis is true. A smaller *p* value strengthens the case for rejecting the null hypothesis.

KNOW THE CONCEPTS

DO YOU KNOW THE BASICS?

Test your understanding of Chapter 3 by answering the following questions:

1. Why do statisticians study coin tossing?

2. If you want to determine for sure whether a coin is fair, why don't you flip the coin a few thousand times?

3. If you flip a coin eight times, which of these patterns is more likely: HTHTHTHT or HHHHHHHH?

4. Why is the probability of getting h heads the same as the probability of getting $n - h$ heads?

5. Suppose you have 100 coins that actually are fair, but you don't know whether they are fair. You will flip each coin 20 times as described in the chapter. Will your investigation lead you to conclude that all 100 coins are fair?

6. Should you make the zone of acceptance very wide in order to minimize the chance of a Type I error?

7. In a practical hypothesis testing situation, how should you decide on the maximum probability of a Type I error that you are willing to tolerate?

TERMS FOR STUDY

alternative hypothesis   probability
critical region   Type I error
factorial   Type II error
hypothesis testing   zone of acceptance
null hypothesis

PRACTICAL APPLICATION

COMPUTATIONAL PROBLEMS

For Exercises 1–3 use the formula given in the chapter to make a table showing the probabilities for the number of heads that will appear if you toss a fair coin:

1. 6 times

2. 7 times

3. 8 times

   The lists in Exercises 4–6 present the probabilities for the number of heads appearing for 50 tosses, 75 tosses, and 100 tosses of a fair coin. In each case you want to test the hypothesis that the coin you toss is fair. Calculate how wide the zone of acceptance should be so that the chance of committing a Type I error (that is, rejecting the fair-coin hypothesis if the coin really is fair) is less than 5 percent.

4. 50 tosses.

h	$\Pr(X = h)$	h	$\Pr(X = h)$
15	.002	26	.108
16	.004	27	.096
17	.009	28	.079
18	.016	29	.060
19	.027	30	.042
20	.042	31	.027
21	.060	32	.016
22	.079	33	.009
23	.096	34	.004
24	.108	35	.002
25	.112		

5. 75 tosses:

b	$\Pr(X = b)$	b	$\Pr(X = b)$
25	.001	38	.091
26	.003	39	.087
27	.005	40	.078
28	.008	41	.066
29	.013	42	.054
30	.021	43	.041
31	.030	44	.030
32	.041	45	.021
33	.054	46	.013
34	.066	47	.008
35	.078	48	.005
36	.087	49	.003
37	.091	50	.001

6. 100 tosses:

b	$\Pr(X = b)$	b	$\Pr(X = b)$
35	.001	44	.039
36	.002	45	.048
37	.003	46	.058
38	.004	47	.067
39	.007	48	.074
40	.011	49	.078
41	.016	50	.080
42	.022	51	.078
43	.030	52	.074

b	$\Pr(X = b)$	b	$\Pr(X = b)$
53	.067	60	.011
54	.058	61	.007
55	.048	62	.004
56	.039	63	.003
57	.030	64	.002
58	.022	65	.001
59	.016		

ANSWERS

KNOW THE CONCEPTS

1. It is helpful to study the principles of probability in a simple situation where we understand the nature of the process; we can then apply these principles to practical situations where the process or population is unknown.

2. You don't flip a coin a few thousand times for the same reason you don't check an entire population: it would be too expensive. (Time is valuable, and it would take a lot of time to flip a coin a few thousand times.)

3. The two patterns are equally likely.

4. The probability of getting h heads is exactly the same as the probability of getting h tails.

5. Even if all the coins are fair, you will probably determine that 12 coins are unfair because our test procedure has a 12 percent chance of saying the coin is unfair when it is really fair. If you test a great many hypotheses in your career as a statistician, you will inevitably make this type of error a certain fraction of the time.

6. If you widen the zone of acceptance, you are increasing the chance of a Type II error.

7. The decision depends on the consequences of each type of error in your particular situation.

PRACTICAL APPLICATION

Here are the formula and directions you need for doing Exercises 1–6:

To find the probability of h heads appearing if you toss a coin n times:

$$\frac{\dfrac{n!}{h!(n-h)!}}{2^n}$$

To test the hypothesis that a coin is fair, set up a zone of acceptance: $(n/2 - c)$ to $(n/2 + c)$, where c is chosen to make the chance of a Type I error less than a specified amount.

Sample calculations are shown below for Exercise 1. The same method is used for Exercises 2 and 3.

1. 6 tosses:

$$b = 0: \frac{\frac{6!}{0!6!}}{64} = \frac{1}{64} = .016$$

$$b = 1: \frac{\frac{6!}{1!5!}}{64} = \frac{6}{64} = .094$$

$$b = 2: \frac{\frac{6!}{2!4!}}{64} = \frac{\frac{6 \times 5 \times 4 \times 3 \times 2 \times 1}{2 \times 1 \times 4 \times 3 \times 2 \times 1}}{64} = \frac{15}{64} = .234$$

$$b = 3: \frac{\frac{6!}{3!3!}}{64} = \frac{\frac{6 \times 5 \times 4 \times 3 \times 2 \times 1}{3 \times 2 \times 1 \times 3 \times 2 \times 1}}{64} = \frac{20}{64} = .313$$

$$b = 4: .234 \qquad b = 5: .094 \qquad b = 6: .016$$

2. 7 tosses:

b	$Pr(X = b)$	b	$Pr(X = b)$
0	.008	4	.273
1	.055	5	.164
2	.164	6	.055
3	.273	7	.008

3. 8 tosses:

b	$Pr(X = b)$	b	$Pr(X = b)$
0	.004	5	.219
1	.031	6	.109
2	.109	7	.031
3	.219	8	.004
4	.273		

4. Zone of acceptance: 18 to 32. With this zone of acceptance the chance of committing a Type I error is .033. (Add all of the probabilities from 18 to 32, and then subtract the result from 1.) If the zone of acceptance is narrowed to the interval from 19 to 31, then the chance of a Type I error increases to .065.

5. Zone of acceptance: 29 to 46.   Chance of Type I error: .037

6. Zone of acceptance: 40 to 60.   Chance of Type I error: .035

4
CALCULATING PROBABILITIES

KEY TERMS

combinations the number of different ways of selecting j objects from a group of n objects when the order in which the objects are chosen does not matter

permutations the number of different ways of selecting j objects from a group of n objects when each distinct way of ordering the chosen objects counts separately

probability of an event the number of outcomes that corresponds to that event divided by the total number of possible outcomes, provided all outcomes are equally likely

sampling with replacement a method for choosing a sample where an item that has been selected is put back in the population and therefore has a chance of being selected again

sampling without replacement a method for choosing a sample where an item that has been selected is not put back in the population and therefore cannot be selected again

INTERPRETATIONS OF PROBABILITY

What exactly is probability? That is a tricky (and sometimes controversial) question.

Consider the statement, "If we flip a coin, the probability is 1/2 that the result will be a head." It is a difficult philosophical question to determine exactly what this statement means. According to the **relative frequency view of probability**, the statement means that the number of heads will be close to 1/2 of the total tosses if you toss the coin a large number of times.

There are some events for which the relative-frequency interpretation is difficult. The weather report often says, "There is a 20 percent chance of rain today." However, we can't have today repeat itself 100 times to see whether it rains 20 of those times.

The **subjective view of probability** states that probability is an estimate of what an individual *thinks* is the likelihood that an event will happen. In that case two individuals might estimate the probability differently. The subjective view makes it possible to talk meaningfully about the probabilities of a wider class of events, but the probabilities become more intangible because we can't objectively specify what they are.

GAMBLER'S INTERPRETATION OF PROBABILITY

Another perspective of probability is the **gambler's view** (remember that the early mathematics of probability was done by gamblers): the probability of an event occurring can be derived by the odds that would have to be offered to you before you would bet that the event does occur. For example, if you are willing to bet at even odds (win or lose the same amount) that it is going to rain tomorrow, you must believe, perhaps unconsciously, that there is at least a 50 percent chance of it raining tomorrow. If you are willing to bet $10 that you can win a game of tennis, but only if you can win at least $30 for risking your $10, then you must believe that there is a 1 out of 4 chance of your winning and a 3 out of 4 chance of losing.

The gambler's view of probability is intuitive, but most people's intuition is inconsistent.

In the mathematical, or axiomatic, approach to probability, the term *probability* is left as an undefined term. A small set of assumptions (axioms) are made about the behavior of probability. These assumptions follow our intuitive idea of what probability means. Then, those assumptions are used to prove theorems.

PROBABILITY SPACES

Now we will develop the formal method of determining the probabilities associated with a random experiment. First, we'll make a list of all the possible results of our experiment. We're going to use the technical term set for this list. *Set* is just a formal name for a collection of objects. Here is an example:

$$\{1, 2, 3, 4, 5, 6\}$$

Sets can be defined by either of two methods. We can use the listing method as we just did. That just involves writing down all of the members of the set. The set members are enclosed in braces: { }. Then it's clear what is in the set and what is not.

A set can also be defined by stating a rule that makes it clear what is in the set. For example, the set above could have been defined by this rule: the set of all possible results of tossing one die.

With small sets, the listing method and the rule method will work equally well. However, with large sets the rule method works much better. For example, it would be very difficult to list all of the members of these sets:

- the set of all whole numbers from 1 to a million

- the set of all possible results of flipping a coin 12 times

We are especially interested in sets that contain all of the possible results of an experiment. The set of all possible results is called the **probability space** (or sometimes the **sample space**). Mathematicians like to use the term *space* for this type of set. Here are some examples of probability spaces:

- experiment: flip coin one time
  probability space: {H, T}

- experiment: flip coin three times
  probability space: {HHH, HHT, HTH, HTT, THH, THT, TTH, TTT}

- experiment: roll one die
  probability space: {1, 2, 3, 4, 5, 6}

- experiment: roll two dice
  probability space: {(1,1)(1,2)(1,3)(1,4)(1,5)(1,6)(2,1)(2,2)(2,3)
                      (2,4)(2,5)(2,6)(3,1)(3,2)(3,3)(3,4)(3,5)(3,6)
                      (4,1)(4,2)(4,3)(4,4)(4,5)(4,6)(5,1)(5,2)(5,3)
                      (5,4)(5,5)(5,6)(6,1)(6,2)(6,3)(6,4)(6,5)(6,6)}

- experiment: draw one card from a deck of 52 cards
  probability space:

    {ace hearts, ace diamonds, ace spades, ace clubs,
      two hearts, two diamonds, two spades, two clubs, etc.}

  (There will be 52 elements if we list them all.)

To avoid the bother of writing "probability space" each time, we'll sometimes use the letter S (short for "space") to stand for a probability space.

The important thing is that every single possible result of the experiment must be included in the probability space. We'll call each possible result an **outcome**. We'll use a small s to represent the total number of outcomes in the probability space S. In the examples above, the first probability space has two possible outcomes and the others have 8, 6, 36, and 52 outcomes, respectively. For now, we'll assume that each outcome is equally likely. (This is called the **classical approach to probability**.) Then, since there are s outcomes, the probability of any one outcome is $1/s$.

Now we'll use a probability space to solve a practical problem. Suppose that we're playing Monopoly, and that our marker is on North Carolina Avenue. We already own Park Place, so we will have it made if we roll a 7 and land on Boardwalk. As we saw earlier, there are 36 possible outcomes for the experiment of rolling two dice. We want to get a 7, so it doesn't make any difference to us whether we roll (1,6) or (2,5) or (3,4) or (4,3) or (5,2) or (6,1). We can put all of these outcomes together in a set. We'll often use capital letters to stand for sets, so we may as well call this one set *A*:

$$A = \{(1,6), (2,5), (3,4), (4,3), (5,2), (6,1)\}$$

We can also define set *A* by the rule method: Set *A* is the set of all possible outcomes from rolling two dice such that the sum of the numbers on the two dice is 7.

Set *A* contains 6 outcomes. If we roll the dice, we have an equal chance of getting any one of the 36 possible outcomes. Since 6 of these outcomes give us what we want (a total of 7 on the dice), the probability of getting 7 is $6/36 = 1/6$.

(1 ,1)	(1 ,2)	(1 ,3)	(1 ,4)	(1 ,5)	(1 ,6)
(2 ,1)	(2 ,2)	(2 ,3)	(2 ,4)	(2 ,5)	(2 ,6)
(3 ,1)	(3 ,2)	(3 ,3)	(3 ,4)	(3 ,5)	(3 ,6)
(4 ,1)	(4 ,2)	(4 ,3)	(4 ,4)	(4 ,5)	(4 ,6)
(5 ,1)	(5 ,2)	(5 ,3)	(5 ,4)	(5 ,5)	(5 ,6)
(6 ,1)	(6 ,2)	(6 ,3)	(6 ,4)	(6 ,5)	(6 ,6)

Figure 4–1

Set *A* is an example of what we will call an *event*. An event is a set that consists of a group of outcomes. In our case, (1,6), (2,5), (3,4), (4,3), (5,2), (6,1) are all outcomes, and the set {(1,6), (2,5), (3,4), (4,3), (5,2), (6,1)} is an event.

An event can also be defined in this way: An event is a **subset** of the probability space. A subset is a set that contains some (or possibly all) members of another set. If set *A* is a subset of set *S*, then every outcome in set *A* is contained in set *S*. For example:

- set: all people living in New York State
  subset: all people living in New York City

YOU SHOULD REMEMBER

1. Probability may be interpreted according to the relative frequency view or the subjective view.

2. A *set* can be defined by listing all its members or by stating a rule that makes clear what the set contains.

3. The set of all possible results of an experiment is called the *probability space*.

4. Each possible result of an experiment is called an outcome.

5. In the *classical approach to probability* each outcome is regarded as equally likely.

PROBABILITY OF AN EVENT

• *PROBABILITY THAT AN EVENT WILL HAPPEN*

Now we're ready to give a formal definition for the **probability of an event** A. First, count the number of outcomes in A. Call that number $N(A)$. (Read this as "N of A," which is short for "number of outcomes in A.") Remember that all outcomes are equally likely and s is the total number of outcomes in the probability space S. Then we can define the probability:

$$\text{Probability that event } A \text{ will occur is } \frac{N(A)}{s}$$

In other words, count the number of outcomes that give you event A, and then divide by the total number of possible outcomes.

It would be helpful to have a shorter way to write "Probability that event A occurs." We will use Pr to stand for probability, and write it like this:

$$\text{Pr}(A) \text{ means "probability that event } A \text{ will occur"}$$

Our result becomes:

$$\text{Pr}(A) = \frac{N(A)}{s}$$

Examples: Determining the Probability of an Event

PROBLEM   What is the probability of getting one head if we toss a coin three times?

SOLUTION   In this case, there are $2^3 = 8$ possible outcomes, so $s = 8$. There are three outcomes that give one head (HTT, THT, TTH), so if A is the event of getting one head, then $N(A) = 3$. Therefore, $\text{Pr}(A) = 3/8$.

PROBLEM   What is the probability of getting a total of 5 if we roll two dice?

SOLUTION   There are 36 possible outcomes, so $s = 36$. Let B be the event of getting 5 on the dice, so B contains four outcomes:

$$B = \{(1,4), (2,3), (3,2), (4,1)\}$$

Then $N(B) = 4$, so $\Pr(B) = 4/36 = 1/9$. (Your chances of getting 5 are worse than your chances of getting 7.)

PROBLEM   What is the probability of drawing an ace if we draw one card from a deck of cards?

SOLUTION   There are 52 possible outcomes, so $s = 52$. Let C be the event of drawing an ace, so C contains four outcomes:

{A hearts, A diamonds, A clubs, A spades}

Then $N(C) = 4$, so $\Pr(C) = 4/52 = 1/13$.

Two special events are interesting. First, let us consider the probability that event S occurs. Remember that S contains all of the possible outcomes of the experiment. Using the formula gives this:

$$\Pr(S) = \frac{N(S)}{s} = \frac{s}{s} = 1$$

This result should be obvious. All it says is, "The probability is 100 percent that the result will be one of the possible results." (Just ask yourself: What is the probability that the result will *not* be one of the possible results?)

Another possible event is the set that contains *no* outcome. You should be able to convince yourself that this set has zero probability of occurring. This set is often called the empty set, because it doesn't have anything in it:

$\Pr(\text{empty set}) = 0$

The empty set is often symbolized by a zero with a slash, /, through it, like this: ∅. Therefore, we can say:

$\Pr(\emptyset) = 0$

• *PROBABILITY THAT AN EVENT WILL NOT HAPPEN*

Now we can develop another important result that is fortunately very obvious. Many times we will want to know the probability that an event will *not* happen. For example, returning to our Monopoly game, suppose we are on North Carolina Avenue and our opponent has a hotel on Boardwalk. In that case we're mainly interested in the probability that we will *not* get a 7. It should be clear that, if there is a 1/6 chance of getting a 7, then there is a 5/6 chance of not getting a 7. We can demonstrate that. Let A be the event of not getting a 7. Then A contains 30 outcomes:

$$\{(1,1)\ (1,2)\ (1,3)\ (1,4)\ (1,5)$$
$$(2,1)\ (2,2)\ (2,3)\ (2,4)\qquad (2,6)$$
$$(3,1)\ (3,2)\ (3,3)\qquad (3,5)\ (3,6)$$
$$(4,1)\ (4,2)\qquad (4,4)\ (4,5)\ (4,6)$$
$$(5,1)\qquad (5,3)\ (5,4)\ (5,5)\ (5,6)$$
$$(6,2)\ (6,3)\ (6,4)\ (6,5)\ (6,6)\}$$

Therefore $N(A) = 30$, so $\Pr(A) = 30/36 = 5/6$. In general, if p is the probability that a particular event A will occur, then $1 - p$ is the probability that the event will not occur.

We will give a special name to the set that contains all of the outcomes that are not in set A. It is called the **complement** of A, written as A^c. (The little c stands for "complement." Read the symbol as "A complement.")

Then:

$$\Pr(A^c) = 1 - \Pr(A)$$

This result is important for calculations, since sometimes it is easier to calculate the probability that an event will not occur than to calculate the probability that it will occur.

Here are some examples of complements:

- If the experiment consists of flipping a coin, and A is the event of getting a head, then A^c is the event of getting a tail.

- If the experiment consists of flipping four coins, and B is the event of getting four heads, then B^c is the event of getting at least one tail.

- If the total set is the set of all 52 cards in a deck of cards, and R is the event of drawing a red card, then R^c is the event of drawing a black card.

- If the total set is the set of all major league baseball teams, and A is the set {Yankees, Mets}, then A^c is the set of all major league teams that are not from New York.

PROBABILITY OF A UNION

Now suppose that nobody owns either Boardwalk or Park Place, and we would like to know the probability that we will land on either of them. If we're currently on North Carolina Avenue, then we need to know the probability that we will get either a 5 or a 7. It often happens in probability that we need to find out the probability that either one of two events will occur. Let's say that A is the event of getting a 7. Then A contains the outcomes

$$\{(1,6), (2,5), (3,4), (4,3), (5,2), (6,1)\}$$

If B is the event of getting a 5, then B contains the outcomes

$$\{(1,4), (2,3), (3,2), (4,1)\}$$

Let's say that C is the event of getting either a 5 *or* a 7. Then C contains these outcomes:

$$\{(1,6), (2,5), (3,4), (4,3), (5,2), (6,1), (1,4), (2,3), (3,2), (4,1)\}$$

C contains 10 outcomes, so $\Pr(C) = 10/36$.

(1 ,1)	(1 ,2)	(1 ,3)	(1 ,4)	(1 ,5)	(1 ,6)
(2 ,1)	(2 ,2)	(2 ,3)	(2 ,4)	(2 ,5)	(2 ,6)
(3 ,1)	(3 ,2)	(3 ,3)	(3 ,4)	(3 ,5)	(3 ,6)
(4 ,1)	(4 ,2)	(4 ,3)	(4 ,4)	(4 ,5)	(4 ,6)
(5 ,1)	(5 ,2)	(5 ,3)	(5 ,4)	(5 ,5)	(5 ,6)
(6 ,1)	(6 ,2)	(6 ,3)	(6 ,4)	(6 ,5)	(6 ,6)

Figure 4–2

There is a special name for the set that contains all of the elements in either or both of two other sets. It is called the **union** of the other two sets. In this case, C is the union of set A and set B. You can think of it in this way: set A and set B get together and join forces to form a union, and the result is set C. In mathematics the word *union* is symbolized by a little symbol that looks like a letter u: $\cup$. Therefore, we can write "C is the union of A and B" as

$$C = A \text{ union } B$$

or

$$C = A \cup B$$

Here are some examples of unions:

- If A is the set of even numbers and B is the set of odd numbers, then $A \cup B$ is the set of all whole numbers.

- If V is the set of vowels and C is the set of consonants, then $V \cup C$ is the set of all letters.

- If A is the set {AH, KH, QH, JH, 10H}, and B is the set {QH, JH, 10H, 9H, 8H}, then $A \cup B$ is {AH, KH, QH, JH, 10H, 9H, 8H}.

There is another interesting fact that we can learn from the dice example. We said that (probability of getting a 7) = $Pr(A)$ = 6/36, (probability of getting a 5) = $Pr(B)$ = 4/36, and (probability of getting a 5 or a 7) = $Pr(A$ or $B)$ = $Pr(A \cup B)$ = 10/36. It looks as though we could just add the probabilities for the two events to get the probability that either one of them will occur, since 10/36 = 6/36 + 4/36. This amazingly simple rule will often work:

$$Pr(A \text{ or } B) = Pr(A \cup B) = Pr(A) + Pr(B)$$

However, this result holds only when there is no possibility that event A and event B can occur at the same time. Here is an example of incorrect reasoning: "Toss a coin twice. Since the probability of getting a head on the first toss is 1/2 and the probability of getting a head on the second toss is 1/2, the probability of getting a head on either the first toss or the second toss is 1/2 + 1/2 = 1." Obviously, that is not the case. In the dice example we could use the simple formula because there is no way to get both a 5 and a 7 on a single toss of a pair of dice. Two events that can never occur together are called **disjoint events** or **mutually exclusive events**.

PROBABILITY OF AN INTERSECTION

Now we will consider an example in which two events can happen together. Suppose you are selecting one card from a deck and you want to know the probability that you will get a red face card — that is, a red jack, queen, or king. Let's say that F is the event of getting a face card. Then F contains these outcomes:

{JH, JD, JC, JS,
QH, QD, QC, QS,
KH, KD, KC, KS}

(Here J = jack, Q = queen, K = king, H = hearts, D = diamonds, C = clubs, S = spades.)

Since $N(F)$ = 12, the probability of getting a face card is 12/52. Let R be the event of getting a red card; then R contains these outcomes:

{AH, 2H, 3H, 4H, 5H, 6H, 7H, 8H, 9H, 10H, JH, QH, KH,
AD, 2D, 3D, 4D, 5D, 6D, 7D, 8D, 9D, 10D, JD, QD, KD}

R contains 26 outcomes, so $Pr(R)$ = 26/52 = 1/2.

Let C be the event that both event F and event R occur—in other words, C is the event that you get a card that is *both* a red card and a face card. Then C contains these six outcomes:

{JD, JH, QD, QH, KD, KH}

Therefore, $\Pr(C) = N(C)/s = 6/52$.

There is a special name for the set that contains all of the elements that are in both of two other sets. It is called the **intersection**. For example, in this case set C is the intersection of set F and set R, because it contains the outcomes that are in both set F and in set R. The symbol of intersection is the symbol for union turned upside down: ∩. Now we can write:

C = set that contains the elements in both A and B;

$C = A$ intersect B; or

$C = A \cap B$

Here are some examples of intersections:

- If V is the set of vowels and C is the set of consonants, then $V \cap C$ is {y}.

- If A is the set of hands with five cards in sequence, and B is the set of hands with five cards of the same suit, then $A \cap B$ is the set of all straight flushes.

- If you flip a coin twice, and A is the event of getting a head on the first toss and B is the event of getting a head on the second toss, then $A \cap B$ is {HH}.

There is no general formula for the probability of the intersection of two events, but Chapter 5 discusses a formula that can sometimes be used. For now, we'll have to count the number of outcomes in the intersection and calculate the probability directly from that.

If two events can't happen together (in other words, they are mutually exclusive events), then their intersection is the empty set. For example, we can't get both a head and a tail on a single coin flip, so if H = event of getting a head, and T = event of getting a tail, then $\Pr(H$ and $T) = \Pr(H \cap T) = 0$. In general, if A and B are mutually exclusive, then $A \cap B = \emptyset$ and $\Pr(A \cap B) = 0$.

Now let us consider the possibility that we will get either a face card *or* a red card when we draw a card from the deck. If F is the event of getting a face card, and R is the event of getting a red card, then we want to know

$$\Pr(F \text{ or } R) = \Pr(F \cup R)$$

We can't use the simple formula $\Pr(F) + \Pr(R)$, because these two events can happen together. We can make a list of all the outcomes in $F \cup R$ (see Figure 4–3.):

{AH, 2H, 3H, 4H, 5H, 6H, 7H, 8H, 9H, 10H,
JH, QH, KH,
JC, QC, KC,
AD, 2D, 3D, 4D, 5D, 6D, 7D, 8D, 9D, 10D,
JD, QD, KD,
JS, QS, KS}

Altogether there are 32 outcomes, so

$$Pr(F \text{ or } R) = Pr(F \cup R) = 32/52$$

AH	AD	AC	AS
2H	2D	2C	2S
3H	3D	3C	3S
4H	4D	4C	4S
5H	5D	5C	5S
6H	6D	6C	6S
7H	7D	7C	7S
8H	8D	8C	8S
9H	9D	9C	9S
10H	10D	10C	10S
JH	JD	JC	JS
QH	QD	QC	QS
KH	KD	KC	KS

Figure 4–3

Now we can figure out a general formula for the probability of $A \cup B$.

$$Pr(A \text{ or } B) = Pr(A) + Pr(B) - Pr(A \text{ and } B)$$

or, written mathematically:

$$Pr(A \cup B) = Pr(A) + Pr(B) - Pr(A \cap B)$$

This formula is good for any two events, whether or not they are mutually exclusive. Notice that, if A and B *are* mutually exclusive, then $Pr(A \text{ and } B) = 0$, so we get the same formula that we had before:

$$Pr(A \text{ or } B) = Pr(A) + Pr(B)$$

Examples: Determining the Probability of Union

PROBLEM   Suppose that, in the middle of a backgammon game, you want to know the probability that you will get a total of 8 or doubles on the dice.

SOLUTION   Let's say that $E1$ is the event of getting 8. Then:

$$E1 = \{(2,6), (3,5), (4,4), (5,3), (6,2)\}, \qquad Pr(E1) = 5/36$$

Let $E2$ be the event of getting a double. Then:

$$E2 = \{(1,1), (2,2), (3,3), (4,4), (5,5), (6,6)\}, \qquad Pr(E2) = 6/36$$

These two events are not mutually exclusive, since you can get both 8 and a double (if the dice turn up (4,4)). Then $(E1 \cap E2)$ is the event of getting (4,4), which, as we have learned, has a probability of 1/36. Now we can use our formula:

Pr(getting a double or 8)

$$= Pr(E1 \text{ or } E2) = Pr(E1) + Pr(E2) - Pr(E1 \text{ and } E2)$$
$$= \quad 5/36 + 6/36 \quad - \quad\quad 1/36$$
$$= 10/36$$

PROBLEM   What is the probability that you will get at least one 6 when you roll two dice?

SOLUTION   We'll call $E1$ the event of getting a 6 on the first die and $E2$ the event of getting a 6 on the second die. Then the event that you will get at least one 6 is $E1 \cup E2$. We know that $Pr(E1) = Pr(E2) = 1/6$. Since $E1 \cap E2$ is the event of getting 6's on both dice, we know that the probability of that happening is 1/36. Therefore, we can use the formula:

$$Pr(E1 \cup E2) = Pr(E1) + Pr(E2) - Pr(E1 \cap E2)$$
$$= \quad 1/6 \quad + \quad 1/6 \quad - \quad\quad 1/36$$
$$= 11/36$$

So your chances of getting at least one 6 are 11/36.

(1 ,1)	(1 ,2)	(1 ,3)	(1 ,4)	(1 ,5)	(1 ,6)
(2 ,1)	(2 ,2)	(2 ,3)	(2 ,4)	(2 ,5)	(2 ,6)
(3 ,1)	(3 ,2)	(3 ,3)	(3 ,4)	(3 ,5)	(3 ,6)
(4 ,1)	(4 ,2)	(4 ,3)	(4 ,4)	(4 ,5)	(4 ,6)
(5 ,1)	(5 ,2)	(5 ,3)	(5 ,4)	(5 ,5)	(5 ,6)
(6 ,1)	(6 ,2)	(6 ,3)	(6 ,4)	(6 ,5)	(6 ,6)

Figure 4–4

YOU SHOULD REMEMBER

1. If there are s outcomes that are all equally likely, and if there are $N(A)$ outcomes that are part of event A, then the probability of event A occurring is

$$\Pr(A) = \frac{N(A)}{s}$$

2. If A is an event and A^C is the opposite event, then

$$\Pr(A^C) = 1 - \Pr(A)$$

3. If A and B are two mutually exclusive events (that is, they cannot happen together), then the probability that either event A or event B will occur is

$$\Pr(A \text{ or } B) = \Pr(A) + \Pr(B)$$

In other words: to calculate the probability that either one of two mutually exclusive events will occur, simply add the probabilities of the two events.

4. If A and B are not mutually exclusive, then

$$\Pr(A \text{ or } B) = \Pr(A) + \Pr(B) - \Pr(A \text{ and } B)$$

MULTIPLICATION PRINCIPLE

When we have a set of outcomes that are all equally likely, the probability that an event A will occur is given by

$$\Pr(A) = \frac{N(A)}{s}$$

where $N(A)$ is the number of outcomes in A and s is the total number of possible outcomes. This means that if we can determine these two numbers—$N(A)$ and s—we're done. We can then directly calculate the probability. An important part of probability, therefore, involves figuring out how to count the outcomes corresponding to a given event. If there are not too many outcomes, we can list them all; but for complicated situations the number of outcomes quickly becomes too large to list.

Suppose we want to choose a car that is one of these four colors; red, blue, green, or white. We are interested in three different body types: 4-door, 2-door, and wagon. How many different types of car do we need to consider? We can make a list:

red 4-door,   red 2-door,   red wagon
blue 4-door,   blue 2-door,   blue wagon
green 4-door, green 2-door, green wagon
white 4-door, white 2-door, white wagon

There are 12 possible types, since $12 = 4 \times 3$.

We can make a general statement of this principle. Suppose we are going to conduct two experiments. The first experiment can have any one of a possible outcomes, the second experiment can have any one of b possible outcomes, and let's suppose that any possible combination of the two results can occur. Then the total number of results of the two experiments is

$$a \times b$$

This rather obvious result is sometimes called the **multiplication principle**. Here are some examples:

- If you flip two coins, each flip has two possible outcomes, so the number of total outcomes is $2 \times 2 = 4$.

- Suppose you toss two dice. Since each die has six possible outcomes, the total number of possible outcomes from the two dice is $6 \times 6 = 36$.

- Suppose there are five candidates in the Republican primary for a particular office, and six candidates in the Democratic primary. Then the total number of possible general-election matchups is $5 \times 6 = 30$.

SAMPLING WITH REPLACEMENT

Now, suppose you have five sweaters in your drawer. Each morning you reach in and randomly select one sweater. In the evening you put the sweater back and mix the sweaters up again. How many different ways can you wear sweaters for the week?

We can use the same principle, only now there are more than two experiments. There are five possible sweaters for you to wear on Sunday. There are also five sweaters for you to wear on Monday, so there is a total of 25 possible different combinations of sweaters you can wear on Sunday and Monday. For each of these possibilities there are five more choices for Tuesday, so there are $25 \times 5 = 125$ possible sweater-wearing patterns for the first 3 days. In fact, for the first week there are

$$5 \times 5 \times 5 \times 5 \times 5 \times 5 \times 5 = 5^7 = 78,125$$

different ways of wearing the sweaters.

From this information we can answer another question: What is the probability that you will wear the same sweater every day? Since there are 78,125 possible outcomes, and only five outcomes in which you wear the same sweater every day, the probability of selecting the same sweater every day is

$$\frac{5}{78,125} = .000064$$

The sweater selection process described here is an example of what is called *sampling*. Sampling means choosing a few items from a larger group called the *population*. In this case the population consists of five sweaters. We are selecting a sample of one sweater on Sunday, one sweater on Monday, and so on, for a total of seven selections. This type of sampling is called **sampling with replacement**. It should be obvious why we use the words "with replacement," since we are replacing the sweater worn that day in the drawer each evening. (Later, we will discuss sampling without replacement.) In general, if you sample n times with replacement from a population of m objects, then there are m^n possible different ways to select the objects.

The key idea of sampling with replacement is that once an item has been selected it can still be selected again. Flipping a coin is an example of sampling with replacement. In this case the population is of size 2: heads and tails. The fact that you've selected heads once doesn't mean you can't select heads again the next time. Therefore if you flip a coin n times there are 2^n possible results.

Rolling a die is another example of sampling with replacement. In this case the population is of size 6. If you roll a 5 on the die once, nothing will prevent you from rolling a 5 the next time. Therefore, there are 6^n total possibilities if you roll a die n times.

Examples: Sampling with Replacement

PROBLEM   Suppose you have to take a 20-question multiple-choice exam in a subject you know absolutely nothing about. Each question has five choices. What is the probability that you will be able to get all of the answers right just by guessing?

SOLUTION   In this case we are sampling 20 times from a population of size 5, so the total number of possible ways of choosing the answers is $5^{20} = 9.5 \times 10^{13}$. There is only one possible outcome in which you have selected all of the right answers, so the probability of getting all of the answers right by pure guessing is $1/(9.5 \times 10^{13}) = 10^{-14}$ (approximately).

PROBLEM   Suppose you are trying to guess the license-plate number of a friend's car. (You haven't seen the car, but you do know that it doesn't have vanity license plates.) Assume that each license plate consists of three letters followed by three digits, such as DGM 235.

SOLUTION First, calculate how many different possibilities there are for the three letters. That is the same as sampling 3 times with replacement from a population of 26 (since there are 26 letters in the alphabet), so there are $26^3 = 17{,}576$ ways of selecting the three letters. Since there are 10 possible digits, there are $10^3 = 1{,}000$ ways of selecting the three digits on the license plate. Each possible letter combination can be matched with each possible digit combination to give a valid license plate, so the total number of license plates is $17{,}576 \times 1{,}000 = 17{,}576{,}000$. Therefore, your chance of guessing the license plate correctly is $1/17{,}576{,}000 = 5.69 \times 10^{-8}$.

PROBLEM You are visiting a 31-flavor ice-cream store. You intend to order a two-scoop cone, but you are having trouble deciding which flavors. How many possibilities are there?

SOLUTION There are 31 possibilities for the top flavor and 31 choices for the bottom flavor, so there are $31 \times 31 = 961$ possible cones.

PROBLEM What is the probability of randomly guessing a 6-letter password? A 12-letter password?

SOLUTION 6 letters: $1/26^6 = 1/308{,}915{,}776$. 12 letters: $1/26^{12} = 1/9{,}543 \times 10^{16}$. If a password contains both upper- and lower-case letters, and digits and other symbols, these probabilities are even lower.

SAMPLING WITHOUT REPLACEMENT

Now, consider a different situation called **sampling without replacement**. Suppose that you have seven T-shirts. Each morning you reach into the drawer and randomly select one T-shirt to wear that day. However, this time, instead of putting the T-shirt back in the drawer in the evening, you put it in the bag of clothes to be washed. (The laundry gets done only once a week.) How many ways can you select the seven shirts for the week?

On Sunday you have seven choices. However, on Monday there are only six clean T-shirts left, so you have only six choices. Therefore, there are $7 \times 6 = 42$ possible ways of choosing the T-shirts that you will wear during the first 2 days. On Tuesday there are only five shirts left, so there are $7 \times 6 \times 5 = 210$ ways of choosing the shirts for the first 3 days. Continuing the process for the rest of the week, we can see that there are $7 \times 6 \times 5 \times 4 \times 3 \times 2 \times 1 = 5{,}040$ ways of selecting the T-shirts for the week.

We've already given a name to this quantity (see Chapter 3): $7 \times 6 \times 5 \times 4 \times 3 \times 2 \times 1$ is called 7 factorial and written as 7!. In this case we know for sure that you will wear each shirt exactly once during the week, so the only question is: In what order will you wear them? In general, if you have n objects, there are $n!$ different ways of putting them in order.

Examples: Sampling without Replacement

PROBLEM   How many different ways are there of shuffling a deck of 52 cards?

SOLUTION   There are 52 possibilities for the top card, 51 possibilities for the second card, and so on, so that altogether there are $52! = 8.07 \times 10^{67}$ ways of shuffling the deck.

PROBLEM   Suppose you have five different dinner menus to choose from for 5 days: hamburgers, hot dogs, pizza, macaroni, and tacos. In how many different orders can you arrange these five meals so that you don't repeat any meals during the 5 days?

SOLUTION   Since there are five meals, the number of different orderings is $5! = 120$.

PROBLEM   Suppose you have invited 20 people to a dinner party at your home. What is the probability that they will arrive at your house in alphabetical order?

SOLUTION   Since there are 20 guests, there are $20! = 2.43 \times 10^{18}$ different possible orders in which they can arrive. There is only one way of putting the guests in alphabetical order, the probability that they will arrive in alphabetical order is therefore $1/(2.43 \times 10^{18}) = 4.12 \times 10^{-19}$.

PROBLEM   An indecisive baseball manager decides to try out every possible batting order before deciding on the order that is best for the team. How many games will it take to test every possible order?

SOLUTION   There are nine batters, so there are $9! = 362,880$ different orders.

YOU SHOULD REMEMBER

1. The multiplication principle states that, if the first of two experiments can have *a* possible outcomes, the second experiment can have *b* possible outcomes, and any combination of these results can occur, then the total number of possible outcomes of the two experiments is

$$a \times b$$

2. In sampling with replacement, once an item has been selected it is returned to the population and can be chosen again.

3. In sampling without replacement, once an item has been selected it is not returned to the population and cannot be chosen again.

PERMUTATIONS

Suppose now that you have 10 T-shirts (and the T-shirts are still washed every week). How many different ways of selecting T-shirts are there during 7 days? Note that in this case you will not wear every shirt every week.

There are 10 choices for the shirt you wear on Sunday, then 9 choices for Monday, 8 choices for Tuesday, and so on down to 4 choices on Saturday. So the total number of choices is

$$10 \times 9 \times 8 \times 7 \times 6 \times 5 \times 4 = 604,800$$

We'd like a shorter way of writing that long expression, so we'll write it like this:

$$10 \times 9 \times 8 \times 7 \times 6 \times 5 \times 4 = \frac{10 \times 9 \times 8 \times 7 \times 6 \times 5 \times 4 \times 3 \times 2 \times 1}{3 \times 2 \times 1}$$

$$= \frac{10!}{3!}$$

What we're doing is choosing a sample of size 7 without replacement from a population of size 10. It's obvious why we call this sampling without replacement, since this time we're *not* replacing the T-shirt in the drawer after it has once been selected. Sampling without replacement means that once an item has been selected it cannot be selected again.

In general, suppose you're going to select j objects without replacement from a population of n objects. Then there are

$$\frac{n!}{(n-j)!}$$

ways of selecting the objects. Each way of selecting the objects is called a **permutation** of the objects, so the formula $n!/(n-j)!$ gives the number of permutations of n things taken j at a time.

The number of permutations of n things taken j at a time is sometimes symbolized by the expression $_nP_j$.

Example: Using Permutations

PROBLEM   The 31-flavor ice-cream store has introduced a new rule: you may not have the same flavor for both scoops of your cone. How many possibilities are there now?

SOLUTION   There are 31 choices for the top flavor, but now only 30 choices for the bottom flavor, so there are $31 \times 30 = 930$ possible cones. In this case we are sampling without replacement. Recall that we found there were 961 possibilities if we sample with replacement;

now there are 31 fewer possibilities because we have eliminated the 31 cases with the same flavor on both top and bottom. Note that the order matters; we would count chocolate on top, vanilla on the bottom as one possibility and vanilla on top, chocolate on the bottom as another possibility. Because the order matters, we say there are 930 permutations of the 31 ice-cream flavors chosen two at a time.

PROBLEM   Suppose that you are attending an eight-horse race, and you are trying to guess the order of the top three finishers without knowing anything about the horses involved. What is the probability that you will guess right?

SOLUTION   Since three horses are to be chosen from the eight horses entered, this situation is equivalent to choosing a sample of size 3 without replacement from a population of size 8. Therefore, there are

$$\frac{8!}{(8-3)!} = \frac{8!}{5!} = 8 \times 7 \times 6 = 336$$

possible finishes. Your chance of randomly guessing the correct order is $1/336 = .003$.

COMBINATIONS

Suppose you are in a card game in which you will be dealt a hand of 5 cards from a deck of 52 cards. There are 52 possibilities for the first card you will draw, then 51 possibilities for the second card, and so on. We can consider this an example of choosing a sample of size 5 without replacement from a population of 52 cards. (Once you've drawn a card, you can't draw that particular card again. If you do draw the same card again, something suspicious is going on.) Therefore, there are

$$\frac{52!}{(52-5)!} = \frac{52!}{47!}$$
$$= 52 \times 51 \times 50 \times 49 \times 48$$
$$= 311,875,200 \text{ ways of drawing the cards}$$

However, suppose you drew these cards:

5C, 8D, 6H, AH, AD

For practical purposes this hand means exactly the same as it would if you drew the cards like this:

8D, 5C, 6H, AH, AD

The second hand contains exactly the same cards, the only difference being that they were picked in a different order. In many card games, the order in which you draw the cards doesn't matter; it's only *which* cards you draw that matters. However, in the way we have been counting the hands, we have counted these two possibilities as separate hands, because they were drawn in different orders. There are, of course, a lot of different orders in which this hand could be drawn.

How many different orderings of these cards are there? We have already discussed this problem. Since there are 5 cards, there are 5! = 120 different ways of arranging the cards in different orders. In fact, for *every* possible hand there are 120 different orderings. Our formula 52!/(52 − 5)! has told us the total number of different orderings of all the hands, but in this case we are interested only in the total number of *different* hands, regardless of the ordering. Therefore, our formula gives us 120 times too many hands, so we have to divide by 120. Therefore:

(total number of distinct 5-card hands that can be drawn from a deck of 52 cards not counting different orderings)

$$= \frac{52!}{(52 - 5)!\ 5!}$$
$$= 2,598,960$$

In general, suppose we are going to select j items without replacement from a population of n items and we're interested only in the total number of selections, without regard to their order. Then the number of possibilities is given by the formula

$$\frac{n!}{(n - j)!\, j!}$$

The number of arrangements without regard to order is called the number of **combinations**. The formula $n!/[(n - j)!j!]$ is said to represent the number of combinations of n things taken j at a time. We will use the formula $n!/[(n - j)!j!]$ frequently in probability and statistics. (Remember that we already used it in Chapter 3.) We'd like a shorter way of writing this formula, so we will symbolize it like this:

$$\binom{n}{j} = \frac{n!}{(n - j)!\, j!}$$

The number of combinations is sometimes symbolized by the expression $_nC_j$. Note that

$$_nC_j = \frac{_nP_j}{j!}$$

This expression is also called the *binomial coefficient* because it is used in a mathematical formula called the binomial theorem.

Here is an example of the formula. Suppose we have five letter blocks and we are going to select three of them. In how many ways can we make the selection? If the blocks have letters A, B, C, D, E, then we can list all of the possible permutations:

ABC, ACB, BAC, BCA, CAB, CBA,
ABD, ADB, BAD, BDA, DAB, DBA,
ABE, AEB, BAE, BEA, EAB, EBA,
ACD, ADC, CAD, CDA, DAC, DCA,
ACE, AEC, CAE, CEA, EAC, ECA,
ADE, AED, DAE, DEA, EAD, EDA,
BCD, BDC, CBD, CDB, DBC, DCB,
BCE, BEC, CBE, CEB, EBC, ECB,
BDE, BED, DBE, DEB, EBD, EDB,
CDE, CED, DCE, DEC, ECD, EDC

There are 60 permutations in this list, a result that agrees with the formula:

$$\frac{5!}{(5-3)!} = \frac{5!}{2!} = 60$$

However, if we look closely at the list we can see that all of the arrangements in a particular row contain exactly the same letters, only arranged in different orders. Each of the 10 rows has different letters in it, so there are 10 different combinations of the letters. That agrees with the formula for combinations:

$$\frac{5!}{(5-3)!\,3!} = \frac{5!}{3!\,2!}$$
$$= 10$$

Here are some examples of these probability functions in Excel.

	A	B	C	D	E
1	cards in deck:	52			
2	orderings (52!):	8.07E + 67	← FACT(B1)		
3	cards in hand:	5			
4	permutations:	311,875,200	← PERMUT(B1,B3)		
5	combinations:	2,598,960	← COMBIN(B1,B3)		

Column C lists the functions that have been entered into column B. Note that Excel uses exponential notation (also called scientific notation) for very big numbers. For example, 8.07E + 67 means 8.07×10^{67}.

Examples: Calculating Combinations

PROBLEM   Previously we found there were 930 possible cones if we sample without replacement where the order matters from the 31-flavor ice-cream store. However, suppose we decide the order doesn't matter. In other words, we would count a cone with chocolate and vanilla as one possibility, regardless of which flavor is on top.

SOLUTION   We need to divide 930 by 2 to take care of the fact that each possibility is counted twice because of the different orderings. Therefore, there are $31 \times 30/2 = 465$ possible ways of choosing the ice cream without replacement where the order doesn't matter. Formally, we can say there are 465 combinations of the 31 flavors chosen two at a time. Using the formula:

$$\binom{31}{2} = \frac{31!}{29!\,2!} = \frac{31 \times 30}{2} = 465$$

PROBLEM   How many 13-card hands can be dealt from a deck of 52 cards?
SOLUTION   Using the formula for the number of combinations of 52 objects taken 13 at a time, we have

$$\frac{52!}{(52-13)!\,13!} = \frac{52!}{39!\,13!}$$
$$= 6.35 \times 10^{11}$$

Now we have all the tools we need to solve many probability problems. There's no sure-fire method that always works, because many problems contain subtle twists.

PROBLEM   Suppose you and your dream lover (whom you're desperately hoping to meet) are both in a group of 20 people, and five people are to be randomly selected to be on a committee. What is the probability that both you and your dream lover will be on the committee?

SOLUTION   The total number of ways of choosing the committee is

$$\binom{20}{5} = 15,504$$

Next, we need to calculate how many possibilities include both of you on the committee. If you've both been selected, then the three other committee members must be selected from the remaining 18 people, and there are

$$\binom{18}{3} = 816$$

ways of doing this. Therefore, the probability that you will both be selected is $816/15,504 = .053$.

PROBLEM Suppose 18 people are going to be randomly divided into two baseball teams. What is the probability that all 9 of the best players will be on the same team?

SOULTION There are $\binom{18}{9} = 48,620$ ways of choosing the team that will bat first. Therefore, the chance of all the best players being on the team that bats first is $1/48,620$. However, there is just as good a chance that all the best players will be on the team that bats second, so the chance they will be on the same team is $2/48,620 = 4 \times 10^{-5}$.

In the next three examples we will develop the formulas that are used in choosing samples. These results will play a crucial role later when we show why samples can give accurate pictures of populations.

PROBLEM A group of nine letter blocks contains five letters from early in the alphabet (A, B, C, D, and E) and four letters from late in the alphabet (W, X, Y, and Z). Five blocks will be selected at random from this group. What is the probability that exactly three of the selected blocks will be early letters?

SOLUTION Since we are choosing five blocks from the group of nine blocks, we can use the formula for combinations to find the number of possible ways of making the selection:

$$\binom{9}{5} = \frac{9 \times 8 \times 7 \times 6 \times 5 \times 4 \times 3 \times 2 \times 1}{4 \times 3 \times 2 \times 1 \times 5 \times 4 \times 3 \times 2 \times 1}$$

$$= \frac{9 \times 8 \times 7 \times 6}{4 \times 3 \times 2 \times 1} = 126$$

Fortunately, this number is small enough that we could list all of the possibilities and then count the number of outcomes with exactly three early letters. However, since most problems will involve far too many outcomes to list, we need a way to count those outcomes without having to list them all. We need to know: how many outcomes are there with three early letters (and two late letters)?

Let's ignore the late letters completely and ask: How many ways are there of choosing three early letters from among the five early letters? We can use the formula for combinations:

$$\binom{5}{3} = 10$$

Now, let's ignore the early letters, and ask: How many ways are there of choosing two late letters from among the four late letters? Again, use the formula for combinations:

$$\binom{4}{2} = 6$$

Now we come to the key insight, which will require you to think a bit before you believe it. Any of the 10 ways of choosing the early letters can be combined with any of the 6 ways of choosing the late letters. Therefore, we need to multiply to find that there are 60 possible ways of choosing three early letters and two late letters. In the future, you will need to accept this on faith, because there will be too many possibilities to list. However, here we can list all 60 possibilities:

	WX	WY	WZ	XY	XZ	YZ
ABC	ABCWX	ABCWY	ABCWZ	ABCXY	ABCXZ	ABCYZ
ABD	ABDWX	ABDWY	ABDWZ	ABDXY	ABDXZ	ABDYZ
ABE	ABEWX	ABEWY	ABEWZ	ABEXY	ABEXZ	ABEYZ
ACD	ACDWX	ACDWY	ACDWZ	ACDXY	ACDXZ	ACDYZ
ACE	ACEWX	ACEWY	ACEWZ	ACEXY	ACEXZ	ACEYZ
ADE	ADEWX	ADEWY	ADEWZ	ADEXY	ADEXZ	ADEYZ
BCD	BCDWX	BCDWY	BCDWZ	BCDXY	BCDXZ	BCDYZ
BCE	BCEWX	BCEWY	BCEWZ	BCEXY	BCEXZ	BCEYZ
BDE	BDEWX	BDEWY	BDEWZ	BDEXY	BDEXZ	BDEYZ
CDE	CDEWX	CDEWY	CDEWZ	CDEXY	CDEXZ	CDEYZ

Note how the possibilities are arranged; each column corresponds to 1 of the 6 ways of selecting the late letters, and each row corresponds to 1 of the 10 ways of selecting the early letters.

The probability of selecting three early letters and two late letters is therefore:

$$\frac{\binom{5}{3} \times \binom{4}{2}}{\binom{9}{5}} = \frac{10 \times 6}{126} = \frac{60}{126} = .476$$

By the same reasoning, we can figure out that the probability of drawing one early letter is given by the formula:

$$\frac{\binom{5}{1} \times \binom{4}{4}}{\binom{9}{5}} = \frac{5 \times 1}{126} = \frac{5}{126} = .040$$

The five outcomes with one early letter are AWXYZ, BWXYZ, CWXYZ, DWXYZ, EWXYZ.

The probability of drawing two early letters is given by the formula:

$$\frac{\binom{5}{2} \times \binom{4}{3}}{\binom{9}{5}} = \frac{10 \times 4}{126} = \frac{40}{126} = .317$$

The 40 outcomes with two early letters are:

	WXY	WXZ	WYZ	XYZ
AB	ABWXY	ABWXZ	ABWYZ	ABXYZ
AC	ACWXY	ACWXZ	ACWYZ	ACXYZ
AD	ADWXY	ADWXZ	ADWYZ	ADXYZ
AE	AEWXY	AEWXZ	AEWYZ	AEXYZ
BC	BCWXY	BCWXZ	BCWYZ	BCXYZ
BD	BDWXY	BDWXZ	BDWYZ	BDXYZ
BE	BEWXY	BEWXZ	BEWYZ	BEXYZ
CD	CDWXY	CDWXZ	CDWYZ	CDXYZ
CE	CEWXY	CEWXZ	CEWYZ	CEXYZ
DE	DEWXY	DEWXZ	DEWYZ	DEXYZ

Each column comes from one of the four ways of choosing three letters from among WXYZ; each row comes from one of the 10 ways of choosing two letters from among ABCDE.

The probability of drawing four early letters is given by the formula:

$$\frac{\binom{5}{4} \times \binom{4}{1}}{\binom{9}{5}} = \frac{5 \times 4}{126} = \frac{20}{126} = .159$$

The 20 outcomes with four early letters are:

ABCDW	ABCDX	ABCDY	ABCDZ
ABCEW	ABCEX	ABCEY	ABCEZ
ABDEW	ABDEX	ABDEY	ABDEZ
ACDEW	ACDEX	ACDEY	ACDEZ
BCDEW	BCDEX	BCDEY	BCDEZ

The probability of drawing five early letters is given by the formula:

$$\frac{\binom{5}{5} \times \binom{4}{0}}{\binom{9}{5}} = \frac{1 \times 1}{126} = \frac{1}{126} = .00794$$

We can summarize these results in a table:

Number of Early Letters in Hand	Number of Outcomes	Probability
1	5	.0397
2	40	.3175
3	60	.4762
4	20	.1587
5	1	.0079
Total	126	1.000

PROBLEM   You are drawing 10 cards at random from a 52-card deck. What is the probability that exactly 4 cards you draw will be hearts?

SOLUTION   First, calculate the total number of ways of selecting the cards, using the formulas for combinations:

$$\binom{52}{10} = \frac{52 \times 51 \times 50 \times 49 \times 48 \times 47 \times 46 \times 45 \times 44 \times 43}{10 \times 9 \times 8 \times 7 \times 6 \times 5 \times 4 \times 3 \times 2 \times 1} = 15,820,024,220$$

Now, determine how many ways there are of drawing 4 hearts from among the 13 hearts in the deck:

$$\binom{13}{4} = \frac{13 \times 12 \times 11 \times 10}{4 \times 3 \times 2 \times 1} = 715$$

If we draw 4 hearts among our 10 cards, then there must be 6 nonhearts. We can determine the number of ways of drawing 6 nonhearts from the 39 nonhearts in the deck:

$$\binom{39}{6} = 3,262,623$$

Now our reasoning is the same as in the previous example, except that there are so many possibilities that we cannot list them all. Each of the 715 ways of choosing the 4 hearts can be combined with each of the 3,262,623 ways of choosing the 6 nonhearts, so in total there are 715 × 3,262,623 = 2,332,775,445 total possible hands with 4 hearts and 6 nonhearts. Therefore, the probability of drawing 4 hearts is:

$$\frac{\binom{13}{4} \times \binom{39}{6}}{\binom{52}{10}} = 2,332,775,445/15,820,024,220 = .147$$

If we let X represent the number of hearts drawn in our 10 card hand, then Figure 4–5 shows the probability that X will equal i, for all values of i from 0 up to 8. (The probability for 9 or 10 is too small to show on the graph.)

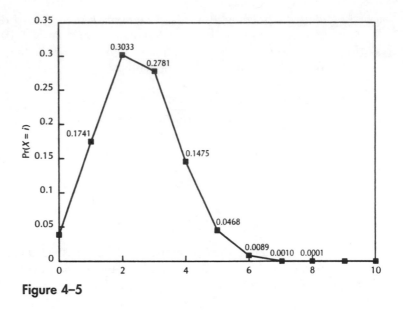

Figure 4–5

We can create a table of these values in Excel. We could use the formula

$$=COMBIN(13,4) * COMBIN(39,6)/COMBIN(52,10)=.147$$

for the probability of drawing 4 hearts, but Excel includes a function that will automatically calculate this probability. The function is called HYPGEOMDIST, which is short for hypergeometric distribution (which will be discussed more on page 173). The function takes four arguments: HYPGEOMDIST(k,ns,M,N) gives the probability of selecting k hearts among the ns hearts in your sample (hand) when there are M hearts in the population (deck), which contains a total of N cards.

We'll put the values for k (the number of hearts in our hand) in column A. These values will run from 0 to 10. First, enter the value 0 into cell A3 and 1 into cell A4. Now, highlight both cells A3 and A4, and then move the mouse pointer to the lower right corner of the highlighted region. Press the left mouse button as you drag the pointer down to the next 10 cells. That will automatically fill in the values from 0 to 10:

	A	B	C	D	E	F
1	Hearts		Deck=	52	Hand=	10
2	in hand		Hearts=	13		
3	0					
4	1					
5	2					
6	3					
7	4					
8	5					
9	6					
10	7					
11	8					
12	9					
13	10					

(Be sure you don't confuse the row numbers on the far left with our actual values in column A.) We've also entered the number of cards in the deck (52, in cell D1), the number of hearts in the deck (13, in cell D2), and the number of cards in the hand (10, in cell F1).

Now enter the formula

$$\text{=HYPGEOMDIST(A3, \$F\$1, \$D\$2, \$D\$1)}$$

into cell B3.

	A	B	C	D	E	F
1	Hearts		Deck=	52	Hand=	10
2	in hand		Hearts=	13		
3	0	0.040186	←HYPGEOMDIST (A3,F1, D2,D1)			
4	1					
5	2					
6	3					
7	4					
8	5					
9	6					
10	7					
11	8					
12	9					
13	10					

Now use the mouse pointer to grab the lower right corner of cell B3 and drag the formula down to cells B4 to B13.

	A	B	C	D	E	F
1	Hearts		Deck=	52	Hand=	10
2	in hand		Hearts=	13		
3	0	0.040186	←HYPGEOMDIST (A3,F1,D2, D1)			
4	1	0.174140	←HYPGEOMDIST (A4,F1,D2, D1)			
5	2	0.303340	←HYPGEOMDIST (A5,F1,D2, D1)			
6	3	0.278062	←HYPGEOMDIST (A6,F1,D2, D1)			
7	4	0.147457	←HYPGEOMDIST (A7,F1,D2, D1)			
8	5	0.046839	←HYPGEOMDIST (A8,F1,D2, D1)			
9	6	0.008922	←HYPGEOMDIST (A9,F1,D2, D1)			
10	7	$9.913085E-4$	←HYPGEOMDIST (A10,F1,D2, D1)			
11	8	$6.028227E-5$	←HYPGEOMDIST (A11,F1,D2, D1)			
12	9	$1.762640E-6$	←HYPGEOMDIST (A12,F1,D2, D1)			
13	10	$1.807835E-8$	←HYPGEOMDIST (A13,F1,D2, D1)			

Because we entered the dollar signs in the cell addresses for cells F1, D2, and D1, they will not change when we copy the formula down to the rest of the column. However, since no dollar sign was entered in the formula for cell A3, that will change each time we copy the formula down, as shown.

PROBLEM Suppose there are N people (M Republicans and $N–M$ Democrats) in the population. We will select a sample of n people (chosen randomly without replacement, and of course the order of selection of the people in the sample doesn't matter). What is the probability that exactly k people in the sample will be Republicans?

SOLUTION The reasoning is exactly the same as in the previous example, only now we have generalized the result.

There are $\binom{N}{n}$ ways of selecting the sample; there are $\binom{M}{k}$ ways of choosing the k Republicans in the sample, and there are $\binom{N-M}{n-k}$ ways of choosing the $n - k$ Democrats in the sample. Therefore, there are $\binom{M}{k} \times \binom{N-M}{n-k}$ ways of selecting the sample with k Republicans and $n - k$ Democrats, so the probability of this happening is given by:

$$\frac{\binom{M}{k}\binom{N - M}{n - k}}{\binom{N}{n}}$$

The previous spreadsheet can be used to calculate these probabilities.

This is the general formula that applies to the selection of samples. We discuss it more in Chapters 7 and 12. However, this formula is cumbersome to work with, so we will also develop some easier shortcuts.

YOU SHOULD REMEMBER

1. The task of calculating probabilities requires calculating the number of possible outcomes that meet a specific condition. Two important concepts in counting outcomes are *permutations* and *combinations*.

2. Permutations: The number of permutations of n things taken j at a time is the number of different possible ways of choosing j objects from the group of n objects when each different way of ordering the chosen objects counts separately. The number of possibilities is

$$\frac{n!}{(n-j)!}$$

---

3. Combinations: The number of combinations of n things taken j at a time is the number of different possible ways of choosing j objects from the group of n objects when the order in which the objects are chosen doesn't matter. The number of possibilities is

$$\binom{n}{j} = \frac{n!}{j! \, (n-j)!}$$

KNOW THE CONCEPTS

DO YOU KNOW THE BASICS?

Test your understanding of Chapter 4 by answering the following questions:

1. When do you add the probabilities of two events?

2. If the probability of getting an order from firm A is .3, and the probability of getting an order from firm B is .4, does this mean there is a probability of .7 that you will get at least one order from firm A and/or firm B?

3. If there is a probability of .25 that firm A will build its new factory in your city, and a probability of .25 that the firm will build its new factory in the other city in your county, does this mean there is a probability of .5 that the firm will build its new factory in one of the cities in your county?

4. If you are checking a sample of electronic parts to determine how many are defective, should you choose the sample with or without replacement?

5. Why are there $n!$ different ways of putting n objects in order?

6. If you are choosing 20 objects from a population of 80 objects, are there more permutations or more combinations?

7. A computer memory consists of bits that have only two possible values: 0 or 1. How many possible data items can be stored in 8 bits? 16 bits?

8. Why is a large random sample likely to be somewhat representative of the population?

9. Why do some computer systems require passwords to include lower- and upper-case letters and numerical digits? Why do they set a minimum length for passwords?

10. You need to travel between n cities. You would like to choose the order in which you visit the cities so as to minimize the total distance. What is the total number of possible routes?

TERMS FOR STUDY

classical approach to probability
combinations
complement
mutually exclusive events
intersection
multiplication principle
outcome
permutations
probability of an event

probability space
relative frequency view of probability
sampling with replacement
sampling without replacement
set
subjective view of probability
subset
union

PRACTICAL APPLICATION

Here are some formulas that you will need for these problems. A and B are events. A^C is the complement of A, that is, the opposite of A. $A \cup B$ means the event "either A or B" while $A \cap B$ means the event "A and B." s is the total number of outcomes, while $N(A)$ is the number of outcomes in the event A. $_nP_j$ is the number of permutations j at a time out of n, and $_nC_j$ is the number of combinations j at a time out of n.

$$\Pr(A) = \frac{N(A)}{s} \text{ when all outcomes are equally likely}$$

$$\Pr(A^c) = 1 - \Pr(A)$$
$$\Pr(A \cup B) = \Pr(A) + \Pr(B) \text{ if } A \text{ and } B \text{ are mutually exclusive}$$
$$\Pr(A \cup B) = \Pr(A) + \Pr(B) - \Pr(A \cap B) \text{ in general}$$

$$_nP_j = \frac{n!}{(n-j)!}$$

$$\binom{n}{j} = {}_nC_j = \frac{n!}{(n-j)!j!}$$

COMPUTATIONAL PROBLEMS

1. What is the probability of getting a 7 or an 11 when two dice are rolled?

2. The town of Wethersfield, Connecticut, has an area of about 14 square miles. What is the probability that a meteorite thrown randomly at the earth will hit Wethersfield? (The surface area of the earth is about 200,000,000 square miles.)

3. What is the probability that a meteorite thrown randomly at the earth will hit an ocean?

4. If you flip a coin five times, what is the probability that you will get a head on either the first, second, or third toss?

5. If you roll a die three times, what is the probability that you will get a 1 on at least one of the three tosses?

6. Seventeenth-century Italian gamblers thought that the chances of getting 9 when they rolled three dice was equal to the chances of getting 10. Calculate these two probabilities to see whether they were right.

7. You're coach of a football team that has just scored a touchdown, so you are now down by 8 points in the fourth quarter. You expect to score one more touchdown in the game. Should you try for a 2-point conversion now, or should you kick a 1-point conversion now and then try a 2-point conversion after your next touchdown? Assume that you have a 100 percent chance of making the 1-point conversion but only a 50 percent chance of making the 2-point conversion.

8. If you toss a coin n times, what is the probability that you will get at least one head?

9. Assume that there are 21 one-hour slots for prime-time television shows during the week. Suppose that the networks select the time slots for their shows at random. If your two favorite shows are on different networks, what is the probability that they will conflict?

10. What is the probability that your two favorite shows will be televised on the same night?

11. What is the probability that your two favorite shows will both be televised on Monday?

12. Suppose your backgammon opponent has points 4, 5, and 6 covered, and you have two pieces on the bar. In order to get back on the board, you need to have both dice result in either 1, 2, or 3. What is the probability that both pieces will get back on the board?

13. Suppose you have a 40 percent chance of getting a job offer from your first-choice firm, a 40 percent chance of getting a job offer from your second-choice firm, and a 16 percent chance of getting a job offer from both firms. What is the probability that you will get a job offer from either firm?

14. Suppose 70 percent of the families in a certain town have children. Of these families, 30 percent have children under 6, and 60 percent have children 6 or over. How many families have children both over 6 and under 6?

15. A hostess has so many guests coming that she needs to use more than one set of plates. She has 22 guests coming, and she has 10 plates in one set and 12 plates in the other set. All of the people will sit at a round table. How many different ways can the plates be set at the table?

16. How many ways can all 32 chess pieces be arranged in a row? (Each color has 8 pawns, 2 rooks, 2 bishops, 2 knights, 1 king, and 1 queen.)

17. Suppose you suddenly find that you have to cook for yourself for 1 week. You have the following kinds of frozen dinners: 4 beef dinners, 2 chicken dinners, and 1 turkey dinner. How many ways can you arrange your menus for the week?

18. A choreographer is planning a dance routine consisting of four star dancers and an eight-member chorus line. The indifferent choreographer regards the four stars as indistinguishable, and likewise the chorus line members as indistinguishable. The dance will end with all 12 dancers in a row. In how many different ways can that row be arranged?

19. How many ways can the four aces be located in a deck of 52 cards?

20. Suppose you are getting dressed in a dark room. In your drawer you have four red socks, three blue socks, and two brown socks. If you randomly select two socks, what is the probability that you will get two socks that match?

21. If you have five pennies and four dimes in your pocket, and you reach in and pick two coins, what is the probability that you will get 20 cents?

22. Messrs. Smith, Jones, and Brown go to a garage sale. At the sale there are nine different bicycle horns. If Smith, Jones, and Brown each buy one horn, how many different possible purchases are there?

23. At a meeting, name tags are being made for four people named John, two people named Julie, and two people named Jane. In how many different ways can the name tags be distributed?

24. At a party five people have blue jackets, four people have brown jackets, and two people have red jackets. If, at the end of the party, each randomly selects a jacket of the correct color, in how many different ways can the jackets be mixed up?

25. If you have 10 large chairs and 5 small chairs to be arranged at a round table, how many different ways are there to arranged them?

26. If you are picking four cards from a standard deck, what is the probability that you will pick an ace, a 2, a 3, and a 4?

27. At a picnic the three indistinguishable Smith children and the two indistinguishable Jones children are sitting on a bench. In how many distinguishable ways can they be arranged on the bench?

28. If you are going to buy something from a vending machine that costs 55 cents, and you have five nickels and three dimes in your pocket, in how many different ways can you put change in the machine?

29. If you have 20 blue balls and 30 red balls in a box, and you randomly pull out 20 balls, what is the probability that they will all be blue?

30. What is $\binom{n}{0}$? Explain intuitively.

31. What is $\binom{n}{1}$? Explain intuitively.

32. What is $\binom{n}{n}$? Explain intuitively.

33. What is $\binom{n}{n-1}$? Explain intuitively.

34. Compare $\binom{n}{j}$ and $\binom{n}{n-j}$. Explain intuitively.

35. How many different possible five-letter words are there?

36. A combination for a lock consists of three numbers from 1 to 30. What is the probability that you could randomly guess the combination?

37. Have It Your Way Burgers, Inc., likes to give its customers a lot of choices, and it likes to keep all possible combinations on hand. Customers have their choice between these options: cheese/no cheese, onion/no onion, pickle/no pickle, well done/medium, ketchup/no ketchup, and there are six possible sizes: tiny, small, junior, medium, hefty, and jumbo. If any option can be selected with any other option, how many hamburgers will Have It Your Way have to keep on hand in order to have every single possibility available?

38. At a Chinese restaurant, you have a choice between five items in column A, six items in column B, and four items in column C. How many possible choices do you have?

39. If you roll three dice, what is the probability of getting at least two numbers the same?

40. Suppose you roll a die six times. What is the probability that no number will occur twice during the six rolls?

41. Suppose you roll a die n times. What is the probability that no number will occur twice during the n rolls?

42. If you roll three dice, what is the probability that they will all turn up the same?

43. If you roll five dice, what is the probability that they will all turn up the same?

44. If you roll a die n times, what is the probability that at least one 1 will turn up?

45. If you draw cards from a well-shuffled deck, what is the probability that you will draw all four kings before drawing the ace of spades?

46. What is the probability that you will draw all four kings before you draw a single ace?

47. Suppose you are playing a card game where you need to get either four in a row of the same suit, or four of a kind. You currently have 5D, 5C, 5H, 6H, and 7H, and you must discard one of these cards. Which card should you discard?

ANSWERS

KNOW THE CONCEPTS

1. You add the probabilities of two events when you want to find the probability that either one of the two events will occur, provided that the two events are disjoint.

2. No. The event of getting an order from firm *A* is not disjoint from the event of getting an order from firm *B*, so you cannot simply add the probabilities to find the probability of getting an order from at least one of the firms.

3. If you assume that the firm will not locate a factory in both cities (meaning that the event of the factory being located in your city is disjoint from the event of the factory being located in the other city), then it is correct to add the probabilities to determine that there is a .5 probability of the factory being located in one of the two cities.

4. You should sample without replacement because there is no need to check the same circuit more than once. However, if the population size is much larger than the sample size, it does not make very much difference whether the sample is chosen with or without replacement.

5. There are *n* possibilities for the first item, *n* − 1 possibilities for the second item, and so on

6. There are more permutations, since each different ordering is counted separately when you are calculating permutations.

7. Use the formula for sampling with replacement: 8 bits: $2^8 = 256$. 16 bits: $2^{16} = 65,536$. An 8-bit code, such as ASCII, can include 256 symbols, which includes all letters of the Latin alphabet and some other symbols. A 16-bit code, such as Unicode, can include symbols from all languages.

8. There are many possible outcomes for choosing the random sample. Of these outcomes, there are many more outcomes that are somewhat representative than there are outcomes that are unrepresentative. (More details on this later.)

9. If the password is longer and is chosen from a larger set of symbols, then the number of possible passwords is much larger, and it becomes much harder for a hacker to guess the password or use a computer to try all possibilities.

10. There are *n*! different orderings of the *n* cities, so you have *n*! different possible routes. Since *n*! rapidly becomes very large, it is a very difficult problem to determine the shortest route. Often *n*! is too large for a computer to check all possibilities in a reasonable amount of time. This problem is known as the traveling salesman problem.

PRACTICAL APPLICATION

1. 2/9

2. .000 000 07

3. 3/4

4. 7/8

5. $1 - (5/6)^3 = .421$

6. Probability of getting 9 is .116; probability of getting 10 is .125.

7. If you go for the 2 points now, you have a 50 percent chance of succeeding, in which case you win the game. If you fail, then you can go for 2 points next time. If you succeed the next time, you will tie; otherwise you will lose. Therefore, if you go for the 2 points this time, you have a 50 percent chance of winning, a 25 percent chance of tying, and a 25 percent chance of losing. If you kick the extra point this time, then you have a 50 percent chance of winning and a 50 percent chance of losing.

8. $1 - (1/2)^n$

9. 1/21

10. 1/7

11. 1/49

12. 1/4

13. Let A be the event of getting hired by the first firm and B be the event of getting hired by the second firm. Then $\Pr(A \text{ or } B) = \Pr(A \cup B) = .40 + .40 - .16 = .64$.

14. 20 percent

15. $\left(\dfrac{1}{22}\right)\left(\dfrac{22}{10}\right)$

16. $\dfrac{32!}{8!\ 8!\ 2!\ 2!\ 2!\ 2!\ 2!\ 2!}$

17. $\dfrac{7!}{4!\ 2!\ 1!} = 105$

18. $\dbinom{12}{4} = 495$

19. $\dfrac{52!}{48!} = 6,497,400$

20. $\dfrac{\dbinom{4}{2} + \dbinom{3}{2} + \dbinom{2}{2}}{\dbinom{9}{2}} = \dfrac{6 + 3 + 1}{36} = \dfrac{5}{18}$

21. $\dfrac{\dbinom{4}{2}}{\dbinom{9}{2}} = 1/6$

22. $9!/6! = 504$

23. $4! \ 2! \ 2! = 96$

24. $5! \ 4! \ 2! = 5,760$

25. $\dbinom{15}{10} = 3,003$

26. $256/270,725$

27. 10

28. 56

29. 2.1×10^{-14}

30. There is only one way to choose zero (that is, no) object from a group of n objects, so $\binom{n}{0}$ is 1.

31. There are n ways to choose one object from a group of n objects.

32. There is only one way to choose all n items.

33. There are n ways to select $n - 1$ objects, since you have n choices as to which object you will not select.

34. They are equal. Choosing j objects from the group is the same as *not* choosing $n - j$ objects.

35. $26^5 = 11,881,376$

36. $1/30^3 = 1/27,000$

37. $2^5 \times 6 = 192$

38. 120

39. $4/9$

40. $6!/6^6 = 120/7,776 = 5/324$

41. $n = 2{:}5/6$; $n = 3{:}5/9$; $n = 4{:}5/18$; $n = 5{:}5/54$; $n = 6{:}5/324$; $n > 6{:}0$.

42. $1/36$

43. $1/6^4 = 1/1,296$

44. $1 - (5/6)^n$

45. $1/5$

46. $1/70$

47. Discard either 5D or 5C. Then you can win with either 4H or 8H.

5

CONDITIONAL PROBABILITY

With random events we're often totally in the dark about what will happen, as we have seen. However, it sometimes happens that we can get some information that sheds light on the issue by telling us whether a particular random event is more or less likely to occur.

For example, suppose we want to know the probability that a total of 8 will turn up when we roll two dice. Ordinarily, we know that the probability this will happen is 5/36. However, suppose we roll one of the dice first. Then we'll have a better idea about how likely we are to get 8. For example, suppose we get a 5 on the first die. Then, to get a total of 8, we need to roll a 3 on the second die, and we know that the probability of this happening is 1/6. Therefore, once we are given the fact that the first die turned up 5, our chances of rolling an 8 have improved from 5/36 to 1/6.

On the other hand, suppose that the first die comes up 1. Then we know that there is no way to roll an 8, no matter what happens with the second die. Therefore, the probability that we will roll an 8, given that we rolled a 1 on the first die, is 0.

Or suppose we're interested in the probability of flipping four heads in a row. We know that ordinarily the probability is 1/16. However, suppose that we've already flipped the coin twice and it turned up heads both times. Once that has happened, the probability of getting two more heads is 1/4. On the other hand, if we flip the coin twice and it comes up heads first and then tails, we know that there is no chance of getting four heads in a row.

Example: Calculating the Probability of a Royal Flush

PROBLEM   Suppose we're interested in the probability of getting a royal flush, that is, a hand consisting of A, K, Q, J, 10, all of the same suit.

SOLUTION

Ordinarily this probability is only $4/2{,}598{,}960 = 1.54 \times 10^{-6}$. However, suppose we have already drawn the ace of hearts and the king of hearts, and we are going to draw three more cards. Then there are $\binom{50}{3} = 19{,}600$ ways of drawing the remaining three cards, so our probability of getting a royal flush has improved to $1/19{,}600 = 5.1 \times 10^{-5}$.

CALCULATING CONDITIONAL PROBABILITIES

All of these situations are examples of **conditional probability**. A conditional probability tells us the probability that a particular event will occur, *if* we already know that another specific event has occurred. In particular, suppose we know that event B has occurred and we want to know the probability that event A will occur. The conditional probability that event A will occur given that event B has occurred is written like this:

$$\Pr(A \mid B)$$

The vertical line means "given that."

Now we have to figure out how to calculate conditional probabilities. In ordinary circumstances the probability that event A will occur is $N(A)/s$, where s is the total number of outcomes and $N(A)$ is the number of events in A. However, we know that not all of these outcomes are possible. We know that event B has occurred, so only the outcomes in event B need to be considered. Therefore, the number of possibilities is $N(B)$. The next question is: How many of these remaining possibilities also have event A occurring? Ordinarily there are $N(A)$ ways for event A to occur, but not all of these are now possible. The outcomes that are in A but not in B cannot occur. Therefore, the number of possible outcomes in which event A can occur is equal to the number of outcomes that are in both event A and event B. But we already gave a name to that event:

$$A \text{ and } B = A \cap B$$

The event in which both A and B occur is called A intersect B. Therefore, the probability that event A will occur given that event B occurs is given by

$$\Pr(A \mid B) = \frac{N(A \cap B)}{N(B)}$$

We can rewrite this formula by dividing both the top and bottom by s:

$$\Pr(A \mid B) = \frac{N(A \cap B)/s}{N(B)/s}$$

$$= \frac{\Pr(A \cap B)}{\Pr(B)}$$

In words, the probability that event A will occur, given that event B occurs, is equal to the probability that both A and B will occur, divided by the probability that B will occur. (Note that this definition does not work when $\Pr(B) = 0$, because then we would be dividing by zero, which is no help at all.)

We can use this formula on the examples we discussed earlier.

Examples: Calculating Conditional Probabilities

PROBLEM   Let A = event of getting a total of 8 on a pair of dice.
Let B = event of getting a 5 on first roll; $\Pr(B) = 1/6$.
Calculate $\Pr(A \mid B)$.

SOLUTION $A \cap B$ = event of getting a 5 on first roll and 8 total.
$A \cap B$ can occur only if we roll (5,3), so $\Pr(A \cap B) = 1/36$. Thus

$$\Pr(A \mid B) = \frac{1/36}{1/6} = 6/36 = 1/6$$

(1 ,1)	(1 ,2)	(1 ,3)	(1 ,4)	(1 ,5)	(1 ,6)
(2 ,1)	(2 ,2)	(2 ,3)	(2 ,4)	(2 ,5)	(2 ,6)
(3 ,1)	(3 ,2)	(3 ,3)	(3 ,4)	(3 ,5)	(3 ,6)
(4 ,1)	(4 ,2)	(4 ,3)	(4 ,4)	(4 ,5)	(4 ,6)
(5 ,1)	(5 ,2)	(5 ,3)	(5 ,4)	(5 ,5)	(5 ,6)
(6 ,1)	(6 ,2)	(6 ,3)	(6 ,4)	(6 ,5)	(6 ,6)

Figure 5–1

PROBLEM   Let A be the event of getting four heads in a row.
Let B be the event of getting two heads in the first two rolls.
Calculate $\Pr(A \mid B)$.

SOLUTION $$\Pr(B) = 1/4$$

$$\Pr(A \cap B) = 1/16$$

$$\Pr(A \mid B) = \frac{1/16}{1/4} = 4/16 = 1/4$$

PROBLEM   Let A be the event of getting a royal flush.
Let B be the event of getting AH, KH on the first two cards.
Calculate $\Pr(A \mid B)$.

SOLUTION

$$\Pr(B) = \frac{\dbinom{50}{3}}{\dbinom{52}{5}}$$

$$= \frac{19,600}{2,598,960}$$

$$= 7.54 \times 10^{-3}$$

$A \cap B$ is the event of getting both KH, AH and a royal flush, so it means getting the hand AH, KH, QH, JH, 10H.

$$\Pr(A \cap B) = 1/2,598,960$$

Therefore,

$$\Pr(A \mid B) = \frac{1/2,598,960}{19,600/2,598,960}$$

$$= 1/19,600$$

PROBLEM   Let A be the event of getting a total of 8 on two dice.
Let B be the event of getting a 1 on the first roll.
Calculate $\Pr(A \mid B)$.

SOLUTION   In this case A and B can't happen together. (We used the term mutually exclusive for two events that cannot occur together.) Therefore, $A \cap B = \emptyset$, so $\Pr(A \cap B) = 0$; then $\Pr(A \mid B) = 0$. In general, when $\Pr(A \cap B)$ is zero, $\Pr(A \mid B)$ is zero. This result should be intuitively clear. It is like asking, "What is the probability that you will flip tails, given the fact that you have already done the flip and it came up heads?"

Another situation occurs if event A is a subset of event B. For example, suppose A is the event of getting a 1 on the dice and B is the event of rolling an odd number. Then A contains the outcome {1}, B contains the outcomes {1, 3, 5}, and $A \cap B$ contains the outcome {1}. Since $A \cap B = A$, then $\Pr(A \cap B) = \Pr(A)$, so $\Pr(A \mid B) = \Pr(A)/\Pr(B)$.

In general, if A is a subset of B, then

$$\Pr(A \mid B) = \frac{\Pr(A)}{\Pr(B)}$$

YOU SHOULD REMEMBER

The conditional probability that event A will occur, given that event B has occurred, is

$$Pr(A \mid B) = \frac{Pr(A \text{ and } B)}{Pr(B)}$$

This can also be written as

$$Pr(A \text{ and } B) = Pr(A \mid B)Pr(B)$$

The vertical line, |, means, "given that."

INDEPENDENT EVENTS

As we have seen, often knowing whether one event has occurred will help tell you whether another event is more likely or less likely. However, there are some cases in which knowing that one event has occurred does not give you a clue about whether another event will occur. For example, suppose you know that a family just had a baby girl. What is the probability that the same parents' next baby will be a girl? In this case, knowing about the last baby does not give you any information about the next baby.

Or suppose that you roll a 3 on the first roll of a die. What is the probability that you will roll a 5 on the next roll? Knowing that the first roll came up 3 does not help you know what will happen on the next roll. In this case, if A is the event of getting a 3 on the first roll and B is the event of getting a 5 on the second roll, then $Pr(A) = 1/6$, $Pr(B) = 1/6$, and $Pr(A \mid B) = 1/6$, since the fact that B has occurred does not affect the probability that A will occur.

We will give a special name to this situation: we will say that these two events are **independent events**. That is a logical term, since two events are independent if they don't affect each other. Knowing that one of the events has occurred does not give you any information about whether the other event will occur.

The formal definition of independence is as follows:

Events A and B are independent if $Pr(A \mid B) = Pr(A)$

Here are some more examples of independent events:

- The probability that you will draw two pairs in a card game is not affected by the fact that you drew two pairs in a card game yesterday.

- The probability that you will roll a 4 on a die is not affected by the fact that you just flipped a head on a coin.

There is an interesting result that we can get from the formula for conditional probability. Note that, in general,

$$\Pr(A \mid B) = \frac{\Pr(A \cap B)}{\Pr(B)}$$

Also, if A and B are independent, then

$$\Pr(A \mid B) = \Pr(A)$$

Therefore, when A and B are independent, we can write:

$$\Pr(A) = \frac{\Pr(A \cap B)}{\Pr(B)}$$

Therefore:

$$\Pr(A \cap B) = \Pr(A)\Pr(B), \quad \text{or} \quad \Pr(A \text{ and } B) = \Pr(A)\Pr(B)$$

This result gives us a nice, simple rule to find the probability of $A \cap B$ if A and B are independent. In other words, if two events are independent, you find the probability that they both occur by multiplying the two individual probabilities.

For example: You have vitally important data on your computer disk. You estimate there is a .01 probability that the system will fail on any day, causing a catastrophic loss of data. You realize you need a backup data system, which will also have a .01 probability of failing. What is the probability that both systems will fail?

If the two systems are independent, then you can simply multiply the probabilities:

Pr(main system fails and backup fails)

= Pr(main system fails) × Pr(backup fails) = .01 × .01 = .0001

However, it is vital to remember the importance of the assumption of independence. Suppose your backup system is located next to the main system. In that case, a single bad event could disable both systems. Therefore, it would not be correct to treat the systems as independent, and the probability of a double failure is much greater than indicated above. The best strategy would be to have the backup system in a different building, so it would be more independent of the main system.

YOU SHOULD REMEMBER

Two events, A and B, are independent if the probability that A will occur is not affected by whether or not B has occurred, and vice versa. In that case:

$$Pr(A \mid B) = Pr(A)$$

$$Pr(A \text{ and } B) = Pr(A) \times Pr(B)$$

In words: To calculate the probability that two independent events will both occur, simply multiply the probabilities of the two events.

Suppose 2 percent of the population has a particular disease. There is a test for the disease, but it is not perfectly accurate. In addition, 3.2 percent of the population tests positive for the disease. There is a 75 percent chance that a person with the disease will test positive. We need to calculate the probability that a person who does test positive really does have the disease.

Let $D+$ be the event of having the disease; $D-$ be the event of not having the disease; $T+$ be the event of testing positive; and $T-$ be the event of testing negative. Then we know:

$$\Pr(D+) = .020$$
$$\Pr(T+) = .032$$
$$\Pr(T+ \mid D+) = .750$$

We need to find $\Pr(D+ \mid T+)$. We can set up a table as follows:

	D+	D−	Total
T+			.032
T−			.968
Total	.020	.980	1.000

We can fill in the totals for the rows and columns with the information we're given, but we don't yet know the remaining numbers in the table. However, we can find

$$\Pr[(D+) \cap (T+)] = \Pr(D+ \text{ and } T+) = \Pr(T+ \mid D+)\Pr(D+) = .75 \times .02 = .0150$$

In other words, the fraction of the population that has the disease and will test positive is .015. Once we know this number, we can fill in its place in the table:

	D+	D–	Total
T+	.015		.032
T–			.968
Total	.020	.980	1.000

Since we know the totals for each row and column, we can now fill in the remaining numbers in the table:

	D+	D–	Total
T+	.015	.017	.032
T–	.005	.963	.968
Total	.020	.980	1.000

From the table we can see $\Pr(D+ \text{ and } T+) = .015$, $\Pr(T+) = .032$, and $\Pr(D+|T+) = \Pr(D+ \text{ and } T+)/\Pr(T+) = .015/.032 = 0.469$. Therefore, less than half the people that test positive actually have the disease.

It is important to remember that the way you state a conditional probability is important: the probability that you will test positive, given that you have the disease [$\Pr(T+|D+)$], is not the same as the probability that you will have the disease, given that you tested positive [$\Pr(D+|T+)$].

We can also solve this problem with a rule known as **Bayes's rule**, which states that for any two events A and B:

$$\Pr(B \mid A) = \frac{\Pr(A \mid B)\Pr(B)}{\Pr(A \mid B)\Pr(B) + \Pr(A \mid B^c)\Pr(B^c)}$$

where B^c means B complement; that is, the event that B does not occur.

To use Bayes's rule for our example, we need to find $\Pr(T+|D-) = \Pr(T+ \text{ and } D-)/\Pr(D-) = .017/.980 = .01735$.

Now calculate:

$$\Pr(D+|T+) = \frac{\Pr(T+|D+)\Pr(D+)}{\Pr(T+|D+)\Pr(D+) + \Pr(T+|D-)\Pr(D-)}$$

$$\Pr(D+|T+) = \frac{.750 \times .020}{.750 \times .020 + .01735 \times .98} = .469$$

YOU SHOULD REMEMBER

Bayes's rule tells how to find the conditional probability $\Pr(B \mid A)$ provided that you know $\Pr(A \mid B)$:

$$\Pr(B \mid A) = \frac{\Pr(A \mid B)\Pr(B)}{\Pr(A \mid B)\Pr(B) + \Pr(A \mid B^c)\Pr(B^c)}$$

KNOW THE CONCEPTS

DO YOU KNOW THE BASICS?

Test your understanding of Chapter 5 by answering the following questions:

1. What is the conditional probability $\Pr(A \mid B)$ if A and B are mutually exclusive events?

2. What is the conditional probability $\Pr(A \mid B)$ if A and B are independent events?

3. If the probability of getting an order from firm A is .3, and the probability of getting an order from firm B is .4, does this mean there is a probability of .12 that you will get an order from both firms?

4. If there is a probability of .25 that firm A will build its new factory in your city, and a probability of .25 that the firm will build its new factory in the other city in your county, does this mean there is a probability of .0625 that the firm will build factories in both cities?

5. If 50 percent of the poor families in a city are single-parent families, what fraction of the single-parent families in the city are poor? What other information do you think you might need to answer the first question?

6. Why would insurance companies care about conditional probabilities?

7. An airplane has a backup hydraulic line in case the primary line fails. Should the backup line be near the primary line?

8. You have a crucial meeting in the morning so you can't oversleep. Should you set two alarm clocks?

TERMS FOR STUDY

Bayes's rule   independent events
conditional probability

PRACTICAL APPLICATION

COMPUTATIONAL PROBLEMS

1. Suppose you have two nickels in your pocket. You know that one is fair and one is two-headed. If you take one out, toss it, and get a head, what is the probability that it was the fair coin?

2. In blackjack, each player is given two cards to start with, and then tries to get a numerical total of 21 in the following way: 2's through 10's are worth their face value, face cards are worth 10, and an ace can be worth either 1 or 11, depending on the player's preference. The player can take more cards, trying to get as close to 21 as possible without going over (in which case the game is lost). Suppose you are dealt a 4 and a 9. If the dealer is dealing from a single deck of 52 cards, and the 4 and the 9 are the only cards that have been dealt from that deck that you know the value of, should you take another card? In other words, what is the probability that if you take another card you won't go over 21?

3. In some versions of blackjack, one of the two cards dealt each player is turned up. Suppose you can see that your fellow players have been dealt two aces, a 5, and a king. You again have a 4 and a 9. Should you draw another card?

4. What is the probability that you will get a royal flush in your next four cards if your first card is the ace of hearts? What is the probability if the next two cards you draw are the king of hearts and queen of hearts? What is the probability if the fourth card you draw is the jack of hearts?

5. What is the probability that you will draw a straight if you have already drawn a 2 and a 3? (A straight consists of five cards in sequence.)

6. If you flip a fair coin twice, and know that at least one head came up, what is the probability of two heads?

7. Suppose you remove all the diamonds from a 52-card deck, put the ace of diamonds back in, shuffle the remaining 40 cards, and pick a card at random. Given that the card you pick is an ace, what is the probability that it is the ace of diamonds?

8. Suppose you roll two dice and pick a card at random from a 52-card deck. Suppose further that the number rolled on the dice is the same as the number on the card. What is the probability that the number is 6?

9. What is the probability that you will win a lottery with a three-digit number, given that you have two digits of the winning number?

10. What is the probability of getting four aces in a poker hand, given that two of the cards in your hand are the ace and king of spades?

11. What is the probability of drawing a jack from a 52-card deck, given that you've drawn a face card?

12. Suppose you roll three dice. Given that one of the dice shows a 5, what is the probability of rolling 14?

13. Consider the experiment of tossing two coins. Let A be the event of getting a head on the first toss.

    (a) Can you name an event that is mutually exclusive but not independent of A?

    (b) Can you name an event that is independent but not mutually exclusive of A?

    (c) Can you name an event that is both mutually exclusive and independent of A?

    (d) Can you name an event that is neither mutually exclusive nor independent of A?

14. Suppose that an election is being conducted with two candidates, Smith and Jones. Of the people in the city 2/3 support Jones, but 5/9 of the people in the country support Smith. Half of the people live in the country and half live in the city. If you randomly start talking with a voter who turns out to be a Jones supporter, what is the probability that that voter lives in the country?

15. Suppose that 5 percent of the people with blood type O are left-handed, 10 percent of those with other blood types are left-handed, and 40 percent of the people have blood type O. If you randomly select a left-handed person, what is the probability that he or she will have blood type O?

16. Suppose that 70 percent of the people with brown eyes have brown hair, 20 percent of the people with green eyes have brown hair, and 5 percent of the people with blue eyes have brown hair. Also, suppose 75 percent of the people have brown eyes, 20 percent have blue eyes, and 5 percent have green eyes. What is the probability that a randomly selected person with brown hair will also have green eyes?

ANSWERS

KNOW THE CONCEPTS

1. If A and B are mutually exclusive, then event A cannot occur if event B has occurred, so $\Pr(A \mid B)$ is 0.

2. If A and B are independent, then knowing that event B has occurred does not affect the probability that event A will occur, so $\Pr(A \mid B) = \Pr(A)$.

3. This reasoning is correct if the two events are independent; in other words, if the chance of getting an order from firm B is not affected by whether or not you get an order from firm A.

4. These two events are presumably mutually exclusive so they cannot be independent. Therefore it is not correct to multiply the two probabilities.

5. You are not given enough information to answer the question. You need to know what fraction of all families are poor and what fraction of all families are single-parent families. For example, if 15 percent of the families are poor and 30 percent of the families are single-parent families, then 25 percent of the single-parent families are poor.

6. It would help the insurance company to know the probability that a customer will file a claim, conditional on observable features that might make filing a claim more or less likely. The rates might be lower for customers with less chance of filing a claim.

7. If the two lines are close together, there is a risk that a single incident might sever both lines. If they are farther apart, then it is more likely that they can be treated as being independent, and if they are independent the probability that both will fail is very small.

8. If the two alarm clocks are independent, then the chances they would both fail is very small. However, if they are both plugged into an electrical outlet, they would both fail if the power goes out. The best course would be to have one plug-in alarm and one battery alarm, since these two most likely can be considered to be independent.

PRACTICAL APPLICATION

1. Let A be the event that a head appeared and B be the event that the coin was fair.

$$\Pr(B) = 1/2 \qquad \Pr(A \mid B) = 1/2 \qquad \Pr(A \mid B^c) = 1$$

$$\Pr(B \mid A) = \frac{\Pr(A \mid B)\Pr(B)}{\Pr(A \mid B)\Pr(B) + \Pr(A \mid B^c)\Pr(B^c)}$$

$$= \frac{(1/2)(1/2)}{(1/2)(1/2) + (1)(1/2)} = 1/3$$

2. $\dfrac{4 + 4 + 4 + 3 + 4 + 4 + 4 + 4}{50} = \dfrac{31}{50}$ yes

3. $\dfrac{2 + 4 + 4 + 3 + 3 + 4 + 4 + 4}{46} = \dfrac{28}{46} = \dfrac{14}{23}$ yes

4. $4!\left(\dfrac{1}{51 \times 50 \times 49 \times 48}\right) = \dfrac{1}{249,900}$

   $2!\times\left(\dfrac{1}{49 \times 48}\right) = \dfrac{1}{1,176}$

   $1/48$

5. There are two ways: A, 2, 3, 4, 5; 2, 3, 4, 5, 6.

$$2 \times 3! \left(\frac{4}{50} \times \frac{4}{49} \times \frac{4}{48} \right) = \frac{8}{1,225}$$

6. Let A be the event of getting at least one head. B is the event of getting two heads. Then

$$\Pr(B \mid A) = \frac{\Pr(A \cap B)}{\Pr(A)} = 1/3$$

7. Let A = ace; $B = AD$;

$$\Pr(B \mid A) = \frac{\Pr(A \cap B)}{\Pr(A)} = \frac{1/40}{4/40} = 1/4$$

10. $3! \left(\dfrac{1}{50} \times \dfrac{1}{49} \times \dfrac{1}{48} \right) = 1/19,600$

11. $\dfrac{1/13}{3/13} = 1/3$

12. A = one 5; B = 14; $\Pr(A)$ = 25/72; $\Pr(A \cap B)$ = 1/36; $\Pr(B \mid A)$ = 2/25.

13. (a) The event of getting tails on the first toss.
    (b) The event of getting heads on the second toss.
    (c) The null set ∅ is both mutually exclusive and independent of every other event. However, there is no way for two events to be both mutually exclusive and independent if one of them is not the null set.
    (d) The event of getting heads on both tosses.

14. Let C mean that a person from the city is chosen, and C_0 that a person from the country is chosen. $\Pr(J \mid C) = 2/3$; $\Pr(J \mid C_0) = 5/9$; $\Pr(C) = \Pr(C_0) = 1/2$; $\Pr(C_0/J) = 2/5$.

15. Let A = let-handed; B = O blood type.

$$\Pr(A \mid B) = .05 \quad \Pr(A \mid B^c) = .10$$

$$\Pr(B) = .40 \quad \Pr(B \mid A) = \frac{(1/20)(2/5)}{(1/20)(2/5) + (1/10)(3/5)}$$

$$= 1/4$$

16. $\Pr(RH \mid BE) = 7/10 \quad \Pr(RH \mid GE) = 1/5$

$\Pr(RH \mid BE) = 1/20 \quad \Pr(RE) = 3/4$

$\Pr(BE) = 1/5 \quad \Pr(GE) = 1/20$

$$\Pr(GE \mid RH) = \frac{(1/5)(1/20)}{(7/10)(3/4) + (1/5)(1/20) + (1/20)(1/5)}$$

$$= .018$$

6

RANDOM VARIABLES

It often happens in probability that the events in which we're interested involve counting something or measuring something. For example, we have been interested in the number of times that "heads" appear when we flip a coin or the number that appears on a pair of dice. In these cases it is easier to talk about **random variables** than about probability spaces and events. If X is the number of heads that appear when you flip a coin three times, then X is a random variable. If Y is the number that appears when you toss one die, then Y is also a random variable. If W represents the number of times that the word *tennis* is used on the 11 o'clock news, then W is a random variable (which can take on values anywhere from zero during the dead of winter to perhaps 50 during Wimbledon). We'll use capital letters to stand for random variables, to avoid confusion with the ordinary variables used in algebra.

Suppose we roll a die and then write down the number Y that appears. This process is called *observing* (or *measuring*) the value of Y. If we roll the die 10 times, we have 10 observations of the random variable Y.

As we have seen, a random event is something which we don't know for sure will happen, but we can often calculate the probability that it will happen. By analogy, a random variable is a variable such that we're not sure what it will equal, but for which we can often calculate the probability that it will equal a particular value. (Formally, a random variable is a variable that takes on a specified value when a particular random event occurs, so it is a function from sets to numbers.)

Although we usually cannot tell exactly what the value of a random variable will be, we often can determine what its value will *not* be. For example, the tennis variable W cannot be $3\frac{1}{3}$ or π or any other rather unusual number; W must be a whole number. The number on the die (Y) must also be a whole number, but it can have only one of six possible values: 1, 2, 3, 4, 5, or 6. Random variables that can take on only isolated values are called **discrete random variables**. (We'll talk later about *continuous random variables*.)

Discrete random variables don't have to take just whole-number values. Suppose we roll two dice, and let T be the average of the two numbers that appear. Then T has the possible values 1, $1\frac{1}{2}$, 2, $2\frac{1}{2}$, 3, $3\frac{1}{2}$, 4, $4\frac{1}{2}$, 5, $5\frac{1}{2}$, and 6.

Examples: Two General Types of Random Variables with Frequent Practical Applications

PROBLEM   Suppose you are interested in a population of N people (or objects). Of these people, M have one particular characteristic and the other $N - M$ do not. If you do not know the value of M, how can you estimate it?

SOLUTION   Observe a random sample of n of these people, and let X be the number of people in the sample who have this characteristic. Then X is a random variable, since its value will depend on which people happen to be chosen to be part of your random sample.

PROBLEM   Suppose you are interested in a large population of people (or objects). Each person has a particular measurable attribute, such as height, income, age, or hours of television watched per week, in which you are interested. What is the value of this attribute, for one specific person in the population?

SOLUTION   Select one person at random, and let X represent the value of the attribute for the person you have chosen. Then X is a random variable since it depends on the distribution of that attribute among the entire population, as well as on the identity of the person you select.

PROBABILITY FUNCTIONS

Now let's figure out what we need to know about random variables. With an ordinary variable, about all we need to know is its value. However, with random variables the situation is much more complicated. First, we need to know which values are possible and which are impossible. For example, if a random variable X can never take the value 3/2, we can write

Probability that $X = 3/2$ is 0

We can write that in a shorter fashion:

$$\Pr(X = 3/2) = 0$$

Once we've made a list of all the possible values, the next thing we would like to know is: How likely is each of these different values? In the case of tossing one die, the situation is very simple: there are only six possible values, and they are all equally likely. We can make a list of these:

$$\Pr(Y = 1) = 1/6$$
$$\Pr(Y = 2) = 1/6$$
$$\Pr(Y = 3) = 1/6$$
$$\Pr(Y = 4) = 1/6$$
$$\Pr(Y = 5) = 1/6$$
$$\Pr(Y = 6) = 1/6$$

We can also make a list of the probabilities for the random variable X, defined as the number of heads turned up in three tosses of a coin:

$$\Pr(X = 0) = 1/8$$
$$\Pr(X = 1) = 3/8$$
$$\Pr(X = 2) = 3/8$$
$$\Pr(X = 3) = 1/8$$

In both of these cases we understand the process that is generating the random variable, so it is easy to calculate the probability of each possible value. In other circumstances, such as the tennis example, we cannot calculate the probabilities because we do not understand the process well enough. (However, later we will discuss ways to estimate the probabilities of these occurrences.)

To make things a little more convenient, we will define a **probability function** for a random variable. The value of the probability function for a particular number is just the probability that the random variable will equal that number. We'll use a small letter f to stand for the probability function. Then we can make this definition:

$$f(a) = \Pr(X = a)$$

(The probability function is also sometimes called the *probability mass function* or *probability density function*.)

When we start talking about more than one random variable at a time, we will write the probability function as $f_x(a)$ to make it clear that f is the probability function for the random variable X.

Here is the probability function for the toss of one die:

$$f(1) = 1/6$$
$$f(2) = 1/6$$
$$f(3) = 1/6$$
$$f(4) = 1/6$$
$$f(5) = 1/6$$
$$f(6) = 1/6$$

(This function is graphed in Figure 6–1).

Figure 6–1

Here is the probability function for flipping a coin three times:

$$f(0) = 1/8$$
$$f(1) = 3/8$$
$$f(2) = 3/8$$
$$f(3) = 1/8$$

Figure 6–2 shows a graph of this function. (In both of these cases $f(a) = 0$ for all values of a except the ones that are listed.)

There is a close connection between the probability function of a random variable and the frequency histogram for the numbers in a sample. For example, suppose we roll a die 6,000 times and then make a frequency

Figure 6–2

Figure 6–3

histogram showing the number of times that each possible result appears (Figure 6–3). The frequency histogram has approximately the same shape as the probability function.

We can quickly establish two obvious properties that a probability function must satisfy:

$$f(a) \leq 1 \text{ for all possible values of } a$$

$$f(a) \geq 0 \text{ for all possible values of } a$$

These two statements point out that there is no such thing as a probability that is greater than 1 or less than 0.

Now, suppose we make a list of all of the possible values and add up their probabilities. If the probabilities add up to less than 1 or more than 1, we will know that something is wrong. The probability must be exactly 1 that X will equal one of its possible values. Therefore, in order for a function f to be a valid probability function for a random variable, the sum of its possible values must be 1: If the possible values are a_1, a_2, a_3, . . . , a_n, then

$$f(a_1) + f(a_2) + f(a_3) + \cdots + f(a_n) = 1$$

For example, when X represents the number of heads that appear on three coin tosses, we can add all of the probabilities:

$$1/8 + 3/8 + 3/8 + 1/8 = 8/8 = 1$$

to show that the sum does indeed equal 1.

It's nice to know what the probability is that X will take on a particular value, but sometimes we don't need to know that. Sometimes we'd like to know what the probability is that X will be less than or equal to a particular value a^*. For example, if you're playing blackjack and you've already drawn a 7 and an 8, then you're mainly interested in the probability that the value of the next card you draw will be less than or equal to 6.

To find the probability that the random variable Y in the case of rolling a die will be less than or equal to 3, we need to add $\Pr(Y = 1) + \Pr(Y = 2) + \Pr(Y = 3) = 1/2$. In general, if a_1, a_2, a_3, . . . , a^* are all of the possible values of Z that are less than or equal to a^*, then

$$\Pr(Z \leq a^*) = f(a_1) + f(a_2) + f(a_3) + \cdots + f(a^*)$$

We will give a special name to the function that tells the probability that Z will be less than or equal to a particular value. We'll call that function the **cumulative distribution function**, and we'll represent it by a capital F:

$$F(a) = \Pr(Z \leq a)$$

We can calculate the cumulative distribution function for the number of heads, X, appearing on three coin tosses:

$$F(a) = \begin{cases} 0 & \text{if } a < 0 \\ 1/8 & \text{if } 0 \leq a < 1 \\ 1/2 & \text{if } 1 \leq a < 2 \\ 7/8 & \text{if } 2 \leq a < 3 \\ 1 & \text{if } 3 \leq a \end{cases}$$

YOU SHOULD REMEMBER

1. A *random variable* is a variable whose value depends on the result of a random experiment.

2. The *probability function* of a discrete random variable is the function that gives the probability that the random variable will take on a particular value. For example, if $x_1, x_2, \ldots, x_m$ are the possible values of a random variable X and $f(x)$ is the probability function, then

$$f(x_1) = \Pr(X = x_1), f(x_2) = \Pr(X = x_2), \text{ and so on}$$

3. The *cumulative distribution function* $F(a)$ gives the probabilities that the random variable will be less than or equal to a particular value:

$$F(a) = \Pr(X \leq a)$$

EXPECTATION

Once we know the probability function or the cumulative distribution function for a particular random variable, we know just about everything we might possibly need to know about it. However, many times we would like to summarize the information that we have about the random variable. We showed that we can summarize a group of numbers by a single number (the average). We will develop a similar concept for a random variable.

Consider the variable X (the number of heads appearing in three coin tosses.) Suppose we measure X eight million times. How many times are we likely to get no head, one head, two heads, or three heads? We can guess that we will probably observe the value $X = 0$ close to one million times, the value $X = 1$ close to three million times, the value $X = 2$ three million times, and the value $X = 3$ one million times. In reality, we would probably not get exactly these numbers, but let us assume for a moment that we performed this experiment eight million times and did get exactly these results. (In general, if you measure a random variable N times, then the number of times that you can expect to get the value a will be equal to $f(a) \times N$.)

Now, we have eight million numbers written down (one number for each of the eight million repetitions of our experiment.) Since we don't want to carry around all eight million numbers, we'd like to summarize all of these values by taking their average:

$$
\begin{array}{ll}
(0 + 0 + 0 + 0 + \cdots & \text{(1 million zeros)} \\
+ 1 + 1 + 1 + 1 + \cdots & \text{(3 million ones)} \\
+ 2 + 2 + 2 + 2 + \cdots & \text{(3 million twos)} \\
+ 3 + 3 + 3 + 3 + \cdots)/8{,}000{,}000 & \text{(1 million threes)}
\end{array}
$$

We can rewrite that in a shorter fashion:

$$
\begin{aligned}
(1{,}000{,}000 &\times 0 \\
+ 3{,}000{,}000 &\times 1 \\
+ 3{,}000{,}000 &\times 2 \\
+ 1{,}000{,}000 &\times 3)/8{,}000{,}000
\end{aligned}
$$

Here's an even shorter version:

$$[1/8 \times 0] + [3/8 \times 1] + [3/8 \times 2] + [1/8 \times 3] = 1\tfrac{1}{2}$$

Therefore, the average of all the values is $1\tfrac{1}{2}$. We can also write that expression in terms of the probability function f:

$$\text{Average} = [f(0) \times 0] + [f(1) \times 1] + [f(2) \times 2] + [f(3) \times 3]$$

We will call this quantity the *expected value* of X, or the **expectation** of X. The expectation of a random variable tells us the average of all the values we would expect to get if we measured the random variable many times. We'll use the capital letter E to stand for expectation, and write this definition:

$$E(X) = \text{expectation of } X$$

The general formula for calculating an expectation is

$$
\begin{aligned}
E(X) &= f(a_1)a_1 + f(a_2)a_2 + f(a_3)a_3 + \cdots + f(a_n)a_n \\
&= \sum_{i=1}^{n} f(a_i)a_i
\end{aligned}
$$

where $a_1, a_2, \ldots, a_n$ are all of the possible values of the random variable X.

The expectation of X is a **weighted average** of all the possible values of X. The weight for each value is equal to the probability that X will take on that value.

The expectation of X is also called the *mean* of X, or the mean of the distribution of X, and it is usually symbolized by the Greek letter μ (mu). Note that $E(X) = \mu$ is not itself a random variable. It is a regular constant number.

The expectation of a random variable does not itself have to be one of the possible values of the random variable. For example, we found that the expectation for the number of heads in three tosses is $1\frac{1}{2}$, but we strongly caution you against betting that the number of heads will ever come out to be $1\frac{1}{2}$ (unless you make the bet with us).

The expectation of the number (Y) that shows up on a die is easy to calculate:

$$\begin{aligned}
E(Y) &= [f(1) \times 1] + [f(2) \times 2] + [f(3) \times 3] \\
&\quad + [f(4) \times 4] + [f(5) \times 5] + [f(6) \times 6] \\
&= [1/6 \times 1] + [1/6 \times 2] + [1/6 \times 3] \\
&\quad + [1/6 \times 4] + [1/6 \times 5] + [1/6 \times 6] \\
&= 3\frac{1}{2}
\end{aligned}$$

There are two important properties of expectations that we can establish. If c is a constant number (in other words, not a random variable), then

$$E(cX) = cE(X)$$

For example, suppose you will win $100 multiplied by the number that appears when a die is tossed. If Y is the random variable representing the number on the die, and W represents your winnings, then $W = 100Y$. We can calculate:

$$E(W) = E(100Y) = 100E(Y) = 100 \times 3.5 = \$350$$

Therefore, your expected winnings from this game are $350.

Suppose we have two random variables X and Y, and we form a new random variable V which is equal to $V = X + Y$. In general, putting two random variables together creates a lot of complications, and we will not talk much about these problems until Chapter 9. However, one property we can establish is

$$E(X + Y) = E(X) + E(Y)$$

There will also be times when we would like to calculate the expectation of a particular function of a random variable.

For example, when X is the number of heads that appear on three coin tosses, we can calculate $E(X^2)$ by multiplying the square of each possible value by the corresponding probability:

$$\begin{aligned}
E(X^2) &= [0 \times 1/8] + [1 \times 3/8] + [4 \times 3/8] + [9 \times 1/8] \\
&= 24/8 = 3
\end{aligned}$$

VARIANCE

Although the expectation of a random variable tells us a lot about its behavior, it doesn't tell the whole story. For example, let's consider one simple "random variable" that really isn't a random variable at all. Suppose U represents the number of times that Wile E. Coyote, the cartoon character, will catch the Roadrunner. Then we know for sure that $U = 0$, so the probability function has the value 1 at $U = 0$ and the value 0 everywhere else. In this case we can easily see that $E(U) = 0$.

Let us consider another random variable, T, which represents the number on the first die you toss minus the number on the second die. Then $f(5) = 1/36$, $f(4) = 2/36$, $f(3) = 3/36$, $f(2) = 4/36$, $f(1) = 5/36$, $f(0) = 6/36$, $f(-1) = 5/36$, $f(-2) = 4/36$, $f(-3) = 3/36$, $f(-4) = 2/36$, $f(-5) = 1/36$. We can easily show that $E(T) = 0$. However, the behavior of the random variable T is much more unpredictable than the behavior of the random variable U.

To consider an even more extreme example, suppose S is a random variable that represents your profit on the following stock market transaction: You pay 1 million dollars for the stock, which has a 50 percent chance of doubling in value and a 50 percent chance of becoming worthless. Then $S = 1$ million with probability 1/2 and $S =$ minus 1 million with probability 1/2. $E(S) = 0$, but, as we can see, the actual value of S will never be close to $E(S)$. Therefore, in addition to the expectation, we need something that tells us how unpredictable a random variable is—in other words, we would like something that tells us whether the random variable is likely to be close to its expectation.

We used the *variance* to measure the dispersion of a list of numbers. We will also use the variance to measure the unpredictability of a random variable. To calculate the variance, we find the squared deviation of each possible value from the expectation. If each possible value has equal probability, then the variance is simply the average of the squared deviations. However, if the probabilities differ, we multiply each squared deviation by the probability of that value and then add up these products to find the variance.

To find the variance where X is the number of heads out of three tosses, set up a table like this:

Possible Value (a_i)	Probability (p)	Squared Deviation $(a_i - E(X))^2$	$p(a_i - E(X))^2$
0	0.125	$(0 - 1.5)^2 = 2.25$	0.2813
1	0.375	$(1 - 1.5)^2 = 0.25$	0.0938
2	0.375	$(2 - 1.5)^2 = 0.25$	0.0938
3	0.125	$(3 - 1.5)^2 = 2.25$	0.2813
		$\text{Var}(X) = \text{sum} =$	0.7500

The variance is therefore 0.75.

Just the same as for the population variance for a list of numbers, the variance of a random variable is represented by σ^2, and the square root of the variance is known as the standard deviation and is represented by σ.

When we calculated the population variance of a list of numbers, it helped to use the formula $\overline{x^2} - \overline{x}^2$ because it saved a bit of calculation. By analogy, the variance of a random variable X can be found by the formula

$$\mathrm{Var}(X) = E(X^2) - [E(X)]^2$$

where $E(X^2)$ is the expected value of X^2. To find that expectation, square each possible value, multiply by the corresponding probability, and then add these products. Here is how it works for the three-coin-toss random variable X:

Possible Value (a_i)	Probability (p)	pa_i	$p(a_i)^2$
0	0.125	$0.125 \times 0 = 0.000$	$0.125 \times 0^2 = 0.000$
1	0.375	$0.375 \times 1 = 0.375$	$0.375 \times 1^2 = 0.375$
2	0.375	$0.375 \times 2 = 0.750$	$0.375 \times 2^2 = 1.500$
3	0.125	$0.125 \times 3 = 0.375$	$0.125 \times 3^2 = 1.125$
Sum:	1	$E(X) = 1.500$	$E(X^2) = 3$

$\mathrm{Var}(X) = \sigma^2 = 3 - 1.500^2 = 0.750$
standard deviation $= \sigma = \sqrt{0.750} = 0.866$

The result is the same as for the previous method. You can see that this type of calculation can be set up on a spreadsheet.

Here are some additional examples. For the random variable U (Wile E. Coyote's success rate):

Possible Value (a_i)	Probability (p)	pa_i	$p(a_i)^2$
0	1.000	$1.000 \times 0 = 0.000$	$1.000 \times 0^2 = 0.000$
Sum:	1	$E(U) = 0$	$E(U^2) = 0$

$\mathrm{Var}(X) = \sigma^2 = 0 - 0^2 = 0$
standard deviation $= \sigma = \sqrt{0} = 0$

If there is only one possible value for the random variable, there is no uncertainty, and so the variance is zero. If, for example, you knew that a certain random variable would always have the value 17, then its variance is zero because there is no uncertainty:

$$\mathrm{Var}(17) = 0$$

Likewise:

$$\text{Var}(10) = 0$$

$$\text{Var}(32) = 0$$

$$\text{Var}(2,598,960) = 0$$

U.S. Treasury bills are considered risk-free investments, so if P is your profit from such an investment, then $\text{Var}(P) = 0$. In general, if c is a constant (not a random variable), then

$$\text{Var}(c) = 0$$

For T, the number on the first die minus the number on the second die:

Possible Value (a_i)	Probability (p)	pa_i	$p(a_i)^2$
5	0.028	$0.028 \times 5 = 0.139$	$0.028 \times 5^2 = 0.694$
4	0.056	$0.056 \times 4 = 0.222$	$0.056 \times 4^2 = 0.889$
3	0.083	$0.083 \times 3 = 0.250$	$0.083 \times 3^2 = 0.750$
2	0.111	$0.111 \times 2 = 0.222$	$0.111 \times 2^2 = 0.444$
1	0.139	$0.139 \times 1 = 0.139$	$0.139 \times 1^2 = 0.139$
0	0.167	$0.167 \times 0 = 0.000$	$0.167 \times 0^2 = 0.000$
−1	0.139	$0.139 \times (-1) = -0.139$	$0.139 \times (-1)^2 = 0.139$
−2	0.111	$0.111 \times (-2) = -0.222$	$0.111 \times (-2)^2 = 0.444$
−3	0.083	$0.083 \times (-3) = -0.250$	$0.083 \times (-3)^2 = 0.750$
−4	0.056	$0.056 \times (-4) = -0.222$	$0.056 \times (-4)^2 = 0.889$
−5	0.028	$0.028 \times (-5) = -0.139$	$0.028 \times (-5)^2 = 0.694$
Sum:	1	$E(T) = 0$	$E(T^2) = 5.833$

$\text{Var}(X) = \sigma^2 = 5.833 - 0^2 = 5.833$
standard deviation $= \sigma = \sqrt{5.833} = 2.415$

For S, the profit from the extremely risky stock market transaction:

Possible Value (a_i)	Probability (p)	pa_i	$p(a_i)^2$
1,000,000	0.5	500,000	500,000,000,000
−1,000,000	0.5	−500,000	500,000,000,000
Sum:	1	$E(S) = 0$	$E(S^2) = 1,000,000,000,000$

$\text{Var}(X) = \sigma^2 = 1,000,000,000,000 - 0^2 = 1,000,000,000,000$
standard deviation $= \sigma = \sqrt{1,000,000,000,000} = 1,000,000$

For our final example, let Y be the number that appears when you toss one die.

Possible Value (a_i)	Probability (p)	pa_i	$p(a_i)^2$
1	0.1667	$0.1667 \times 1 = 0.1667$	$0.1667 \times 1^2 = 0.1667$
2	0.1667	$0.1667 \times 2 = 0.3333$	$0.1667 \times 2^2 = 0.6667$
3	0.1667	$0.1667 \times 3 = 0.5000$	$0.1667 \times 3^2 = 1.5000$
4	0.1667	$0.1667 \times 4 = 0.6667$	$0.1667 \times 4^2 = 2.6667$
5	0.1667	$0.1667 \times 5 = 0.8333$	$0.1667 \times 5^2 = 4.1667$
6	0.1667	$0.1667 \times 6 = 1.0000$	$0.1667 \times 6^2 = 6.0000$
Sum:	1	$E(Y) = 3.5000$	$E(Y^2) = 15.1667$

$\text{Var}(X) = \sigma^2 = 15.1667 - 3.5000^2 = 2.9167$
standard deviation $= \sigma = \sqrt{2.9167} = 1.7078$

YOU SHOULD REMEMBER

1. The expectation of a random variable is the average value that would occur if you observed the random variable many times. It can be found from this formula:

$$E(X) = x_1 f(x_1) + x_2 f(x_2) + \cdots + x_m f(x_m)$$

where $f(x_i) = \text{Pr}(X = x_i)$. The expectation of a random variable is also called the mean of its distribution, and it is symbolized by the Greek letter μ (mu).

2. The formula for the variance of a random variable is

$$\text{Var}(X) = E((X - \mu)^2) = E(X^2) - (E(X))^2$$

A larger value of the variance means that there is a larger chance that the random variable is far away from its mean. The variance is symbolized by σ^2 (sigma squared).

BERNOULLI TRIALS

Now we'll discuss another simple random variable that illustrates all of these concepts. Let us consider a Mad Scientist who repeats a particular experiment each day. There is a probability p that the experiment will succeed on any particular trial; let's suppose that $p = 1/5$. (An experiment like this that can have only two possible results, success or failure, is called a **Bernoulli trial**.) Let Z be the random variable that is equal to the number of successes on a particular day. Then Z has only two possible values: 0 and 1. We can easily calculate the complete probability function:

$$f(0) = \Pr(Z = 0) = 1 - p$$
$$f(1) = \Pr(Z = 1) = p$$
$$f(a) = 0 \quad \text{for all other values of } a$$

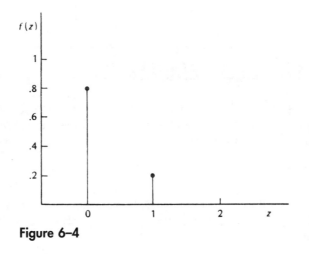

Figure 6–4

Figure 6–4 shows a graph of this probability function for $p = 1/5$.
  Next, we can calculate the cumulative distribution function:

$$F(a) = 0 \qquad \text{if } a < 0$$
$$F(a) = 1 - p \quad \text{if } 0 \le a < 1$$
$$F(a) = 1 \qquad \text{if } a \ge 1$$

Figure 6–5 illustrates this function for $p = 1/5$.

Figure 6–5

The expectation can be found from:

$$E(Z) = 0 \times \Pr(Z = 0) + 1 \times \Pr(Z = 1) = [0 \times (1 - p)] + [1 \times p] = p$$

We can use the shortcut formula to calculate the variance:

$$E(Z^2) = 0^2 \times \Pr(Z = 0) + 1^2 \times \Pr(Z = 1) = [0^2(1 - p)] + [1^2 p] = p$$
$$\mathrm{Var}(Z) = E(Z^2) - (E(Z))^2$$
$$= p - p^2$$
$$= p(1 - p)$$

Note that, if $p = 0$, we know for sure that $Z = 0$; and if $p = 1$, we know for sure that $Z = 1$. In either case, $\mathrm{Var}(Z)$ is 0, as we know must be the case.

Note that the variance is maximized when $p = 1/2$ because then the uncertainty is the greatest.

> # YOU SHOULD REMEMBER
>
> If you conduct an experiment that has a probability p of success, and Z is a random variable that will be 1 if the experiment succeeds and 0 if the experiment fails, then Z is a Bernoulli random variable:
>
> $$E(Z) = p \qquad Var(Z) = p(1-p)$$

VARIANCE OF A SUM

In this section we will develop two useful properties of variances. First, if c is a constant, we can show that

$$Var(cX) = c^2Var(X)$$

Note that the constant c is squared when it is pulled outside the variance. Compare this with the formula for expectation: $E(cX) = cE(x)$.

Second, we would like a formula for the **variance of a sum**.

Suppose we toss two dice, letting X_1 be the number on the first die and X_2 be the number on the second die, and let $T_2 = X_1 + X_2$. We can calculate the expected value and variance of T_2:

i	# of outcomes	$Pr(T_2 = i)$	$i \times Pr(T_2 = i)$	$i \times Pr(T_2 = i)$
2	1	1/36	2/36	0.0556
3	2	2/36	6/36	0.1667
4	3	3/36	12/36	0.3333
5	4	4/36	20/36	0.5556
6	5	5/36	30/36	0.8333
7	6	6/36	42/36	1.1667
8	5	5/36	40/36	1.1111
9	4	4/36	36/36	1.0000
10	3	3/36	30/36	0.8333
11	2	2/36	22/36	0.6111
12	1	1/36	12/36	0.3333
Total	36	36/36	252/36	7

To find the variance:

i	# of outcomes	$\Pr(T_2 = i)$	$i^2 \times \Pr(T_2 = i)$	$i^2 \times \Pr(T_2 = i)$
2	1	1/36	4 × 1/36	0.1111
3	2	2/36	9 × 2/36	0.5000
4	3	3/36	16 × 3/36	1.3333
5	4	4/36	25 × 4/36	2.7778
6	5	5/36	36 × 5/36	5.0000
7	6	6/36	49 × 6/36	8.1667
8	5	5/36	64 × 5/36	8.8889
9	4	4/36	81 × 4/36	9.0000
10	3	3/36	100 × 3/36	8.3333
11	2	2/36	121 × 2/36	6.7222
12	1	1/36	144 × 1/36	4.0000
Total	36	36/36	1974/36	$E(T_2^2) = 54.8333$

We find $\text{Var}(T_2)$ is $54.8333 - 7^2 = 5.83333$.

We found earlier (on page 143) that the variance of the number on one die is 2.91667.

Note that $5.83333 = 2.91667 + 2.91667$, so we are tempted to say:

$$\text{Var}(T_2) = \text{Var}(X_1 + X_2) = \text{Var}(X_1) + \text{Var}(X_2)$$

Unfortunately, we quickly realize this does not work as a general rule. For example, if X is the number on top, and B is the number on the bottom of a die, then $X + B$ always equals 7, so $\text{Var}(X + B) = 0$, which is not the same as $\text{Var}(X) + \text{Var}(B)$. The difference is that the random variables on the two different dice are **independent**—that is, knowing the value of one, the random variables provides you with no clue about the value of the other. On the other hand, the numbers on the top and bottom of a die are strongly related, so that if you know one of the numbers you also can tell what the other one is.

We can use the rule:

$$\text{Var}(X + Y) = \text{Var}(X) + \text{Var}(Y)$$

if X and Y are independent random variables. In Chapter 9 we will discuss a general formula for the variance of a sum that always works.

YOU SHOULD REMEMBER

1. $E(cX) = cE(X)$
2. $\text{Var}(cX) = c^2\text{Var}(X)$
   (In 1 and 2, c can be any constant; X is any random variable)
3. $E(X + Y) = E(X) + E(Y)$
   (In 3, X and Y can be any two random variables)
4. $\text{Var}(X + Y) = \text{Var}(X) + \text{Var}(Y)$
   (In 4, X and Y must be *independent* random variables)

RANDOM SAMPLES AND THE LAW OF LARGE NUMBERS

Suppose we roll two dice. We'll let X_1 be the number that appears on the first die and X_2 be the number that appears on the second die. Then X_1 and X_2 are two random variables that are *independent and identically distributed*. They are independent because the dice don't affect each other at all, so knowing the value of X_1 does not tell us anything about X_2. They are identically distributed because they both have exactly the same probability function:

$$\Pr(X_1 = 1) = \Pr(X_2 = 1) = 1/6 \qquad \Pr(X_1 = 4) = \Pr(X_2 = 4) = 1/6$$
$$\Pr(X_1 = 2) = \Pr(X_2 = 2) = 1/6 \qquad \Pr(X_1 = 5) = \Pr(X_2 = 5) = 1/6$$
$$\Pr(X_1 = 3) = \Pr(X_2 = 3) = 1/6 \qquad \Pr(X_1 = 6) = \Pr(X_2 = 6) = 1/6$$

We will often deal with independent, identically distributed random variables. Suppose X is a random variable that we can observe n times, calling the first observation X_1, the second observation X_2, and so on, up to the last observation X_n. X could be a random variable involving dice, in which case we can measure X by rolling dice; or it could represent the height of a person selected at random from a specified population, in which case we can measure X n different times by selecting n people; or X might represent any of the many other possible types of random variables that we could have. In any case the sequence

$$X_1, X_2, X_3, \ldots, X_n$$

is called a **random sample** *of size n* taken from the distribution X.

In our case we are rolling two dice, so (X_1, X_2) form a random sample of size 2. We know that $E(X_1) = E(X_2) = 3.5$ and $\text{Var}(X_1) = \text{Var}(X_2) = 2.9167$. Now let's create a new random variable called T_2:

$$T_2 = X_1 + X_2$$

In other words, T_2 can be defined in this way: Roll two dice, and let T_2 be the sum of the numbers that appear on the dice.

We can find the expected value and variance:

$$E(T_2) = E(X_1 + X_2) = E(X_1) + E(X_2) = 3.5 + 3.5 = 7$$
$$\text{Var}(T_2) = \text{Var}(X_1 + X_2) = \text{Var}(X_1) + \text{Var}(X_2) = 2.9167 + 2.9167 = 5.833$$

These are the same results as on page 147.

(Remember that the formula $E(X_1 + X_2) = E(X_1) + E(X_2)$ works for *any* two random variables, but the formula $\text{Var}(X_1 + X_2) = \text{Var}(X_1) + \text{Var}(X_2)$ works only because X_1 and X_2 are independent.) As you might have expected, the variance of $X_1 + X_2$ is greater than the variance of either X_1 or X_2 alone.

Now suppose we toss one die, and let Y_2 be a random variable equal to *twice* the number that appears $(Y_2 = 2X)$. We can use this formula

$$E(cA) = cE(A) \quad \text{(where } A \text{ can be any random variable}$$
$$\text{and } c \text{ can be any constant)}$$

to tell us that $E(Y_2) = 2E(X) = 2 \times 3.5 = 7$. The expected value of Y_2 (which is double the number that appears on one die) is the same as the expected value of T_2 (the sum of the numbers that appear on two dice). However, the variance of Y_2 is different from the variance of T_2. We can use the formula

$$\text{Var}(cA) = c^2 \text{Var}(A)$$

to find that

$$\text{Var}(Y_2) = \text{Var}(2X) = 2^2 \text{Var}(X) = 4\text{Var}(X) = 11.667$$

Note that the variance of Y_2 is bigger than the variance of T_2. If we make a graph of the two probability functions, we can see why.

$\Pr(Y = 2) = 1/6$	$\Pr(Y = 8) = 1/6$
$\Pr(Y = 4) = 1/6$	$\Pr(Y = 10) = 1/6$
$\Pr(Y = 6) = 1/6$	$\Pr(Y = 12) = 1/6$

(See Figure 6–6.)

Figure 6–6

In each case the range of possible values is from 2 to 12. However, you can see that Y_2 is more likely than T_2 to have an extreme value such as 2 or 12. This is an example of a very important statistical property: If you add two independent random variables, the sum is relatively more likely to take on a value near the middle of its distribution than an extreme value. An extreme value will occur only if *both* random variables have extreme values in the same direction. For example, the random variable T_2 will take on the value 2 only if *both* X_1 and X_2 take on the value 1.

Now let's roll 100 dice, letting X_1 be the value that appears on the first dice, and so on, up to X_{100}. Then $X_1, X_2, \ldots, X_{100}$ are all independent and all identically distributed, so they form a random sample of size 100 from the distribution of X. We'll let T_{100} be the sum of all the numbers:

$$T_{100} = X_1 + X_2 + \cdots + X_{100}$$

We can calculate $E(T_{100})$ and $\text{Var}(T_{100})$:

$$\begin{aligned}
E(T_{100}) &= E(X_1 + X_2 + \cdots + X_{100}) \\
&= E(X_1) + E(X_2) + \cdots + E(X_{100}) \\
&= 3.5 + 3.5 + \cdots + 3.5 \\
&= 350
\end{aligned}$$

$$\begin{aligned}
\text{Var}(T_{100}) &= \text{Var}(X_1 + X_2 + \cdots + X_{100}) \\
&= \text{Var}(X_1) + \text{Var}(X_2) + \cdots + \text{Var}(X_{100}) \\
&= 2.9167 + 2.9167 + \cdots + 2.9167 \\
&= 291.67
\end{aligned}$$

(It would be very tedious to calculate the exact probability function of T_{100}, but we will see in Chapter 8 that there is a good way to get a close approximation.)

• CALCULATING THE AVERAGE VALUE

Now suppose we are interested in the *average* number that appears when we roll some dice. We'll let A_2 represent the average of the two numbers that appear when we roll two dice, and we'll let A_{100} be the average of the numbers that appear when we roll 100 dice. Then

$$A_2 = \frac{T_2}{2} \quad \text{and} \quad A_{100} = \frac{T_{100}}{100}$$

We can calculate the expectation and variance:

$$E(A_2) = E\left(\frac{T_2}{2}\right) = \frac{1}{2} E(T_2) = \frac{1}{2} \times 7 = 3.5$$

$$E(A_{100}) = E\left(\frac{T_{100}}{100}\right) = \frac{1}{100} E(T_{100}) = \frac{1}{100} \times 350 = 3.5$$

$$\text{Var}(A_2) = \text{Var}\left(\frac{T_2}{2}\right) = \left(\frac{1}{2}\right)^2 \text{Var}(T_2) = \frac{1}{4} \text{Var}(T_2) = 1.4584$$

$$\begin{aligned}
\text{Var}(A_{100}) &= \text{Var}\left(\frac{T_{100}}{100}\right) \\
&= \left(\frac{1}{100}\right)^2 \text{Var}(T_{100}) \\
&= 0.029167
\end{aligned}$$

Note that the expected value of each average is 3.5, which is also equal to $E(X)$. This is exactly what we would have expected. Remember that we initially said that the expected value of X was the average value we would expect to get if we observed X many, many times. However, we can see that the variance of A_2 is less than the variance of X, and the variance of A_{100} is much less than the variance of X. This means that, if we roll 100 dice, the average value will be very close to 3.5. If we roll one or two dice, then there is a reasonable chance that the average value will be as small as 1 or as large as 6. We can state this result as an important rule:

The variance of the average value of a large number of independent, identically distributed random variables will be much less than the variance of any one of the random variables taken individually.

To show that this is true in general, we'll let $X_1, X_2, \ldots, X_n$ be a random sample of size n taken from a distribution of a random variable X that has mean μ and variance σ^2. In other words,

$$\mu = E(X_1) = E(X_2) = E(X_3) = \cdots = E(X_n)$$

and

$$\sigma^2 = \text{Var}(X_1) = \text{Var}(X_2) = \cdots = \text{Var}(X_n).$$

Then we'll let $\bar{x}$ represent the sample average for this sample:

$$\bar{x} = \frac{X_1 + X_2 + \cdots + X_n}{n}$$

Because $\bar{x}$ is formed by adding a bunch of random variables, $\bar{x}$ is itself a random variable. We can find its expectation and variance:

$$E(\bar{x}) = E\left(\frac{X_1 + X_2 + \cdots + X_n}{n}\right)$$

$$= \frac{1}{n} E(X_1 + X_2 + \cdots + X_n)$$

$$= \frac{1}{n} [E(X_1) + E(X_2) + \cdots + E(X_n)]$$

$$= \frac{1}{n} [\mu + \mu + \cdots + \mu]$$

$$= \frac{1}{n} (n\mu)$$

$$E(\bar{x}) = \mu$$

In other words, the expected value of the sample average is equal to the mean of the distribution of X.

We can find the variance:

$$\mathrm{Var}(\bar{x}) = \mathrm{Var}\left(\frac{X_1 + X_2 + \cdots + X_n}{n}\right)$$

$$= \left(\frac{1}{n}\right)^2 \mathrm{Var}(X_1 + X_2 + \cdots + X_n)$$

$$= \left(\frac{1}{n}\right)^2 [\mathrm{Var}(X_1) + \mathrm{Var}(X_2) + \cdots + \mathrm{Var}(X_n)]$$

$$= \left(\frac{1}{n}\right)^2 [\sigma^2 + \sigma^2 + \cdots + \sigma^2]$$

$$= \left(\frac{1}{n}\right)^2 (n\sigma^2)$$

$$\mathrm{Var}(\bar{x}) = \frac{\sigma^2}{n}$$

• *THE LAW OF LARGE NUMBERS*

The variance of the sample average is less than the variance of each random variable taken individually. The larger the sample size (n) becomes, the smaller the variance of $\bar{x}$ becomes. In other words, as the sample size increases, you can become more and more confident that the value of $\bar{x}$ will come close to the value of μ. This result is called the **law of large numbers**. We will see that it plays a crucial role in the theory of statistical inference.

YOU SHOULD REMEMBER

If you have n independent, identically distributed random variables (X_1, $X_2, \ldots, X_n$), all chosen from a distribution with mean μ and variance σ^2, then these random variables are said to form a random sample of size n from the distribution of X. Let $\bar{x}$ be the average of all of these values. Then

$$E(\bar{x}) = \mu \qquad \mathrm{Var}(\bar{x}) = \frac{\sigma^2}{n}$$

• *RISKY DECISIONS*

In business you often need to make decisions that involve risk. If you can estimate the probabilities of different occurrences then you can estimate the expected value and the standard deviation of different decisions. Here are two spreadsheets illustrating your choice between two decisions. There are five possible states in the future. You don't know which state will actually occur, but you do know that state 1 has probability .1, state 2 has probability .2, state 3 has probability .4, state 4 has probability .2, and state 5 has probability .1. Your profit will be different depending on which state occurs. In each of the two worksheets below, the profit from each of the five states is given. Calculate the expected value and the standard deviation of the profit for each of the two decisions, and then think about which decision you should make.

Decision 1:

State	Probability (p)	Profit (X)	pX	pX^2
1	0.10	100.00	10	1,000
2	0.20	200.00	40	8,000
3	0.40	300.00	120	36,000
4	0.20	400.00	80	32,000
5	0.10	500.00	50	25,000
Sum:	1		xx	$E(X) = 300$	$E(X^2) = 102,000$

$\text{Var}(X) = E(X^2) - [E(X)]^2 = 102{,}000 - 300^2 = 12{,}000$
standard deviation $= \sigma = 109.5445$

Decision 2:

State	Probability (p)	Profit (X)	pX	pX^2
1	0.10	0.00	0	0
2	0.20	10.00	2	20
3	0.40	20.00	8	160
4	0.20	30.00	6	180
5	0.10	3,000.00	300	900,000
Sum:	1		xx	$E(X) = 316$	$E(X^2) = 900,360$

$\text{Var}(X) = E(X^2) - [E(X)]^2 = 900{,}360 - 316^2 = 800{,}504$
standard deviation $= \sigma = 894.7089$

Decision 2 has a slightly higher expected value, but it involves considerably more risk. Your decision depends on your tolerance of risk.

KNOW THE CONCEPTS

DO YOU KNOW THE BASICS?

Test your understanding of Chapter 6 by answering the following questions:

1. Why is the expected value of a random variable defined by the expression $\Sigma\ a_i\ f(a_i)$?

2. Why is the graph of a probability function for a discrete random variable like a frequency diagram?

3. Suppose X is a random variable representing the height of a person selected at random from a population. What is its mean and variance?

4. Suppose you took a sample of 30 people and calculated their average height (A). What is $E(A)$? How does the variance of A compare with the variance of X?

5. Let X be a random variable, and let $\bar{x}$ be the average of several independent random variables with the same distribution as X. Why is the variance of $\bar{x}$ smaller than the variance of X?

6. Why must the probabilities for a discrete random variable add up to 1?

7. What value of p makes the variance of a Bernoulli random variable as large as possible? Why?

8. If you roll a die several thousand times, the average of the numbers that appear will be close to 3.5 (according to the law of large numbers). If you find that the average after the first thousand rolls is 3.6, does this mean that you will be more likely to get values less than 3.5 in future rolls?

9. Which is more likely to be the result of tossing 5 dice: 6,6,6,6,6; or 2,4,4,5,2.

10. If an employee shows up late for work every day and claims to have bad luck with traffic and red lights every day, what should you think?

11. Since a casino cannot predict how much any individual customer might win, how can it be confident of collecting more money from customers than it pays out?

12. If two stocks have different amounts of risks, why would anyone buy the riskier stock?

TERMS FOR STUDY

Bernoulli trial
cumulative distribution function
discrete random variable
expectation
law of large numbers

probability function
random sample
random variable
standard deviation
variance

PRACTICAL APPLICATION

COMPUTATIONAL PROBLEMS

For each exercise below, you are given the probability function for a random variable X. Calculate the expectation and variance of the random variable.

1.

X	f(X)
1	.250
2	.250
3	.250
4	.250

2.

X	f(X)
10	.500
20	.250
30	.125
40	.125

3.

X	f(X)
−1	.500
1	.500

4.

X	f(X)
1	.100
2	.200
3	.300
4	.400

5.

X	f(X)
20	.100
25	.200
30	.400
35	.200
40	.100

6.

X	f(X)
−10	.990
1,000	.010

7.

X	f(X)
−100	.900
10,000	.100

8.

X	f(X)
−5,000	.100
0	.600
3,000	.300

9.

X	f(X)
−30	.200
0	.750
500	.050

10.

X	f(X)
1	.100
2	.100
3	.100
4	.100
5	.100
6	.100
7	.100
8	.100
9	.100
10	.100

11. Your store sells fans. However, you need to order the fans before you know whether next month will be hot or cool. You need to choose whether to order a large number or a small number of fans. If it's hot, you'll sell a large number; but if it's cool you'll sell a small number. Develop a formula for the expected value and variance of the profit for each of the two decisions. Let Q_H be the quantity you sell if it is hot and Q_C be the quantity you sell if it is cool. Let p_H and p_C be the respective probabilities. X is the random variable representing the amount you sell.

Let P be the price you can sell the fans for, K be the cost you have to pay the supplier for each fan, and R be the amount you can receive if you return fans to the supplier. Note $P > K > R$.

12. You are trying to decide whether to place a large order or a small order. There are two possible future states of nature: high demand or low demand. The following table gives the probability of each state, and your profit if you make each decision in each state:

Probability	State	Small Order	Large Order
0.60	Low demand	Profit = 200	Profit = 0
0.40	High demand	Profit = 200	Profit = 500

Calculate the expected value and the variance if you make a small order, and calculate the expected value and the variance if you make a large order.

13. A store needs to order products before it knows what the demand will be. There are four possible "states of nature." The demand may be low (quantity demanded = 100, with probability 0.20); below average (quantity demanded = 150, with probability 0.20); above average (quantity demanded = 200, with probability 0.40); or high (quantity demanded = 250, with probability 0.20).

There are four decisions you can make: order a small amount (100), order a below average amount (150), order an above average amount (200), or order a large amount (250).

You must pay 5 dollars for each item you order. You can sell each item for 9 dollars (up to the quantity demanded amount). Each unsold item can be returned for a credit of 2 dollars.

Create an Excel table showing your profit for each decision for each possible state of nature. The profit table will look like this:

Probability	$Q_O = 100$	$Q_O = 150$	$Q_O = 200$	$Q_O = 250$
0.2000 $Q_D = 100$				
0.2000 $Q_D = 150$				
0.4000 $Q_D = 200$				
0.2000 $Q_D = 250$				

The columns represent decisions: Q_O is the amount ordered. The rows represent states of nature: Q_D is the quantity demanded.

Hint: Each entry in the column for $Q_O = 100$ is 400, since if quantity ordered is less than demand, then profit is

(selling price − acquisition cost) × (quantity ordered)

Hint: In the upper right corner of the table (Q_D = 100, Q_O = 250) the profit is −50. When $Q_O > Q_D$, the profit is

(selling price) × (quantity demanded) − (acquisition cost) × (quantity ordered) + (return credit) × (quantity ordered − quantity demanded)

Finally, use this table to calculate the expected value and the variance for the profit for each of the four decisions.

ANSWERS

KNOW THE CONCEPTS

1. The expectation of a random variable is the average value that would appear if you observed the random variable many times. This average value will be a weighted average of all possible values of the random variable, with greater weight being attached to the possible values that have a greater probability of occurring.

2. If you observed the random variable many times and drew a frequency diagram for the results of those observations, the diagram would look like the density function.

3. The mean of X will be the average height of all persons in the population, and the variance of X will be the variance of the heights of all persons in the population.

4. The mean of A will be the average height of the persons in the population, but the variance of A will be much smaller than the variance of the population heights.

5. If you observe the random variable many times, you will get some values that are greater than the mean and some values less than the mean. The average of all these values is more likely to be close to the mean.

6. There is probability 1 that the random variable will take on one of its possible values, so the sum of the probabilities for all of the possible values must be 1.

7. The value $p = 1/2$. When p is closer to 1/2, there is greater uncertainty as to whether any particular trial will be a success or a failure.

8. No. The probabilities for future rolls are not affected by past rolls.

9. The two patterns are equally likely. You might think that the first pattern is less likely because its average value is 6.0, whereas the average value of the second pattern is 3.4. We know that 3.4 is much more likely than 6.0 to be the average result from tossing 5 dice. However, that does not mean

that any particular way of getting an average of 3.4 is more likely than any particular way of getting 6.0. The reason that 3.4 is a more likely value for the average is that there are many possible outcomes that lead to an average of 3.4, whereas there is only one outcome that leads to an average of 6.0. (Note that there are $6^5 = 7,776$ outcomes when you toss five dice.)

10. Everybody has bad luck at times. However, if you average out over many observations, the random ("luck") element will tend to average out, according to the law of large numbers. Therefore, it is not very plausible that the employee is late because of bad luck every day.

11. The law of large numbers makes it possible to estimate average payouts.

12. Investors might buy a stock if it has a higher expected rate of return. A general feature of financial markets is that riskier investments need a higher expected rate of return to encourage people to invest in them.

PRACTICAL APPLICATION

The formulas you need to do Exercises 1–10 are as follows:

$$\text{expectation: } E(X) = \sum_{i=1}^{n} f(a_i)a_i$$

$$\text{variance: } \text{Var}(X) = E(X^2) - (E(X))^2$$

The calculations for Exercise 1 are shown below. The same methods are used for Exercises 2–10.

1. $E(X) = [1 \times .25] + [2 \times .25] + [3 \times .25] + [4 \times .25] = 2.5$

$E(X^2) = [1 \times .25] + [4 \times .25] + [9 \times .25] + [16 \times .25] = 7.5$

$\text{Var}(X) = 7.5 - 2.5^2 = 1.25$

$E(X)$	$\text{Var}(X)$
2. 18.75	110.938
3. 0	1
4. 3	1
5. 30	30
6. 0.1	10,099
7. 910	9,180,900
8. 400	5,040,000
9. 19	12,319
10. 5.5	8.25

11. $E(X) = \mu = p_H Q_H + p_C Q_C$

$E(X^2) = p_H Q^2_H + p_C Q^2_C$

$\text{Var}(X) = \sigma^2 = E(X^2) - (E(X))^2$

Large order: Profit $= PX - KQ_H + R(Q_H - X) = (P - R)X - (K - R)Q_H$

$E(profit) = (P - R)\mu - (K - R)Q_H$

$Var(profit) = (P - R)^2\sigma^2$

If you place a large order, and the weather is hot, then $X = Q_H$ and your profit is $(P - K)Q_H$. In general, a larger value for R reduces the risk because you receive more for each unsold fan you return.

Small order: Profit $= PQ_C - KQ_C = (P - K)Q_C$

If you place a small order, you will not have to return any fans and there is no uncertainty about your profit, but you will have to turn away customers if it is hot and demand for fans is high.

12. Small order:

$E(X) = 0.60 \times 200 + 0.40 \times 200 = 200$

$E(X^2) = 0.60 \times 200^2 + 0.40 \times 200^2 = 40,000$

$Var(X) = 40,000 - 200^2 = 0$

Large order:

$E(X) = 0.60 \times 0 + 0.40 \times 500 = 200$

$E(X^2) = 0.60 \times 0^2 + 0.40 \times 500^2 = 100,000$

$Var(X) = 100,000 - 200^2 = 60,000$

13. Profit table

Probability		$Q_O = 100$	$Q_O = 150$	$Q_O = 200$	$Q_O = 250$
0.2000	$Q_D = 100$	400	250	100	-50
0.2000	$Q_D = 150$	400	600	450	300
0.4000	$Q_D = 200$	400	600	800	650
0.2000	$Q_D = 250$	400	600	800	1,000

Profit times probability table

Probability		$Q_O = 100$	$Q_O = 150$	$Q_O = 200$	$Q_O = 250$
0.2000	$Q_D = 100$	80	50	20	-10
0.2000	$Q_D = 150$	80	120	90	60
0.4000	$Q_D = 200$	160	240	320	260
0.2000	$Q_D = 250$	80	120	160	200
Expected value $= E(X) =$ Sum:		400	530	590	510

Profit squared times probability table

Probability		$Q_O = 100$	$Q_O = 150$	$Q_O = 200$	$Q_O = 250$
0.2000	$Q_D = 100$	32,000	12,500	2,000	500
0.2000	$Q_D = 150$	32,000	72,000	40,500	18,000
0.4000	$Q_D = 200$	64,000	144,000	256,000	169,000
0.2000	$Q_D = 250$	32,000	72,000	128,000	200,000
	$E(X^2)$ = Sum:	160,000	300,500	426,500	387,500
$E(X^2) - (E(X))^2$ = Variance:		0	19,600	78,400	127,400

7

THE BINOMIAL DISTRIBUTION

KEY TERMS

binomial distribution the discrete probability distribution that applies when an experiment is conducted n times with each trial having a probability p of success and each trial being independent of every other trial

Several types of random variables are used so frequently that they have been given special names. One of the most important random variable distributions is called the *binomial distribution*.

THE BINOMIAL DISTRIBUTION

We'll return to the situation where a scientist conducts an experiment that has two possible results: success or failure. The probability of success for each trial is p, and the probability of failure is $1 - p$. If the experiment is conducted 10 times, how many trials do you think will result in success? If the probability of success p equals .8, you'll intuitively expect there would be 8 successes. We'll show that to be true.

First we'll ask this question: If the scientist conducts the experiment two times, what is the probability that both trials will result in success? If A is the event of getting a success on the first trial and B is the event of getting a success on the second trial, then $\Pr(A) = p$ and $\Pr(B) = p$. The event of getting successes on both trials can be written as $A \cap B$ (A intersect B; see Chapter 4). We will make an important assumption: each trial is independent. This means that the chance of getting a success on any particular trial is not affected by the results of any of the other trials. If the trials are independent, then we can multiply the two probabilities:

$$\Pr(A \cap B) = \Pr(A \text{ and } B) = \Pr(A)\Pr(B) = p^2$$

Therefore, the probability of obtaining successes on both the first trial and the second trial is p^2. We can use the same reasoning to show that the probability of obtaining successes on all 10 trials is p^{10}. For example, if $p = .8$, then the probability of 10 successes is $.8^{10} = .107$. Even though the chance of success on any particular trial is good, the chance of 10 successes occurring in 10 trials is very slim.

We can also show that the probability of all 10 trials resulting in failure is $(1 - p)^{10}$. For example, if $p = .8$, then the chance of 10 failures in 10 trials is $.2^{10} = .0000001$.

What is the probability of obtaining one success and nine failures? This question is complicated, so let's first ask a simpler question: What is the probability that the first trial succeeds, and the other nine fail? That probability is $.8 \times .2^9 = 4.096 \times 10^{-7}$.

Make sure you understand the difference between these two questions:

- What is the probability that only the *first* trial succeeds?

- What is the probability that exactly 1 of the 10 trials succeeds?

To find the probability of exactly one trial succeeding, we need to add together the probability that only the first trial succeeds (4.096×10^{-7}), plus the probability that only the second trial succeeds (also 4.096×10^{-7}), and so on. There are 10 possibilities, so:

$$\Pr(\text{one success}) = 10 \times .8 \times .2^9 = 4.096 \times 10^{-6}$$

You can probably guess what comes next: we calculate the probability of exactly two successes, in a similar manner. The probability that the first two succeed (and the remaining eight fail) is

$$.8^2 \times .2^8 = 1.638 \times 10^{-6}$$

This is also the probability that any specified pattern of 2 successes and 8 failures will occur. The next question is: How many such patterns are there? In other words, how many ways are there of choosing 2 positions from among 10 possible positions? We have already seen the answer to that question. Use the formula for combinations:

$$\binom{10}{2} = 45$$

Therefore, the probability of exactly two successes is:

$$\binom{10}{2} \times .8^2 \times .2^8 = 7.373 \times 10^{-5}$$

Now we can give a general formula for a special type of random variable distribution: the **binomial distribution**. The binomial distribution applies to any situation in which several independent trials are conducted, each of which can have one of two possible outcomes. We will call the two possible outcomes "success" and "failure," although in some cases these may be arbitrary designations. Suppose the scientist performs the experiment n times. Let X represent the number of successes. If the probability of success for each trial is p, then the probability that there will be i successes is

$$\Pr(X = i) = \binom{n}{i} p^i (1 - p)^{n-i}$$

This formula gives the probability function for the binomial random variable. Formally, X is said to be a random variable having a binomial distribution with parameters n and p. Remember:

$$\text{The expression } \binom{n}{i} \text{ means } \frac{n!}{i!(n-i)!}$$

If n is large, it can be difficult to perform the calculations in the formula. In Chapter 8 we will see that it is possible to use another distribution called the *normal distribution* to calculate approximate values for the binomial distribution.

Here are the calculations for our case ($p = .8$ and $n = 10$):

i	$\Pr(X = i)$	Cumulative Probability (Pr X less than or equal to i)
0	1.024E-07	1.024E-07
1	4.096E-06	4.198E-06
2	0.00007	0.00008
3	0.00079	0.00086
4	0.00551	0.00637
5	0.02642	0.03279
6	0.08808	0.12087
7	0.20133	0.32220
8	0.30199	0.62419
9	0.26844	0.89263
10	0.10737	1.00000

(The table rounds the results to five decimal places, except for very small values that are given in exponential notation.)

We can see that the probability of getting exactly 6 successes in 10 trials is approximately .088.

This formula is a more general version of the formula we used in Chapter 3 to calculate the probability that a specified number of heads would result if we tossed a coin n times. The number of heads that will appear has a binomial distribution with $p = .5$.

The binomial distribution function is built into Excel. If X has a binomial distribution with parameters n and p, then $\Pr(X = k)$ is found from the formula

$$=\text{BINOMDIST(k,n,p,FALSE)}$$

The cumulative distribution function $\Pr(X \le k)$ is written

$$=\text{BINOMDIST(k,n,p,TRUE)}$$

Here is an example.

	A	B	C	D
1	Binomial		n =	10
2	Distribution		p =	0.8
3	k	Pr(X = k)		Cumulative
4	0	0.0000001	← BINOMDIST(A4,D1,D2,FALSE)	0.0000001
5	1	0.0000041	← BINOMDIST(A5,D1,D2,FALSE)	0.0000042
6	2	0.0000737	← BINOMDIST(A6,D1,D2,FALSE)	0.0000779
7	3	0.0007864	← BINOMDIST(A7,D1,D2,FALSE)	0.0008644
8	4	0.0055050	← BINOMDIST(A8,D1,D2,FALSE)	0.0063694
9	5	0.0264241	← BINOMDIST(A9,D1,D2,FALSE)	0.0327935
10	6	0.0880804	← BINOMDIST(A10,D1,D2,FALSE)	0.1208739
11	7	0.2013266	← BINOMDIST(A11,D1,D2,FALSE)	0.3222005
12	8	0.3019899	← BINOMDIST(A12,D1,D2,FALSE)	0.6241904
13	9	0.2684355	← BINOMDIST(A13,D1,D2,FALSE)	0.8926258
14	10	0.1073742	← BINOMDIST(A14,D1,D2,FALSE)	1.0000000

The cumulative values in column D use exactly the same formula that is shown for column B, except with the FALSE changed to TRUE.

• *CALCULATING THE EXPECTATION AND VARIANCE OF A BINOMIAL RANDOM VARIABLE*

We would like to calculate the expectation and variance for a binomial random variable. There is a clear intuitive explanation for the expectation. If, for example, you conduct an experiment 100 times where the probability of success for each trial is .75, you would expect, on average, to obtain 75 successes. In general, if X is a binomial random variable with parameters n and p, then the expected number of successes is np. We can easily show that this is the case. Let's suppose A_1 is a random variable that has only two possible values: A_1 will be 1 if trial 1 is a success, and A_1 will be 0 if trial 1 is a failure. Likewise, A_2 will be 1 if trial 2 is a success and 0 if trial 2 is a failure. We define $A_3, A_4, \ldots, A_n$ in the same way. Then

$$X = A_1 + A_2 + \cdots + A_n$$

The number of successes is just equal to the sum of all of the A's. We know from Chapter 6 that each A is a Bernoulli random variable, so

$$E(A_1) = p \quad \text{and} \quad \text{Var}(A_1) = p(1 - p)$$

Because each A is independent, we know that

$$E(X) = E(A_1) + E(A_2) + \cdots + E(A_n) = np$$

$$\text{Var}(X) = \text{Var}(A_1) + \text{Var}(A_2) + \cdots + \text{Var}(A_n) = np(1 - p)$$

Figure 7–1 shows a graph of a probability function for a sample binomial distribution ($n = 10$, $p = .8$).

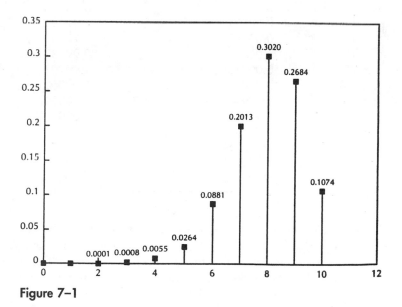

Figure 7–1

• *APPLICATIONS OF THE BINOMIAL DISTRIBUTION*

Examples: Applying the Binomial Distribution

PROBLEM   Suppose you are taking a 20-question multiple-choice exam. Each question has four possible answers, so the probability is .25 that you can answer a question correctly by guessing. What is the probability that you can get at least 10 questions right by pure guessing?

SOLUTION   To solve this problem, we need to calculate the probabilities for a binomial distribution with $n = 20$ and $p = .25$:

k	$Pr(X = k)$	Cumulative Probability (Pr X less than or equal to k)
0	0.00317	0.00317
1	0.02114	0.02431
2	0.06695	0.09126
3	0.13390	0.22516
4	0.18969	0.41484
5	0.20233	0.61717
6	0.16861	0.78578
7	0.11241	0.89819
8	0.06089	0.95907
9	0.02706	0.98614
10	0.00992	0.99606
11	0.00301	0.99906
12	0.00075	0.99982
13	0.00015	0.99997
14	0.00003	1.00000
15	3.426E-06	1.00000
16	3.569E-07	1.00000
17	2.799E-08	1.00000
18	1.555E-09	1.00000
19	5.457E-11	1.00000
20	9.095E-13	1.00000

The table gives the probabilities rounded to five decimal places, except that exponential notation is used for very small values. By looking at the cumulative column, we can see that there is a probability of .98614 that you will get 9 or fewer questions right. Therefore, the probability of getting at least 10 right is 1 − .9861 = .01386. It would seem in this case that studying is a better strategy than random guessing. (Of course, you can look at the bright side—there is only about a 9 percent probability that you will get fewer than 3 answers correct.)

PROBLEM   Suppose you are running an airline that flies planes seating 200 people each. On average, 7 percent of the people who make reservations fail to show up for their flights. It seems wasteful to take only 200 reservations for each flight, because you know that then there will probably be some empty seats left. You decide to gamble by taking more than 200 reservations. If more than 200 people happen to show up, however, you will be in big trouble. Suppose you have decided that you are willing to run a 5 percent risk of having too many people show up for a flight. How many reservations can you accept while still keeping the probability of an overflow less than 5 percent?

SOLUTION   We can regard each reservation as a "trial," and we can call each time a person with a reservation shows up for the flight a "success." (We are assuming that no people show up without making reservations.) If we let X be the number of people who show up for a particular flight, then X has a binomial distribution where n is the number of reservations and $p = .93$. Suppose you take 210 reservations. Then we can calculate these probabilities (rounded to three decimal places):

	Binomial Probability with $n = 210$ and $p = .93$
$Pr(X = 201)$	.034
$Pr(X = 202)$	.020
$Pr(X = 203)$	.011
$Pr(X = 204)$	.005
$Pr(X = 205)$	.002
$Pr(X = 206)$	.001

The probability that X will be greater than 206 is negligible. There will be an overflow if 201 or more people show up, so if we add up all of the probabilities in our table we can find that the probability of an overflow is about 7 percent. You want the overflow probability to be less than 5 percent, however, so you must take fewer than 210 reservations.

We can repeat the same calculations for 209 reservations; we find that the overflow probability is about 4 percent. Therefore, you should take 209 reservations for each flight since that is the largest number of reservations you can take and still have less than a 5 percent chance of an overflow.

PROBLEM An insurance company has 150 customers. Each customer has a probability of .03 of filing a claim this year. The company must pay $1,000 for each claim. If all customers are independent of each other, calculate the probabilities for a certain number of claims, and then calculate the expected value and variance of the number of claims and the amount spent on claims.

SOLUTION Let X be the number of claims filed. Using the binomial distribution with $n = 150$ and $p = .03$, the expected value for the number of claims is $E(X) = np = 150 \times .03 = 4.50$, and the variance for the number of claims is $\text{Var}(X) = np(1 - p) = 150 \times .03 \times (1 - .03) = 4.365$.

Let c be the cost of each claim (which is constant), and K be the amount spent on claims. Then $K = cX$, so the expected value is $E(K) = E(cX) = cE(X) = 1,000 \times 4.5 = 4,500$. The variance is $\text{Var}(K) = \text{Var}(cX) = c^2\text{Var}(X) = 1,000^2 \times 4.3650 = 4,365,000$. (Remember to square the constant c when it is pulled outside the variance.)

Using the Excel function BINOMDIST(a2, 150, .03, false) we can find the probabilities. (Assume cell a2 contains 0, cell a3 contains 1, and so on.) Then enter the formula in cell b2 and copy down. The cumulative column is created with the same formula except the last argument is "true."

i (Claims)	$\Pr(X = i)$	Cumulative
0	0.01037	0.01037
1	0.04811	0.05848
2	0.11084	0.16932
3	0.16912	0.33844
4	0.19222	0.53066
5	0.17359	0.70426
6	0.12975	0.83400
7	0.08255	0.91655
8	0.04564	0.96219
9	0.02227	0.98446
10	0.00971	0.99417
11	0.00382	0.99799
12	0.00137	0.99936
13	0.00045	0.99981
14	0.00014	0.99995
15	0.00004	0.99999

There is a probability of .99999 that the number of claims will be 15 or fewer, so the leaders of the company can sleep more easily with the knowledge that the chance of a large number of claims is very small. (Remember that the assumption that all customers are independent is crucial to this calculation.)

YOU SHOULD REMEMBER

1. Suppose you conduct some form of "experiment" n times. The probability of success for any one trial is p. Let X be a random variable representing the number of successes that occur. Then X is said to have a binomial distribution with parameters n and p.

2. The probabilities for X are given by the formula

$$\Pr(X = i) = \binom{n}{i} p^i (1-p)^{n-i}$$

3. The expectation and variance for X are given by these formulas:

$$E(X) = np \qquad \text{Var}(X) = np(1-p)$$

• *CALCULATING THE PROPORTION OF SUCCESSES*

Often we will be interested not only in the number of success in n trials but also the proportion of successes. If we let X represent the number of successes and p represent the proportion of successes, then $p = X/n$. We can find $E(P)$ and $\text{Var}(P)$ as follows:

$$E(P) = E\left(\frac{X}{n}\right) = \frac{1}{n}E(X) = \frac{1}{n} \times np = p$$

$$\text{Var}(P) = \text{Var}\left(\frac{X}{n}\right) = \left(\frac{1}{n}\right)^2 \quad \text{Var}(X) = \frac{1}{n} \times np(1-p) = \frac{p(1-p)}{n}$$

The expected value of the proportion of successes is just equal to p, the probability of success. For example, if the probability that a machine will work correctly is 3/4, then you would expect that it would work 3/4 (75 percent) of the times you operate it.

* * * * *

We will now consider two more important types of random variable distributions: the Poisson distribution and the hypergeometric distribution.

THE POISSON DISTRIBUTION

Let X be the number of telephone calls that arrive at a particular office in an hour. X is a random variable, and it turns out that its probability function often looks like this:

$$f(k) = e^{-\lambda} \frac{\lambda^k}{k!} \quad (k = 0, 1, 2, 3, \ldots)$$

A random variable with this distribution is called a *Poisson random variable*. (The symbol λ is the Greek letter lambda, which is used as the parameter for the **Poisson distribution**, and e represents a special mathematical number equal to about 2.71828.)

The Poisson distribution has the unusual property that its expectation is equal to its variance. Both are equal to λ. Figure 7–2 shows a graph of this Poisson probability function.

Note that, in theory, there is an infinite number of possible values for X, but the probability that X will equal k becomes very small as k becomes large.

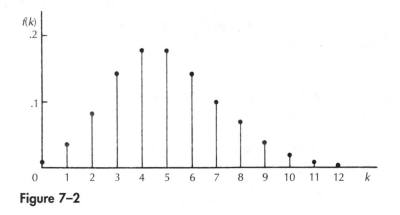

Figure 7–2

• APPLICATION OF THE POISSON DISTRIBUTION: QUEUING THEORY

A *queue* is essentially a line of people or things that are being processed. People form queues at stores and banks when they line up to make their transactions at the cash register or teller, respectively. New people or things join the back of the line and leave the front of the line when it is their turn. Products are constructed in assembly lines that are queues. Cars entering a highway form queues. Queues are sometimes described as being FIFO: first in, first out.

If we assume a constant rate of arrival λ, e.g., 10 persons per hour joining the line with no more than one person arriving at a given moment, then the number of people that join the line over a period of time T is a Poisson distribution with a mean of λT. So if 10 persons per hour join the line, then over 8 hours the number of people that join the line is a Poisson distribution with a mean $10 \times 8 = 80$.

Describing the number of people leaving the line over a given period of time is harder since it is possible that the line will sometimes be empty. If that happens, then how fast people can be served doesn't matter: there aren't any people to serve. If, on the other hand, the line is never empty and there is a constant rate of people being served, μ, then the number of people leaving the line over a period of time T is a Poisson distribution with a mean of μT. If 12 persons per hour leave the line, which is never empty, then over 8 hours the number of people leaving the line will follow a Poisson distribution with a mean $12 \times 8 = 96$.

Whether or not the line is ever empty, you would want $\lambda \leq \mu$ or the line will keep growing without bound.

Multiple channel queues (with more than one line to choose from) quickly become more complicated to analyze. What we've described above is a *single channel queue.*

THE HYPERGEOMETRIC DISTRIBUTION

Now we will introduce a discrete random variable distribution with an intimidatingly long name: the **hypergeometric distribution**. However, we have actually seen its probability function already (in Chapter 4), before we knew what it was called. The hypergeometric distribution applies to this situation:

- There are N objects in the population.

- The population is divided into two types: M objects of type A and N-M objects of type B.

- A random sample of size n is chosen without replacement from this population.

- Let X be a random variable equal to the number of type A objects in the sample. Then X has the hypergeometric distribution with parameters N, M, and n.

The probability function is:

$$\Pr(X = i) = \frac{\binom{M}{i}\binom{N-M}{n-i}}{\binom{N}{n}}$$

There are some obvious restrictions that apply to this formula:

$$0 \leq M \leq N; \quad 0 \leq n \leq N; \quad 0 \leq i \leq n; \quad 0 \leq i \leq M$$

We will not formally derive the formula for the expected value, but we can intuitively predict what it will be. Suppose a population of 1,000 parts contains 50 defective parts. If we select a random sample of 100 parts, how many would you expect to be defective? Since 5 percent of the population is defective, we would guess 5 percent of the sample, or 5 parts, are likely to be defective.

In general, the expectation for a hypergeometric random variable is given by this formula:

$$E(X) = \frac{nM}{N}$$

If we let $p = M/N$, the proportion of items in the population of type A, then the expectation is:

$$E(X) = np$$

That formula looks familiar; it suggests there is a similarity between the hypergeometric distribution and the binomial distribution. Suppose that we chose our sample of 100 parts with replacement: that is, once we had randomly selected 1 part and recorded whether or not it was defective, we put it back in the population so there was a chance of selecting that same part again. In that case, X (the number of defective parts) has a binomial distribution with parameters n and p. The binomial distribution works when we sample with replacement because each selection is independent.

The hypergeometric distribution applies when we sample without replacement. In that case the selections are not independent.

The variance of the hypergeometric distribution is given by the formula:

$$n \left(\frac{M}{N} \right) \left(1 - \frac{M}{N} \right) \left(\frac{N-n}{N-1} \right)$$

Since $p = M/N$, the hypergeometric variance is:

$$np(1-p)\left(\frac{N-n}{N-1} \right)$$

This is the same as the variance of the binomial distribution except for the factor $(N - n)/(N - 1)$. If N is much larger than n, then the fraction $(N-n)/(N-1)$ will be close to 1, and the hypergeometric variance will be close to the binomial variance. In that case, it doesn't matter whether the sample is selected with or without replacement. Therefore, if N is much larger than n, a binomial distribution with parameters n and $p = M/N$ can be used as an approximation to the hypergeometric distribution with parameters N, M, and n. This is helpful because the binomial distribution is easier to deal with. (Later, we will see that the binomial distribution can be approximated by the normal distribution.)

KNOW THE CONCEPTS

DO YOU KNOW THE BASICS?

Test your understanding of Chapter 7 by answering the following questions:

1. Provide an intuitive explanation for the formula that gives the mean of the binomial distribution.

2. Why is the binomial distribution appropriate when a sample is chosen with replacement?

3. Suppose a worker attempts 80 identical tasks each day. Is it appropriate to regard the number of successful tasks as coming from a binomial distribution?

4. Is it appropriate to use the binomial distribution to represent the number of free throws made by a basketball team in a single game?

5. Are the binomial probabilities symmetric? In other words, is the probability of j successes the same as the probability of j failures?

6. Consider the airline reservation example in the text. Do you think you should try to make the probability of an overflow decrease almost to zero?

For questions 7–9, consider a hypergeometric distribution with population of size N, sample of size n, and M objects from the population having the desired characteristic. Compare that with a binomial distribution with n trials and probability of success M/N.

7. In what circumstance will the binomial distribution be appropriate? When will the hypergeometric distribution be appropriate?

8. When will the binomial distribution and the hypergeometric distribution give almost the same results?

9. Will the variance of the hypergeometric distribution be greater than or less than the variance of the binomial distribution? Explain.

10. An insurance company cannot forecast which customers will file claims. Under what circumstances can it accurately forecast the dollar value of the claims it will need to pay?

11. If a multiple-choice test contains questions with 5 choices for each item, how can the scoring system be designed so that a student who randomly guesses on every question will have an expected score of 0?

12. How does the risk to an insurance company change when it has more customers?

TERMS FOR STUDY

binomial distribution   Poisson distribution
hypergeometric distribution

PRACTICAL APPLICATION

COMPUTATIONAL PROBLEMS

1. Suppose that 1,000 meteorites hit the earth each year. What is the probability that the town of Wethersfield, Connecticut will be struck by two meteorites in 11 years? (See Chapter 4, Exercise 2.)

2. What is the probability of getting three primes in five rolls of a die?

3. In tossing a fair coin, what is the probability of getting at least four heads in five tosses?

4. Pensylvania has a daily lottery. A three-digit number is chosen every night. What is the probability of getting a number less than 100 more than five times in 1 week?

5. You're hunting Moby Dick. Each day you send out one small boat with harpooners from your ship. (You never catch Moby Dick, just because Moby Dick *is* Moby Dick.) The probability is 2/3 that the small boat will be sunk on any particular day. You plan to hunt Moby Dick for 4 days. What is the probability that you will lose three or more small boats?

6. Assume that you've been given a 100-question true/false exam on a subject that you know nothing about. If you guess randomly, what is the probability of getting at least 75 answers correct?

7. How many times must you toss a fair coin for the probability to be greater than 1/2 that you will get at least two heads?

8. Assume that 10 percent of the population is left-handed. If three people are chosen at random, what is the probability that at least one will be left-handed?

9. What is the probability that two of the next three presidents of the United States will have been born on a Sunday?

10. Assume that 2/5 of the population have O+ blood type. If you randomly choose six people, what is the probability that four of them are O+?

11. Assume that 45 percent of the Smiths in the world are women. If you randomly run into three Smith siblings, what is the probability that at least two are sisters?

12. Suppose you are running an insurance company. You have N customers. There is a probability $p = .05$ that any particular customer will file a claim in a year, in which case you have to pay $C = \$1,000$. You collect a premium of $50 per year from each customer.

   (a) What is the expected value for your profits each year?
   (b) Suppose you have $N = 20$ customers. What is the probability that your profits will be $2,000? What is the probability they will be $1,000? 0? −$1,000? −$2,000? −$3,000?

13. Calculate the mean and variance of a hypergeometric random variable with parameters $N = 1,000$, $M = 300$, and $n = 25$.

14. Suppose that you pull 15 balls out of a jar containing 30 white balls and 15 black balls. How many white balls would you expect to pull out on the average?

15. Let X be a random variable representing the number of times the word *platypus* is said on a given day. Assume X has a Poisson distribution with parameter $\lambda = 1/2$. What is $\Pr(X > 1)$?

16. What is the maximum value for $\Pr(X = n)$ if X is a Poisson random variable with parameter $\lambda > 0$?

17. If X is a Poisson random variable with parameter $\lambda = 10$, what is $\Pr(1 \le X \le 3)$?

18. Given that 20 books in a shipment of 200 books to a bookstore contain misprints, and you buy 3 of the 200 books, what is the probability that one of your books will contain a misprint?

19. You're dressing in the dark because of a power failure. You have two black socks and six red socks in a drawer. You pull out three socks. What is the probability that two are black?

20. Let X be a Poisson random variable with parameter $\lambda = 3$, representing the number of people who use a given dictionary in a given library on a given day. If $F(a)$ is the cumulative distribution function, what is $F(4)$?

21. A dictionary has 300 pages. What is the probability that, if you look up five words at random, two of them will be on pages with page numbers ending in zero? (Assume that the two words you look up are on different pages.)

22. (a) An insurance company has 10,000 customers. The probability that each customer will file a claim is .05. Each customer is independent of every other customer. Let X be the number of claims that are filed. Calculate $E(X)$ and $Var(X)$.

(b) A different insurance company has 10,000 customers. The probability that each customer will file a claim is .05. Each customer will only file a claim if a natural disaster strikes. If the natural disaster strikes, then all customers will file a claim. If it does not strike, then no customers will file a claim. The probability of the disaster hitting is .05. Let X be the number of claims that are filed. Calculate $E(X)$ and $Var(X)$.

(c) Which insurance company faces the greatest risk?

ANSWERS

KNOW THE CONCEPTS

1. On average you would expect the number of successes to be equal to the number of trials times the probability of success.

2. Consider it a "trial" each time you select one item from the population. Replace each item after it has been selected, and mix the population items before the next selection. Then each selection is independent, and the probabilities are the same for all selections, so the binomial distribution is appropriate.

3. The trials may not all be independent. For example, the worker may be more tired near the end of the day. Therefore, the binomial distribution might not be appropriate.

4. The probability of success will be different for each player, so the binomial distribution is not appropriate.

5. The probabilities are symmetric if $p = .5$; otherwise they are not.

6. You may reduce the probability of an overflow by reducing the number of reservations, but this will reduce your revenue. When you make your decision, you must balance the risk of overflow with the need to have the planes as full as possible.

7. The binomial distribution is appropriate if you select a sample of size n with replacement from the population described. The hypergeometric distribution is appropriate if you select a sample of size n without replacement.

8. If you select a sample without replacement from a population that is much larger than the sample, then the probabilities from the hypergeometric

distribution will be very similar to the probabilities from the binomial distribution.

9. The variance of the hypergeometric distribution will be smaller by the factor $(N - n)/(N - 1)$. The variance associated with the sample will be slightly smaller if you select the sample without replacement.

10. If the customers are independent, then the law of large numbers will allow the insurance company to make a good forecast of the amount of claims it must pay if it has a large number of customers. However, if the customers are not independent (as would be the case if a single disaster might strike all customers), then it is much more difficult for the insurance company.

11. If students are penalized 0.25 point per wrong answer, then their score will be $X - 0.25(n - X)$ where X is the number of correct answers and n is the number of questions (assuming they answer each question). If answers are selected randomly, the expected value of X is $0.2n$, since the probability of answering a question correctly by guessing is .2. Then the expected value of the score becomes

$$E(X - 0.25(n - X)) = E(X) - 0.25n + 0.25E(X)$$
$$= 0.2n - 0.25n + 0.25 \times 0.2n = 0$$

However, if you are able to eliminate some of the possible answers from consideration, then your probability of guessing the correct answer improves.

12. In the situation where all customers are independent and all have the same probability of filing a claim, the binomial distribution applies, and the variance for the number of claims is $np(1 - p)$, which increases in proportion to the number of customers n. However, the standard deviation increases in proportion to the square root of n. Since the revenue increases roughly in proportion to n, an insurance company with more customers has less risk.

PRACTICAL APPLICATION

1. The number of meteorites that hit Wethersfield will have a binomial distribution with $p = .000\,000\,07$ and $n = 11,000$. The probability of two hits is 2.96×10^{-7}. Interestingly enough, the town of Wethersfield *was* hit by two meteorites in an 11-year period.

2. $\dbinom{5}{3}\left(\dfrac{1}{2}\right)^3\left(\dfrac{1}{2}\right)^2 = \dfrac{5}{16}$

3. $\dbinom{5}{4}\left(\dfrac{1}{2}\right)^4\left(\dfrac{1}{2}\right) + \dbinom{5}{5}\left(\dfrac{1}{2}\right)^5\left(\dfrac{1}{2}\right)^0 = \dfrac{3}{16}$

4. $\binom{7}{6}\left(\frac{1}{10}\right)^6\left(\frac{9}{10}\right) + \binom{7}{7}\left(\frac{1}{10}\right)^7\left(\frac{9}{10}\right)^0 = \frac{1}{156,250}$

5. $\binom{4}{3}\left(\frac{2}{3}\right)^3\left(\frac{1}{3}\right) + \binom{4}{4}\left(\frac{2}{3}\right)^4\left(\frac{1}{3}\right)^0 = \frac{16}{27}$

6. $\sum_{k=75}^{100} \binom{100}{k} \times \frac{1}{2^{100}}$

9. $\binom{3}{2}\left(\frac{1}{7}\right)^2\left(\frac{6}{7}\right) = \frac{18}{343}$

7. 4

8. $1 - (.9)^3 = .271$

10. $\binom{6}{4}\left(\frac{2}{5}\right)^4\left(\frac{3}{5}\right)^2 = \frac{432}{3125}$

11. $\binom{3}{2}\left(\frac{9}{20}\right)^2\left(\frac{11}{20}\right) + \binom{3}{3}\left(\frac{9}{20}\right)^3\left(\frac{11}{20}\right)^0 = .425$

12. Let X = number of claims. $E(X) = Np$ expected value of profits = $50N - 1000Np = 0$.

Profits	Claims	Probability
2,000	–	0
1,000	0	0.3585
0	1	0.3774
−1,000	2	0.1887
−2,000	3	0.0596
−3,000	4	0.0133

13. Mean = 7.5   Variance = 5.12

14. Mean = 10

15. $\Pr(X > 1) = 1 - (3/2)e^{-1/2}$

16. $\Pr(X = n) = e^{-\lambda}\lambda^n/n!$, where $n \le \lambda < n + 1$

17. $e^{-10}(680/3)$

18. $\dfrac{\binom{20}{1}\binom{180}{2}}{\binom{200}{3}} = .245$

20. $e^{-3}(131/8)$

19. $\dfrac{\binom{2}{2}\binom{6}{1}}{\binom{8}{3}} = .107$

21. $\dfrac{\binom{30}{2}\binom{270}{3}}{\binom{300}{5}} = .072$

22. (a) X has a binomial distribution.
$E(X) = np = 10,000 \times 0.05 = 500$
$Var(X) = np(1 - p) = 10,000 \times 0.05 \times 0.95 = 475$

(b) Create the table of possible values:

a_i	$Pr(X = a_i)$	$a_i \times Pr(X = a_i)$	$a_i^2 \times Pr(X = a_i)$
0	0.95	0	0
10,000	0.05	500	5,000,000
Sum	1	500	5,000,000

$E(X) = 500$
$E(X^2) = 5,000,000$
$Var(X) = E(X^2) - [E(X)]^2 = 5,000,000 - 500^2 = 4,750,000$

(c) The company in part (b) faces a much bigger risk, since there is a small but still nontrivial probability that *all* customers will file a claim. For the company in part (a), the probability that all customers will file a claim is negligible ($.05^{10,000}$, about $10^{-13,010}$). Note the crucial difference: In part (a), the customers are independent. In part (b), a single event could make all customers file a claim.

8

THE NORMAL DISTRIBUTION AND RELATED DISTRIBUTIONS

KEY TERMS

central limit theorem a theorem that states that the average of a large number of independent, identically distributed random variables will have a normal distribution

continuous random variable a random variable that can take on any real-number value within a certain range; it is characterized by a probability function curve such that the area under the curve between two numbers represents the probability that the random variable will be between those numbers

normal distribution the most important continuous random variable distribution; its probability function is bell-shaped; many real populations are distributed according to the normal distribution

uniform distribution a continuous random variable distribution that takes values between two boundaries a and b; every value between a and b is equally likely to occur.

THE UNIFORM DISTRIBUTION

Suppose that a student (named Jones) comes to class randomly. The class meets for 90 minutes, and Jones comes at any time during that 90-minute time period, without ever actually missing a class. Let X be how late (in minutes) Jones is for any given class.

X has some interesting properties. We know that X has to be between 0 and 90. Assume that Jones is equally likely to arrive at any time during the class. Then every value between 0 and 90 is equally likely.

With that assumption, we can work out some probabilities.

1. $\Pr(0 \leq X \leq 90) = 1$ since X always lies between 0 and 90.
2. $\Pr(0 \leq X \leq 45) = 0.5$ since Jones stands a $1/2$ chance of arriving during the first half of class.
3. $\Pr(0 \leq X \leq 30) = 0.333$ since Jones stands a $1/3$ chance of arriving during the first third of class.
4. $\Pr(0 \leq X \leq 10) = 0.111$ and so on.

We can figure out a formula for the probability that X lies between c and d, where $0 \leq c \leq d \leq 90$. It is the fraction of the 90-minute class that is spent between c and d, namely

$$\Pr(c \leq X \leq d) = \frac{d - c}{90}$$

The smaller the interval from c to d is, the smaller the probability.

What is the probability that Jones arrives to class *exactly* 15 minutes late? In that case $c = d = 15$ and $\Pr(15 \leq X \leq 15) = \Pr(X = 15) = 0$. The probability is 0 that Jones will arrive exactly 15 minutes late. Since there is nothing particularly special about the number 15, we have by the same reasoning that $\Pr(X = c) = 0$ for any number c between 0 and 90.

X has a *uniform distribution* when X is equally likely to take values between two boundaries a and b where $a < b$ and never takes values less than a or larger than b. If $a \leq c \leq d \leq b$, then $\Pr(c \leq X \leq d) = (d - c)/(b - a)$.

The uniform distribution is not a discrete random variable, as were the binomial random variables we discussed in Chapter 7. Instead, a uniform random variable is an example of a different type of random variable called a continuous random variable. We will examine continuous random variables more closely in later sections. However, we have already seen one of their most important (and confusing) properties: Finding the probability makes sense only when a continuous random variable takes a range of values. The probability that a continuous random variable takes a single value will always be 0.

THE BELL-SHAPED CURVE

Suppose you make a graph of the probabilities of the numbers of heads you will expect to see if you repeatedly flip a coin 15 times. (See Figure 8–1.) Or

Figure 8–1

Figure 8–2

suppose you select 1,000 people off the street and make a frequency diagram of their heights (Figure 8–2).

These graphs look similar. This bell-shaped curve, called the *normal curve*, is the most important curve in statistics. There are many examples of quantities that are distributed according to the normal curve:

- the height, weight, or IQ of a population
- the results of the measurement of a physical quality, such as the molecular weight of a chemical, where each measurement involves a random error.
- the total that appears if you toss many dice
- the number of weekly customers at many businesses

The normal distribution often applies in situations where extreme values are less likely to occur than moderate values. The normal distribution can also be used as an approximation to the binomial distribution, and it applies whenever you add together a bunch of identical, independently distributed random variables. Like the uniform distribution, the normal distribution is a continuous distribution.

Discrete random variables are easier to understand intuitively. However, continuous random variables are usually easier to handle mathematically. If a discrete distribution has many possible values that are close together, then it can usually be approximated by a continuous distribution.

YOU SHOULD REMEMBER

1. The most important curve in statistics is the bell-shaped, or normal, curve, which shows the distribution of such quantities as the height of a population or the number of "heads" that appear if a coin is flipped many times.

2. A continuous random variable can take on any real-number value within a certain range. Examples include the length of time until an automobile battery "dies" and the height to which a beginning ballet student can leap.

CONTINUOUS CUMULATIVE DISTRIBUTION FUNCTIONS

Now we have to figure out how to describe the behavior of continuous random variables. There are many similarities between discrete random variables and continuous random variables, but there are also some important differences. We can estimate the probability that the person we select from the phone book will have a height less than 6 feet. Or we could calculate the probability that the person will have a height greater than 50 feet (which is, of course, zero). Therefore we can define a cumulative distribution function for a continuous random variable, just the same as we did for a discrete random variable. We'll use a capital letter, such as F, to stand for a cumulative distribution function, so we can make the definition

$$F(a) = \Pr(X \leq a)$$

where X is the random variable we are discussing.

A continuous cumulative distribution function satisfies the same requirements that we found for a discrete cumulative distribution function:

1. $F(a)$ is always between 0 and 1.
2. As a becomes very large, $F(a)$ approaches 1.
3. As a becomes very small (approaches minus infinity), $F(a)$ approaches 0.
4. $F(a)$ is never decreasing.

Two important practical properties are as follows:

If we want to find the probability that X will be greater than a particular value a, we can use the formula

$$\Pr(X > a) = 1 - \Pr(X < a) = 1 - F(a)$$

If we want to find the probability that X will be between two particular values b and c, we can use the formula

$$\Pr(b < X < c) = \Pr(X < c) - \Pr(X < b) = F(c) - F(b)$$

Warning: Do *not* use these two formulas for discrete random variables. They work only for continuous random variables.

Figure 8–3 shows a cumulative distribution function for the heights of a group of people.

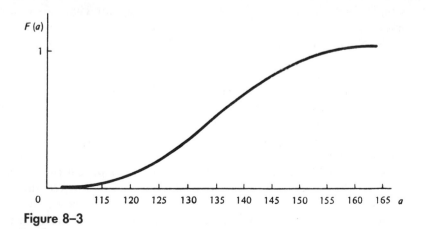

Figure 8–3

For example, let's consider the uniform random variable Y that has an equal chance of taking any value between 0 and 3. Then the probability that Y will be less than 1 is 1/3, the probability that Y will be between 1 and $1\frac{1}{2}$ is 1/6, and so on. If we make a graph of the cumulative distribution function for Y, it looks like the function shown in Figure 8–4.

Figure 8–4. Cumulative distribution function for uniform continuous random variable

Since the probability that a continuous random variable will take on a specific value is zero, we need to develop a new approach to represent these variables. To start with, remember that there is a connection between the probability function for a discrete random variable and the frequency diagram for a sample. So we'll start by drawing a frequency diagram. Figure 8–5 shows the frequency diagram for the weights of American League baseball players in 2009. The bell-shaped normal curve is also drawn on the diagram, indicating that the frequency diagram roughly follows the bell curve. (You would not expect an exact fit.) Note that the height of each bar represents the number of people whose weights are between two specified values. For example, the height of the bar between 180 and 190 is the number of people in the sample whose weights are between 180 and 190.

If we have a very large population, we will get a more accurate picture of the distribution if we make the categories narrower. However, if we make the categories half as wide, then the bars would become about half as tall (since there would be fewer people in a narrower category). In order to keep the bars from shrinking in height as we shrink the width, we'll double the height when we cut the width in half. This means we will make the area of each bar proportional to the number of people in that category. Another way to say it: the

Figure 8–5

height of each bar will be proportional to the frequency in that category divided by the width of the category (just as we did for the histogram in Chapter 2).

We'll keep making the bars narrower and narrower, until eventually it appears that we have a smooth curve. See Figure 8–6. We will call this curve the *probability density function* for the continuous random variable. The curve will be higher where X is more likely, and the curve will be lower where X is less likely. The probability that X will be between two values a and b will be the area under the curve between a and b. Since there is a probability of 1 that the random variable will be somewhere between negative infinity and positive infinity, the total area under the curve must be 1.

If you know some calculus, you will recognize that we are talking about integration. If you don't, don't worry—we will use technology to do our area computations so you won't have to do them by hand.

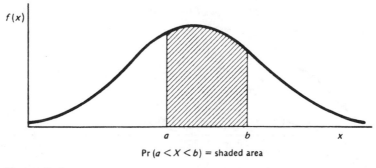

Pr $(a < X < b)$ = shaded area

Figure 8–6

THE NORMAL DISTRIBUTION

• *PROPERTIES OF THE NORMAL DISTRIBUTION*

The **normal distribution** is an example of a continuous random variable distribution. In fact, there are many different normal distributions. A normal distribution can be identified by specifying two numbers: the mean and the variance (or standard deviation). The mean μ is located at the peak of the distribution. The variance σ^2 determines the shape of the distribution—whether it will be spread out or whether most of the area will be concentrated near the peak.

Figure 8–7 shows four normal distributions that have the same variance but different means.

Figure 8–8 shows four normal distributions that have the same mean but different variances. The area under each of these curves is 1, as it must be for a continuous probability distribution. The upper and lower ends of the curve are called the *tails* of the distribution. The tails never actually touch the axis. Therefore, the normal random variable could conceivably take on any value, including values far away from the mean. However, you can see that there is not very much area under the curve out in the tails, so the chance of the observed value appearing far from the mean is remote.

• *ADDITION PROPERTY OF NORMAL RANDOM VARIABLES*

An important property of a normal random variable is the addition property. If X is a normal random variable with mean μ and variance σ^2, and $Y = aX + b$, where a and b are two constants, then Y has a normal distribution with mean $a\mu + b$ and variance $a^2\sigma^2$.

Also, suppose X and Y are two independent random variables with normal distributions. (Two random variables are independent if they don't affect each other. We'll define exactly what independence means in Chapter 9.) Suppose that

$$E(X) = \mu_x, \quad \text{Var}(X) = \sigma_x^2, \quad E(Y) = \mu_y, \quad \text{and} \quad \text{Var}(Y) = \sigma_y^2.$$

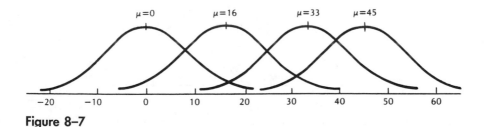

$\mu=0 \qquad \mu=16 \qquad \mu=33 \qquad \mu=45$

−20 −10 0 10 20 30 40 50 60

Figure 8–7

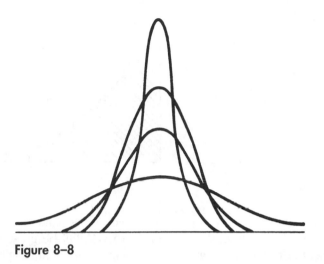

Figure 8–8

If we form a new random variable by adding these two together, $V = X + Y$, then V will also have a normal distribution. (We already know that $E(V) = \mu_x + \mu_y$ and $\text{Var}(V) = \sigma_x^2 + \sigma_y^2$.)

YOU SHOULD REMEMBER

1. The normal distribution is a common random variable distribution that arises in many situations where extreme values are less likely than moderate values.

2. The graph of the density function of a normal random variable forms a bell-shaped curve with its peak located at the mean (μ).

3. The variance (σ^2) determines the shape of the curve; a larger value of the variance means that the curve will be spread out more.

For example, suppose you decide to enter the hamburger business by opening restaurants at two different locations. The number of hamburgers that you sell each day at the downtown location is given by a normal random variable with mean 200 and variance 1,600. The number of hamburgers sold at the suburban location has a normal distribution with mean 100 and variance 400. Then the total number of hamburgers that you will sell at both restaurants has a normal distribution with mean 300 and variance 2,000.

To find the probabilities associated with the normal distribution we must be able to calculate the area under the curve. Consider a normal random variable X with mean $\mu = 20$ and standard deviation $\sigma = 5$. (See Figure 8–9.) If we need to find the probability that X will be greater than 20, we need to find the area under the curve above 20. Because the distribution is symmetric,

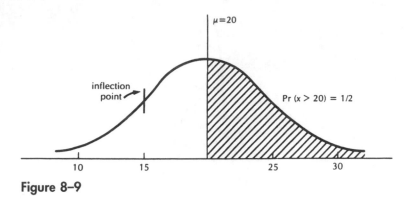

Figure 8–9

the total area under the curve above the mean is the same as the total area below the mean. Therefore, the probability that X will be greater than 20 is .5. Likewise, the probability that any normal random variable will be greater than its mean is equal to .5.

• *THE STANDARD NORMAL DISTRIBUTION*

In most cases when we need to know the area under a normal curve we will need to look in a table, or use a computer or calculator. It would be impossible to prepare a separate table for every normal distribution with every possible mean and every possible variance. Fortunately, we can find the results for any normal distribution by looking at a table for the normal distribution that has mean $\mu = 0$ and variance $\sigma^2 = 1$. This special normal distribution is called the **standard normal distribution**.

Suppose that Z is a random variable with a standard normal density function. Figure 8–10 shows a graph of the density function for Z. Suppose also that we need to know the probability that Z is between 0 and 1. Then we need to calculate the area under the curve between 0 and 1. (See Figure 8–11.)

Unfortunately, there is no simple formula that tells us what this area is. We have to look up the results in a table such as Table A3–1 at the back of the book or use Excel.

The table gives the cumulative distribution function, which tells you the probability that Z will be less than a particular value, z. [The Greek uppercase letter Φ (phi) is often used to represent this function. $\Phi(a)$ equals $\Pr(Z < a)$.] The function satisfies this property: $\Phi(-a) = 1 - \Phi(a)$. (See Figure 8–12).

The probability that Z will be between any two numbers a and b can be found from the formula

$$\Pr(a < Z < b) = \Phi(b) - \Phi(a)$$

We have already figured out that $\Phi(0) = .5$. We can see from the table that $\Phi(1) = .8413$. Therefore, the probability that Z will be between 0 and 1 is $.8413 - .5000 = .3413$.

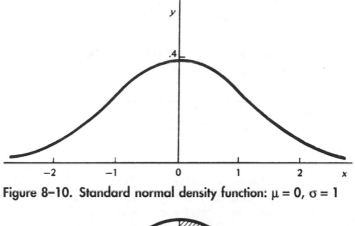

Figure 8–10. Standard normal density function: μ = 0, σ = 1

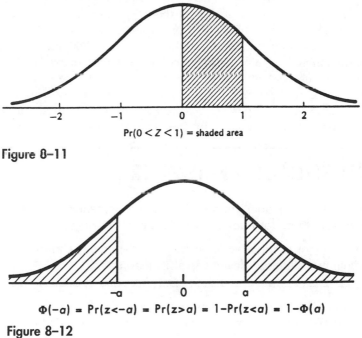

Pr(0 < Z < 1) = shaded area

Figure 8–11

Φ(−a) = Pr(z<−a) = Pr(z>a) = 1−Pr(z<a) = 1−Φ(a)

Figure 8–12

Because of the symmetry of the density function, we can see that there is also a .3413 probability that Z will be between −1 and 0. (See Figure 8–13.) We can add these two probabilities together:

$$\Pr(-1 < Z < 0) + \Pr(0 < Z < 1) = .3413 + .3413$$
$$\Pr(-1 < Z < 1) = .6826$$

Therefore, there is a 68 percent chance that a standard normal random variable will be between −1 and 1. In other words, there is a 68 percent chance that the

Pr(−1<Z<0) = Pr(0<Z<1)

Figure 8–13

value of a standard normal random variable will be within one standard deviation of its mean. (In this case the mean is 0 and the standard deviation is 1.)

This particular property also holds for *any* normal random variable, regardless of its mean and standard deviation: there is a 68 percent chance that any normal random variable will be within one standard deviation of its mean. For example, if X is a normal random variable with mean 200 and standard deviation 30, then there is a 68 percent chance that X will be between 170 and 230.

We can also use the table to show that there is a 95 percent chance that Z will be between −1.96 and 1.96. In general, we can say that any normal random variable has a 95 percent chance of being less than about two standard deviations away from its mean. (See Figure 8–14.)

YOU SHOULD REMEMBER

1. Any normal random variable has a 68 percent chance of being within one standard deviation of its mean.

2. Any normal random variable has a 95 percent chance of being within two standard deviations of its mean.

It will often be helpful to know the probability that a standard normal random variable will be between a and $−a$, where a is a particular number. To make things more convenient, Table A3–2 at the back of the book lists these values. For example, the table shows that there is a .3830 probability that Z will be between −0.5 and 0.5.

The value of the standard normal random variable could conceivably be anything, since the density function never quite touches the axis. There is no number k such that $Pr(Z > k) = 0$. However, you can calculate in Excel that there is only a .0002 probability that Z will be greater than 3.5. Larger values are even less likely, so we don't have to worry too much about the likelihood that Z might take on extreme values.

We can use the standard normal tables to find the probabilities for any normal random variable by using the following trick: Suppose Y has a normal

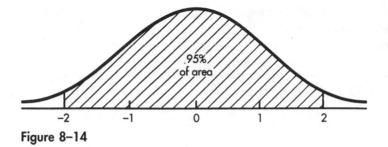

Figure 8–14

distribution with mean 6, standard deviation 3, and variance 9, and we need to know the probability that Y will be between 5 and 8. We can create the random variable Z:

$$Z = \frac{Y - 6}{3}$$

which will have a normal distribution with mean 0 and variance 1 because of the addition property.

Now:

$$\Pr(5 < Y < 8) = \Pr\left(\frac{5 - 6}{3} < \frac{Y - 6}{3} < \frac{8 - 6}{3}\right)$$
$$= P(-1/3 < Z < 2/3)$$
$$= \Phi(.6667) - \Phi(-.3333)$$
$$= .7486 - (1 - .6293)$$
$$= .7486 - .3707$$
$$= .3779$$

In general, if X is a normal random variable with mean μ and variance σ^2, then $(X - \mu)/\sigma$ is a standard normal random variable.

Then:

$$\Pr(X < a) = \Pr\left(\frac{X - \mu}{\sigma} < \frac{a - \mu}{\sigma}\right) = \Pr\left(Z < \frac{a - \mu}{\sigma}\right)$$

For example, suppose we would like to know the probability that you will sell more than 230 hamburgers at your downtown store. Let X_1 represent the number of hamburgers. In this case $\mu = 200$, $\sigma^2 = 1,600$, and $\sigma = 40$. Let's create the standard normal random variable Z_1:

$$Z_1 = \frac{X_1 - 200}{40}$$

$$\Pr(X_1 > 230) = \Pr\left(\frac{X_1 - 200}{40} > \frac{230 - 200}{40}\right) = \Pr\left(Z > \frac{3}{4}\right)$$

If X_1 is greater than 230, then Z_1 is greater than 3/4. Table A3–1 tells us that the probability of this occurring is $1 - \Pr(Z_1 < .75) = 1 - .7734 = .2266$.

Now, suppose we would like to know the probability that you will sell a total of more than 330 hamburgers at the two locations. Let X be the total number of hamburgers. Then $\mu = 300$, $\sigma^2 = 2{,}000$, and $\sigma = 44.72$. Set up the standard normal random variable:

$$Z = \frac{X - 300}{44.72}$$

$$\Pr(X > 330) = \Pr\left(\frac{X - 300}{44.72} > \frac{330 - 300}{44.72}\right) = \Pr(Z > .67)$$

If $X > 330$, then $Z > .67$, and the probability of this happening is .2514.

You can calculate values for the normal distribution with Excel. NORMS-DIST(a) gives $\Pr(Z < a)$, where Z has a standard normal distribution. NORM-SINV(p) gives the value a such that $\Pr(Z < a) = p$. For example, entering =NORMDIST(1.96) will give the value 0.97500; entering =NORMSINV(0.975) will give the value 1.95996.

You can use the NORMDIST function for normal random variables with different means and variances. NORMDIST(a,mu,sigma,TRUE) gives $\Pr(X < a)$, where X has a standard normal distribution with mean *mu* and standard deviation *sigma*. NORMINV(p,mu,sigma) gives the value a such that $\Pr(X < a) = p$. For example, entering =NORMDIST(12,10,2,TRUE) will give the value 0.84134; entering =NORMINV(0.841345,10,2) will give the value 12.0000.

Entering NORMDIST(x,0,1,FALSE) gives the height of the standard normal curve for the value x. We can use this function to make a graph of the curve. Enter the value −3 into cell A1, and enter −2.95 into cell A2. Now highlight A1 and A2, then drag the corner down the spreadsheet until you reach the value positive 3. Now enter the formula =NORMDIST(A1,0,1,FALSE) into cell B1, and copy that formula down as far as you copied the first one. The top part of the screen will look like this (we won't show the whole screen to save space):

	A	B
1	−3	0.004432
2	−2.95	0.005143
3	−2.9	0.005953
4	−2.85	0.006873
5	−2.8	0.007915

Now highlight all the values in columns A and B, and go to the chart wizard. Choose an XY (scatter) graph, and choose the version where it only draws curves connecting the data points (with no markers for individual data points). Then view your graph, and you will see the density function for the standard normal distribution.

YOU SHOULD REMEMBER

1. A standard normal random variable is a normal random variable with mean 0 and variance 1. Table A3–1 in the back of the book can be used to calculate the probability that a standard normal random variable will be between two numbers.

2. The standard normal distribution can also be used to find the probabilities for any normal random variable. If X is a normal random variable with mean μ and variance σ^2, the $(X - \mu)/\sigma$ has a standard normal distribution.

3. The random variable $Z = (X - \mu)/\sigma$ has a standard normal distribution. The function $\Phi(a)$ is the cumulative distribution function of Z:

$$\Phi(a) = \Pr(Z < a)$$

This function satisfies these properties:

$$\Phi(0) = .5$$
$$\Phi(-a) = 1 - \Phi(a)$$
$$\Pr(Z > b) = 1 - \Phi(b)$$
$$\Pr(a < Z < b) = \Phi(b) - \Phi(a)$$
$$\Pr(a < X < b) = \Phi\left(\frac{b - \mu}{\sigma}\right) - \Phi\left(\frac{a - \mu}{\sigma}\right)$$

4. If you multiply a normal random variable by a constant, then the result will still be a normal random variable. If you add together two independent normal random variables, then the result will still be a normal random variable.

5. In general, if X_1 has a normal distribution with mean μ_1 and variance σ_1^2, and X_2 has a normal distribution with mean μ_2 and variance σ_2^2, and X_1 and X_2 are independent, then this random variable:

$$c_1 X_1 + c_2 X_2 + c_3$$

will have a normal distribution with mean $(c_1 \mu_1 + c_2 \mu_2 + c_3)$ and variance $(c_1^2 \sigma_1^2 + c_2^2 \sigma_2^2)$, where c_1, c_2, and c_3 can be any constants.

CENTRAL LIMIT THEOREM

Now we will present an amazing property of the normal distribution. Suppose X is a random variable with any distribution. X could have a strange distribution that does not look at all like the normal distribution, and it can be either discrete or continuous. As usual, let $E(X) = \mu$ and $\text{Var}(X) = \sigma^2$. Take a random sample of size n from this distribution: $X_1, X_2, X_3, \ldots, X_n$. Let $\bar{x}$ equal the average of all of these numbers. In Chapter 6 we found that $E(\bar{x}) = \mu$ and $\text{Var}(\bar{x}) = \sigma^2/n$. Now for the amazing part:

As the sample size becomes very large, the distribution of $\bar{x}$ will be approximately the same as the normal distribution.

This result is called the **central limit theorem**. The astonishing feature of this theorem is that it applies to any random variable. (If X happens to have a normal distribution to begin with, then $\bar{x}$ will have a normal distribution for any sample size.)

We can establish two very simple corollaries. If we just add all of the x's together, the result will also have a normal distribution, this time with mean $n\mu$ and variance $n\sigma^2$. Or, if we calculate the random variable

$$Z = \frac{(\bar{x} - \mu)}{\sigma/\sqrt{n}} = \frac{\sqrt{n}(\bar{x} - \mu)}{\sigma}$$

then Z will have a standard normal distribution.

Since the binomial distribution can be thought of as the sum of a group of independent two-valued random variables, the central limit theorem says that the binomial probability function begins to look like the normal distribution as n becomes large. Note that this works even though the binomial distribution is a discrete distribution and the normal distribution is a continuous distribution. Table 8–1 illustrates what happens as n increases, and the binomial probability function is illustrated in Figure 8–15.

Of course, there are some limitations to the normal approximation. A normal random variable might be anywhere between minus infinity and plus infinity, whereas a binomial random variable must be between 0 and n. However, the probability that a normal random variable will take on such extreme values is very small, so there is no cause for worry. In practice, the normal approximation is all right when $n > 30$, provided that $np > 5$ and $n(1 - p) > 5$.

For another example, consider the probability function for the number that is the result of the role of a die. (See Table 8–2 and Figure 8–16.)

Table 8-1. Comparison of Normal and Binomial Probability Density Functions

	Pr($X = k$)			$p = .5$				
	$n = 6$		$n = 10$		$n = 20$		$n = 30$	
k	Binomial	Normal	Binomial	Normal	Binomial	Normal	Binomial	Normal
1	.0938	.0859	.0098	.0103	—	.0001	—	—
2	.2344	.2334	.0439	.0417	.0002	.0003	—	—
3	.3125	.3257	.1172	.1134	.0011	.0013	—	—
4	.2344	.2334	.2051	.2066	.0046	.0049	—	—
5	.0938	.0859	.2461	.2523	.0148	.0146	.0001	.0002
6			.2051	.2066	.0370	.0360	.0006	.0007
7			.1172	.1134	.0739	.0725	.0019	.0020
8			.0439	.0417	.1201	.1196	.0055	.0056
9			.0098	.0103	.1602	.1614	.0133	.0132
10					.1762	.1784	.0280	.0275
11					.1602	.1614	.0509	.0501
12					.1201	.1196	.0806	.0799
13					.0739	.0725	.1115	.1116
14					.0370	.0360	.1354	.1363
15					.0148	.0146	.1445	.1457

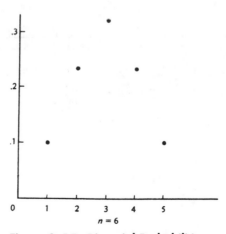

Figure 8–15. Binomial Probabilities *(continued)*

Figure 8–15. Binomial Probabilities

Table 8-2

Number of Dice:	1		2		3		4		5	
Number on Dice	Number of Ways	Probability	Number of Ways	Probability	Number of Ways	Probability	Number of Ways	Probability	Number of Ways	Probability
1	1	.167								
2	1	.167	1	.028						
3	1	.167	2	.056	1	.005				
4	1	.167	3	.083	3	.014	1	.001		
5	1	.167	4	.111	6	.028	4	.003	1	...
6	1	.167	5	.139	10	.046	10	.008	5	.001
7			6	.167	15	.069	20	.015	15	.002
8			5	.139	21	.097	35	.027	35	.005
9			4	.111	25	.116	56	.043	70	.009
10			3	.083	27	.125	80	.062	126	.016
11			2	.056	27	.125	104	.080	205	.026
12			1	.028	25	.116	125	.096	305	.039
13					21	.097	140	.108	420	.054
14					15	.069	146	.113	540	.069
15					10	.046	140	.108	651	.084
16					6	.028	125	.096	735	.095
17					3	.014	104	.080	780	.100
18					1	.005	80	.062	780	.100
19							56	.043	735	.095
20							35	.027	651	.084
21							20	.015	540	.069
22							10	.008	420	.054
23							4	.003	305	.039
24							1	.001	205	.026
25									126	.016
26									70	.009
27									35	.005
28									15	.002
29									5	.001
30									1	...

Figure 8–16 *(continued)*

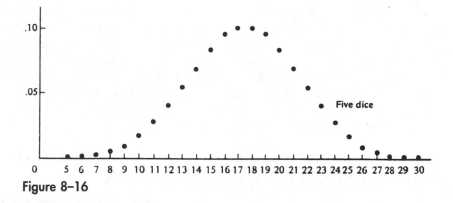

Figure 8–16

This function doesn't look at all like the normal distribution. However, if you roll two dice, the function for the result looks a bit more like the normal distribution, and if you increase the number of rolls, the function looks more and more like the normal density function.

YOU SHOULD REMEMBER

1. The central limit theorem states that the average of a large number of independent, identically distributed random variables will have a normal distribution.

2. This theorem applies to any random variable distribution.

For example, if we toss five dice, we can approximate the sum T with a normal distribution with mean $\mu = 5 \times 3.5 = 17.50$ and standard deviation $\sigma = \sqrt{5 \times 2.9167} = 3.8188$. To find the probability that T will be between 15 and 20, find the area under the normal curve from 14.5 to 20.5:

$$\Pr(14.5 < T < 20.5) = \Pr\left(\frac{14.5 - 17.50}{3.8188} < \frac{T - \mu}{\sigma} < \frac{20.5 - 17.50}{3.8188}\right)$$
$$= \Pr(-0.7856 < Z < 0.7856)$$
$$= .7852 - .2148 = 0.5704$$

The exact figure for the probability (from Table 8–2) is $(651 + 735 + 780 + 780 + 735 + 651)/6^5 = 0.5571$.

* * * * *

Now you can understand why we spent so much time talking about normal distributions. They really are *normal* in the sense that many things that we want to measure have the bell-shaped probability density function associated with a normal random variable, and, because of the central limit theorem, we can count on that happening whenever we are summing or averaging independent measurements of the same thing over and over again.

We will now discuss three more random variable distributions that are related to the normal distribution: the chi-square distribution, the t distribution, and the F distribution. These distributions seem rather esoteric at first, but they turn out to be important tools in statistics.

THE CHI-SQUARE DISTRIBUTION

Suppose Z is a standard normal random variable (that is, it has mean 0 and variance 1). Then suppose that $\chi = Z^2$. (χ is the Greek letter chi.) This means that χ will also be a continuous random variable. Its probability density function is shown in Figure 8–17.

Figure 8–17

The mean of this random variable is easy to calculate. Since Z has a standard normal distribution, by definition $E(Z) = 0$ and $\text{Var}(Z) = 1$. Since $\text{Var}(Z) = E(Z^2) - E(Z^2) = E(Z^2)$, it follows that $E(Z^2) = E(\chi) = 1$. The variance of χ turns out to be 2.

The variable χ is, strictly speaking, called a **chi-square random variable** with one **degree of freedom**. Suppose we square many independent normal random variables and then take their sum, calling the result χ_n:

$$\chi_n = Z_1^2 + Z_2^2 + \cdots + Z_n^2$$

Then χ_n is said to have the chi-square distribution with n degrees of freedom. You're probably wondering why we use the term "degrees of freedom." You can think of it this way. Each of the normal random variables acts like a number that you can choose freely, so since you have n of these numbers, it's as if you have n different free choices that you can make.

Here are formulas for the expectation and variance:

$$E(\chi_n) = n$$
$$\text{Var}(\chi_n) = 2n$$

Figure 8–18 shows several different chi-square distributions with different degrees of freedom.

Figure 8–18

(continued)

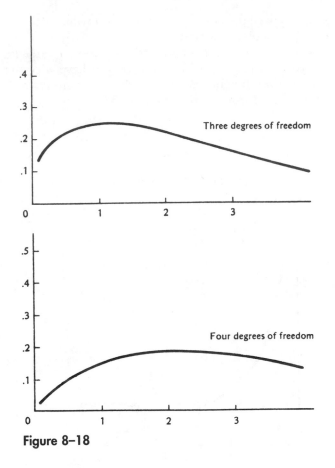

Figure 8–18

When the number of degrees of freedom is small, the density function is severely asymmetric. As the number of degrees of freedom increases, the density function gradually becomes more and more symmetric. As n becomes very large, the chi-square distribution begins to resemble a normal distribution. (This follows from the central limit theorem.) Note that a chi-square random variable can never be negative.

Unfortunately, there is no simple expression for the cumulative distribution function for a chi-square random variable. The only way to calculate values of $F(y)$ is to use a computer. Table A3–3 lists some results.

The chi-square random variable is very important in statistical estimation. For example, the distribution of the sample variance of a random sample drawn from the normal distribution will be closely related to a chi-square distribution. (See Chapter 11.) Also, this distribution provides the basis for an important statistical test known as the chi-square test. (See Chapter 13.)

THE *t* DISTRIBUTION

Another important distribution related to the normal distribution is the **t distribution**. Suppose that Z and Y are independent random variables. Let Z be a standard normal random variable (mean 0, variance 1) and Y a chi-square variable with m degrees of freedom. Let us make the definition

$$T = \frac{Z}{\sqrt{Y/m}}$$

Then it is said that the variable T has the *t distribution with m degrees of freedom*. (The *t* distribution is sometimes called *Student's distribution*.)

The distribution is not just for students; Student was the pseudonym used by William Gossett when he first wrote about the distribution in 1908. He was a statistician employed by Guinness Brewing Company who was fearful of losing his job if he published under his own name.

Figure 8–19 shows a sample *t* density function.

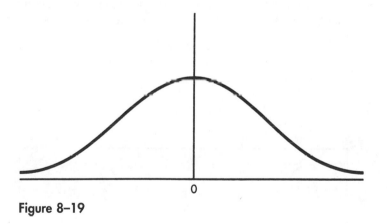

Figure 8–19

The density function has a bell shape that is roughly similar to the standard normal distribution. Like the standard normal distribution, a *t* distribution is symmetric about its peak at 0. In general, though, the *t* distribution has thicker tails than the normal distribution. In other words, a *t* random variable has a higher chance of being far from 0 than does a standard normal random variable. However, as the number of degrees of freedom (m) increases, the *t* distribution approaches very close to the standard normal distribution. See Tables A3–4 and A3–5 in Appendix 3.

THE F DISTRIBUTION

Now we will mention one other distribution related to the chi-square distribution that has important uses in statistics. If X and Y are independent chi-square random variables with degrees of freedom m and n, respectively, then the random variable

$$F = \frac{X/m}{Y/n}$$

is said to have the F distribution *with m and n degrees of freedom*. Note that the order of m and n makes a big difference.

Figure 8–20 illustrates an example of the density function for a random variable with an F distribution with 10 and 4 degrees of freedom. Like the chi-square distribution, an F random variable can never be negative. The F distribution is used in analysis of variance and regression, as we will see in chapters 15 to 17. We are generally interested in knowing the value that separates the top 5 percent of the area from the rest of the area, as shown in Figure 8–21 for an F distribution with 3 and 30 degrees of freedom. We can see from Table A3-6 in Appendix 3 that this random variable has a 95 percent chance of being less than 2.92.

Figure 8–20. F Distribution with 10 and 4 Degrees of Freedom

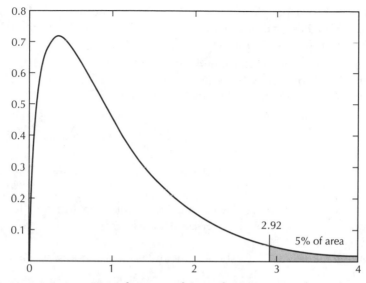

Figure 8–21. F Distribution with 3 and 30 Degrees of Freedom

YOU SHOULD REMEMBER

1. The chi-square, *t*, and *F* distributions are distributions related to the normal distribution that are used extensively in statistical inference.

2. In order to identify a specific chi-square or *t* distribution you must specify the value of the *degrees of freedom*.

3. In order to identify a specific *F* distribution you must specify the degrees of freedom for the numerator and the degrees of freedom for the denominator.

KNOW THE CONCEPTS

DO YOU KNOW THE BASICS?

Test your understanding of Chapter 8 by answering the following questions:

1. Would it be appropriate to represent the weekly sales totals for an automobile dealer by a normal distribution?

2. If the heights of people in a population have a normal distribution with mean 66 inches and standard deviation 5 inches, is it possible that someone in the population has a height of 86 inches?

3. When can the normal distribution be used as an approximation to the binomial distribution? Why is that approximation appropriate? What are the advantages in making that approximation?

4. Can you explain intuitively why the central limit theorem is true?

5. If you add together two random variables that have normal distributions, will the result have a normal distribution?

6. Why must the area under the density function for a continuous random variable always be equal to 1?

7. Why is it impossible for the cumulative distribution function for a continuous random variable to ever be decreasing?

For questions 8 to 10, let Z be a standard normal random variable.

8. Is $\Pr(Z < 1)$ the same as the $\Pr(Z \leq 1)$?

9. Why is $\Pr(Z < -a) = \Pr(Z > a)$?

10. Why is $\Pr(Z > a) = 1 - \Pr(Z < a)$?

11. Does this rule work for all random variables: $\Pr(X > a) = 1 - \Pr(X < a)$?

12. What is the largest possible value for a random variable with a standard normal distribution?

13. Why can the value of a sample average ($\bar{x}$) be approximated by the normal distribution? What conditions must apply for this approximation to be valid?

14. Which of these random variable distributions might produce negative values: standard normal, t, chi-square, and F?

15. If the clothing sizes of the population follow a normal distribution, approximately what range of sizes does a clothing store need to have on hand in order to include sizes for 95 percent of the population?

TERMS FOR STUDY

central limit theorem	degrees of freedom	standard normal
chi-square distribution	F distribution	distribution
continuous random variable	normal distribution	t distribution

---

PRACTICAL APPLICATION

COMPUTATIONAL PROBLEMS

1. Suppose the annual rainfall in a city has a normal distribution with mean 40 and standard deviation 5. What is the probability that the city will get

less than 33 inches of rain next year? What is the probability that the city will get more than 38 inches of rain?

2. Suppose that the score that a student will get on an entrance exam is a random variable selected from a normal distribution with mean 550 and variance 900. If you need a score of 575 to get into a certain college, what is the probability that you will get in? If instead you need a score of 540, what is the probability that you will get in?

3. You're coach of a football team that faces a third-down situation with 4 yards needed for a first down. If you select a play involving a runoff tackle, the number of yards you will gain on the play is given by a normal random variable with mean 2.5 and standard deviation 1. What is the probability that you will make the first down if you run this play?

4. Consider the same situation as in Exercise 3. Another play you might run is a tricky end-around double reverse. The results of this play are given by a normal random variable with mean 3 and variance 6. What is the probability that you will make the first down if you run this play?

5. Suppose you are measuring the speed of light. The result of your measurement is given by a normal random variable whose mean is the true value and whose standard deviation is 5×10^9 centimeters per second. What is the probability that your measurement will be within 2×10^9 centimeters per second of the true value?

6. Suppose you are running a lemonade stand. The number of glasses of lemonade that you sell each day is given by a normal random variable with mean 15 and standard deviation 10. What is the probability that you will sell at least 120 glasses of lemonade in a week (7 days)? What is the probability that you will sell at least 100 glasses? Is it all right to represent a variable such as the number of glasses of lemonade as a normal random variable?

In Exercises 7–15, let X *be a normal random variable with parameters* μ *and* σ^2, *density function* $f_x(x)$, *and cumulative distribution function* $F_X(a)$. *Use Table A3-1 to calculate* $\Phi(x)$.

7. If $\mu = 0$ and $\sigma^2 = 100$, what is $\Pr(5 < X < 10)$?

8. If $\mu = -3$ and $\sigma^2 = 9$, and $F_X(a) = .6$, what is a?

9. If $\mu = 0$ and $F_X(5) = .8$, what is σ^2?

10. If $\mu = 3$, why can't $F_X(4) = .4$?

11. If $\mu = 73$ and $\sigma^2 = 81$, what is $\Pr(|X| > 100)$?

12. If $\mu = 25$ and $\sigma^2 = 100$, what is $\Pr(X = 25)$?

13. If $\mu = 1$ and $\sigma^2 = 64$, for what values of a is $.1 < F_X(a) < .3$?

14. If $f_x(X)$ takes a maximum value of 5 at $x = 10$, what are μ and σ^2?

15. If X is a normal random variable with mean μ_1 and standard deviation σ_1, and Y is a normal random variable with mean μ_2 and standard deviation σ_2, what is $\Pr(Y > X)$?

16. Suppose you have your choice between two jobs. Your monthly earnings from an industrial job will have a normal distribution with mean $15,000 and standard deviation $2,000. Your monthly earnings from a traveling sales job will have a normal distribution with mean $12,000 and standard deviation $10,000. What is the probability that you would earn more from the traveling sales job?

17. Suppose you manage a bank where the amounts of daily deposits and daily withdrawals are given by independent random variables with normal distributions. For deposits, the mean is $12,000 and the standard deviation is $4,000; for withdrawals, the mean is $10,000 and the standard deviation is $5,000. For a particular day, calculate the probability of each of the following events:

(a) Deposits will be greater than $13,000.
(b) Withdrawals will be greater than $13,000.
(c) Withdrawals will be greater than deposits.
(d) Withdrawals will exceed deposits by $5,000.

18. Suppose you have found that the heights of the adults in a town of 10,000 people are distributed according to a normal distribution with mean 5 feet 8 inches and standard deviation 5 inches.

(a) How many people are taller than 6'6"?
(b) How many people are between 6'0" and 6'6"?
(c) How many people are between 5'8" and 6'0"?
(d) How many people are between 5'4" and 5'8"?
(e) How many people are shorter than 5'4"?

19. Suppose that the lifetime of a particular electronic circuit has a normal distribution with mean 50,000 hours and standard deviation 8,000 hours.

(a) If you select one of these circuits at random, what is the probability that it will last less than 30,000 hours?
(b) What is the probability that your randomly selected circuit will last more than 55,000 hours?
(c) Suppose you buy two circuits. When the first circuit fails, you will replace it with the second circuit. Let X be a random variable representing the lifetime of the first circuit plus the lifetime of the second circuit. What is the distribution of X? What is its mean? What is its variance?
(d) What is the probability that X will be greater than 80,000 hours?

20. Suppose you are a banquet manager. The number of people who arrive at your Chamber of Commerce banquet is given by a normal distribution with mean 65 and standard deviation 4. How many places may you set if the probability of an overflow must be less than 3 percent?

21. Consider a city of 100,000 families. If you took the common logarithms of the income for each family, you would find that the resulting numbers had a normal distribution with mean 4.3010 and standard deviation 0.3. (If you are not already familiar with logarithms, you may look ahead to the discussion in Chapter 15.) How many families in the city have incomes between $10,000 and $15,000? Between $15,000 and $20,000? Between $20,000 and $25,000? Between $25,000 and $30,000?

22. Suppose that the grade that a student receives in an individual course is not very accurate, since there are many random factors that could cause the grade to be higher or lower than the student's true abilities would indicate. Suppose that the grade is given by a random variable with a normal distribution with mean 3.5 and variance 1/16. What is the probability that the student's grade for an individual course will be between 3.4 and 3.6? Now, suppose a student takes 36 courses, whose grades all have the same normal distribution. What is the probability that the average grade for all of the courses will be between 3.4 and 3.6?

23. What is the probability that a chi-square random variable with 3 degrees of freedom will be greater than 4?

24. What is the probability that a chi-square random variable with 5 degrees of freedom will be less than 2?

25. What is the probability that a random variable with a t distribution with 5 degrees of freedom will be between 0 and 1?

26. What is the probability that a random variable with a t distribution with 10 degrees of freedom will be between −2 and −1?

27. Suppose someone tells you that he observed the value 16 as the result of a chi-square random variable with 12 degrees of freedom. Do you believe him?

28. If someone tells you that she observed the value 5 for a chi-square random variable with 16 degrees of freedom, do you believe her?

29 If someone tells you that he observed the value −2.3 for a random variable that was selected from a t distribution with 3 degrees of freedom, do you believe him?

30 If someone tells you that she observed the value 0.7 for a random variable selected from a t distribution with 12 degrees of freedom, do you believe her?

31. A plane will carry 350 passengers. The passengers come from a population whose weight is given by a normal distribution with mean $\mu = 189$ pounds, and standard deviation $\sigma = 33$ pounds.

    (a) What is the probability the average weight of all passengers will be greater than 190 (meaning the total weight is over 66,500)?
    (b) What is the probability the average weight of all passengers will be greater than 192 (meaning the total weight is over 67,200)?
    (c) What is the probability the average weight of all passengers will be greater than 195 (meaning the total weight is 68,250)?

32. Use the Excel NORMSDIST function to create a table with three columns. The first column is a;
the second column is $\Pr(Z < a)$ [written in Excel as =NORMSDIST(A1)];
the third column is $1{,}000{,}000 \times (1 - \Pr(Z < a))$.
The table has 7 rows, corresponding to these values of a: 1, 2, 3, 4, 4.5, 5, 6.

33. The height of the normal distribution curve is given by the formula

$$y = \frac{1}{\sigma\sqrt{2\pi}}\, e^{-0.5[(x-\mu)/\sigma]^2}$$

where π is a special number with value about 3.14159, and e is a special number with value about 2.71828. This function can be calculated in Excel:

$$\text{NORMDIST}(x,\ \mu,\ \sigma,\ \text{FALSE})$$

The FALSE means to find the height of the curve rather than the area under the curve.

Create a graph showing four different normal distributions with the same mean but different standard deviations.

ANSWERS

KNOW THE CONCEPTS

1. The sales figures are likely to follow the normal distribution approximately. It would be necessary to observe the sales figures for several weeks and then draw a frequency diagram to see whether the normal distribution looked appropriate. Note that the normal distribution cannot exactly represent this situation since the normal distribution is a continuous distribution but the number of sales must always be a whole number.

2. It would be extremely unlikely for someone to have a height that is four standard deviations above the mean, but it is not impossible.

3. The normal distribution can be used as an approximation to the binomial distribution when the number of trials is large. The binomial distribution can be treated as the sum of n independent, identical Bernoulli random variables, so the central limit theorem applies. This approximation is advantageous because the calculations based on the normal distribution are easier than the calculations using the binomial distribution formula.

4. If you observe a random variable many times and take the average value, it is unlikely that this average will take on a value far from the mean of the distribution. For example, the average will only be far above the mean if most of the observed values are above the mean, which is unlikely. The normal distribution applies to many such situations where extreme values are less likely than moderate values.

5. The result will have a normal distribution if the two random variables are independent. If they are not independent, then you do not know for sure what the distribution of the sum will be.

6. The probability is 1 that the random variable will take on a value between minus infinity and plus infinity, so the area under the curve from minus infinity to plus infinity must be 1.

7. If $a < b$, and X is a continuous random variable, then $Pr(X < a)$ must be less than (or equal to) $Pr(X < b)$. For example, $Pr(X < 2)$ must be less than or equal to $Pr(X < 3)$.

8. Yes. If X is any continuous random variable and a is any number, then $Pr(X < a) = Pr(X \leq a)$. This property is not true for discrete random variables.

9. Because the standard normal curve is symmetric about zero, the area under the curve to the right of a must be equal to the area under the curve to the left of $-a$.

10. Since Z must be either greater than a or less than a, it follows that $Pr(Z > a)$ must equal $1 - Pr(Z < a)$.

11. This rule works for continuous random variables. It does not work for discrete random variables because a discrete random variable might be exactly equal to a.

12. There is no upper bound for the value of a standard normal, but we can see from the table that the chance of a standard normal random variable being greater than 3 is very small.

13. The central limit theorem applies, as long as n is large enough, each observation is independent of the other observations, and all observations come from the same distribution. There are no restrictions on what that distribution must be.

14. Standard normal and t.

15. Size values starting with the mean minus twice the standard deviation, up to the mean plus twice the standard deviation.

PRACTICAL APPLICATION

1. .08; .66

2. .20; .63

3. .07

4. .34

5. .31

6. .28; .58. The normal distribution can represent this situation only approximately, since the number of glasses sold is a discrete random variable.

7. .15

8. −2.25

9. 35.43

10. $F(3) = F(\mu) = \Phi(0) = .5$, which is greater than $F(4) = .4$, thereby contradicting the fact that F must be an increasing function.

11. 0

12. 0

13. $-9.24 < a < -3.16$

14. Mean = 10   Variance = .0064

15. $1 - \Phi\left(\dfrac{\mu_1 - \mu_2}{\sqrt{\sigma_1^2 + \sigma_2^2}}\right)$

16. .39

17. (a) .4013   (b) .2743   (c) .3783   (d) .1379

18. (a) 227   (b) 1,892   (c) 2,881   (d) 2,881   (e) 2,119

19. (a) .0062   (b) .2676   (c) Normal distribution   Mean = 100,000
    Variance = 128,000,000   (d) .9616

20. 73

21. 17,850; 16,280; 12,550; 9,690

22. .3108; 9836

23. A bit less than .25

24. About .10

25. About .30

26. About .15

27. There is a probability of about .2 that this random variable might be as big as 16, so you can believe the person.

28. There is less than a .005 probability that this random variable will be less than 5, so you should not believe this claim.

29. Since there is only a .05 probability that this random variable will be smaller than −2.3, this value is implausible, but you cannot reject it with certainty.

30. Yes.

31. Let $\bar{x}$ be the average weight of the passengers. Then $E(\bar{x}) = \mu = 189$, $\text{Var}(\bar{x}) = \sigma^2/n = 33^2/350 = 1,089/350 = 3.1114$, and the standard deviation of $\bar{x}$ is $\sqrt{3.1114} = 1.7639$.

   (a) $\Pr(\bar{x} > 190) = \Pr\left(Z > \dfrac{190 - 189}{1.7639}\right) = \Pr(Z > 0.5669)$

   $= 1 - \Pr(Z < 0.5669) = 0.2854$

   (b) $\Pr(\bar{x} > 192) = \Pr\left(Z > \dfrac{192 - 189}{1.7639}\right) = \Pr(Z > 1.7008)$

   $= 1 - \Pr(Z < 1.7008) = 0.0445$

   (c) $\Pr(\bar{x} > 195) = \Pr\left(Z > \dfrac{195 - 189}{1.7639}\right) = \Pr(Z > 3.4015)$

   $= 1 - \Pr(Z < 3.4015) = 0.0003$

32. The last column can be interpreted as defects per million.

a	Pr(Z < a)	1,000,000 × (1 − Pr(Z < a))
1	0.841344746	158,655.25
2	0.977249868	22,750.13
3	0.998650102	1,349.90
4	0.999968329	31.67
4.5	0.999996602	3.40
5	0.999999713	0.29
6	0.999999999	0.000987

If the production process is performing well, each item produced will be very similar. If you measure a particular characteristic of each item, then the distribution of those measurements will be very narrow, such as a normal distribution with a small value of σ. If σ is small relative to the tolerance for the process, then a defective item (one that is outside the tolerance range) must be several "sigmas" away from the mean. The term "six sigma" quality control implies that the spread of the process is so narrow that an item must be more than six sigmas away from the mean to be defective. However, in practice a standard of 4.5 sigmas is used, which allows for a rate of 3.4 defects per million items produced. For many processes this is considered a good level of quality control for the production process. (If defects are life-threatening, it would help to have an even higher standard.)

9

DISTRIBUTIONS WITH TWO RANDOM VARIABLES AND CORRELATION

KEY TERMS

correlation an indication of the degree of association between two quantities; its value is always between −1 and 1

covariance an indication of the degree of association between two quantities; it is related to the correlation but is not constrained to be between −1 and 1

independent random variables two random variables that do not affect each other; knowing the value of one of the random variables does not provide any information about the other variable

JOINT PROBABILITY FUNCTIONS

Two random variables may be related, so knowing the value of one may help predict the value of the other, or they may be independent of each other.

Suppose we have two discrete random variables X and Y, and we are interested in the probabilities that they will take on particular values. Just as in the case of one random variable, we can define a probability function and a cumulative distribution function.

Let's say that X has six possible values: X_1, X_2, X_3, X_4, X_5, and X_6. Also, we'll say that Y has six possible values: Y_1, Y_2, Y_3, Y_4, Y_5, Y_6. Now, let's conduct a random experiment in which we observe values for X and Y. The result of the experiment consists of two numbers: the observed value of X and the observed value of Y. Then there are 36 possible outcomes for the experiment. (In general, if there are m possible values for X and n possible values for Y, there will be mn possible results.) To characterize the experiment completely, we need to calculate the probability for each one of the 36 possible results. We can arrange our results in a table.

For example, suppose that X is the number that shows up on the top of a die when it is rolled and Y is the number on the bottom of the die. Then the probability table is as follows:

Y	X = 1	X = 2	X = 3	X = 4	X = 5	X = 6
1	0	0	0	0	0	1/6
2	0	0	0	0	1/6	0
3	0	0	0	1/6	0	0
4	0	0	1/6	0	0	0
5	0	1/6	0	0	0	0
6	1/6	0	0	0	0	0

(The table looks like this because the numbers on any two opposite faces of a die add up to 7.)

For another example, suppose that X and Z are the numbers that appear on two different dice. Then the probability table looks like this:

Z	X = 1	X = 2	X = 3	X = 4	X = 5	X = 6
1	1/36	1/36	1/36	1/36	1/36	1/36
2	1/36	1/36	1/36	1/36	1/36	1/36
3	1/36	1/36	1/36	1/36	1/36	1/36
4	1/36	1/36	1/36	1/36	1/36	1/36
5	1/36	1/36	1/36	1/36	1/36	1/36
6	1/36	1/36	1/36	1/36	1/36	1/36

(In this case, obviously, each of the 36 outcomes is equally likely.)

When there are many possible values for either X or Y, it will be too cumbersome to make a table. In general, though, we can define a **joint probability function** $f(x, y)$ like this:

$$f(x, y) = \Pr[(X = x) \text{ and } (Y = y)]$$
$$= \Pr[(X = x) \cap (Y = y)]$$

In this case f is a function of two variables. (An ordinary probability function is a function of only one variable.) Note that $f(x, y) = 0$ if (x, y) is not a possible result for X and Y. The sum of all of the possible values of the function $f(x, y)$ must be 1.

We can also define the **joint cumulative distribution function**:

$$F(x, y) = \Pr[(X \leq x) \text{ and } (Y \leq y)]$$
$$= \Pr[(X \leq x) \cap (Y \leq y)]$$

The joint cumulative distribution function for two continuous random variables can be defined in the same way. The joint density function for two continuous random variables can be pictured as follows. Imagine a little hill spread out across a flat plane with an x axis and a y axis marked on it. The total volume under the hill must be 1. Then the probability that the values of X and Y will be within any specified rectangle of the plane is equal to the volume of the hill above that rectangle.

Visualizing joint probability density functions for continuous random variables is hard because they are three-dimensional. Figure 9–1 is a perspective diagram illustrating the joint density function $f(x, y) = 12x^2y^3$, where $0 \leq x \leq 1$ and $0 \leq y \leq 1$.

Figure 9–1

Excel will attempt to create these graphs for you if you have entered a two-dimensional table with the values for $f(x, y)$. Choose the "surface graph" option from the graph type menu. Figure 9–2 shows Excel's version of the joint density function for two independent, normal, random variables. Excel will use color to indicate the heights of different points.

MARGINAL PROBABILITY FUNCTIONS FOR INDIVIDUAL RANDOM VARIABLES

Suppose that we are interested in the value of X but don't care about the value of Y. (For example, most people don't really care what number shows

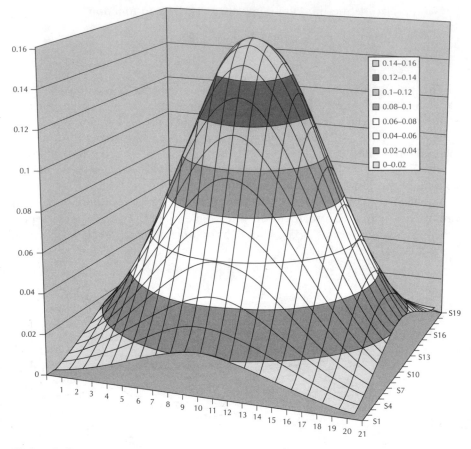

Figure 9–2

up on the bottom of a die they have just tossed.) In that case, the joint probability function gives us far more information than we want. What we'd like to do is to figure out some way to derive the regular probability function for X alone. (We will write $f_X(x)$ to stand for the probability function of X.) Let's look at the joint probability function for X and Y shown above. We should be able to use this information to find the probability that X will equal 1. As you can see from the table, there are six possible outcomes of the experiment that have X equal to 1:

$$(X = 1, \ Y = 1); \ (X = 1, \ Y = 2); \ (X = 1, \ Y = 3);$$
$$(X = 1, \ Y = 4); \ (X = 1, \ Y = 5); \ (X = 1, \ Y = 6)$$

To get the probability that X will equal 1, we need to add all these probabilities. We get $0 + 0 + 0 + 0 + 0 + 1/6 = 1/6$.

Now, look at the table that gives us the joint probability function for X and Z. Again we can get the probability that X will equal 1 by adding all of the terms in the first column: $1/36 + 1/36 + 1/36 + 1/36 + 1/36 + 1/36 = 1/6$. Likewise, by adding up each of the other columns in the tables we can find $Pr(X = 2)$, $Pr(X = 3)$, and so on.

In general, if there are n possible values for Y, then

$$
\begin{aligned}
Pr(X = x) = {} & Pr[(X = x) \text{ and } (Y = y_1)] \\
& + Pr[(X = x) \text{ and } (Y = y_2)] + \cdots \\
& + Pr[(X = x) \text{ and } (Y = y_n)]
\end{aligned}
$$

We can write this relation in terms of the joint probability function:

$$
\begin{aligned}
f_X(x) &= f(x, y_1) + f(x, y_2) + \cdots + f(x, y_n) \\
&= \sum_{i=1}^{n} f(x, y_i)
\end{aligned}
$$

An individual probability function derived from a joint function in this way is sometimes called a **marginal probability function**.

We can also find the marginal probability function for y:

$$
f_Y(y) = f(x_1, y) + f(x_2, y) + \cdots + f(x_m, y)
$$

Here are the results for our random variables X, Y, and Z.

Y	$X = 1$	$X = 2$	$X = 3$	$X = 4$	$X = 5$	$X = 6$	$f_Y(y)$
1	0	0	0	0	0	1/6	1/6
2	0	0	0	0	1/6	0	1/6
3	0	0	0	1/6	0	0	1/6
4	0	0	1/6	0	0	0	1/6
5	0	1/6	0	0	0	0	1/6
6	1/6	0	0	0	0	0	1/6
$f_X(x)$:	1/6	1/6	1/6	1/6	1/6	1/6	

The row totals (in the far right column) give the marginal probability of Y, and the column totals (in the bottom row) give the marginal probability of X.

Z	$X = 1$	$X = 2$	$X = 3$	$X = 4$	$X = 5$	$X = 6$	$f_z(z)$
1	1/36	1/36	1/36	1/36	1/36	1/36	1/6
2	1/36	1/36	1/36	1/36	1/36	1/36	1/6
3	1/36	1/36	1/36	1/36	1/36	1/36	1/6
4	1/36	1/36	1/36	1/36	1/36	1/36	1/6
5	1/36	1/36	1/36	1/36	1/36	1/36	1/6
6	1/36	1/36	1/36	1/36	1/36	1/36	1/6
$f_x(x)$:	1/6	1/6	1/6	1/6	1/6	1/6	

Notice that the marginal probability functions for X, Y, and Z are all the same, even though the joint probability function for X and Y is much different from the joint probability function for X and Z.

With continuous random variables, it is necessary to use the calculus technique called *integration* to find a marginal probability function from a joint probability function.

CONDITIONAL PROBABILITY FUNCTIONS

Often we know the value of one of two random variables and would like to know the value of the other. Sometimes knowing the value of one random variable will help us when we try to guess the value of the other one. For example, if we know that the variable Y discussed above has the value of 4, then we know for sure that X has the value 3. However, knowing that Z (the number on another die) is 4 does not tell us anything about the value of X.

The **conditional probability function** for X tells us what the probability function for X is, given that Y has a specified value. Note that this concept is very much like the conditional probabilities that we discussed in Chapter 5. We will write "the conditional probability of X given that Y has the value of y^*" like this:

$$f(x \mid (Y = y^*)) \quad \text{or} \quad f(x \mid y^*)$$

(Remember that the vertical line, $|$, means "given that.") Then we can use the definition of conditional probability to find that

$$f(x \mid Y = y^*) = \frac{\Pr((X = x) \text{ and } (Y = y^*))}{\Pr(Y = y^*)}$$

$$= \frac{f(x, y^*)}{f_Y(y^*)}$$

In other words, the conditional probability function is equal to the joint probability function $f(x, y^*)$ divided by the marginal probability function of y. For example, suppose $Y = 3$. Then $f_Y(3) = 1/6$, so

$$f(x \mid Y = 3) = \begin{cases} \dfrac{0}{1/6} & \text{when } x = 1 \\[2ex] \dfrac{0}{1/6} & \text{when } x = 2 \\[2ex] \dfrac{0}{1/6} & \text{when } x = 3 \\[2ex] \dfrac{1/6}{1/6} & \text{when } x = 4 \\[2ex] \dfrac{0}{1/6} & \text{when } x = 5 \\[2ex] \dfrac{0}{1/6} & \text{when } x = 6 \end{cases}$$

YOU SHOULD REMEMBER

1. The *joint probability function* for two discrete random variables lists the probabilities for each pair of possible values for the two variables.

2. A *marginal probability function* is a probability function for a single random variable.

3. A *conditional probability function* is a probability function for one random variable, given that another random variable has a specified value.

4. Both the marginal probability function and the conditional probability functions can be calculated from the joint probability function.

INDEPENDENT RANDOM VARIABLES

It would be nice if we could tell whether two random variables affect each other. We will say that two random variables X and Y are **independent random variables** if knowing the value of Y does not tell us anything about the value of X, and vice versa. This means that the conditional probability for X, given Y, is equal to the regular marginal probability for X (since knowing the value of Y does not change any of the probabilities for X). Therefore, if X and Y are independent,

$$f(x \mid y) = f_X(x)$$

We know from the definition of conditional probability that

$$f(x \mid y) = \frac{f(x, y)}{f_Y(y)}$$

Therefore, when X and Y are independent,

$$f_X(x) = \frac{f(x, y)}{f_Y(y)}$$
$$f(x, y) = f_X(x)f_Y(y)$$

When the two variables are independent, the joint probability function can be found simply by multiplying together the two marginal probability functions. This means that independent random variables are much easier to deal with. In general, it is very difficult to reconstruct the joint probability function for two individual random variables if we are given their marginal probability functions. (In fact, it is impossible unless we have some additional information about how the two random variables are related.)

In the examples above, X, Y, and Z all have identical marginal probability functions. However, the joint probability for X and Y is much different from the joint probability function for X and Z, since X and Z are independent but X and Y are not.

Here is an example of the joint probability function for two independent random variables U and V:

V	U = 1	U = 2	U = 3	U = 4	$f_v(v)$
1	.02	.04	.06	.08	.2
2	.02	.04	.06	.08	.2
3	.06	.12	.18	.24	.6
$f_u(u)$	.1	.2	.3	.4	1.0

The marginal probability function for U can be found by adding each column, and the marginal probability function for V can be found by adding each row. You can see that for each entry in the table $f(u, v)$ is equal to $f_u(u)f_v(v)$, so the two random variables are independent.

Here is another useful result that works if two random variables are independent. If U and V are independent, then

$$E(UV) = E(U)E(V)$$

In other words, the expectation of their product is just equal to the product of their individual expectations. This is another reason why life is much simpler when we have independent random variables.

YOU SHOULD REMEMBER

1. Two random variables are independent if knowing the value of one of the variables does not provide any information about the value of the other variable.

2. Mathematically, two random variables are independent if their joint probability function can be found by multiplying the two marginal probability functions.

COVARIANCE AND CORRELATION

• *COVARIANCE*

Suppose X and Y are two random variables that are not independent. We would like to be able to measure how closely they are related. If X and Y are very closely related, learning the value of X tells you a lot about the value of Y. If they are only slightly related, then knowing the value of X helps a little, but not much, when we try to guess the value of Y.

The quantity that measures the degree of dependence between two random variables is called the **covariance**. The covariance of X and Y, written as $\text{Cov}(X, Y)$, is defined as follows:

$$\text{Cov}(X, Y) = E[[X - E(X)][Y - E(Y)]]$$

Suppose that, when X is larger than $E(X)$, we know the Y is also larger than $E(Y)$. In that case, $E[[X - E(X)][Y - E(Y)]]$ will be positive. In general, when two random variables tend to move together, their covariance is positive. And if two random variables tend to move in the opposite direction (for example, if X tends to be big at the same time Y is small, and vice versa), their covariance is negative.

There is a shortcut formula for calculating covariances that is much easier to use than the defining formula:

$$E[[X - E(X)][Y - E(Y)]]$$
$$= E[XY - Y\,E(X) - X\,E(Y) + E(X)E(Y)]$$
$$= E(XY) - E[Y\,E(X)] - E[X\,E(Y)] + E(X)E(Y)$$
$$= E(XY) - E(X)E(Y) - E(X)E(Y) + E(X)E(Y)$$
$$\text{Cov}(X, Y) = E(XY) - E(X)E(Y)$$

To find the covariance, you find the expected value of X times Y and then subtract the expected value of X times the expected value of Y.

We can calculate $E(XY)$ for X, the number on top of the die, and Y, the number on the bottom. There are only six possibilities with nonzero probabilities; each possibility has a probability of 1/6:

Probability	X	Y	XY	Prob × XY
1/6	1	6	6	6/6 = 1
1/6	2	5	10	10/6 = 5/3
1/6	3	4	12	12/6 = 2
1/6	4	3	12	12/6 = 2
1/6	5	2	10	10/6 = 5/3
1/6	6	1	6	6/6 = 1
				$E(XY)$ = sum = $9\frac{1}{3}$ = 9.333

Since $E(X) = E(Y) = 3.5$, we have:

$$\text{Cov}(X, Y) = 9.333 - 3.5 \times 3.5 = -2.917$$

The covariance is negative, because larger values of X are associated with smaller values of Y.

From the shortcut formula you can see immediately that $\text{Cov}(X, Y) = 0$ if X and Y are independent. (Use the result $E(XY) = E(X)\,E(Y)$ if X and Y are independent.) Therefore $\text{Cov}(X, Z) = 0$ when X and Z are the numbers on two different dice. [However, unfortunately it works out that just showing that $\text{Cov}(X, Y) = 0$ is not enough to ensure that X and Y are independent.]

• *CORRELATION*

If $\text{Cov}(X, Y)$ is nonzero, then we know that X and Y are not independent. However, the size of $\text{Cov}(X, Y)$ does not tell us much, because it depends mostly on the size of X and Y. We define a new quantity, called the **correlation**, that we can use directly to tell how strong the relation between X and

Y is. We will write the correlation between X and Y as $r(X, Y)$ if the data comes from a sample. (The Greek letter rho (ρ) is often used to stand for correlation if you have population data.) The definition of the correlation coefficient is

$$r(X,Y) = \frac{\text{Cov}(X,Y)}{\sqrt{\text{Var}(X)\text{Var}(Y)}} = \frac{\text{Cov}(X,Y)}{\sigma_x\sigma_y}$$

(Note the similarity to the formula in Chapter 2 for the correlation for a list of observations of the two variables.)

The most important property of the correlation coefficient is that its value is always between -1 and 1. If X and Y are independent, then clearly their correlation is zero. If the correlation coefficient is positive, we know that, when X is big, Y is also likely to be big. They are then said to be **positively correlated**. X and Y are more closely related the closer the correlation coefficient is to 1. On the other hand, if the correlation is negative, then Y is more likely to be small when X is big. They are **negatively correlated**, and the negative relationship is stronger if the correlation coefficient is closer to -1.

Example: Determining the Correlation

PROBLEM   Suppose we flip three pennies and three nickels. Let U be the total number of heads that appear, and let V be the number of heads on the pennies. Calculate the joint probability table and the correlation.

SOLUTION   The joint probability table looks like this:

V	U = 0	U = 1	U = 2	U = 3	U = 4	U = 5	U = 6	f(v)
0	1/64	3/64	3/64	1/64	0	0	0	1/8
1	0	3/64	9/64	9/64	3/64	0	0	3/8
2	0	0	3/64	9/64	9/64	3/64	0	3/8
3	0	0	0	1/64	3/64	3/64	1/64	1/8
f(u)	1/64	6/64	15/64	20/64	15/64	6/64	1/64	1

We can calculate $E(UV)$ by creating these two additional tables. First, create a table for the values of UV:

V	U = 0	U = 1	U = 2	U = 3	U = 4	U = 5	U = 6
0	0	0	0	0	0	0	0
1	0	1	2	3	4	5	6
2	0	2	4	6	8	10	12
3	0	3	6	9	12	15	18

Next, create a table where you multiply each value of UV (from the second table) by the probability of obtaining that value (from the first table):

V	$U = 0$	$U = 1$	$U = 2$	$U = 3$	$U = 4$	$U = 5$	$U = 6$
0	0	0	0	0	0	0	0
1	0	3/64	18/64	27/64	12/64	0	0
2	0	0	12/64	54/64	72/64	30/64	0
3	0	0	0	9/64	36/64	45/64	18/64

Now take the sum of the values in this table, and we find that $E(UV) = 336/64 = 5.25$.

We already know that $E(U) = 3$ and $E(V) = 3/2$. Therefore, $Cov(U, V) = 5.25 - 3 \times 3/2 = .75$. We also have found that $\sigma_U = 1.225$, and $\sigma_V = .8660$. That means that $r(U, V) = .75/(1.225 \times .8660) = .7070$. The correlation is positive, because larger values of U are associated with larger values of V.

• PERFECTLY CORRELATED RANDOM VARIABLES

Suppose the joint density function for X and Y is as follows:

Y	$X = 0$	$X = 1$	$X = 2$	$X = 3$	$X = 4$	$X = 5$	$X = 6$	
0	1/7	0	0	0	0	0	0	1/7
4	0	1/7	0	0	0	0	0	1/7
8	0	0	1/7	0	0	0	0	1/7
12	0	0	0	1/7	0	0	0	1/7
16	0	0	0	0	1/7	0	0	1/7
20	0	0	0	0	0	1/7	0	1/7
24	0	0	0	0	0	0	1/7	1/7
	1/7	1/7	1/7	1/7	1/7	1/7	1/7	1

In this case it is clear that Y is always equal to $4X$. We can calculate that $E(X) = 3$, $\sigma_X = 2$, $E(Y) = 12$, $\sigma_Y = 8$, and $E(XY) = 52$. Therefore, $Cov(X, Y) = 52 - 3 \times 12 = 16$, and the correlation is $16/(2 \times 8) = 1$.

In general, if the correlation between two random variables is equal to 1, then there is a relationship between them of this general form:

$$Y = aX + b$$

where a and b are constants, and $a > 0$. This is called a linear relationship, because all of the points representing possible values of X and Y would be on a straight line with a positive slope if you drew their graph.

If we have the relationship $Y = aX + b$, but $a < 0$, then the correlation is -1. Again the points showing possible values would fit on a straight line, this time with a negative slope. For example, we can find the correlation between the top and bottom numbers of a die to be $-2.917/\sqrt{2.917 \times 2.917} = -1$.

There are often situations where we observe the outcomes of the random process but we don't know the nature of the relationship between the two variables. In that case, we turn to **regression analysis** to estimate the nature of the relationship; that topic is covered in Chapter 15.

VARIANCE OF A SUM

We can now derive a general formula for $\text{Var}(X + Y)$:

$$
\begin{aligned}
\text{Var}(X + Y) &= E[(X + Y)^2] - [E(X + Y)]^2 \\
&= E[X^2 + 2XY + Y^2] - [E(X) + E(Y)]^2 \\
&= E(X^2) + 2E(XY) + E(Y^2) \\
&\quad - (E(X))^2 - 2E(X)E(Y) - (E(Y))^2 \\
&= E(X^2) - (E(X))^2 + E(Y^2) - (E(Y))^2 \\
&\quad + 2[E(XY) - E(X)E(Y)]
\end{aligned}
$$

Since $E(X^2) - (E(X))^2 = \text{Var}(X)$, and $E(Y^2) - (E(Y))^2 = \text{Var}(Y)$, and $E(XY) - E(X)E(Y) = \text{Cov}(X, Y)$, we have:

$$
\text{Var}(X + Y) = \text{Var}(X) + \text{Var}(Y) + 2\,\text{Cov}(X, Y)
$$

If X and Y are independent, then $\text{Cov}(X, Y) = 0$, and we have $\text{Var}(X + Y) = \text{Var}(X) + \text{Var}(Y)$, as we had earlier (page 147). If $\text{Cov}(X, Y)$ is positive, then X tends to have larger values at the same time Y has larger values, and the uncertainty of their sum becomes even greater. However, if $\text{Cov}(X, Y)$ is negative, then X tends to have larger values at the same time Y has smaller values, which tends to reduce the uncertainty of their sum.

For example, suppose you own stock in Worldwide Fastburgers, Inc. Your profit from the stock is a random variable (W) with mean 1,000 and variance 400. You would like to buy some more stock, and you are trying to decide between Have It Your Way Burgers, Inc., and Fun and Good Times Pizza, Inc. Both stocks also have profits that are random variables with mean 1,000 and variance 400. Which one should you choose? Let H represent your profit if you choose Have It Your Way Burgers, and let F represent your profit if you choose Fun and Good Times Pizza.

The expected value of your profit will be the same regardless of which one you choose. However, you should also like the variance of your profit to be as small as possible, since a smaller variance means that your stock holding is less risky. To calculate the total variance of your portfolio, you need to look at the covariance between Worldwide Burgers and the other two companies. Suppose that $Cov(W, H) = 380$. The covariance is positive, meaning that both firms will prosper if the hamburger market is strong, but both firms will suffer if the hamburger market is weak. Suppose also that $Cov(W, F) = -200$. The negative covariance means that the pizza market is booming when the hamburger market is in a slump, and vice versa.

If you buy the Have It Your Way Burger stock, then the total variance of your profit will be

$$\begin{aligned}
Var(W + H) &= Var(W) + Var(H) + 2\,Cov(W, H) \\
&= \quad 400 \quad + \quad 400 \quad + \quad 2 \times 380 \\
&= 1,560
\end{aligned}$$

If you buy the pizza stock, then the variance will be

$$\begin{aligned}
Var(W + F) &= Var(W) + Var(F) + 2\,Cov(W, F) \\
&= \quad 400 \quad + \quad 400 \quad + \; 2 \times (-200) \\
&= 400
\end{aligned}$$

Clearly, it is much less risky to buy the pizza stock. In general, you can lower the risk of your stock holdings by diversifying and buying stocks that have negative covariances with each other. In other words, don't put all your eggs in one basket.

Now consider X and Y, where X is the number on top of the die and Y is the number on the bottom. We have previously found $Var(X) = Var(Y) = 2.917$ and $Cov(X, Y) = -2.917$. Now, to find the variance of their sum:

$$Var(X + Y) = Var(X) + Var(Y) + 2\,Cov(X, Y) = 2.917 + 2.917 - (2 \times 2.917) = 0$$

This makes sense, because we know $X + Y = 7$ always, so there is no uncertainty about what $X + Y$ will be (even if there is lots of uncertainty about the value of X and the value of Y).

STOCK PORTFOLIOS

Now we'll consider the general problem of allocating funds in a stock portfolio with two stocks: stock A, with expected return k_A and standard deviation σ_A; and stock B, with expected return k_B and standard deviation σ_B. You will allocate a fraction x_A of the portfolio value into stock A and x_B into B. Since these are the only two choices, $x_A + x_B = 1$. The total return on the portfolio T is:

$$T = x_A A + x_B B$$

We can find the expected return on the total portfolio:

$$E(T) = E(x_A A + x_B B) = x_A E(A) + x_B E(B) = x_A k_A + x_B k_B$$

Next, we'll find the variance of the total portfolio:

$$\text{Var}(T) = \text{Var}(x_A A + x_B B) = \text{Var}(x_A A) + \text{Var}(x_B B) + 2\,\text{Cov}(x_A A, x_B B)$$

Since

$$\text{Cov}(A, B) = E(AB) - E(A)E(B)$$

we can work out this formula:

$$\text{Cov}(x_A A, x_B B) = E(x_A A x_B B) - E(x_A A)E(x_B B)$$
$$\text{Cov}(x_A A, x_B B) = x_A x_B E(AB) - x_A x_B E(A)E(B)$$
$$= x_A x_B [E(AB) - E(A)E(B)]$$
$$= x_A x_B \text{Cov}(A, B)$$

Then the formula for variance becomes:

$$\text{Var}(T) = x_A^2 \text{Var}(A) + x_B^2 \text{Var}(B) + 2x_A x_B \text{Cov}(A, B)$$

Cov(A, B) equals $r_{AB}\sigma_A\sigma_B$, where r_{AB} is the correlation between A and B.

$$\text{Var}(T) = x_A^2 \sigma_A^2 + x_B^2 \sigma_B^2 + 2x_A x_B r_{AB}\sigma_A\sigma_B$$

The standard deviation of the total portfolio (σ_T) becomes:

$$\sigma_r = \sqrt{x_A^2 \sigma_A^2 + x_B^2 \sigma_B^2 + 2x_A x_B r_{AB}\sigma_A\sigma_B}$$

Consider a situation where A is the safer stock but B has a higher expected rate of return: $k_A = .06$, $\sigma_A = .03$, $k_B = .12$, $\sigma_B = .08$. We'll consider three different values of r_{AB}. Figure 9–3 illustrates the possible values of the risk and return for your portfolio if the stocks have a correlation of −1. In general, investors wish to increase their rate of return but reduce their risk, so they

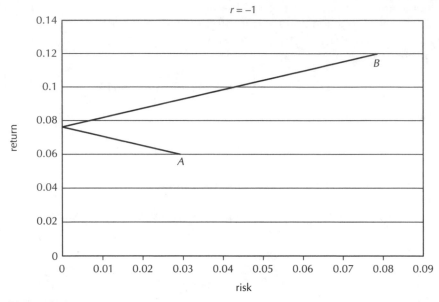

Figure 9–3

would prefer to move toward the upper left corner of the risk/return diagram. Point *A* represents the situation where you hold your entire portfolio in stock *A*, and *B* represents the point where you hold your entire portfolio in stock *B*. Moving from point *A* toward point *B* indicates you are increasing the share of *B* in your portfolio, which will increase your rate of return. In the case where the stocks have a perfect negative correlation, designing a portfolio with a zero standard devation is possible—in other words, you can eliminate the risk of the portfolio.

However, two stocks having a perfect negative correlation would be very unusual. Figure 9–4 illustrates the situation where the correlation r_{AB} is zero. Diversifying your portfolio so as to allow you to have both a higher return and less risk than you would have by investing exclusively in stock *A* is possible.

Figure 9–5 illustrates the case where the stocks are perfectly correlated ($r_{AB} = 1$). In this case, the lowest risk occurs if you invest the entire portfolio in stock *A*, and reducing the risk with diversification is not possible.

Figure 9–4

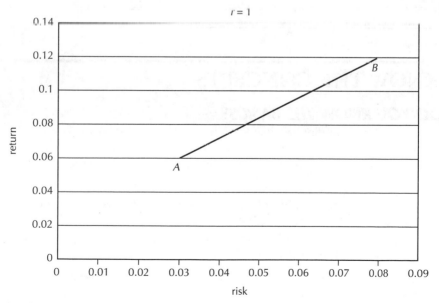

Figure 9–5

YOU SHOULD REMEMBER

1. The covariance of two random variables is a measure of their association. If the covariance is *positive*, then large values of one of the random variables are likely to be associated with large values of the other random variable. If the covariance is *negative*, then large values of one of the random variables are likely to be associated with small values of the other random variable. If the two random variables are *independent*, then the covariance is zero. The covariance can be calculated from this formula:

$$\text{Cov}(x, y) = E(XY) - E(X)E(Y)$$

2. The correlation is a quantity similar to the covariance except that it is scaled so as always to be between −1 and 1. If the two random variables are independent, the correlation is zero. If there is a perfect linear relationship between the two random variables, the correlation is either −1 or 1, depending on whether the covariance is positive or negative.

3. If X and Y are two random variables, then the variance of their sum can be found from this formula:

$$\text{Var}(X + Y) = \text{Var}(X) + \text{Var}(Y) + 2\,\text{Cov}(X, Y)$$

KNOW THE CONCEPTS

DO YOU KNOW THE BASICS?

Test your understanding of Chapter 9 by answering the following questions:

1. What is the sum of all of the probabilities in a joint probability table?

2. How can you tell if two random variables are independent?

3. Do you think the number of new cars sold in a city is independent from the number of used cars sold?

4. Can you calculate the marginal density function for two random variables if you are given their joint density function?

5. Can you calculate the joint density function for two random variables if you are given their marginal density function?

6. In what circumstances could you completely eliminate the risk of a portfolio with two stocks?

7. Is holding a mortgage-backed security that includes a small portion of the payment from 1,000 mortgages more or less risky than lending money to one mortgage borrower?

TERMS FOR STUDY

conditional probability function
correlation
covariance
independent random variables
joint cumulative distribution function
joint probability function
marginal probability function

negatively correlated
perfectly correlated
positively correlated

PRACTICAL APPLICATION

COMPUTATIONAL PROBLEMS

1. Roll three dice (one red, one blue, and one green). Let X equal the sum of the numbers on the red and blue dice, and let Y equal the sum of the numbers on the blue and green dice. Find the joint distribution of X and Y.

2. Roll two dice (one red and one blue). Let X be the sum of the numbers on the two dice, and let Y be the number on the red die. Find the joint distribution of X and Y.

For Exercises 3–6 calculate the marginal probability functions for X *and* Y, *the covariance between* X *and* Y, *and the correlation between* X *and* Y. *In each case the table gives the joint probability function.*

3. X	Y = 0	Y = 2	Y = 4	Y = 6
−2	.1	0	.1	.2
4	0	.1	0	.1
5	.1	0	.1	.2

4. X	Y = 3	Y = 5	Y = 9
−2	.15	.05	0
−1	.05	0	.2
0	0	.1	0
1	.15	0	.2
2	0	.1	0

5.

X	$Y = 1$	$Y = 4$	$Y = 5$	$Y = 6$	$Y = 9$
0	.1	0	.1	0	0
5	0	.1	0	0	.15
9	0	.05	0	0	0
11	0	.3	0	.05	0
13	.15	0	0	0	0

6.

X	$Y = -9$	$Y = -4$	$Y = -3$	$Y = -1$	$Y = 0$
-3	0	.1	0	.05	.1
2	.05	0	0	0	0
4	0	0	.1	0	.05
5	0	0	0	.05	0
7	0	.25	.05	0	.2

7. Suppose the joint probability function for X and Y is given by the following table, Find $f_X(x)$ and $f_Y(y)$.

X	$Y = 1$	$Y = 2$	$Y = 3$	$Y = 4$
1	.2	.1	.1	0
2	0	0	0	0
3	0	.1	.1	.2
4	0	0	.1	.1

8. Roll two dice. Let X represent the sum of the numbers on the top of the dice, and let Y represent the sum of the numbers on the bottom of the dice. Determine the joint probability function.

9. In a lottery based on a randomly selected three-digit number, let X be the first two digits of the number and Y be the last two. Describe $f_{XY}(x, y)$.

10. Suppose the following table gives the joint probability function for two random variables X and Y:

X	$Y = 7$	$Y = 10$	$Y = 13$	$Y = 14$
1	.1	0	.1	0
2	0	0	0	.15
5	0	.25	0	.1
9	.1	.1	.1	0

Find the joint cumulative distribution function.

11. Why can't

$$g(x, y) = \begin{cases} .1 & x = 2, \quad y = 3/2 \\ .3 & x = 1/2, y = 4 \\ .5 & x = 2, \quad y = 1 \\ .2 & x = 4, \quad y = 1 \\ 0 & \text{everywhere else} \end{cases}$$

be a joint probability function?

12. Calculate the covariance and correlation between X and Y when X represents the number on the top of a die and Y represents the number on the bottom of the die.

13. Calculate the covariance and correlation between X and Z when they represent the numbers that appear when two separate dice are tossed.

Exercises 14–16 refer to the random variables U and V whose joint probability is given on page 226.

14. Calculate the marginal probability functions for U and V.

15. Find the conditional probability function for U, given that $V = 2$.

16. Find the conditional probability function for V, given that $U = 3$.

17. A, B, and C are random variables representing the returns from three different stock investments, and T is the random variable representing the total return on your investment:

$$T = x_a A + x_b B + x_c C$$

where x_a, x_b, and x_c are the shares of each stock (so $x_a + x_b + x_c = 1$). Find $E(T)$ and $\text{Var}(T)$.

18. Obtain data on the daily closing prices for two stocks and calculate the correlation between them.

ANSWERS

KNOW THE CONCEPTS

1. 1

2. If two random variables are independent, then their joint probability function is found by multiplying their individual marginal probability functions.

3. Probably the two numbers are not independent, but you would need to collect some observations and then conduct a chi-square test (which will be discussed in Chapter 13) in order to tell for sure.

4. Yes, by addition.

5. In general, no. However, if you know that the two random variables are independent, then you can calculate the joint probability function by multiplying.

6. If the correlation of the returns equals −1. This is unlikely to happen in practice, but this analysis does indicate how the risk of a portfolio can be reduced by diversification.

7. Because the mortgage-backed security includes portions of so many loans, the random individual risks associated with each loan will largely cancel out. Therefore, the diversification means that the security is safer than an individual mortgage. However, diversification is no protection against systematic risk. For example, if housing prices fall across the country, then a diversified portfolio of mortgage loans will not protect against the risk of not being paid back because of the fall in the value of the collateral. Also, if loan originators don't care much about whether the loan will be repaid (because they are selling the loan instead of keeping it on their own balance sheet), then there is an element of systematic risk. These types of problems happened during the U.S. mortgage crisis in 2008.

PRACTICAL APPLICATION

1.

X	Y = 2	Y = 3	Y = 4	Y = 5	Y = 6	Y = 7	Y = 8	Y = 9	Y = 10	Y = 11	Y = 12
2	1/216	1/216	1/216	1/216	1/216	1/216	0	0	0	0	0
3	1/216	2/216	2/216	2/216	2/216	2/216	1/216	0	0	0	0
4	1/216	2/216	3/216	3/216	3/216	3/216	2/216	1/216	0	0	0
5	1/216	2/216	3/216	4/216	4/216	4/216	3/216	2/216	1/216	0	0
6	1/216	2/216	3/216	4/216	5/216	5/216	4/216	3/216	2/216	1/216	0
7	1/216	2/216	3/216	4/216	5/216	6/216	5/216	4/216	3/216	2/216	1/216
8	0	1/216	2/216	3/216	4/216	5/216	5/216	4/216	3/216	2/216	1/216
9	0	0	1/216	2/216	3/216	4/216	4/216	4/216	3/216	2/216	1/216
10	0	0	0	1/216	2/216	3/216	3/216	3/216	3/216	2/216	1/216
11	0	0	0	0	1/216	2/216	2/216	2/216	2/216	2/216	1/216
12	0	0	0	0	0	1/216	1/216	1/216	1/216	1/216	1/216

2.

X	Y = 1	Y = 2	Y = 3	Y = 4	Y = 5	Y = 6
2	1/36	0	0	0	0	0
3	1/36	1/36	0	0	0	0
4	1/36	1/36	1/36	0	0	0
5	1/36	1/36	1/36	1/36	0	0
6	1/36	1/36	1/36	1/36	1/36	0
7	1/36	1/36	1/36	1/36	1/36	1/36
8	0	1/36	1/36	1/36	1/36	1/36
9	0	0	1/36	1/36	1/36	1/36
10	0	0	0	1/36	1/36	1/36
11	0	0	0	0	1/36	1/36
12	0	0	0	0	0	1/36

3.

x:	−2	4	5	
$f(x)$:	.4	.2	.4	

y:	0	2	4	6
$f(y)$:	.2	.1	.2	.5

The covariance and correlation are 0.

4.

x:	−2	−1	0	1	2
$f(x)$:	.2	.25	.1	.35	.1

y:	3	5	9	
$f(y)$:	.35	.25	.4	

$Cov(X, Y) = .49$ $r(XY) = .139$

5.

x:	0	5	9	11	13
$f(x)$:	.2	.25	.05	.35	.15

y:	1	4	5	6	9
$f(y)$:	.25	.45	.1	.05	.15

$Cov(X, Y) = -2.5$ $r(X, Y) = -.214$

6.

x:	−3	2	4	5	7
$f(x)$:	.25	.05	.15	.05	.50

y:	−9	−4	−3	−1	0
$f(y)$:	.05	.35	.15	.1	.35

$Cov(X, Y) = -.17$ $r(X, Y) = -.018$

7.

x:	1	2	3	4
f(x):	.4	0	.4	.2

y:	1	2	3	4
f(y):	.2	.2	.3	.3

8.

Y	X = 2	X = 3	X = 4	X = 5	X = 6	X = 7	X = 8	X = 9	X = 10	X = 11	X = 12
2	0	0	0	0	0	0	0	0	0	0	1/36
3	0	0	0	0	0	0	0	0	0	2/36	0
4	0	0	0	0	0	0	0	0	3/36	0	0
5	0	0	0	0	0	0	0	4/36	0	0	0
6	0	0	0	0	0	0	5/36	0	0	0	0
7	0	0	0	0	0	6/36	0	0	0	0	0
8	0	0	0	0	5/36	0	0	0	0	0	0
9	0	0	0	4/36	0	0	0	0	0	0	0
10	0	0	3/36	0	0	0	0	0	0	0	0
11	0	2/36	0	0	0	0	0	0	0	0	0
12	1/36	0	0	0	0	0	0	0	0	0	0

9. For each possible value of X there will be 10 possible values for Y.

10.

	y < 7	7 ≤ y < 10	10 ≤ y < 13	13 ≤ y < 14	14 ≤ y
x < 1	0	0	0	0	0
1 ≤ x < 2	0	.1	.1	.2	.2
2 ≤ x < 5	0	0	.1	.2	.35
5 ≤ x < 9	0	0	.35	.45	.7
9 ≤ x	0	.2	.55	.75	1

11. Because the sum of the values is greater than 1.

12. $Cov(X, Y) = -2.917$ $r(X, Y) = -1$

13. $Cov(X, Z) = 0$ $r(X, Z) = 0$

14.

$$E(T) = E(x_aA + x_bB + x_cC)$$
$$= E(x_aA) + E(x_bB) + E(x_cC)$$
$$= x_aE(A) + x_b E(B) + x_cE(C)$$

$$\text{Var}(T) = E(T^2) - [E(T)]^2$$

$$\text{Var}(T) = E[(x_aA + x_bB + x_cC)^2] - [x_aE(A) + x_bE(B) + x_cE(C)]^2$$
$$\text{Var}(T) = E[x_a^2A^2 + x_b^2B^2 + x_c^2C^2$$
$$+ 2x_ax_bAB + 2x_ax_cAC + 2x_bx_cBC]$$
$$- [x_a^2E(A)^2 + x_b^2E(B)^2 + x_c^2E(C)^2$$
$$+ 2x_ax_bE(A)E(B) + 2x_ax_cE(A)E(C) + 2x_bx_cE(B)E(C)]$$
$$\text{Var}(T) - x_a^2E(A^2) + x_b^2E(B^2) + x_c^2E(C^2)$$
$$+ 2x_ax_bE(AB) + 2x_ax_c E(AC) + 2x_bx_cE(BC)$$
$$- x_a^2E(A^2) - x_b^2E(B)^2 + x_c^2E(C)^2$$
$$- 2x_ax_bE(A)E(B) - 2x_ax_cE(A)E(C) - 2x_bx_cE(B)E(C)$$
$$\text{Var}(T) = x_a^2E(A^2) - x_a^2E(A)^2$$
$$+ x_b^2E(B^2) - x_b^2E(B)^2$$
$$|\ x_c^2E(C^2)\quad x_c^2E(C)^2$$
$$+ 2[x_ax_bE(AB) - x_ax_bE(A)E(B)$$
$$+ x_ax_cE(AC) - x_ax_cE(A)E(C)$$
$$+ x_bx_cE(BC) - x_bx_cE(B)E(C)]$$

$$\text{Var}(T) = x_a^2[E(A^2) - E(A)^2] + x_b^2[E(B^2) - E(B)^2] + x_c^2[E(C^2) - E(C)^2]$$
$$+ 2[x_ax_b[E(AB) - E(A)E(B)] + x_ax_c[E(AC) - E(A)E(C)]$$
$$+ x_bx_c[E(BC) - E(B)E(C)]]$$
$$\text{Var}(T) = x_a^2\text{Var}(A) + x_b^2\text{Var}(B) + x_c^2\text{Var}(C)$$
$$+ 2[x_ax_b \text{Cov}(A, B) + x_ax_c \text{Cov}(A, C) + x_bx_c \text{Cov}(B, C)]$$

10 STATISTICAL ESTIMATION

KEY TERMS

consistent estimator an estimator that tends to converge toward the true value as the sample size becomes larger

estimator a quantity based on observations of a sample whose value is taken as an indicator of the value of an unknown population parameter (for example, the sample average $\bar{x}$ is often used as an estimator of the unknown population mean μ)

maximum likelihood estimator an estimator with the following property: if the true value of the unknown parameter has this value, then the probability of obtaining the sample that was actually observed is maximized

statistical inference the process of using observations of a sample to estimate the properties of the population

unbiased estimator an estimator whose expected value is equal to the true value of the parameter it is used to estimate

ESTIMATING THE MEAN

We'd like to investigate gasoline consumption by the N people that live in Central County. If we could investigate the entire population, we would have a list of N numbers. We could enter that list into our spreadsheet and calculate the population mean μ and the population standard deviation σ.

However, most likely it will be too expensive to check with everyone in the entire population. We could randomly select one person, measure his or her gas consumption, and call the result X_1. Then X_1 is a random variable, whose mean is equal to the population mean μ and whose standard deviation is equal to the population standard deviation σ. We could use X_1 as an estimator for the value of μ, but you would be very skeptical that we would have a reliable estimate with a sample of only one person. Clearly we should choose a random sample with a bunch of people. In the next chapter we'll see how a larger sample provides us with more accurate estimates. For now, let n represent the size of the sample, and let

$$X_1, X_2, X_3, \ldots, X_n$$

represent the values we observed in the sample.

Let $\bar{x}$ be the sample average:

$$\bar{x} = \frac{X_1 + X_2 + X_3 + \ldots + X_n}{n}$$

$$= \frac{\Sigma X_i}{n}$$

We'll select the sample with replacement. Because we choose the sample with replacement, then each X_i can be treated as independent from all the others, and they all come from the same distribution. For such a random sample that is independent and identically distributed, we found

$$E(\bar{x}) = \mu$$
$$\text{Var}(\bar{x}) = \frac{\sigma^2}{n}$$

See page 153.

Also, because of the central limit theorem we can expect $\bar{x}$ to have a normal distribution for any reasonably large sample.

The same procedure applies to investigating any measurable quantity for any population.

Some other examples of inferential statistics include the following:

- Suppose that the distribution of the heights of all of the people in the country can be described by a normal distribution. However, we don't know in advance what the mean (μ) of the distribution is. Instead, we will have to estimate it.

- Suppose you are conducting a scientific experiment to measure the molecular weight of a chemical. On the average, you can expect that the result of the measurement will be the true value of the weight. However, any particular measurement is subject to random errors. It is often reasonable to suppose that the actual result of each measurement has a normal distribution whose mean is the true value of the quantity you are measuring.

- Suppose we know that the number of successes of an experiment can be characterized by a binomial distribution, but we don't know in advance the value of the probability-of-success parameter (p). We wish to use our observations of the results of the experiment to estimate the value of p.

- Suppose we know that a person's scores on two different kinds of tests are given by random variables with unknown correlation. We will try to estimate the correlations.

We will consider the general problem of trying to estimate the mean (μ) of a random variable X. An unknown population quantity such as μ is called a **parameter**. The quantity $\bar{x}$ is an example of a **statistic**. A *statistic* is a particular function of the items in a random sample. When a statistic is used to estimate the value of some unknown quantity, it's called an **estimator**. In this case, $\bar{x}$ is used as an estimator for the quantity μ. Often a small hat sign ($\hat{\mu}$) is placed over a quantity to indicate that it is an estimator for a parameter. The statement "$\hat{\mu} = \bar{x}$" means, "We are using the sample average $\bar{x}$ as an estimator for the population mean μ." An **estimate** is the value of an estimator in a particular circumstance. If the sample we observe consists of the numbers 5, 7, 4, 10, 12, and 4, then $\bar{x} = \hat{\mu} = 7$ is an estimate for the population mean.

Because an estimator is itself a random variable, it comes from a random variable distribution that is called the *sampling distribution*. We'll see some examples of sampling distributions later in this chapter.

What we'll do now is show that the sample average $\bar{x}$ has some appealing properties when it is used to estimate the mean.

YOU SHOULD REMEMBER

1. *Statistical inference* is the process of using information from observations of a sample to estimate characteristics of the population from which the sample was drawn.

2. A *statistic* is a quantity calculated using observed values from a sample.

3. An estimator is a statistic that is used to estimate the value of an unknown population quantity. For example, the sample average $\bar{x} = (X_1 + \cdots + X_n)/n$ is used as an estimator for the unknown population mean. The unknown population value is called a parameter.

MAXIMUM LIKELIHOOD ESTIMATORS

We have already seen how the value of the population average μ can affect the probabilities associated with a sample average $\bar{x}$. For example, if $\mu = 10,000$, it's just not very likely that $\bar{x} = 7$. Thus if we don't know what the value of μ really is but we get a sample average $\bar{x} = 7$, we can probably rule out $\mu = 10,000$ as a possibility.

If we're trying to use $\bar{x}$ as a tool to figure out what μ really is, we should pick the value for the μ that is most likely to give us the $\bar{x}$ that we ended up with from our sample. If $\bar{x} = 7$, then we can reason as follows: if $\mu = 10{,}000$, we aren't likely to get $\bar{x} = 7$, so 10,000 is a bad estimate for μ. The chances of $\mu = 100$ and us getting $\bar{x} = 7$ are better, so 100 is a better estimate for μ. The value of μ that gives us the greatest probability of getting $\bar{x} = 7$ is $\mu = 7$. In this case, we say that $\bar{x}$ is a *maximum likelihood estimator* for μ, because its value corresponds to the value of μ that is most likely to give the sample average that we got.

The method of maximum likelihood can also be used for many other types of problems. In general, suppose that a is an unknown parameter in a particular probability distribution. Then in many cases we can calculate the **maximum likelihood estimator** for a. For example, we can show that the maximum likelihood estimator of the variance ($\hat{\sigma}^2$) from a normal distribution is

$$\hat{\sigma}^2 = \frac{(X_1 - \bar{x})^2 + (X_2 - \bar{x})^2 + \cdots + (X_n - \bar{x})^2}{n}$$

If we are trying to estimate the probability of success p for a random variable with a binomial distribution, then the maximum likelihood estimator is also the obvious one:

$$\frac{\text{number of successes}}{\text{number of attempts}}$$

Another important property of maximum likelihood estimators is called the *invariance property*. Suppose that $\hat{a}$ is the maximum likelihood estimator for a parameter a, but we really want to know the maximum likelihood estimator of $\sqrt{a}$. If we were forced to make a guess, we would probably estimate that $\sqrt{a}$ is equal to $\sqrt{\hat{a}}$, and fortunately we would be right. For example, the maximum likelihood estimator of the standard deviation ($\hat{\sigma}$) is just the square root of the sample variance. In general, if $h(a)$ is any function of a parameter a, then the maximum likelihood estimator of $h(a)$ is just $h(\hat{a})$.

CONSISTENT ESTIMATORS

Another important property that we would like our estimators to have is the consistency property. You've undoubtedly been confused by inconsistent people, and you can be just as confused by inconsistent estimators. Here is what we mean by the consistency property for estimators. Suppose we are able to increase our sample size greatly and thereby acquire many more observations of the random variable X. In that case, do we know that the new value of $\bar{x}$ will be closer to the mean μ, or is there a chance that it might be farther away?

A **consistent estimator** is an estimator whose variance approaches 0 as the sample size increases. In this way, we can ensure that our estimator will be very close to its expected value (which is just the parameter that we're looking for if the estimator is unbiased) by choosing a large enough sample size.

Fortunately, $\bar{x}$ does satisfy the property of being a consistent estimator of the population mean.

UNBIASED ESTIMATORS

Another important question we might ask about an estimator is this: Do we expect that the result of this estimator will be the true value? An estimator is said to be *unbiased* if the expectation value of the estimator is equal to the true value of the parameter we are trying to estimate.

If X_1, X_2, X_3, . . . , X_n form a random sample—that is, they are independent, identically distributed random variables—then we previously found (page 152) that

$$E(\bar{x}) = \mu$$

That is, the expected value of the sample average is equal to the population mean. This means that the sample average is an unbiased estimator of the population mean. (However, it does not mean that the sample average for any particular sample is guaranteed to equal the population mean—only the expected value equals the mean.)

Recall the formula for the sample variance s^2:

$$s^2 = \frac{(X_1 - \bar{x})^2 + (X_2 - \bar{x})^2 + (X_3 - \bar{x})^2 + \ldots + (X_n - \bar{x})^2}{n - 1}$$

$$= (\overline{x^2} - (\bar{x})^2)\left(\frac{n}{n - 1}\right)$$

It can be shown that

$$E(s^2) = \sigma^2$$

In other words: the expected value of the sample variance is equal to the population variance. This means that the sample variance meets the condition of being an unbiased estimator of the population variance. In fact, this property is the reason for using $n - 1$ (rather than n) in the denominator for the sample variance formula. (See Exercise 8 for the proof of this fact for the case where $n = 2$.)

In general, there can be many different unbiased estimators for the same parameter. When possible, we would like to select an estimator that has as small a variance as possible. Since an estimator is a statistic calculated from a random sample, it is a random variable whose variance we can calculate. (The distribution of an estimator is often called the **sampling distribution** of that estimator.)

For example, suppose two people are trying to estimate the value of an unknown population mean μ. One person randomly selects two items and uses the measure $A_2 = (X_1 + X_2)/2$. Since $E(A_2) = \mu$, it is an unbiased estimator. However, the other person randomly selects 100 items and uses their average: $A_{100} = (X_1 + \ldots + X_{100})/100$. Both estimators are unbiased, but A_{100} is clearly a much better estimator than A_2 because its variance is smaller ($\sigma^2/100$ as opposed to $\sigma^2/2$). The mere fact that an estimator is unbiased does not mean that it is the best one to use.

YOU SHOULD REMEMBER

1. There are several desirable characteristics that estimators can have if they provide good estimates of the population parameters.

2. A *maximum likelihood estimator* has the following property: if the true value of the unknown parameter has this value, then the probability of obtaining the sample that was actually observed is maximized.

3. A *consistent estimator* is an estimator whose value will converge to the true value as the sample size becomes very large.

4. An *unbiased estimator* is an estimator whose expected value is equal to the true value.

---

* * * * *

In this chapter we discussed ways of obtaining a single number that can be used to estimate the value of an unknown parameter. Such an estimate is called a **point estimate**. Often we will need to know whether the true value of the parameter is likely to be near the point estimate or whether there is a chance that the true value could be far from the point estimate. To answer that question we need to calculate an **interval estimate**, which we will discuss in the next chapter.

KNOW THE CONCEPTS

DO YOU KNOW THE BASICS?

Test your understanding of Chapter 10 by answering the following questions:

1. In statistical inference, what is the term for an unknown population quantity? What is the term for a known quantity calculated from the observations in a sample?

2. After you have calculated an estimate in a particular situation, do you know how accurate that estimate is?

3. Why is it desirable to use an estimator that has a small variance? Should you pick the estimator with the smallest possible variance?

4. Why does the formula for the sample variance (version 2) divide by $n - 1$ instead of by n?

5. Can you think of a situation where it would be best to use an estimator that is not unbiased?

6. What is the difference between point estimates and interval estimates?

TERMS FOR STUDY

consistent estimator

estimate

estimator

interval estimate

maximum likelihood estimator

parameter

point estimate

sampling distribution

statistic

statistical inference

unbiased estimator

PRACTICAL APPLICATION

COMPUTATIONAL PROBLEMS

1. Let X be a normal random variable with mean 7 and standard deviation 3. Suppose you collect 16 observations of X and then calculate the sample average $\bar{x}$. What is the probability that $\bar{x}$ will be between 7 and 7.5? Between 7.5 and 8? Between 8 and 8.5? Between 8.5 and 9? Between 9 and 9.5?

2. Suppose X_1, X_2, and X_3 are independent, identically distributed random variables with mean μ and variance σ^2. Let $V = 3/4X_1 + 1/8X_2 + 1/8X_3$. Calculate $E(V)$ and $\text{Var}(V)$. Is V an unbiased estimator of μ?

3. Let $W = 1/2X_1 + 1/2X_2 + 1/2X_3$ (X_1, X_2, and X_3 are defined in Exercise 2). Calculate $E(W)$ and $\text{Var}(W)$. Is W an unbiased estimator of μ?

4. Let X be a binomial random variable with parameters n and p. Let $\hat{p} = X/n$. Calculate $E(\hat{p})$. Is $\hat{p}$ an unbiased estimator of p?

5. What is $\text{Var}(\hat{p})$? (See Exercise 4.)

6. Suppose you conduct an experiment n times. Each trial has a probability p of success. Let X_1 be equal to 1 if trial i is a success, and let X_1 be equal to 0 if trial i is a failure. Let $A_2 = (X_1 + X_2)/2$. Calculate $E(A_2)$ and $\text{Var}(A_2)$. Do you think A_2 is a very good estimator for p?

7. Calculate $E(X_1)$ and $\text{Var}(X_1)$ (X_1 is defined in Exercise 6). Is X_1 a very good estimator for p?

8. Let X_1 and X_2 be two independent, identically distributed random variables drawn from a distribution with mean μ and variance σ^2. Calculate

$$E\left[\frac{(X_1 - \bar{x})^2 + (X_2 - \bar{x})^2}{n - 1}\right]$$

where $\bar{x} = (X_1 + X_2)/n$ and $n = 2$.

9. Let X be a random variable with mean μ and variance σ^2. Calculate $E(X^2)$. Let $X_1, X_2, \ldots, X_n$ be a random sample of size n drawn from this distribution. Let $\overline{x^2} = (X_1^2 + X_2^2 + \cdots + X_n^2)/n$. Calculate $E(\overline{x^2})$. Is $\overline{x^2}$ an unbiased estimator of μ^2?

10. If a random variable X had N possible values: $a_1, a_2, a_3, \ldots, a_N$, and each possible value is equally likely, determine $E(X)$ and $\text{Var}(X)$.

ANSWERS

KNOW THE CONCEPTS

1. The unknown population quantity is called a parameter; the quantity calculated from the sample is called a *statistic*.

2. You do not know for sure how accurate the estimate is unless you have been able to check the entire population to learn the true value. When we discuss confidence intervals in the next chapter, we will learn how to determine the likelihood that the estimated value is close to the true value.

3. An estimator with a small variance is less likely to deviate randomly from the true value it is trying to estimate. However, that does not mean you should always choose the estimator with the smallest possible variance. You need to make sure that the estimator is likely to be near the true value. It is often desirable to choose the unbiased estimator that has the lowest variance.

4. Division by $n - 1$ produces an unbiased estimator.

5. An estimator with a small amount of bias but a small variance might be preferable to an unbiased estimator with a large variance.

6. A point estimate indicates a single value for the unknown parameter; an interval estimate expresses a range of likely values for the parameter.

PRACTICAL APPLICATION

1. Sample average $\bar{x}$ will have a normal distribution with mean 7 and standard deviation $3/\sqrt{16} = 3/4$. Then $z = 4/3(x - 7)$ will have a standard normal distribution. For $\bar{x}$ to be between 7 and 7.5, z will be between 0 and 0.67, which will occur with probability 249.

$$\Pr(7.5 < \bar{x} < 8.0) = .160$$
$$\Pr(8.0 < \bar{x} < 8.5) = .069$$
$$\Pr(8.5 < \bar{x} < 9.0) = .019$$
$$\Pr(9.0 < \bar{x} < 9.5) = .003$$

You can see that $\bar{x}$ will probably be near 7, which is the true value of the mean. Therefore, if you observe the value $\bar{x} = 7$ when you have taken observations from a distribution with unknown mean, you will be quite willing to estimate that the true value of the mean is 7. This is the concept behind maximum likelihood estimators.

2. $E(V) = \mu$, so V is an unbiased estimator of μ.
   $\text{Var}(V) = (38/64)\sigma^2$. Note that $\text{Var}(V) > \text{Var}(\bar{x})$, where $\bar{x} = (X_1 + X_2 + X_3)/3$. Therefore, $\bar{x}$ is a better estimator of the mean.

3. $E(W) = (3/2)\mu$, so W is not an unbiased estimator of μ.
   $\text{Var}(W) = (3/4)\sigma^2$.

4. $E(\hat{p}) = E(X/n) = E(X)/n = np/n = p$. Therefore, $\hat{p}$ is an unbiased estimator of p.

5. $\text{Var}(\hat{p}) = \text{Var}(X/n) = \text{Var}(X)/n^2 = np(1 - p)/n^2 = p(1 - p)/n$

6. $E(A_2) = E[(X_1 + X_2)/2] = E(X_1 + X_2)/2 = p$
   $\text{Var}(A_2) = p(1 - p)/2$

   A_2 is an unbiased estimator of p. However, if we let $\hat{p} = X/n_1$ where X is the total number of successes in n trials, then we know that $\hat{p}$ is a much better estimator of p. $\text{Var}(\hat{p}) = p(1- p)/n$, which is smaller than $\text{Var}(A_2)$. It is obvious why A_2 is not a very good estimator: it is based only on the results of the first two trials, whereas $\hat{p}$ is based on the results of all n trials.

7. $E(X_1) = p$ and $\text{Var}(X_1) = p(1 - p)$. Although X_1 is an unbiased estimator of p, it is even worse than the estimator discussed in Exercise 6. It is not a good idea to conduct the experiment once and then estimate that

$p = 1$ if the experiment was a success and that $p = 0$ if the experiment was a failure.

8. Since $n = 2$, $n - 1 = 1$. Therefore:

$$E[(X_1 - \bar{x})^2 + (X_2 - \bar{x})^2]$$

$$= E\left[\left(X_1 - \frac{X_1}{2} - \frac{X_2}{2}\right)^2 + \left(X_2 - \frac{X_1}{2} - \frac{X_2}{2}\right)^2\right]$$

$$= E\left[\left(\frac{X_1}{2} - \frac{X_2}{2}\right)^2 + \left(\frac{X_2}{2} - \frac{X_1}{2}\right)^2\right]$$

$$= E\left[2\left(\frac{X_1}{2} - \frac{X_2}{2}\right)^2\right]$$

$$= 2E\left(\frac{X_1^2}{4} - \frac{X_1 X_2}{2} + \frac{X_2^2}{4}\right)$$

$$= 2\left[\frac{E(X_1^2)}{4} - \frac{E(X_1 X_2)}{2} + \frac{E(X_2^2)}{4}\right]$$

$$= 2\left[\frac{E(X^2)}{2} - \frac{E(X_1)E(X_2)}{2}\right]$$

$$= E(X^2) - [E(X)]^2$$

$$= \text{Var}(X)$$

Note: $E(X_1 X_2) = E(X_1)E(X_2)$ because X_1 and X_2 are independent. Also, $E(X_1) = E(X_2) = E(X)$ because they have identical distributions. This calculation shows (for $n = 2$) that the sample variance formed by dividing by $n - 1$ is an unbiased estimator of the variance.

9. Since $\text{Var}(X) = \sigma^2 = E(X^2) - \mu^2$, it follows that $E(X^2) = \sigma^2 + \mu^2$. You can also show that $E(\bar{X}^2) = \sigma^2 + \mu^2$, so $\bar{x}^2$ is not an unbiased estimator of μ^2.

10. The probability of each possible value is $1/N$. The expectation is the sum of each possible value multiplied by its probability:

$$E(X) = \sum\left(\frac{1}{N}\right)a_i = \frac{\Sigma a_i}{N} = \mu$$

where μ is the average of all of the possible values.

$$E(X^2) = \sum\left(\frac{1}{N}\right)a_i^2 = \frac{\Sigma a_i^2}{N} = \overline{a^2}$$

where $\overline{a^2}$ is the average of the squares of the possible values. The variance is

$$E(X^2) - (E(X))^2 = \overline{a^2} - \mu^2 = \sigma^2$$

where σ^2 is the variance of the list of numbers $a_1, a_2, a_3, \ldots, a_N$.

This problem applies when you are observing some measurable quantity for a population of N items. It shows the connection between the mean and variance of a list of numbers, and the mean and variance of the random variable representing one item randomly chosen from that population.

11
CONFIDENCE INTERVALS

KEY TERMS

confidence interval an interval based on observations of a sample and so constructed that there is a specified probability that the interval contains the unknown true value of a parameter (for example, it is common to calculate confidence intervals that have a 95 percent chance of containing the true value)

confidence level the degree of confidence associated with a confidence interval; the probability that the interval contains the true value of the parameter

---

In Chapter 10 we discussed how to use observations of a random variable to get information about an unknown parameter for the distribution that generates that variable. However, we still have to face one important question: Is such an estimate likely to be very close to the true value?

For example, suppose you are trying to estimate the fraction of days that it rains in Florida. You naturally would use the estimator

$$\frac{\text{(number of days you've been in Florida when it rained)}}{\text{(number of days you've been in Florida)}}$$

However, if you've been in Florida only one day and it rained that day, your estimate that it rains in Florida every day is not likely to be very accurate. If you've spent 10 years in Florida, you'll be able to estimate the fraction of rainy days much more accurately.

The value of a statistic that is used as an estimator depends on the values of a group of random variables, meaning that the estimator is itself a random variable. It would help if we could figure out what the distribution of the estimator looks like. For example, let's suppose we are using the sample average $\bar{x}$ to estimate the population mean:

$$\bar{x} = \frac{X_1 + X_2 + \cdots + X_n}{n}$$

By the central limit theorem, $\bar{x}$ has a normal distribution for a reasonably sized sample. We have already found (see pages 152) that $E(\bar{x}) = \mu$ and $\text{Var}(\bar{x}) = \sigma^2/n$.

CALCULATING CONFIDENCE INTERVALS FOR THE MEAN WHEN THE VARIANCE IS KNOWN

Now that we know the distribution of $\bar{x}$, we can be more precise about how good our estimate is. We know that the true value of μ is likely to be close to $\bar{x}$, but how close is close? Is $\bar{x}$ likely to be 1 unit away from μ? Or is it likely to be 50 units away? We'd like to know the probability that the distance from $\bar{x}$ to μ will be less than some specific value c. In other words, we want to know the probability that the true value of μ is between $(\bar{x} - c)$ and $(\bar{x} + c)$.

Obviously, the probability depends a lot on the value of c that we choose. (See Figure 11–1). If we choose a very large value of c, we can be almost certain that the true value of μ will be in the interval. For example, we could set c to be infinity. Then the probability that μ will be in the interval is 100 percent, since obviously μ must be between $(\bar{x} - \text{infinity})$ and $(\bar{x} + \text{infinity})$. However, an interval that wide is not very useful. If we make the interval narrower by choosing a smaller value for c, we can be more precise about the true value of μ. However, when we make the interval narrower, there is a greater chance that μ won't even be contained in the interval.

The normal procedure in statistics works like this. First, we choose the probability that we want—in other words, we set in advance the probability that μ will be in the interval. Often this probability is set at 95 percent. Then we calculate how wide the interval must be so that there is a 95 percent chance that it contains the true value. This type of interval is called a **confidence interval**, and .95 is the **confidence level**.

Figure 11–1

Now we need to calculate the value of c that satisfies the equation

$$\Pr(\bar{x} - c < \mu < \bar{x} + c) = .95$$

or

$$\Pr(-c < \bar{x} - \mu < c) = .95$$

Once we know the value of c, we know how wide the confidence interval must be. This means that our job is to calculate the value of c. Let's create a new random variable called Z:

$$Z = \frac{\bar{x} - \mu}{\sqrt{\sigma^2/n}}$$
$$= \sqrt{n}\,\frac{\bar{x} - \mu}{\sigma}$$

Using the properties we established for normal random variables, we know that Z has a standard normal distribution (mean 0 and variance 1; see Chapter 8). We can rewrite the equation:

$$\Pr\left(\frac{-c\sqrt{n}}{\sigma} < \sqrt{n}\,\frac{\bar{x} - \mu}{\sigma} < \frac{c\sqrt{n}}{\sigma}\right) = .95$$
$$\Pr\left(\frac{-c\sqrt{n}}{\sigma} < Z < \frac{c\sqrt{n}}{\sigma}\right) = .95$$

This problem calls for the standard normal probability table. Let's define a as follows: $a = c\sqrt{n}/\sigma$. Then

$$\Pr(-a < Z < a) = .95$$

Now we need to look in Table A3–2 until we find a value of a that satisfies this equation. Scanning down the columns, we can see that in this case the correct value for a is 1.96.

Now we can find the value for c:

$$c = \frac{1.96\sigma}{\sqrt{n}}$$

Thus we know how wide the confidence interval should be. There is a 95 percent chance that the interval from $\bar{x} - 1.96\sigma/\sqrt{n}$ to $\bar{x} + 1.96\sigma/\sqrt{n}$ will contain the true value of μ.

Two features of this result are appealing to common sense. First, the confidence interval is wider (that is, more uncertain) if σ is bigger. If the variance of each individual observation is bigger, then it will be harder for us to pin down the true value of μ. Second, the confidence interval is smaller if n is bigger. This means that as we take more and more observations we will be able to predict the true value of μ more accurately.

We can be even more cautious if we want to. Suppose that we want to be 99 percent sure that our confidence interval contains the true value of μ. Then we will have to settle for a wider, less precise interval. Or, if we wanted to be less careful, we could have calculated a smaller confidence interval that had a lower probability of containing the true value.

The confidence intervals that we talk about here and later on are symmetric in the following way: the probability that the left end point of the interval is greater than our parameter (μ here) is the same as the probability that the right end point of the interval is less than the parameter. In theory you could construct an asymmetric confidence interval, but symmetric confidence intervals are the narrowest ones possible, and thus more precise.

General Procedure for Calculating Confidence Intervals for the Mean When You Have n Observations from a Normal Distribution with Known Standard Deviation σ

1. Decide on the confidence interval you want. If you are more cautious, pick a higher level (.95 is one of the most common levels).

2. Look up the value of a in Table A3–2. If CL is the confidence level, then

$$\Pr(-a < Z < a) = CL$$

3. Calculate $\bar{x}$ and $a\sigma/\sqrt{n}$.

   The confidence interval is from $\bar{x} - a\sigma/\sqrt{n}$ to $\bar{x} + a\sigma/\sqrt{n}$.

YOU SHOULD REMEMBER

1. When we calculate an estimate for an unknown population parameter, we need to know how accurate that estimate is likely to be.

2. It is valuable to calculate a *confidence interval*—that is, an interval constructed so that there is a fixed probability that the interval will contain the unknown value of the population parameter.

3. This fixed probability is known as the *confidence level*, and it is often set at 95 percent.

4. A narrow confidence interval is better because it means that you are able to make a more precise estimate of the true value of the parameter.

5. In general, the confidence interval will become narrower as the number of observations increases.

CALCULATING CONFIDENCE INTERVALS BY USING THE *t* DISTRIBUTION

There is one major difficulty with calculating confidence intervals in the way just described. Often we don't know the true value of σ^2. Our first guess might be that we could use the sample variance to estimate the value of σ^2. It turns out that, if the sample size (n) is large enough (for example, if $n > 30$), we can use the same confidence interval formula as in the preceding section, with the sample variance s^2 used in place of σ^2. However, for small samples we need to develop a new method.

Remember that our initial confidence interval calculation was based on the fact that

$$Z = \frac{\sqrt{n}\,(\bar{x} - \mu)}{\sigma}$$

has a standard normal distribution. Let's create a new random variable that we'll call T:

$$T = \frac{\sqrt{n}\,(\bar{x} - \mu)}{s}$$

Note that T is exactly the same as Z except that the known value s has been substituted in place of the unknown value of σ. We would expect the distribution of T to be very similar to a standard normal distribution.

In Chapter 8, we found that the t distribution is similar to the normal distribution. Our statistic T will have a t distribution with $n - 1$ degrees of freedom.

Now we can calculate the width of the confidence interval. We need to find the value of c that satisfies the equation

$$\Pr(\bar{x} - c < \mu < \bar{x} + c) = .95$$

Using our definition of the statistic T, we can rewrite the equation like this:

$$\Pr\left(\frac{-c\sqrt{n}}{s} < T < \frac{c\sqrt{n}}{s}\right) = .95$$

We define a to be equal to $c\sqrt{n}/s$.

Now we have to look in a table of the t distribution. We need to find a value of a such that

$$\Pr(-a < T < a) = .95$$

For example, if $n - 1 = 8$, we can see from Table A3–5 that $a = 2.306$. Once we find a, we can find c from the formula

$$c = s\,\frac{a}{\sqrt{n}}$$

Therefore, the 95 percent confidence interval for μ is from $\bar{x} - sa/\sqrt{n}$ to $\bar{x} + sa/\sqrt{n}$.

Example: Finding the Confidence Interval by Using the t Distribution

PROBLEM We have been given a list of 750 major cities around the world and would like to estimate the average population of these cities.

SOLUTION Choose a random sample of 20 of these cities. To choose the cities, use a computer random-number generation program. Here is one example of 20 randomly selected world cities:

Population	City
473,800	Bangui, Central African Republic
8,243,400	Bombay, India
550,000	Bucaramanga, Colombia
160,800	Cádiz, Spain
1,170,000	Cheng-chou, China
1,279,200	Curitiba, Brazil
4,884,200	Delhi, India
923,300	Goiânia, Brazil
1,144,000	Ibadan, Nigeria
1,056,400	Kitakyushu, Japan
346,900	Miami, USA
285,000	Nouakchott, Mauritania
1,287,000	Recife, Brazil
818,300	Sakai, Japan
484,700	Scarborough, Canada
112,300	Thunder Bay, Canada
348,000	Toulouse, France
336,500	Tucson, USA
566,000	Vilnius, Lithuania
266,500	Wiesbaden, Germany

To calculate a 95 percent confidence interval for the mean, we first need to calculate $\bar{x} = 1,236,845$ and $s = 1,939,221.09740$. Since $n = 20$, we need to look in Table A3–5 for $20 - 1 = 19$ degrees of freedom, to find $a = 2.093$. Therefore, the confidence interval is $1,236,845 \pm 2.093 \times 1,939,221.09740/\sqrt{20}$, or 329,272–2,144,417.

This interval is so wide that it is not very useful. The problem is that there is a very large variance among the population of cities; there are some very large cities and a lot of smaller cities. The city populations do not follow the normal distribution, but we know from the central limit theorem that $\bar{x}$ will have a normal distribution anyway. As you can guess, the way to find a narrower confidence interval is to take a larger sample.

Note: It is correct to say, "There is a 95 percent chance that the interval $\bar{x} - sa/\sqrt{n}$ to $\bar{x} + sa/\sqrt{n}$ contains the true value of μ." The two end points of the interval are random variables. However, once you have performed the calculation, it is not correct to say, "There is a 95 percent chance that the interval 329,272 to 2,144,417 contains the true value of μ." Since μ is not a random variable, it does not make sense to talk about the probability that it takes on values in a certain range.

If you calculate many 95 percent confidence intervals during your career, you would expect that about 95 percent of them will be "correct," in the sense that the true value of the parameter is contained in the interval. However, that also means that about 5 percent of them will be incorrect, and you won't know which ones.

Figure 11–2 illustrates what might happen if you calculated 20 confidence intervals for the same quantity with the same sample size, but with different random samples each time. The vertical line represents the true value of the parameter. The horizontal lines represent the 20 different confidence intervals. Note that 19 of the intervals contain the true value, but one does not. This is about what you would expect for 95 percent confidence intervals. Remember that in reality you will only do one of these calculations, and you won't know the true value.

Note that the widths of the intervals vary because the sample variance will be different for different samples. In order to get a narrower interval, observe a larger sample. However, even with a larger sample you will expect about 5 percent of the intervals will be incorrect. In order to reduce this percent, you need to increase the confidence level. If you calculate many 99 percent confidence intervals, only about 1 percent of them would be incorrect, but remember that a 99 percent interval is wider than a 95 percent interval, for a given sample size.

One example of a sample with very narrow confidence intervals is the monthly Current Population Survey, which is used to estimate the unemployment rate and other statistics. The online publication *Employment and Earnings* contains information on how the confidence intervals are calculated; see *www.bls.gov/opub/ee/*.

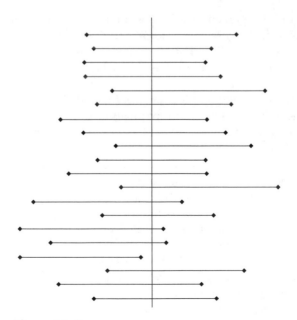

Figure 11–2

Procedure to Calculate Confidence Intervals Using the *t* Distribution When You Have *n* Observations of the Random Variable *X*

(Use for small samples when σ is unknown.)

1. Decide on the confidence level CL (.95 is one of the most common levels).

2. Calculate $\bar{x}$:

$$\bar{x} = \frac{x_1 + x_2 + \cdots + x_n}{n}$$

3. Calculate *s*:

$$s = \sqrt{\frac{(x_1 - \bar{x})^2 + (x_2 - \bar{x})^2 + \cdots + (x_n - \bar{x})^2}{n-1}}$$

$$= \sqrt{\frac{n}{n-1}(\overline{x^2} - \bar{x}^2)}$$

4. Look up the value of *a* in Table A3–5.

$$\Pr(-a < T < a) = CL$$

where *T* has a *t* distribution with $n - 1$ degrees of freedom. (Note that, if *n* is larger than 30, the *t* distribution is almost the same as the standard normal distribution.)

The confidence interval for μ is from $\bar{x} - sa/\sqrt{n}$ to

$$\bar{x} + sa/\sqrt{n}.$$

CALCULATING THE CONFIDENCE INTERVAL FOR THE VARIANCE

Suppose you have a sample taken from an approximately normal population whose variance you would like to estimate. We know how to calculate the sample variance. Now we would like to determine a confidence interval for σ^2. It turns out that

$$Y^2 = \frac{(n-1)s^2}{\sigma^2}$$

is a chi-square random variable with $n - 1$ degrees of freedom. For any two positive numbers a and b we know that

$$\Pr(a < Y^2 < b) = \Pr\left(a < \frac{(n-1)s^2}{\sigma^2} < b \right)$$

$$= \Pr\left(\frac{(n-1)s^2}{b} < \sigma^2 < \frac{(n-1)s^2}{a} \right)$$

For example, here are the heights (in centimeters) of 25 students selected at random from Millard Fillmore Elementary School:

135, 139, 128, 143, 122, 123, 142, 135, 140,
141, 115, 133, 128, 137, 142, 128, 135,
142, 129, 133, 141, 137, 125, 127, 138

We can find that s^2 is 56.427. We will construct a 90 percent confidence interval for the variance. We need to find two numbers a and b such that

$$\Pr(Y^2 < a) = .05 \quad \text{and} \quad \Pr(Y^2 < b) = .95$$

Looking in Table A3–3 for a chi-square distribution with $25 - 1 = 24$ degrees of freedom, we find $a = 13.85$ and $b = 36.4$. Then the confidence interval is from $(n - 1)s^2/b = 37.20$ to $(n - 1)s^2/a = 97.78$.

Procedure to Calculate the Confidence Interval for the Variance

1. Decide on the confidence level (CL).

2. Calculate $\bar{x}$, $\overline{x^2}$, and $s_1^2 = \overline{x^2} - \bar{x}^2$.

3. Use Table A3–3 to find a and b such that, if Y^2 is a chi-square random variable with $n - 1$ degrees of freedom, then

$$\Pr(Y^2 < a) = \frac{1 - CL}{2} \quad \text{and} \quad \Pr(Y^2 < b) = \frac{1 + CL}{2}$$

For example, if CL = .90, then $\Pr(Y^2 < a) = .05$ and $\Pr(Y^2 < b) = .95$
The confidence interval for σ^2 is from $(n - 1)s^2/b$ to $(n - 1)s^2/a$.

CALCULATING THE CONFIDENCE INTERVAL FOR THE DIFFERENCE BETWEEN TWO MEANS

Often a situation will arise where you want to compare two populations with respect to some random variable. Here are some examples:

- average income in two different cities

- sales revenue of two companies

- number of readers of two newspapers

In all of these examples it would be of interest to estimate the difference of the means, $\mu_a - \mu_b$, of the two random variables X_a (mean μ_a, variance σ_a^2) and X_b (mean μ_b, variance σ_b^2). This is done by calculating the difference of the sample means, $\bar{x}_a - \bar{x}_b$. As before, the question of accuracy arises. How close is $\bar{x}_a - \bar{x}_b$ to the unknown value of $\mu_a - \mu_b$? Again we turn to confidence intervals.

Let X_a have sample mean $\bar{x}_a$ and sample size n_a; and similarly for X_b, $\bar{x}_b$, and n_b. If X_a and X_b are normal random variables, then so is $\bar{x}_a - \bar{x}_b$, which has mean $\mu_a - \mu_b$ and variance $(\sigma_a^2/n_a + \sigma_b^2/n_b)$. As above, we create a new random variable Z:

$$Z = \frac{(\bar{x}_a - \bar{x}_b) - (\mu_a - \mu_b)}{\sqrt{\sigma_a^2/n_a + \sigma_a^2/n_b}}$$

which has a standard normal distribution. Then look in the Appendix: Table A3–2 to find the value of a such that

$$\Pr(-a < Z < a) = \text{CL}$$

where CL is the confidence level. Then calculate c:

$$c = a\sqrt{\sigma_a^2/n_a + \sigma_b^2/n_b}$$

The confidence interval for $\mu_a - \mu_b$ is then:

$$(\bar{x}_a - \bar{x}_b) \pm c$$

For example, here is a set of sales figure (in thousands) for a given newspaper in two nearby towns over a period of days:

Town A: 25, 13, 14, 19, 23, 30, 35, 29, 28, 17, 17, 16, 13, 18, 20
Town B: 10, 12, 15, 13, 7, 6, 11, 5, 9, 14, 15, 18, 17, 16,
12, 12, 10, 11, 13, 14

Assume that $\sigma_a^2 = 40$ and $\alpha_b^2 = 14$. Then we can calculate that $\bar{x}_a = 21.13$, $n_a = 15$, $\bar{x}_b = 12.00$, $n_b = 20$, and $\bar{x}_a - \bar{x}_b = 9.13$. Using a 99 percent confidence interval, we find that $a = 2.58$, $c = 2.58 \sqrt{40/15 + 14/20} = 4.73$, and the confidence interval is from 4.40 to 13.86.

We then have the following procedure (similar to the one used to calculate the confidence interval for the mean of one variable):

Procedure to Calculate the Confidence Interval for the Difference Between Two Means (σ_a, σ_b known)

1. Decide on the confidence level you want (such as 95 percent).

2. Look up the value of a in Table A3–2.

3. Calculate $\bar{x}_a - \bar{x}_b$.

4. Calculate $c = a\sqrt{\sigma_a^2/n_a + \sigma_b^2/n_b}$

   The confidence interval is $(\bar{x}_a - \bar{x}_b) \pm c$.

Again, if the sample sizes are large enough, the sample variances can be substituted for σ_a^2 and σ_b^2 when the latter are unknown. For small samples we turn to the t distribution. Here, however, we must make two more assumptions, namely, that $\sigma_a^2 = \sigma_b^2$, and that the samples are selected independently. (With small sample sizes, it would be very easy to lose the randomness essential to good statistics.)

Remember that we're not assuming that we know σ_a^2 or σ_b^2. We are just assuming that they are equal. If you do know them, good. If not, we can approximate them by the *pooled estimate* s_p^2:

$$s_p^{\,2} = \frac{(n_a - 1)s_a^{\,2} + (n_b - 1)s_b^{\,2}}{(n_a - 1) + (n_b - 1)}$$

We will use s_a^2 to mean the sample variance of sample a:

$$s_a^{\,2} = \frac{(\overline{x_a^{\,2}} - \bar{x}_a^{\,2})n_a}{n_a - 1}$$

Likewise, s_b^2 is the sample variance for sample b. Also, s_p^2 is a weighted average of s_a^2 and s_b^2, so that, if n_a is much larger than n_b, then s_p^2 is closer to s_a^2 than s_b^2, and vice versa.

Now, in the above formula for large samples, if $\sigma_a^2 = \sigma_b^2$, we have

$$Z = \frac{(\bar{x}_a - \bar{x}_b) - (\mu_a - \mu_b)}{\sqrt{\sigma_a^2/n_a + \sigma_b^2/n_b}}$$

$$= \frac{(\bar{x}_a - \bar{x}_b) - (\mu_a - \mu_b)}{\sqrt{\sigma_a^2(1/n_a + 1/n_b)}}$$

We substitute in our pooled estimator s_p^2 in the place of σ_a^2 and create a new t statistic:

$$T = \frac{(\bar{x}_a - \bar{x}_b) - (\mu_a - \mu_b)}{\sqrt{\sigma_p^2(1/n_a + 1/n_b)}}$$

This t statistic has $(n_a - 1) + (n_b - 1) = n_a + n_b - 2$ degrees of freedom. If we know what the value of σ_a^2 is, we insert it for s_p^2 (no need to estimate if we've got the real thing).

We find the value of a from Table A3–5 so that

$$\Pr(-a < T < a) - CL$$

where CL is the confidence level and T has a t distribution with $n_a + n_b - 2$ degrees of freedom. Then we calculate c:

$$c = a\sqrt{s_p^2\left(\frac{1}{n_a} + \frac{1}{n_b}\right)}$$

Then the confidence interval for $\mu_a - \mu_b$ is

$$(\bar{x}_a - \bar{x}_b) \pm c$$

For example, here are the sales figures (in thousands) for two different brands of kites for randomly selected months:

Brand A: 15, 20, 33, 27
Brand B: 23, 42, 39

Assume that $\sigma_a^2 = \sigma_b^2$. We can calculate that $\bar{x}_a = 23.75$, $\bar{x}_b = 34.67$, $\bar{x}_a - \bar{x}_b = -10.92$, $s_a^2 = 62.25$, $s_b^2 = 104.3$, and $s_p^2 = 79.08$. Using a 95 percent confidence interval for $n_a + n_b - 2 = 5$ degrees of freedom, we find that

$a = 2.571$, $c = 2.571 \sqrt{79.08(1/4 + 1/3)} = 17.46$, and the confidence interval is from -28.38 to 6.54.

Procedure to Calculate the Confidence Interval for the Difference between Population Means When We Have Small Samples with Equal Population Variances

1. Decide on the confidence interval (such as 95 percent).

2. Calculate $\bar{x}_a - \bar{x}_b$.

3. Calculate s_p^2:

$$s_p^2 = \frac{(n_a - 1)s_a^2 + (n_b - 1)s_b^2}{n_a + n_b - 2}$$

4. Look up the value of a in Table A3–5 for $n_a + n_b - 2$ degrees of freedom.

5. Calculate c:

$$c = a\sqrt{s_p^2\left(\frac{1}{n_a} + \frac{1}{n_b}\right)}$$

The confidence interval is $(\bar{x}_a - \bar{x}_b) \pm c$.

KNOW THE CONCEPTS

DO YOU KNOW THE BASICS?

Test your understanding of Chapter 11 by answering the following questions:

1. Why shouldn't you calculate a confidence interval with a very high confidence level, such as 99.99 percent?

2. Why is a confidence interval more valuable than a single point estimate?

3. Name three ways to make a confidence interval narrower.

4. When should you calculate a confidence interval using the t distribution instead of the normal distribution?

5. If you double the number of observations, will you be able to cut the width of the confidence interval in half?

6. Which of these statements is true about a 95 percent confidence interval?

   (a) The true parameter value has a 95 percent chance of being in the interval.
   (b) The interval has a 95 percent chance of containing the true parameter value.

7. Will the formula for the confidence interval for the mean work even if the quantity being measured does not follow the normal distribution?

8. Which of the following sample selection methods will work best for calculating a confidence interval?

   (a) Checking with your friends
   (b) Setting up a web page that asks people to e-mail to you
   (c) Calling people whose phone numbers are selected by a random number generator
   (d) Asking the students in a class
   (e) Asking the customers of your business

9. You will perform n different confidence interval calculations (each time using the 95 percent confidence level). Let X be the number of these confidence interval calculations that are correct—that is, the interval contains the true value of the parameter it is trying to estimate. What is the distribution of X?

10. Can observations of the prices of a particular stock provide you with a reliable confidence interval calculation?

TERMS FOR STUDY
confidence interval   confidence level

PRACTICAL APPLICATION

COMPUTATIONAL PROBLEMS
Each of the following lists of numbers represents weekly net revenue figures for one company. Assume that for each company the net revenue figures have a normal distribution with unknown mean and unknown variance. Calculate a 95 percent confidence interval for the true value of the mean.

1.	23	12	1	6	4
	16	28	14	6	28
	15	18	6	2	14
	19	11	15	20	20

2.	5	48	6	49	0
	11	44	47	35	13
	10	4	50	7	22
	1	40	4	4	26
	8	18	35	23	12
3.	12	1	22	8	24
	25	22	21	13	12
	18	8	0	16	20
	11				
4.	10	20	19	30	17
	28	26	26	29	28
	6	4			
5.	23	8	18	29	14
	20	1	19	19	28
	18	16	30	4	19

For each of the following exercises you are given the total of a list of observations, the average of these observations, and the standard deviation (s_2) of these observations. Calculate a 95 percent confidence interval and a 99 percent confidence interval for the unknown value of the mean of each distribution.

6. Total: 523.114
   Average: 52.311
   s_2: 8.813

7. Total: 1,571.322
   Average: 104.755
   s_2: 3.002

8. Total: 1,150.295
   Average: 127.811
   s_2: 4.611

9. Total: 4,528.186
   Average: 283.012
   s_2: 8.386

10. Total: 2,957.990
    Average: 147.899
    s_2: 1.688

ANSWERS

KNOW THE CONCEPTS

1. An interval with that high a confidence level generally is too wide to be useful.

2. A point estimate contains no information about how accurate the estimate is likely to be.

3. More observations; smaller value of the population variance; lower confidence level.

4. The t distribution should be used when the population variance is unknown and the number of observations is less than 30.

5. No. The width of the confidence interval is proportional to $1/\sqrt{n}$.

6. The second statement (b) is correct. The interval is random. The true parameter value is not random.

7. Because of the central limit theorem, the sample average $\bar{x}$ will follow the normal distribution for a large enough sample size, regardless of whether or not the individual items being measured are distributed according to the normal distribution.

8. Method (c) is the method most likely to generate a random sample (although there are also problems with phone polls, as discussed in the next chapter).

9. A binomial distribution with parameters n and $p = .95$.

10. If the future will be similar to the past, then you can view observations from the past as a random sample of all observations (past and future). However, if the future is significantly different, your past observations won't help you predict the future value.

PRACTICAL APPLICATION

Calculations are shown below for Exercise 1 and Exercise 6. Similar methods can be used for Exercises 2–5 and 7–10, respectively.

1. $\bar{x} = (23 + 12 + 1 + 6 + 4 + 16 + 28 + 14 + 6 + 28$
$+ 15 + 18 + 6 + 2 + 14 + 19 + 11 + 15 + 20 + 20)/20$
$= 13.9$

$\overline{x^2} = (23^2 + 12^2 + 1^2 + 6^2 + 4^2 + 16^2 + 28^2 + 14^2 + 6^2$
$+ 28^2 + 15^2 + 18^2 + 6^2 + 2^2 + 14^2 + 19^2 + 11^2$
$+ 15^2 + 20^2 + 20^2)/20$
$= 253.7$

$s_2 = \sqrt{253.7 - 13.9^2} \times \sqrt{19/20} = 7.98$

From Table A3–5 we can find that $a = 2.093$ for a t distribution with 19 degrees of freedom. Therefore the .950 confidence interval is

$$13.9 \pm 2.093 \times 7.98/\sqrt{20} \quad \text{or} \quad 10.165 - 17.635$$

2. Average = 20.880 $s_2 = 17.405$
.950 confidence interval = 13.695 − 28.065

3. Average = 14.562 $s_2 = 7.763$
.950 confidence interval = 10.427 − 18.698

4. Average = 20.250 s_2 = 9.255
   .950 confidence interval = 14.369 − 26.131

5. Average = 17.733 s_2 = 8.455
   .950 confidence interval = 13.050 − 22.416

95% Confidence Intervals	99% Confidence Intervals
6. $52.311 \pm 2.262 \times 8.813/\sqrt{10}$	$52.311 \pm 3.250 \times 8.813/\sqrt{10}$
46.007–58.615	43.254–61.368
7. 103.092–106.417	102.447–107.063
8. 124.266–131.355	122.654–132.968
9. 278.544–287.479	276.834–289.190
10. 147.110–148.689	146.819–148.979

12
POLLS AND SAMPLING

KEY TERMS

cluster sampling a sampling method where the population is divided
into clusters; some clusters are selected at random, and then some
members of the chosen clusters are selected at random to make up the
sample

stratified sampling a sampling method where the population is divided
into strata that are as much alike as possible

OPINION POLLS

How can we find out how many people in a population have a particular
characteristic? For example, we might want to know how many voters support
our favorite presidential candidate. Or we might be interested in some general
characteristics of people in a certain state—for example, how many are children, how many live in cities, or how many are employed.

One way to find the answers to these questions is to check with everybody. This method will be very accurate. Since we're asking *everybody*, we
can get a detailed view of the entire population. This method is used sometimes. An election is held every four years in the United States to find out the
presidential preferences of all voters. Every 10 years a census is held to obtain
detailed information about all of the people in the country.

However, there are disadvantages to the ask-everybody method. The main
one is that this method is very expensive. Elections and censuses are costly.
Also, there will often be times when we would like to obtain information
about the population but we can't wait until the next census or the next
election.

Another possible method is to ask some people who are part of a sample.
If the sample is representative of the entire population, we can use the characteristics of the people in the sample to estimate the characteristics of the
people in the population. For example, opinion poll interviewers typically

check with about 1,000 people in an attempt to estimate the opinions of all 300 million people in the country.

Are these results likely to be accurate? At first glance you might be suspicious. The poll takers are talking to only about 1 out of every 300,000 people. You probably think it is unlikely that each person in the poll has the same opinions as his or her 300,000 closest neighbors. However, polls do seem to be fairly accurate. The election results predicted by polls are usually close to the actual results (with a few notable exceptions).

Now we will look at the theory that explains why these results tend to be accurate. We'll let N stand for the number of people in the population we are investigating. We'll assume that M of these people favor our candidate. Our goal is to estimate M/N—the fraction of people who support our candidate. Let $p = M/N$. We'll ask a sample of n people. X will represent the number of people in the sample who favor our candidate. If our poll is any good, X/n will be close to M/N. Let $\hat{p} = X/n$.

For example, suppose that we are trying to estimate the preferences of people in a town with a population of 30,000. We will ask all the people in a sample of 500 which candidate they support. Suppose that in reality there are 16,500 people who support our candidate (16,500 is 55 percent of the total population). If it turns out that 270 people (54 percent) in the sample support our candidate, then the sample did a good job of representing the entire population. On the other hand, if 330 people (66 percent) in the sample are on our side, then the sample is quite unrepresentative and our poll will give us very misleading results.

• *METHODS FOR SELECTING A SAMPLE*

It makes a big difference how the sample is selected, since the value of X will depend on exactly who is in the sample. We need to figure out a good system for choosing the sample so that it will be representative of the population as a whole. We can't just start asking our friends, since our friends might be more likely to be on our side. We can't select just one neighborhood and interview everyone there, since people in one particular neighborhood are not likely to be representative of the diverse characteristics of all of the people in the town.

There are subtle problems with other systems as well. We can't just mail out a lot of postcards and ask people to return them, since the people on our side might be more likely to take the trouble to send the cards back. We might decide that we can make our sample representative by deciding in advance that we want our sample to contain certain quotas of people with particular characteristics. For example, we might decide that we want our sample to contain 50 percent women, 15 percent minorities, and 0.5 percent veterinarians. However, that method still doesn't answer the question about how to select the sample, since it doesn't tell us which minorities or which women or which veterinarians to include in the sample. We obviously can't set in advance a quota for the number of people in the sample who favor our candidate, since we don't know what that fraction is until after we've taken the sample.

It turns out that the best system for selecting the sample is to have no system at all—in other words, select the sample completely at random. By selecting the sample randomly, we can make sure that it has no systematic bias. We should design the sampling system so that each person has an equal chance of being selected. Not only that, we should design the system so that every single possible sample that we might conceive of has an equal chance of being the sample that we actually choose.

How are we going to do this? One way is to write everyone's name on a slip of paper, put the papers in little capsules, and then put all of the capsules in a large drum. If we mix up the capsules very thoroughly and then pull n capsules out of the drum, we will have a random sample of n people. However, even this approach is difficult if N is very large. For one thing, we would need a very large drum. Another problem is that it is difficult to mix the capsules well if there are a large number of them. If the capsules are not mixed well, then the people whose names were put in last have a greater chance of being selected and we will no longer have a pure random sample.

Something akin to this actually did happen with the draft lottery in the United States in 1970. People were assigned draft numbers on the basis of their birth dates, with a low number indicating a greater chance of being inducted. The 366 dates were put into capsules, mixed, and drawn and assigned lottery numbers 1, 2, etc. Apparently, the capsules were not mixed very well—people born in December had lottery numbers that averaged 121.5, which is pretty far away from the average of #1 366 = 183.5. Steps were taken with the 1971 draft lottery to make the results more random by drawing both the date and the lottery number from drums, after mixing them more thoroughly.

An easier method is to give everyone in the population a number. Then we can select a bunch of random numbers and interview the people whose numbers we've chosen. How do we select the random numbers? It's not as easy as it sounds. We can't just start making up numbers, since it is hard for a person to make up a long string of numbers without falling into some sort of pattern. (Try it yourself sometime.) We could use a die if we needed only numbers from 1 to 6, but to get a larger group of numbers we need a better system.

In the old (precomputer) days, the best way was to use a table of random digits. A random-digit table is a table that has been created by someone whose job it is to create random numbers. The numbers have been tested to make sure that they pass certain tests of randomness. Nowadays, you can have a computer generate the random numbers. Most computer systems have built-in random-number generators. The numbers that they generate are not true random numbers, since they are generated according to a fixed rule.

However, the rule is unpredictable enough that for all practical purposes the numbers seem to have been selected totally at random.

YOU SHOULD REMEMBER

1. It is expensive to survey everyone in the population, so samples are selected.

2. The proportion of people in a sample with a particular characteristic is used to estimate the proportion of people in the population with the same characteristic.

3. The best method for choosing a sample is to select the sample at random, that is, in such a way that every possible sample is equally likely to be chosen.

• USING THE BINOMIAL DISTRIBUTION

We will choose the sample without replacement, since we don't want to run the risk of annoying someone by calling them twice. We already know the probability distribution to use: the hypergeometric distribution. We know:

$$\Pr(X = i) = \frac{\binom{M}{i}\binom{N-M}{n-i}}{\binom{N}{n}}$$

where N = size of population; M = number of items in the population we're interested in; n = size of sample; $p = M/N$; $E(X) = np$, $\text{Var}(X) = np(1 - p)(N - n)/(N - 1)$.

The hypergeometric calculations are very cumbersome to deal with. To make the calculations easier, let's change our sampling procedure slightly. We'll still select 1,000 names from the drum. However, this time after we select each name we'll put it back in the drum and mix all of the names again. That means that a person who has been selected once in the sample might be selected again, and would thus be interviewed twice. (That person probably would be annoyed, which is one reason why this method is not used in practice.) There is even a minuscule chance that we will select the same person 1,000 times.

Once again we'll let X represent the number of people in the sample who favor our candidate. Let's call it a "success" if a particular person in the sample favors our candidate. Then we know exactly what the distribution of X looks like—it has a binomial distribution with parameters n and $p = M/N$.

It turns out that if the population size is much larger than the sample size we can use the binomial distribution even if we sample without replacement. For example, let's suppose that, in a population of 200 million, half of the people are on our side and half are on the other side. Then there is a probability of 1/2 that the first person we select will support our candidate. Suppose that the first person we select does support our candidate. If we sample with replacement, there is a probability of .5 that the second person we select will also be on our side. If we sample without replacement, there is a probability of

$$\frac{99,999,999}{199,999,999} = .4999999975$$

that the second person will support our candidate. So it does make a slight difference whether we sample with replacement or without replacement—but not much. Therefore, we can approximate the hypergeometric distribution by a binomial distribution.

CONFIDENCE INTERVAL FOR PROPORTION

• *USING THE NORMAL DISTRIBUTION*

The binomial distribution itself is rather cumbersome, so while we're making approximations we may as well go all the way and approximate the binomial distribution with a normal distribution. We know that this works when n becomes large. (See Chapter 8.)

Let $\hat{p}$ be the sample proportion X/n, where X is the number of people in the sample that support our candidate. Since X can be approximated by a normal distribution with mean np and variance $np(1 - p)$, it follows that $\hat{p}$ has a normal distribution with mean p and variance $p(1 - p)/n$.

Figures 12–1 and 12–2 illustrate what happens as we increase the sample size from 100 to 1,000. In both cases the population proportion is $p = .28$. The curve illustrates the density function for $\hat{p}$; note how the density function becomes taller and narrower for larger sample sizes. This illustrates that the probabilities for $\hat{p}$ become concentrated closer to the value of p as n becomes larger.

In reality, we will usually not know the true value of p, but we can calculate a confidence interval for it.

Let c represent half of the width of the confidence interval, as in the previous chapter. The confidence interval will be centered around $\hat{p}$. It is defined by this equation:

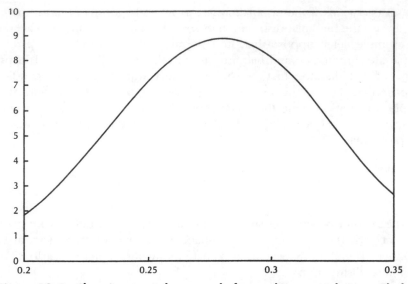

Figure 12–1. Choosing a random sample from a large population with the population proportion equal to 0.28 and the sample size equal to 100

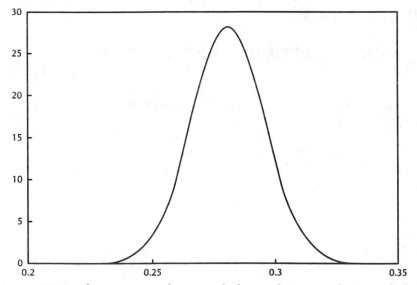

Figure 12–2. Choosing a random sample from a large population with the population proportion equal to 0.28 and the sample size equal to 1,000

$$\Pr(\hat{p} - c < p < \hat{p} + c) = .95$$

Subtract p from all three parts of the inequality:

$$\Pr(-c < p - \hat{p} < c) = .95$$

Multiply all three parts by -1:

$$\Pr(c > \hat{p} - p > -c) = .95$$

Reverse the order:

$$\Pr(-c < \hat{p} - p < c) = .95$$

We have a normal random variable ($\hat{p}$) minus its mean (p); as you might guess, the next step is to divide by its standard deviation $\sqrt{p(1-p)/n}$.

$$\Pr\left[\frac{-c}{\sqrt{\dfrac{p(1-p)}{n}}} < \frac{\hat{p} - p}{\sqrt{\dfrac{p(1-p)}{n}}} < \frac{c}{\sqrt{\dfrac{p(1-p)}{n}}}\right] = .95$$

The middle expression can be replaced by the standard normal random variable Z; then make this definition:

$$a = \frac{c}{\sqrt{\dfrac{p(1-p)}{n}}}$$

Then:

$$\Pr(-a < Z < a) = .95$$

From the table at the back of the book, we see that $a = 1.96$ (we would use a different value of a if the confidence level were different from .95). Therefore:

$$c = 1.96\sqrt{\frac{p(1-p)}{n}}$$

The population proportion p is unknown, but we can substitute the sample proportion $\hat{p}$ in its place. Therefore, the 95 percent **confidence interval for the proportion** p is:

$$\hat{p} - 1.96\sqrt{\frac{\hat{p}(1-\hat{p})}{n}} \quad \text{to} \quad \hat{p} + 1.96\sqrt{\frac{\hat{p}(1-\hat{p})}{n}}$$

For example, let $\hat{p} = .62$ and $n = 200$. The confidence interval is from

$$.62 - 1.96\sqrt{\frac{.62 \times .38}{200}} \quad \text{to} \quad .62 + 1.96\sqrt{\frac{.62 \times .38}{200}}$$

or from

$$.552 \text{ to } .687$$

This can be written .62 plus or minus .067, and $c = .067$ is often called the margin of error for the poll.

General Procedure for Confidence Interval for Proportion

Let n be the number of items in the sample, X be the number of items in the sample with the characteristic you're interested in, $\hat{p} = X/n$ be the proportion of people in the sample with that characteristic, and p be the unknown proportion of people in the population with that characteristic.

1. Determine the confidence level you want.

2. Look up the value of a in Table A3–2. (If the confidence level is 95 percent, then $a = 1.96$.)

3. Calculate $c = a\sqrt{\hat{p}(1-\hat{p})/n}$.

The confidence interval is from $\hat{p} - c$ to $\hat{p} + c$.

One minor concern about our analysis is that our approximation might break down if the population is not much larger than the sample. Recall that we can approximate the hypergeometric distribution with parameters N, M, and n by the binomial distribution with parameters $p = M/N$ and n, provided N is much larger than n. Fortunately, in many realistic cases, the population is much large than the sample, so the approximation works just fine. To analyze situations where the approximation does not work, we need to consider the formula we saw in Chapter 7 that gives the variance of the hypergeometric distribution:

$$n\left(\frac{M}{N}\right)\left(1-\frac{M}{N}\right)\left(\frac{N-n}{N-1}\right)=np(1-p)\left(\frac{N-n}{N-1}\right)$$

As long as N is much larger than n, then the fraction $(N-n)/(N-1)$ will be close to 1, and the binomial approximation works fine. Otherwise, we can approximate the hypergeometric distribution with a normal distribution using this standard deviation:

$$\sqrt{np(1-p)\left(\frac{N-n}{N-1}\right)}$$

The expression $\sqrt{(N-n)/(N-1)}$ is called the **finite population correction factor**. If the population is much larger than the sample, then it can be ignored. Otherwise, use this formula for the confidence interval for p:

$$\hat{p}\pm1.96\sqrt{\frac{\hat{p}(1-\hat{p})}{n}}\sqrt{\frac{N-n}{N-1}}$$

We can make a table of these results. (See Table 12–1.)

Table 12-1. Percent Error for Sample

N	$n = 100$	$n = 500$	$n = 1,000$	$n = 5,000$	$n = 10,000$	$n = 50,000$
10,000	9.8	4.3	2.9	1.0	0	—
50,000	9.8	4.4	3.1	1.3	0.9	0
100,000	9.8	4.4	3.1	1.4	0.9	0.3
500,000	9.8	4.4	3.1	1.4	1.0	0.4
50,000,000	9.8	4.4	3.1	1.4	1.0	0.4
200,000,000	9.8	4.4	3.1	1.4	1.0	0.4

The table assumes that $p = .5$. If the true value of p is different from .5, then the errors will be less than the values listed in the table. The table lists the percentage-point error. For example, for population size 50,000 and sample size 5,000, the table gives the value 1.3. This means that there is a 95 percent chance that the sample proportion will be within 1.3 percentage points of the true value (in other words, between .487 and .513).

• *ANALYZING THE PERCENT ERROR IN TERMS OF SAMPLE SIZE*

You can see some interesting results if you scan through the table. If you take a sample of 1,000 people, there is a 95 percent chance that the poll result will be within 3.1 percentage points of the true value. If you increase the sample size to 5,000, the error falls to only 1.4 percent. Therefore, the table does tend to reinforce one's faith in polls.

Another interesting result you can see is that a sample of 1,000 does just as well when the population is 200 million as it does when the population is 50,000. You might expect that the sample would become less accurate as the population becomes larger, but this is not the case.

However, the reverse is also true. If you want to get an accurate sample of a population of 50,000, you need just as large a sample as you would if you had a population of 200 million. Making the population smaller does not reduce the number of people you need in the sample in order to get a representative sample. You can get a good cross section of 200 million people by interviewing one person in every 40,000; but if you try to interview one person in 40,000 when the population is 50,000, you will end up with a very unrepresentative sample. What this means is that if you want an accurate view of the opinions of people in every state you will need a much larger sample than you would if you needed to know only the opinions of the entire country.

Another important fact to note is that, although the error goes down as the sample size becomes larger, it reaches a point where large increases in the sample size lead to only small decreases in the error. Therefore, when you decide on what size sample to use, you need to take two factors into consideration. Adding more people will make the sample a bit more accurate, but the cost of taking the sample becomes larger if more people are included.

YOU SHOULD REMEMBER

1. The accuracy of a poll depends on the size of the sample, not the size of the population (provided that the population size is large).

2. If the population is much larger than the sample, then the sample proportion will have an approximately normal distribution.

The confidence interval formula given earlier works when the population size N is much larger than the sample size n [so $(N - n)/(N - 1)$ is close to 1] and the sample size is larger than 30. If the sample size is smaller than 30, then the normal approximation is not as accurate, so you need to perform some tricky calculations involving the binomial distribution that we will not discuss in this book.

An opinion poll cannot measure the population proportion if the population proportion is very small. Suppose you would like your poll to be able to tell you the proportion of suburban veterinarians aged 50 to 55 in the nation. The population proportion is very small, and you are quite likely to find that there are zero suburban veterinarians aged 50 to 55 in a national sample of 2,000 people. In that case you don't have the slightest idea what the actual value is (other than the fact that it must be very small, but you knew that even before you took the poll).

In general, if $np > 5$ and $n(1 - p) > 5$, then the confidence intervals discussed above based on the normal approximation work fine. For example, suppose $n = 200$ and $p = .025$. Then $np = 5$ and we can calculate the probabilities: (see Figure 12–3)

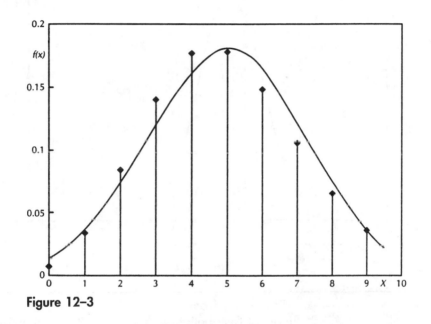

Figure 12–3

	Probability from Binomial Distribution	Normal Approximation
$Pr(X = 0)$	.006	.014
$Pr(X = 1)$	.032	.035
$Pr(X = 2)$	.083	.072
$Pr(X = 3)$	.140	.120
$Pr(X = 4)$	.177	.163
$Pr(X = 5)$	.178	.181
$Pr(X = 6)$	.148	.163
$Pr(X = 7)$	.105	.120
$Pr(X = 8)$	.065	.072
$Pr(X = 9)$	.036	.035
$Pr(X = 10)$	.017	.014

The normal approximation still works quite well, and the value of X will probably be close to its expected value of 5. However, now suppose that $n = 200$ and $p = .001$. Then we can find that $E(X) = np = 0.2$. Obviously the actual value of X cannot be equal to 0.2 because it must be a whole number. Here are the probabilities: (See Figure 12–4)

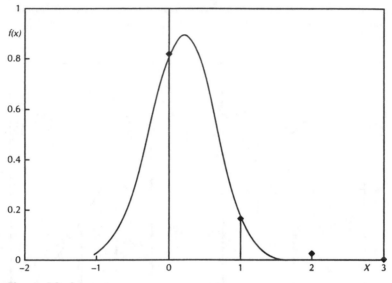

Figure 12–4

	Probability from Binomial Distribution	Normal Approximation
$Pr(X = -1)$	—	.024
$Pr(X = 0)$	.819	.807
$Pr(X = 1)$	.164	.180
$Pr(X = 2)$	.016	0
$Pr(X = 3)$	.001	0

The most likely value of X is zero. In this case the normal approximation breaks down because the actual value of X can never be negative even though the normal approximation says it can.

YOU SHOULD REMEMBER

If $\hat{p}$ is the sample proportion and n is the number of items in the sample, then a 95 percent confidence interval for the population proportion is

$$\hat{p} \pm 1.96\sqrt{\frac{\hat{p}(1-\hat{p})}{n}}$$

This formula works if the sample was a pure random sample, that is, if all possible samples were equally likely to have been selected.

TYPES OF SAMPLING METHODS

It is very important to remember that all of these methods work only when the sample is a pure random sample. If the sample is not a pure random sample, all bets are off. A good example of a nonrandom sample was the 1936 *Literary Digest* presidential election poll. The *Literary Digest* had 2 million people respond to its poll, which is a much larger number than would have been needed to get an accurate result if the sample had been selected randomly. However, the poll predicted that Alfred Landon would be an easy winner, whereas in fact Franklin D. Roosevelt won by a landslide. The problem was that the *Digest* sample was not a random sample. The magazine mailed out cards to people whose names were obtained from telephone lists and other sources, but the people who had telephones at that time were not representative of the population as a whole. If a sample is not selected randomly there is no way to estimate how far off it might be.

• *CLUSTER SAMPLING*

For statistical purposes it is best to use a pure random sample. However, there are practical reasons why that is often impossible. Modern opinion polls cannot select their samples by putting the name of every person in the country in a hat. For one thing, there is no such thing as a list of names for the whole country. Even if there were, it would be very expensive to interview 3,000 randomly selected people scattered all over the country. Instead, the polls follow a method called **cluster sampling**. In cluster sampling the population is divided into different clusters and the sample is taken only from selected clusters rather than the entire population. Ideally each cluster would be as representative as possible of the entire population. In practice, clusters are selected geographically. Some regions are selected at random, and then some sub-regions, and finally some households, are selected. This procedure guarantees that the people in the sample live in clusters, making it possible for one interviewer to interview quite a few people.

• STRATIFIED SAMPLING

Another sampling method is called **stratified sampling**. If the population can be grouped into subgroups that all consist of individuals who are very much alike, a representative sample can be obtained by interviewing a random sample of people in each group. This procedure can produce very accurate samples, but it works only when the population can be divided into homogeneous groups.

• CONVENIENCE SAMPLING

Many other types of sampling methods are also used. Statistical analysis is often incorrectly applied to these samples as if they were pure random samples. We might call these sampling methods **convenience sampling**. For example, colleges often conduct psychological experiments on samples of freshman psychology students. Since there is no reason to expect that freshman psychology students are at all representative of the entire freshman population (let alone the population as a whole), it is inappropriate to make statistical inferences about the population based on these experiments. To take another example, if you set up a table at a shopping mall and ask passersby to stop long enough to fill out a survey form, it is unlikely that you will end up with a random sample of the population. Similarly, magazines often report shocking statistics about behavior based on a survey of their subscribers, but since the subscribers are not a random sample of the population, it is impossible to make valid statistical inferences about the population as a whole from these surveys.

Some television stations conduct pseudopolls by having viewers pay to call a 900 telephone number to vote one way or the other. These polls are worse than misleading because they falsely create the impression of being similar to a real poll. There is no reason why anybody should care about the opinions of the particular group of people who happen to feel like paying to call the phone number that day. Since there has been no random selection, it is not at all appropriate to generalize these results to the larger population.

Many polls never risk the embarrassment of being shown to be wrong because the entire population is seldom checked. However, election prediction polls can be compared with the voting results for the entire voting population.

Opinion polls that try to predict the results of elections have even bigger problems. Not everyone votes, so the poll would rather not count the opinion of anyone who decides not to vote. Therefore, the polls ask some questions that they use to guess whether a person will vote. And there is another obvious problem. If many people change their minds after the poll but before the election, the poll will not be able to predict the election results very well.

Traditional telephone polls have not included cell phones, so that could be a source of systematic bias. A newer type of poll is an automated poll, in which a machine dials the phone number, a recorded voice explains the poll, and the person replies by pushing buttons. This type of poll has the advantage that it is cheaper than using a live interviewer, and all people hear the question asked with exactly the same voice. However, these polls have the disadvantage that there is no way to verify the identity of the person responding (for example, a child too young to vote may pretend to be an adult and answer the questions). Another issue is that some voters might lie about who they intend to vote for if they think one answer is more socially acceptable. An automated poll might be more likely to get them to reveal their true feelings.

Despite these issues, polls were fairly accurate during the presidential elections in 2008 and many previous years. However, it would have been impossible for a poll to predict the result of the 2000 election with its razor-thin margin.

Any report giving the result of a poll should include a statement describing the number of people interviewed, the method of doing the interviews, and the dates the poll was taken. The margin of error should be given, but it should be made clear there is no guarantee that the true value is within the margin of error. There should be a disclaimer describing the confidence interval that goes something like this: "The margin of error of this poll is 3 percentage points. This means that if the same procedure were repeated 20 times, one would expect that 19 of these times the true result for the entire population would be within the stated margin of error." In other words, if the poll finds 54 percent of the people support candidate X, then the 95 percent confidence interval is from 51 percent to 57 percent.

Another example of a national sample is the **Current Population Survey**, which is conducted each month by the Census Bureau for the Bureau of Labor Statistics. Among other things, the Survey is used to calculate the unemployment rate every month. The Bureau of Labor Statistics wants to know about the characteristics of the unemployed—how long they have been unemployed, what kind of jobs they used to have, and so on. To get data on that many different categories, the Current Population Survey needs to use a much larger sample than it would need if it just wanted to know the total number of unemployed people in the country. For this reason, the Current Population Survey uses a sample of about 50,000 households.

YOU SHOULD REMEMBER

1. In practice it is expensive to select pure random samples, so two other sampling methods, cluster sampling and stratified sampling, are used.

2. In *cluster* sampling the population is divided into clusters; some clusters are selected at random, and then some members of the chosen clusters are selected at random to make up the sample.

3. In *stratified sampling* the population is divided into strata that are as much alike as possible.

4. It is not appropriate to apply statistical analysis to samples that consist of the persons or other units who were most conveniently accessible to the interviewer.

MARKETING SURVEYS

A business can stay in business only if it meets the needs and desires of its customers. A business engages in *marketing research* when it tries to determine what those needs and desires are. Marketing researchers can obtain data from a variety of sources: published data from the government and other sources; data generated by the business itself; data gathered from questions asked of a focus group; data gathered from a marketing experiment; and data from a survey. Consult a textbook on marketing research for more details about this process. In this section, we will consider some of the issues involved with one of the tools of marketing research: a survey.

As always, the statistical analysis of a survey is possible only if the survey respondents were selected randomly. One major problem with surveys is the percentage of nonrespondents. Since determining how the opinions of the nonrespondents might differ from those that did respond is difficult, using the results of the sample to generalize to the population is difficult. There are some indications that people are less willing to respond to surveys than they used to be. Partly this is because people are hit with such a barrage of marketing messages these days that they tend to try to avoid them. Junk e-mail and phone solicitors in particular tend to turn people against responding to phone surveys or mass e-mails. Unethical survey takers do not help when they mislead respondents into thinking they are taking a survey when in reality they are listening to a sales call. The proliferation of surveys in recent years might also contribute to people being less willing to respond. When surveys were relatively rare, you might have felt special at being selected to take part. When your dinner is interrupted each night by sales calls, you're more likely to ignore all calls, even legitimate surveys.

A survey taker needs to decide what kind of survey to take: in person, phone, or mail. Each one has advantages and disadvantages. In person interviews provide a good opportunity for the interviewer to interact with the respondent, but they are expensive and won't work if the questions are too personal. Mail surveys provide the advantage that the respondents can fill out the surveys at their leisure and can give thoughtful responses, but they are the easiest for respondents to ignore. E-mail surveys may become more popular as more people in the population have access to e-mail. However, people who have to spend a lot of time deleting spam (junk e-mail) will likely be less willing to cooperate with e-mail surveys. Phone surveys tend to be cheaper than in person surveys and have better response rates than mail surveys, so many survey takers choose this method.

Care needs to be taken in designing the questions in the survey. Open-ended questions give the respondents the opportunity to answer in their own words. These questions provide more opportunities to learn about the attitudes of the respondents. However, the answers are harder for the interviewer to record, and they are harder to summarize statistically. Structured questions provide the respondents with choices, like a multiple-choice exam. The choices might be yes or no; or they might be strongly agree, agree, disagree, or strongly disagree; or they might be a rating scale from 0 to 10. These questions are easier to fill out than open-ended questions. However, interpreting the scale used might be more complicated.

If you want a true view of people's preferences, avoid leading questions that tend to imply what the desired answer is. For example, avoid asking, "Given the many pressing needs here at home, should the U.S. reduce the military budget?" or "Given the dangerous situation in the world today, should the U.S. increase the defense budget?"

Other issues to consider:

- If people have a middle option, such as strongly agree, agree, neither agree nor disagree, disagree, or strongly disagree, people may choose the middle option to avoid thinking about the question or to avoid revealing their true feelings.

- Sometimes people may give the answer that they think the interviewer wishes to hear or the socially acceptable answer rather than reveal their true opinions.

- Many people are understandably embarrassed to talk about personal products, so it is hard for a survey taker to learn the true opinions of the people.

- Many people are understandably concerned about protecting their privacy and may not reveal correct information about some questions (for example, if you ask them about their incomes).

- The respondents will not know the answer to some questions, even about their own behavior. For example, questions such as, "How many lattes did you buy last month?" or "How often do you buy toothpaste?" may lead to incorrect answers out of genuine ignorance on the part of the respondents. They may be unwilling to admit their ignorance to the interviewer and so answer anyway with a made-up answer.

• The order of the questions can make a difference in the responses.

• The survey taker should test the questions by asking them to a test group before beginning the actual survey. Revise the questions if the tests reveal unintentional ambiguities or some of the problems listed above.

• The interviewers may make errors in recording the results. If the interviewers are poorly paid and poorly supervised, they might not care very much about the quality of the job they do.

KNOW THE CONCEPTS

DO YOU KNOW THE BASICS?

Test your understanding of Chapter 12 by answering the following questions:

1. If a friend refused to believe in the accuracy of polls, could you convince him?

2. What is the problem with applying statistical analysis to convenience samples?

3. If you need to choose a representative sample of 100 people, could you do so by choosing one name at random and then picking the following 99 names from the phone book?

4. When you take a sample, should you set quotas for different groups to make sure that the sample represents the population?

5. Why does a poll have problems if the population proportion is very small?

6. What are some of the different types of errors that can arise with polls, making them unrepresentative of the population?

7. When should you use the finite population correction factor?

8. When you are conducting a poll, should you select your sample with or without replacement?

9. Does the accuracy of the sample depend on the size of the population or on the size of the sample?

10. If you double the sample size, how much more accurate will your sample become?

11. Why is it impossible for national opinion polls to select pure random samples?

12. What would happen if the monthly unemployment rate was estimated with a sample size of 1,000 people?

13. Why does the Census Bureau use statistical adjustment for some census totals?

14. Are the assumptions that are required in order to approximate the hypergeometric distribution with the binomial distribution very realistic?

15. Can past observations be used as a random sample of a time interval that includes the future? (Note: There is, obviously, no way to obtain observations from the future.)

16. Why are television networks concerned when many people watch shows in hotel rooms, dormitory lobbies, and restaurants?

17. Which is harder to measure: television ratings or radio ratings?

TERMS FOR STUDY

cluster sampling
confidence interval for proportion
convenience sampling

Current Population Survey
finite population correction factor
stratified sampling

PRACTICAL APPLICATION

COMPUTATIONAL PROBLEMS

For each of the following exercises you are given the sample size (n) and the number of items in the sample that have the characteristic you are interested in (m). Calculate 95 percent and 99 percent confidence intervals for the unknown value of the proportion of items in the entire population that have this characteristic. Assume that the population size is much larger than the sample size.

	n	m		n	m		n	m
1.	100	36	7.	53	45	13.	824	422
2.	200	72	8.	97	16	14.	560	328
3.	500	180	9.	48	43	15.	705	451
4.	1,000	360	10.	56	18	16.	234	128
5.	5,000	1,800	11.	158	100	17.	657	503
6.	10,000	3,600	12.	652	311			

18. Estimate how large the sample size should be if the margin of error needs to be 5 percent. What if it needs to be 2 percent? What if it needs to be 0.5 percent? What if it needs to be 0.1 percent? For purposes of this estimate, assume $\hat{p} = .5$.

ANSWERS

KNOW THE CONCEPTS

1. Try this argument: If you take a random sample of 1,000 people from a large population, the chance that this sample will be highly unrepresentative is about as good as the chance that you can flip 1,000 coins with the number of heads being far from 500.

2. Statistical inference techniques are not valid with nonrandom samples, as the 1936 polls demonstrated.

3. This would not be a pure random sample, since all possible samples of 100 people were not equally likely to have been chosen.

4. You should not set quotas. There is no way that you could set a quota for every conceivable population characteristic. The samples most likely to be representative of the population are pure random samples.

5. When the population proportion for a particular characteristic is very small, the expected number of items in the sample with that characteristic will be 0 or 1. Since the number of items in the sample must be a whole number, the sample proportion will not be able to represent the population proportion.

6. Any random sample is subject to some uncertainty. In practice any sample is also subject to difficulties such as the fact that some of the people selected may not want to participate in the sample, or they may not give truthful answers.

7. The finite population correction factor is used when the sample is not significantly smaller than the population. One rule is as follows: You do not need to use this correction factor if the sample is less than one-twentieth the size of the population.

8. The sample should be chosen without replacement. However, if the population size is much larger than the sample size, it does not make much difference whether the sample is chosen with or without replacement.

9. The accuracy of the sample depends primarily on the size of the sample, not the size of the population.

10. Doubling the sample will increase the accuracy of the sample, but it will not cause the width of the confidence interval to be cut in half. The width of the confidence interval is proportional to $1/\sqrt{n}$.

11. A pure random sample would be scattered all over the country, and it would be too expensive for the interviewers to reach all the persons.

12. The margin of error would be about 3 percent, which would make it very difficult to use the data. If the reported unemployment rate was 7 percent with a margin of error of 3 percent, then the true rate might be as low

as 4 percent or as high as 10 percent. In reality the rate is estimated using a much larger sample.

13. They are trying to correct for the fact that some people might be missed by the census process, which is trying to count everyone.

14. This approximation is valid if the population is much larger than the sample, which is often the case.

15. You would have to assume that the future will not be systematically different from the past. In that case, past observations can be treated as a random sample. If there will be a systematic change in the future, then it will not work to treat past observations as a random sample.

16. The ratings measurements traditionally only included people watching from home, so they may understate the total audience for a show.

17. Radio is harder because people are more likely to listen to radio for short periods of time before changing the station or doing something else. People are unlikely to remember all of the times they listened to a particular radio station during a week. New measurement technology will automatically keep track of when a person listens to the radio.

PRACTICAL APPLICATION

Use the formulas for the confidence interval for the proportion:

$$\hat{p} \pm 1.96 \sqrt{\frac{\hat{p}(1-\hat{p})}{n}} \text{ (95 percent)}, \qquad \hat{p} \pm 2.6 \sqrt{\frac{\hat{p}(1-\hat{p})}{n}} \text{ (99 percent)}$$

Below are the calculations for Exercise 1. The other exercises can be done similarly.

1. 95 percent interval:
   $.36 \pm 1.96 \sqrt{.36 \times .64/100}$;   .266–.454
   99 percent interval:
   $.36 \pm 2.6 \sqrt{.36 \times .64/100}$;   .236–.484

	95% Confidence Interval	99% Confidence Interval
2.	.293–.427	.272–.448
3.	.318–.402	.305–.415
4.	.330–.390	.321–.399
5.	.347–.373	.342–.378
6.	.351–.369	.348–.372
7.	.753–.945	.722–.976
8.	.091–.239	.068–.262

9.	.809–.982	.782–1.000
10.	.199–.444	.160–.482
11.	.558–.708	.534–.732
12.	.439–.515	.427–.527
13.	.478–.546	.467–.557
14.	.545–.627	.532–.639
15.	.604–.675	.593–.686
16.	.483–.611	.463–.631
17.	.733–.798	.723–.808

18. For a 95 percent confidence interval, the margin of error c is

$$c = 1.96 \sqrt{\frac{\hat{p}(1 - \hat{p})}{n}}$$

Solve for n:

$$c^2 = 1.96^2 \left(\frac{\hat{p}(1 - \hat{p})}{n} \right)$$

$$n = 1.96^2 \left(\frac{\hat{p}(1 - \hat{p})}{c^2} \right)$$

For $\hat{p} = .5$, this becomes

$$n = 1.96^2 \left(\frac{.5(1 - .5)}{c^2} \right)$$

$$n = \frac{1.96^2 \times .25}{c^2}$$

for $c = 0.050$, $n = 384$
for $c = 0.020$, $n = 2,401$
for $c = 0.005$, $n = 38,416$
for $c = 0.001$, $n = 960,400$

13

HYPOTHESIS TESTING

KEY TERMS

null hypothesis the hypothesis that is being tested in a hypothesis-testing situation; often the null hypothesis is of the form "There is no relation between two quantities"

test statistic a quantity calculated from observed quantities used to test a null hypothesis; the test statistic is constructed so that it will come from a known distribution if the null hypothesis is true; therefore the null hypothesis is rejected if it seems implausible that the observed value of the test statistic could have come from that distribution

In Chapter 3 we considered a specific hypothesis-testing problem: If you toss a coin many times, how can you tell whether or not the coin is fair? Now we'll consider a more general treatment of the methodology that statisticians use when they formulate and test hypotheses.

Remember that the hypothesis that we want to test is called the **null hypothesis** (or H_0), and the hypothesis that says, "The null hypothesis is wrong" is called the **alternative hypothesis**. Examples of null hypotheses include:

- A coin is fair.

- The mean number of raisins in boxes of a particular brand of raisin cereal is 7.

- The difference in effectiveness between four cold medicines occurred entirely by chance.

- The rate of appointments to the U.S. Supreme Court fits the Poisson distribution.

If we decide to reject the null hypothesis, this means that we are almost sure the hypothesis is not true. More specifically, we usually design our test so that there is only a 5 percent chance that we will reject the hypothesis if it is really true. However, if we decide to accept the hypothesis, this does not mean for sure that the hypothesis is true. It just means that we have not yet found statistical evidence to reject it.

One important principle of hypothesis testing: you should state your hypothesis before you collect the data. If you state your hypothesis after you have collected the data, then you can easily mistake a coincidence for a specific result. For example, suppose you collect some data and observe that 20 percent of the people in your sample are named Johnson. Then you state the null hypothesis that 20 percent of the people in the population are named Johnson, and proceed to test it on your data. Obviously you will accept the hypothesis, because the hypothesis was stated after the data was collected.

You will need to modify your hypotheses as you collect more data, but the point is that you can't use data to test a hypothesis if that hypothesis was based on the same data in the first place. The solution is: collect more data. If the hypothesis seems to work even for data that was collected after it was stated, you might be onto something.

Another important principle: you should state your significance level before collecting the data. This way you will be sure you are objective and don't decide on the significance level after seeing the test statistic value, where you can alter its value depending on what you hope the result will be.

TEST STATISTICS

The normal procedure in statistics is to calculate a specific quantity called a **test statistic**. There are several common test statistics. The one that you use depends on the problem you are facing.

The test statistic is designed so that, *if* the null hypothesis is true, the test statistic will be a random variable that comes from a known distribution. After you observe the test statistic you have to ask: "Would you believe that this test statistic value came from this distribution?" If the observed test statistic value is implausible, then you must answer: "I find that hard to believe." Then you must reject the hypothesis.

For example, suppose you toss a coin 100 times, and let X be the number of heads. Then the reasoning works like this (an example from classical logic is also included for comparison):

STATEMENT 1

If the coin is fair, X has a binomial distribution with $n = 100$ and $p = .5$.

STATEMENT 1

If an animal is a frog, then it is green.

STATEMENT 2
The value of $X = 90$ is observed; I find it hard to believe that X came from a binomial distribution with $n = 100$, $p = .5$.

STATEMENT 2
Fozzie has been observed, and he is not green.

CONCLUSION
I find it hard to believe that the coin is fair.

CONCLUSION
Fozzie is not a frog.

The logical structure of each argument is the same. The difference is that the statement "Fozzie is not green" is made with certainty; the statement "X probably did not come from a binomial distribution with $n = 100$, $p = .5$" is not made with certainty. As is usually the case in statistics, some doubt remains.

In this chapter we will see several examples of test statistics in practical problems.

• TESTING A NULL HYPOTHESIS

For example, suppose you are testing a null hypothesis using a test statistic Z. Suppose you know that Z will have a standard normal distribution if the null hypothesis is true. Calculate the value of Z. If, for example, the value of Z turns out to be .878, then everything is fine. There is a reasonably good chance of drawing the number .878 from a standard normal distribution. Since the observed value is not particularly implausible, you have no grounds for rejecting the hypothesis.

However, suppose the observed value of the test statistic Z turns out be 3. Then you should begin to get suspicious. You can see from the standard normal table that there is a probability of only .0026 that a standard normal random variable will be outside 3. (We will use the terms *inside* and *outside* in the following fashion. We will say that Z is *inside* a value c if $-c < Z < c$. We will say that Z is *outside* a value c if $Z < -c$ or if $Z > c$. In other words, Z is inside c if $|Z| < c$, and Z is outside c if $|Z| > c$.) You should say to the advocates of the null hypothesis, "You can't pull the wool over my eyes. I know that this test statistic value is very unlikely to have occurred if the null hypothesis were true, so I'm going to reject the hypothesis."

The null hypothesis advocates might respond, "If you reject the null hypothesis, you will be committing a Type I error, since we think that the null hypothesis is really true. We admit that we had bad luck with our test statistic, and it turned out to have an implausible value. But it is still possible that you might draw the number 3 from a standard normal distribution."

• AVOIDING TYPE I AND TYPE II ERRORS

Of course, there is no way that you can prove them wrong. There still is a slight possibility that the null hypothesis might be true, so you could commit a Type I error by erroneously rejecting the hypothesis. But that is the risk that you will have to take. (Remember that a **Type I error** occurs if you reject the null hypothesis when it is really true. A **Type II error** occurs if you accept the null hypothesis when it is really false. See Chapter 3.) Normally, we design our test so that the risk of committing a Type I error is less than 5 percent. The risk of committing a Type I error is called the **level of significance** of the test and is symbolized by α. Therefore, we can say that our test is designed to be at the 5 percent significance level.

From the standard normal tables we can see that there is a 95 percent chance that Z will be inside 1.96. For this reason we will design our test so that the null hypothesis is accepted if Z is inside 1.96 and rejected otherwise. Therefore, we will call the region inside 1.96 the **zone of acceptance** and the region outside 1.96 the **rejection region** or **critical region**. (See Figure 13–1.) Sometimes the number that is the boundary between the critical region and the zone of acceptance is called the **critical value** of the test statistic. In this case the critical values are 1.96 and −1.96.

We can see that with this test

$$\text{Pr(rejecting } H_0 \text{ if it is really true)}$$
$$= \Pr[(Z > 1.96) \text{ or } (Z < 1.96)]$$
$$= .025 + .25$$
$$= .05$$

which is the result we want. If the observed value of the test statistic turns out to be outside 1.96, we will say that we can reject the hypothesis at the 5 percent significance level.

However, suppose that we want to be more cautious. Suppose that it is very costly for us to reject the hypothesis erroneously, so we want to make sure that the probability of this event happening is only 1 percent. Then we

Figure 13–1

0.5%
of area

0.5%
of area

−2.58

0

2.58

Rejection
region

99% of area
Zone of acceptance

Rejection
region

Figure 13–2

need to widen the zone of acceptance. (See Figure 13–2.) There is a 99 percent chance that Z will be inside 2.58. Therefore, we can ensure that there is only a 1 percent chance of committing a Type I error if we design our test so that the zone of acceptance runs from −2.58 to 2.58. If the value of the test statistic turns out to be −2.6, we can reject the hypothesis at the 1 percent significance level. (Unfortunately, this is confusing terminology, since a *more* significant test corresponds to a lower significance level.)

However, suppose the value of the test statistic Z turns out to be 2. In that case we cannot reject the hypothesis at the 1 percent level. If we want a test at that level, we must accept the hypothesis. However, as we saw earlier, with a test statistic of 2 we can reject the hypothesis at the 5 percent level. Test statistics like this one are in a sort of gray area. Is the hypothesis really true? Nobody knows, and this time we are not even sure whether to accept the hypothesis. If we're willing to risk a 5 percent chance of a Type I error, we can reject the hypothesis. However, if we are more cautious we will have to accept the hypothesis.

The situation is much more clear-cut when the test statistic is 3 or larger. In that case we can reject the hypothesis at every significance level.

It will be helpful to remember these critical values: If Z has a standard normal distribution when the null hypothesis is true, then

- if $-1.96 < Z < 1.96$, accept the hypothesis at the 5 percent level.
- if $-2.58 < Z < 2.58$, accept the hypothesis at the 1 percent level.

The previous example illustrates a **two-tailed test**, because the rejection region includes both tails of the distribution of the test statistic. We will also see some examples of **one-tailed tests**, where the null hypothesis is rejected only if the test statistic takes on an extreme value in one direction. In that case, the rejection region contains only one tail of the distribution (it may be either the right tail or the left tail, depending on the specific circumstances).

When a hypothesis test is performed, the *p*-value is the probability of getting a sample as extreme as the given one or worse, given that the null hypothesis is true. If the *p*-value is very small (specifically, if it is smaller than the significance level), then the null hypothesis should be rejected.

For example, suppose you are performing a right-tailed hypothesis test based on a standard normal (Z) random variable. If the test statistic value is $Z = 3$, then the *p* value is .0013 (the area to the right of 3, found from the table on page 527). A *p* value this small gives you strong evidence to reject the null hypothesis. A smaller *p* value increases your confidence that rejecting the null hypothesis is the right thing to do.

If you were performing a two-tailed test and found a test statistic of 3, then the *p* value would be .0026 (the area in both tails that are outside the range -3 to 3).

The power of a hypothesis test is the probability that the null hypothesis will be rejected, expressed as a function of the parameter being investigated. (You can't express the probability of a Type II error as a single number, since its value will vary as the true parameter value changes.) For example, if you were testing for the value of the population mean μ, then ideally the power function would equal 0 at the true value of μ, and 1 everywhere else. This power function would guarantee that the correct decision would always be made, but you can seldom expect such a nice situation in practice. In general, increasing your sample size will improve the power function by making it more like the ideal power function.

YOU SHOULD REMEMBER

1. These are the key definitions you need to know in hypothesis testing:

   null hypothesis: the hypothesis you want to test (symbolized by H_0)

   alternative hypothesis: the hypothesis that says, "The null hypothesis is wrong"

   Type I error: saying that the null hypothesis is *false* when it is really *true*

   Type II error: saying that the null hypothesis is *true* when it is really *false*

   level of significance (α): the probability of a Type I error

> **2.** The normal hypothesis-testing procedure is to calculate a quantity, based on your observations, called a *test statistic*.
>
> **3.** If the null hypothesis is true, then the test statistic will be a random variable with a known distribution.
>
> **4.** If it seems plausible that the calculated value could have come from this distribution, then you accept the null hypothesis.
>
> **5.** If the calculated test-statistic value is not likely to have come from this distribution, then you reject the null hypothesis.
>
> **6.** A smaller value for the *p* value increases your confidence that rejecting the null hypothesis is the correct decision.

TESTING THE VALUE OF THE MEAN

Suppose that we know the variance, but not the mean, of a distribution. We need to test the hypothesis that μ equals a particular value μ^*. Using the H_0 notation we would write:

$$H_0: \mu = \mu^*$$

For example, suppose that we're quality control inspectors investigating the number of raisins in each (small) box of a raisin cereal. If there are too few raisins in the box, customers will complain. If there are too many, the company will lose money on each box of cereal sold. The raisins are put into the boxes by an Automatic Raisin Packer. We know that the machine works in such a way that the number of raisins in each box has a normal distribution with variance 16.16. On the average, each box is supposed to have 7 raisins. Our mission is to test the null hypothesis that the mean μ is equal to 7. We have $n = 13$ observations for the mean:

$$9,\ 11,\ 6,\ 10,\ 7,\ 4,\ 0,\ 7,\ 8,\ 6,\ 8,\ 2,\ 18$$

The sample average $\bar{x}$ is 7.38. Is that close enough to 7 so that we should accept the hypothesis? Or is it too far away? We know that if the hypothesis is true, $\bar{x}$ will have a normal distribution with mean $\mu = 7$ and variance $16.16/n$. Therefore,

$$Z = \frac{\sqrt{n}\,(\bar{x} - \mu^*)}{\sigma} = \frac{\sqrt{13}\,(7.38 - 7)}{4.02}$$

will have a standard normal distribution. Therefore, Z will be our test statistic. In our case, the computed value of Z is .341, which is well within the zone of acceptance. Consequently we can accept the hypothesis that $\mu = 7$.

Of course, in general we cannot use the statistic $Z = \sqrt{n}\ (\bar{x} - \mu^*)/\sigma$, because we ordinarily won't know the true value of σ. However, if the null hypothesis $\mu = \mu^*$ is true, then the test statistic

$$t = \sqrt{n}\ \frac{\bar{x} - \mu^*}{s}$$

will have a t distribution with $n - 1$ degrees of freedom. (See Chapter 11.)

For example, suppose that you have the following data points representing the weights of 27 sample players on a particular football team:

$$160,\ 185,\ 235,\ 208,\ 170,\ 185,\ 204,\ 180,\ 205,$$
$$215,\ 185,\ 188,\ 180,\ 220,\ 220,\ 221,\ 205,\ 235,$$
$$225,\ 190,\ 180,\ 205,\ 250,\ 210,\ 230,\ 210,\ 218$$

You want to test the hypothesis that these weights were selected from a normal distribution with mean 220. You need to calculate the two statistics $\bar{x} = 204.4$ and $s = 22.1$. Then you can calculate the test statistic t:

$$t = \frac{204.4 - 220}{22.1}\sqrt{27} = -3.67$$

If the hypothesis is true, t will have a t distribution with 26 degrees of freedom. If you look up the results in Table A3–5, you can see that the critical value for a 1 percent test is 2.779. In other words, you can reject the null hypothesis at the 1 percent level if the value of the test statistic is outside 2.779. Since -3.67 is in the rejection region, you have good statistical evidence to reject the hypothesis that the sample of football players was selected from a population with mean 220.

The Excel function TDIST(ABS(-3.67),26,2) will calculate the p value for this test, where -3.67 is the test statistic value, there are 26 degrees of freedom, and it is a two-tailed test. (In the next section we'll see when to use a one-tailed test.) In this case the p value is 0.0011. The small value supports our decision to reject the null hypothesis.

Suppose a different sample gives these values: $\bar{x} = 215.7$, $s = 19.8$, and $n = 27$. Again testing the null hypothesis that the mean is 220, we have the test statistic

$$t = \frac{215.7 - 220}{19.8}\sqrt{27} = -1.13$$

This falls within the zone of acceptance, so we accept the null hypothesis. Using the Excel function TDIST(ABS(−1.13),26,2) we find the *p* value is 0.2688. Since this is larger than 0.10, we would accept the null hypothesis at either the 10, 5, or 1 percent level; we would even accept it at the 26 percent level if we chose that extremely unusual significance level.

General Procedure to Test the Hypothesis That the Mean μ = μ*, When You Have Observed *n* Values Taken from a Normal Distribution

Method 1. Use this method if you *know* the variance (σ²) of the distribution.

1. Calculate the sample average $\bar{x}$.

2. Calculate the test statistic Z:

$$Z = \frac{\sqrt{n}(\bar{x} - \mu^*)}{\sigma}$$

3. If you want to test the hypothesis at the 5 percent significance level, then accept the hypothesis that μ = μ* if Z is between −1.96 and 1.96; otherwise reject the hypothesis.

4. If you want to test the hypothesis at another significance level, then look in Table A3–2 to find the critical value for Z.

Method 2. Use this method if you *don't know* the variance of the distribution.

1. Calculate the sample average $\bar{x}$.

2. Calculate the sample variance s^2:

$$s^2 = \frac{(X_1 - \bar{x})^2 + (X_2 - \bar{x})^2 + \cdots + (X_n - \bar{x})^2}{n-1}$$

3. Calculate the statistic *t*:

$$t = \sqrt{n}\frac{(\bar{x} - \mu^*)}{s}$$

4. The *t* statistic will have a *t* distribution with *n* − 1 degrees of freedom. Look in Table A3–5 to find the critical value for the *t* distribution with the appropriate degrees of freedom.

There is a close connection between hypothesis testing for means and the confidence intervals for means we developed in Chapter 11. We could calculate a 95 percent confidence interval for the unknown mean weight of the population of football players:

$$204.4 - 2.056 \times 22.1/\sqrt{27} \quad \text{to} \quad 204.4 + 2.056 \times 22.1/\sqrt{27}$$

or

$$195.7 \quad \text{to} \quad 213.1$$

Suppose that we wanted to test the hypothesis that $\mu = 210$ at the 5 percent significance level. The value 210 is inside the confidence interval, and if we calculate the t statistic:

$$\frac{\sqrt{27}(204.4 - 210)}{22.1} = -1.32$$

you can see that we would accept this hypothesis.

On the other hand, suppose we wanted to test the hypothesis that $\mu = 215$. The value 215 is outside the confidence interval, so you probably can guess that we would reject the hypothesis. If you calculate the t statistic:

$$\frac{\sqrt{27}(204.4 - 215)}{22.1} = -2.49$$

you can see that it is in the critical region, so our guess was correct and we would indeed reject the hypothesis.

In general, when we have calculated a 95 percent confidence interval for the mean, we will accept at the 5 percent significance level any null hypothesis where the hypothesized value of the mean is inside the confidence interval. Likewise we will reject any hypothesis where the hypothesized value of the mean is outside the confidence interval. (If we wanted to test the hypothesis at the 1 percent significance level, we would accept the hypothesis if the hypothesized value for the mean was inside the 99 percent confidence interval.)

YOU SHOULD REMEMBER

1. To test the hypothesis that the mean μ of a random variable with a normal distribution is equal to μ^*, calculate this test statistic:

$$\frac{\sqrt{n}(\bar{x} - \mu^*)}{s}$$

> If the null hypothesis is true, this statistic will have a *t* distribution with *n* − 1 degrees of freedom.
>
> **2.** If you have calculated a 95 percent interval for μ, then you will accept the hypothesis μ = μ* at the 5 percent level if μ* is contained in the confidence interval.

THE ONE-TAILED TEST

Suppose that you are a quality control inspector for a semiconductor firm that buys silicon wafers from a particular supplier. Each wafer has a certain number of defects. If there are too many defects, you must reject the wafer. The supplier tells you that, on the average, there are 11 defects per wafer. Your job is to find out whether the supplier is right. You have checked the number of defects for a sample of 17 wafers, with these results:

$$7, 16, 19, 12, 15, 9, 6, 16, 14, 7, 2, 15, 23, 15, 12, 18, 9$$

You want to test the hypothesis that the number of defects on each wafer has a normal distribution with mean μ = 11. However, suppose it turns out that you can reject the hypothesis that μ = 11 because the sample average is significantly *less* than 11. In that case you'll be totally happy—you surely won't complain to the supplier if the number of defects is less than is advertised. Therefore, you don't really want to test the null hypothesis that μ = 11.

Instead, you want to test the null hypothesis that μ ≤ 11. If you can reject this null hypothesis, then you will complain to the supplier. You can use the same *t* statistic again. The only difference is that, this time, you will reject the null hypothesis only if the value of the *t* statistic is in the region where the top 5 percent of the area is located. Figure 13–3 illustrates the rejection

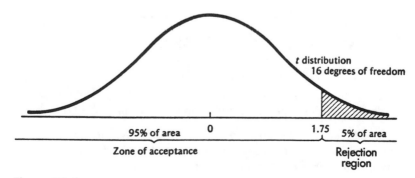

t distribution
16 degrees of freedom

95% of area   0   1.75   5% of area

Zone of acceptance   Rejection region

Figure 13–3

region and the zone of acceptance for this test. For your problem you will have a *t* distribution with 16 degrees of freedom. If you look in Table A3–4, you can see that the rejection region is located for values of *t* above 1.746.

This type of test is called a **one-tailed test**, because the rejection region consists of only one tail of the distribution. In a one-tailed test the null hypothesis is rejected only if the test statistic has a value significantly greater than expected. (Or we could do a one-tailed test using only the left-hand tail, in which case the null hypothesis is rejected only if the test-statistic value is significantly less than expected.)

The type of test that we did before is called a **two-tailed test**. In a two-tailed test, you reject the null hypothesis if the test-statistic value is either very low or very high. Which type of test you should use depends on your situation. Normally, if the null hypothesis involves an inequality, such as $\mu \geq \mu^*$ or $\mu \leq \mu^*$, you will want to use a one-tailed test. If the null hypothesis involves an equality, such as $\mu = \mu^*$, then you will use a two-tailed test.

In the semiconductor case, the sample average $\bar{x} = 12.647$. The value of *s* is 5.396, so the test-statistic value is

$$T = \sqrt{n}\,\frac{\bar{x} - 11}{s} = 1.26$$

Therefore, we can accept the null hypothesis since 1.26 < 1.75.

The Excel function TDIST(ABS(1.26),16,1) reports that the *p* value is 0.1129, so we would accept the null hypothesis at the 10, 5, or 1 percent levels. (Recall we have 16 degrees of freedom and this is a one-tailed test.)

Suppose another sample provides the results $\bar{x} = 15.3$, $s = 4.4$, and $n = 17$. The test statistic value is

$$t = \frac{15.3 - 11}{4.4}\,\sqrt{17} = 4.03$$

The *p* value is 0.000484 (from TDIST(ABS(4.03),16,1)). The small value provides strong evidence for rejecting the null hypothesis.

YOU SHOULD REMEMBER

1. A *two-tailed test* is used to test a hypothesis involving an equality, such as $\mu = \mu^*$. The hypothesis is rejected if the calculated test statistic falls in either the upper tail or the lower tail of the *t* distribution.

2. A *one-tailed test* is used to test a hypothesis involving an inequality, such as $\mu < \mu^*$. The hypothesis is rejected only if the calculated test statistic falls in the appropriate tail.

TESTING HYPOTHESES ABOUT THE PROBABILITY OF SUCCESS

Now we return to the problem of attempting to tell whether or not a coin is fair. You probably won't really study coin tossing during your professional career, but the same concept applies to other processes where you need to estimate the probability of success. To make things easier, let's assume that we have performed enough tosses so that we can approximate the binomial distribution by the normal distribution. In that case, if the hypothesis $p = p^*$ is true, then the number of heads (X) will have a normal distribution with mean $\mu = p^*N$ and variance $\sigma^2 = Np^*(1 - p^*)$. The variable $Z = (X - \mu)/\sigma$ will have a standard normal distribution.

Now, suppose that we have tossed the coin 10,000 times, and we ended up with 5,056 heads. Should we accept the hypothesis that the coin is fair? The fair-coin hypothesis says that $p = .5$, so X will have a normal distribution with $\mu = 5,000$ and $\sigma^2 = 10,000/4$. We need to calculate the test statistic Z:

$$Z = \frac{X - 5,000}{\sqrt{10,000/4}} = \frac{56}{50} = 1.12$$

This value is within the 95 percent zone of acceptance, so we can accept this hypothesis at the 5 percent significance level.

For another example, suppose that 4,884 heads resulted from the 10,000 tosses. In that case the value of the test statistic is $-116/50 = -2.32$. This value is outside 1.96, so we can reject the fair-coin hypothesis at the 5 percent level (and the person who supplied the coin has some explaining to do). However, the value -2.32 is not outside the zone of acceptance at the 1 percent level, so if we want to be more cautious we cannot reject the fair-coin hypothesis. The p value is 0.0203, from the Excel formula $2*(1 - $ NORMSDIST (ABS $(-2.32)))$.

Let's return to the first situation, in which 5,056 heads appeared in 10,000 flips. Suppose that we don't actually believe that the coin is fair. Instead, we think that the coin is unbalanced so that heads are slightly more likely to appear. In particular, we'll test the hypothesis that $p = .51$. If this null hypothesis is true, then X will have a normal distribution with mean 5,100 and variance $10,000 \times .51 \times .49 = 2,499$. In this case the value of our test statistic is $-44/49.98 = -0.880$. This value is well within the zone of acceptance, so we can't reject the hypothesis that $p = .51$. However, we have already found that we also can't reject the hypothesis that $p = .5$. It is not possible that both of these hypotheses can be right, but we have no way to tell the two apart using only the information available to us. You probably could have guessed that it would be very difficult to tell the difference between these two hypotheses.

Even if you decide to accept the null hypothesis, this does not mean that there is not some other hypothesis that can also adequately account for the data. If you want to make a very convincing case that your hypothesis is true, then you will have to be able to reject all of the likely competing hypotheses. Since we haven't been able to do that in the coin example, we cannot say for sure that the coin is fair.

Some writers will say that you "fail to reject," rather than "accept," the null hypothesis, to emphasize that the mere fact that your test statistic falls in the zone of acceptance does not mean that you can guarantee that this null hypothesis is true, rather than some other possible null hypothesis.

We have only one hope—if we flip the coin many, many times, then finally we will reach the point where we can tell the difference between the hypotheses $p = .5$ and $p = .51$.

For example, suppose you flip the coin 39,000 times, with 19,680 heads. If the null hypothesis is $p = .5$, our test statistic becomes

$$(19,680 - 39,000 \times .5)/\sqrt{39,000 \times .5 \times .5} = 180/\sqrt{9750} = 1.82,$$

which falls in the acceptance region. If the null hypothesis is $p = .51$, our test statistic becomes

$$(19,680 - 39,000 \times .51)/\sqrt{39,000 \times .51 \times .49} = -210/\sqrt{9746.1} = 2.12,$$

which falls in the rejection region. Therefore, with 39,000 tosses we are finally able to distinguish between the hypotheses $p = .5$ and $p = .51$. However, in the real world you often cannot increase your sample size greatly. If you find yourself with two competing hypotheses neither of which can be rejected by the available data, then you're stuck.

YOU SHOULD REMEMBER

1. It is easier to prove that a hypothesis is wrong than to prove that it is right.

2. If neither of two competing hypothesis can be proved wrong, an impasse has been reached.

TESTING FOR THE DIFFERENCE BETWEEN TWO MEANS

Suppose that you have two different populations whose means you want to compare. Assume that the random variables X_a (mean μ_a, variance σ_a^2) and

X_b (mean μ_b, variance σ_b^2) have approximately normal distributions. If you take samples of sizes n_a and n_b, respectively, then the sample means $\bar{x}_a$ and $\bar{x}_b$ are normal random variables and their difference is a normal random variable with mean $\mu_a - \mu_b$ and variance $\sigma_a^2/n_a + \sigma_b^2/n_b$.

Often we will want to test hypotheses about the difference between the population means: $\mu_a - \mu_b$. For example, our null hypothesis might be that the population means are equal:

$$\mu_a = \mu_b \quad \text{or} \quad \mu_a - \mu_b = 0$$

More generally, let our null hypothesis be that

$$\mu_a - \mu_b = D$$

If the population variances σ_a^2 and σ_b^2 are known, we can form the test statistic Z:

$$Z = \frac{\bar{x}_a - \bar{x}_b - D}{\sqrt{\sigma_a^2/n_a + \sigma_b^2/n_b}}$$

which will have a standard normal distribution if the null hypothesis is true.

For example, suppose we have two six-sided dice, A and B, which may be biased. We suspect that die A gives, on average, a value 0.7 larger than that of die B. Die A is rolled 20 times and gives the following values:

$$4, 5, 3, 6, 3, 5, 6, 3, 3, 6, 5, 1, 4, 2, 6, 1, 5, 5, 6, 2$$

Die B is rolled 15 times and gives the following values:

$$4, 3, 5, 4, 3, 2, 5, 1, 4, 1, 5, 6, 3, 6, 1$$

The manufacturer tells us that $\sigma_a^2 = 3.0$ and $\sigma_b^2 = 2.8$. We will assume that the manufacturer is statistically honest even though the dice may be shady. We can calculate our test statistic:

$$\bar{x}_a = 4.05, \quad \bar{x}_b = 3.53, \quad \sqrt{\frac{\sigma_a^2}{n_a} + \frac{\sigma_b^2}{n_b}} = .580$$

Therefore:

$$Z = \frac{4.05 - 3.53 - 0.7}{0.58} = -0.310$$

Since this result is within the zone of acceptance, we will accept the null hypothesis.

If the population variances are unknown, we must turn once again to the t statistic. If the null hypothesis is true, and if we also know that $\sigma_a^2 = \sigma_b^2$, then

$$T = \frac{(\bar{x}_a - \bar{x}_b) - D}{\sqrt{s_p^2(1/n_a + 1/n_b)}}$$

has a t distribution with $n_a + n_b - 2$ degrees of freedom, where

$$s_p^2 = \frac{(n_a - 1)s_a^2 + (n_b - 1)s_b^2}{n_a + n_b - 2}$$

(See Chapter 11.)

Examples: Testing for the Difference Between Two Means

PROBLEM   Upon sober reflection, we decide that the values for σ_a^2 and σ_b^2 given us by the dice manufacturer mentioned above were not reliable. We also decide that it is reasonable to assume that $\sigma_a^2 = \sigma_b^2$. Once again we will test the hypothesis that $\mu_a - \mu_b = 0.7$.

SOLUTION   We can calculate that

$$s_a^2 = 2.892, \quad s_b^2 = 2.981, \quad s_p^2 = 2.930$$

and

$$T = \frac{4.05 - 3.53 - 0.7}{\sqrt{2.930(1/20 + 1/15)}} = -0.308$$

which will have a t distribution with 33 degrees of freedom if our hypothesis is correct. Checking Table A3–5, we see that we will accept the null hypothesis at the 5 percent level since −0.308 is inside the critical value of 2.030. The p value is 0.7600, from TDIST (ABS(−0.308),33,2).

General Procedure for Hypothesis Testing for the Difference Between Two Means

Method 1 (if the values of σ_a^2 and σ_b^2 are known):

1. Calculate $\bar{x}_a$ and $\bar{x}_b$.

2. Calculate the test statistic Z:

$$Z = \frac{\bar{x}_a - \bar{x}_b - D}{\sqrt{\sigma_a^2/n_a + \sigma_b^2/n_b}}$$

3. If you want to test the hypothesis at the 5 percent significance level, then accept the hypothesis that $\mu_a - \mu_b = D$ if Z is between -1.96 and 1.96; otherwise reject the hypothesis.

4. If you want to test the hypothesis at another significance level, then look in Table A3–2 to find the critical value for Z.

Method 2 (if the values of σ_a^2 and σ_b^2 are unknown but assumed to be equal):

1. Calculate $\bar{x}_a$ and $\bar{x}_b$.

2. Calculate the sample variances (version 2) for both samples: s_a^2 and s_b^2.

3. Calculate the pooled estimator s_p^2:

$$s_p^2 = \frac{(n_a - 1)s_a^2 + (n_b - 1)s_b^2}{n_a + n_b - 2}$$

4. Calculate the test statistic T:

$$T = \frac{\bar{x}_a - \bar{x}_b - D}{\sqrt{s_p^2(1/n_a + 1/n_b)}}$$

5. If the null hypothesis is true, then T will have a t distribution with $n_a + n_b - 2$ degrees of freedom. Look in Table A3–5 to find the critical values for the appropriate t distribution.

STATISTICALLY SIGNIFICANT VERSUS IMPORTANT

The use of the term "significant" can often be misleading. For example, suppose you read this statement: "A study has been conducted of juggling ability, which found the statistically significant result that broccoli lovers have greater juggling ability than broccoli haters."

If this statement was worded precisely, it would say: "Our study indicates that, at the 5 percent significance level, we can reject the null hypothesis that the mean juggling ability is the same for broccoli lovers and broccoli haters." This means we believe the means of the two groups are not exactly the same, but this does not necessarily mean that there is any important difference between the means. The two means may differ by a trivial amount. Suppose the broccoli lovers are group a and the haters are group b. A sample of 1,000 from each group has taken a juggling test, with these results:

$$n_a = 1,000 \qquad n_b = 1,000$$
$$\bar{x}_a = 64 \qquad \bar{x}_b = 62$$
$$\sigma_a = 20.3 \qquad \sigma_b = 20.3$$

Now, test the hypothesis that $\mu_a = \mu_b$:

$$Z = \frac{\bar{x}_a - \bar{x}_b}{\sqrt{\sigma_a^2/n_a + \sigma_b^2/n_b}} = \frac{2}{\sqrt{.824}} = 2.2$$

This value of Z falls in the rejection region, so we reject the null hypothesis that the two means are the same (at the 5 percent significance level). The p value is 0.0278, from 2*(1 − NORMSDIST(2.2)). Whenever you have a large enough sample, there is a good chance you will find a statistically significant difference between the means. However, the sample averages are very close to each other, so even if there is a statistically significant difference there is not really any important difference. One way we can determine if the difference is important is to calculate $\Pr(A > B)$, where A is the score of a randomly selected broccoli lover and B is the score of a randomly selected broccoli hater:

$$\Pr(A > B) = \Pr((A - B) > 0)$$

Let $U = A - B$; U has a normal distribution with $E(U) = 2$ and

$$\text{Var}(U) = 20.3^2 + 20.3^2 = 824.18.$$
$$\text{Standard deviation} = \sqrt{824.18} = 28.709$$
$$\Pr(U > 0) = \Pr(Z > (0 - 2)/28.709) = .5279$$

Therefore, there is only about a 53 percent chance that a randomly selected broccoli lover will demonstrate greater juggling ability than a randomly selected broccoli hater.

This issue is important because unfortunate stereotypes often arise from the use of the word *significant* in statistical studies. For example, studies often find statistically significant differences in certain abilities between men and women, but the variation in ability within each sex is much greater than the variation between the means of the two sexes. It would be wrong to use the results of such a study to prejudge the ability of any particular individual.

PAIRED SAMPLES

Suppose you are investigating whether a random sample of students score higher on tests given on Friday or on Monday. The sample of 8 students gives this result:

Initials	Friday test (a)	Monday test (b)	Difference
M.Y.	98	90	8
B.K.	94	84	10
R.T.	91	90	1
G.A.	88	83	5
R.S.	86	80	6
T.J.	82	77	5
L.S.	80	76	4
J.B.	76	72	4

Your first temptation might be to use the test procedure for the difference of two means, using the null hypothesis $\mu_a - \mu_b = 0$, as in the preceding section:

$$s_p^2 = \frac{(n_a - 1)s_a^2 + (n_b - 1)s_b^2}{n_a + n_b - 2} = \frac{7 \times 7.3957^2 + 7 \times 6.6027^2}{8 + 8 - 2} = 48.491$$

$$T = \frac{x_a - x_b - 0}{\sqrt{s_p^2(1/n_a + 1/n_b)}} = 1.54$$

This result is inside the acceptance region for a t distribution with $8 + 8 - 2 = 14$ degrees of freedom, which could lead you to believe there is no statistically significant difference in test scores on the different days of the week.

However, glancing at the table, you can see that each student has a higher score on Friday than on Monday, which suggests there is a problem with the previous analysis. The problem is: there is so much variability in the scores between the different students that it tends to overwhelm the difference between the different days. The preceding analysis is inappropriate, because we are not dealing with a random sample from Friday and an independent random sample on Monday. Instead, we have a paired sample; that is, a sample where we have pairs of values, one each for Friday and Monday, for each student. In this case, we should perform the following t test:

1. Assume that the difference in scores between Monday and Friday for each student comes from a normal distribution with mean μ_D and variance σ_D^2.

2. The null hypothesis is that $\mu_D = 0$.

3. Let X_{Di} be the difference in scores for student i. Calculate the average $\overline{x_D} = (\Sigma X_{Di})/n$; this average will have a normal distribution with mean μ_D and variance σ_D^2/n.

4. Calculate the test statistic:

$$\frac{\overline{x_D}}{s_D / \sqrt{n}} = \frac{\sqrt{n}\,(\overline{x_D})}{s_D}$$

where s_D is the sample standard deviation (with $n - 1$ in the denominator) for the differences.

If the null hypothesis is true, this test statistic will come from a t distribution with $n - 1$ degrees of freedom.

For our example, we have $\overline{x_D} = 5.375$; $s_D = 2.722$; $n = 8$, and:

$$T = \frac{\sqrt{8} \times 5.375}{2.722} = 5.58$$

This is well within the rejection region, so we reject the null hypothesis that there is no difference between Friday scores and Monday scores. The p value is very low: 0.000833.

TESTING FOR THE DIFFERENCE BETWEEN TWO PROPORTIONS

Suppose now that we perform two series of tests. Suppose that test A is performed n_a times, with each test having an unknown probability p_a of success. If X_a is the number of successes, then $\hat{p}_a = X_a/n_a$ is an estimate of p_a. If n_a is large, then the central limit theorem says that $\hat{p}_a$ will have a normal distribution with mean p_a and variance $p_a(1 - p_a)/n_a$. Similarly, if X_b is the number of successes in n_b trials for test B, each with probability p_b of success, then, for large n_b, $\hat{p}_b = X_b/n_b$ has a normal distribution with mean p_b and variance $p_b(1 - p_b)/n_b$. Then $\hat{p}_a - \hat{p}_b$ also has a normal distribution with mean $(p_a + p_b)$ and variance equal to $[p_a(1 - p_a)/n_a + p_b(1 - p_b)/n_b]$.

If $p_a - p_b = D$, then this quantity:

$$\frac{\hat{p}_a - \hat{p}_b - D}{\sqrt{p_a(1 - p_a)/n_a + p_b(1 - p_b)/n_b}}$$

has a standard normal distribution. If we hypothesize that $p_a - p_b = D$, then we want to test this hypothesis using the above statistic. Unfortunately, we need to know the values of p_a and p_b to calculate that statistic. But, if we knew these values, we wouldn't need to test the hypothesis in the first place.

How far off would we be if we substituted $\hat{p}_a$ for p_a and $\hat{p}_b$ for p_b? If n_a is large, then $|\hat{p}_a - p_a|$ will be small (by the law of large numbers), $|(p_a - \hat{p}_a) \times (1 - p_a - \hat{p}_a)|$ will be still smaller, and $|(p_a - \hat{p}_a)(1 - p_a - \hat{p}_a)/n_a)|$ will be even smaller. The same reasoning applies to substituting $\hat{p}_b$ for p_b, and thus, if the null hypothesis is true and $p_a - p_b = D$, then the statistic Z:

$$Z = \frac{\hat{p}_a - \hat{p}_b - D}{\sqrt{\hat{p}_a(1 - \hat{p}_a)/n_a + \hat{p}_b(1 - \hat{p}_b)/n_b}}$$

has a standard normal distribution.

Examples: Testing for the Difference Between Two Proportions

PROBLEM Suppose that two manufacturers, Abercrombie and Bayes, supply electric light bulbs to your multinational corporation, which has many lamps. You suspect that Bayes's bulbs are less reliable than Abercrombie's and, in fact, that the probability of a Bayes bulb being defective is .001 greater than that of a defective Abercrombie bulb. Is your suspicion justified?

SOLUTION A random sample of 1,000 of Abercrombie's bulbs turns up 15 defective bulbs, while a random sample of 2,000 of Bayes's bulbs turns up 36 defective bulbs. Then

$$\hat{p}_a = \frac{15}{1,000} = .015 \qquad \hat{p}_b = \frac{36}{2,000} = .018$$

$$\frac{\hat{p}_a(1 - \hat{p}_a)}{n_a} = .0000148 \qquad \frac{\hat{p}_b(1 - \hat{p}_b)}{n_b} = .00000883$$

and the value of Z is

$$Z = \frac{.015 - .018 - (-.001)}{\sqrt{.0000148 + .00000883}}$$
$$= -.412$$

Thus you would accept the hypothesis that $p_a - p_b = -.001$ at the 5 percent significance level, since $-1.96 < -.412 < 1.96$.

If $D = 0$, however, we can find a better estimate for p_a and p_b (which are assumed to be equal in this case). We will use the estimator $\hat{p} = (X_a + X_b)/(n_a + n_b)$. Substituting this for $\hat{p}_a$ and $\hat{p}_b$ in the denominator, we get

$$Z = \frac{\hat{p}_a - \hat{p}_b}{\sqrt{\hat{p}(1 - \hat{p})(1/n_a + 1/n_b)}}$$

PROBLEM   Suppose we wish to test the null hypothesis that $p_a = p_b$.
SOLUTION   Then

$$\hat{p} = \frac{15 + 36}{1,000 + 2,000} = .017 \qquad Z = \frac{.015 - .018}{.005007} = -.599$$

$$\sqrt{\hat{p}(1 - \hat{p})\left(\frac{1}{n_a} + \frac{1}{n_b}\right)} = .005007$$

Thus we would accept the null hypothesis at the 5 percent level, since $-1.96 < -.599 < 1.96$.

General Procedure for Testing the Hypothesis That $p_a - p_b = D$, Given That Test *A* Has X_a Successes in n_a Trials, Test *B* has X_b Successes in n_b Trials, and n_a and n_b Are Large

Method 1 (if *D* does not equal zero):

1. Calculate $\hat{p}_a$ and $\hat{p}_b$:

$$\hat{p}_a = \frac{X_a}{n_a} \quad \text{and} \quad \hat{p}_b = \frac{X_b}{n_b}$$

2. Calculate *Z*:

$$Z = \frac{\hat{p}_a - \hat{p}_b - D}{\sqrt{\hat{p}_a(1 - \hat{p}_a)/n_a + \hat{p}_b(1 - \hat{p}_b)/n_b}}$$

3. If you want to test the hypothesis at the 5 percent significance level, then accept the hypothesis if *Z* is between -1.96 and 1.96; otherwise reject the hypothesis.

4. If you want to test the hypothesis at another significance level, then look in Table A3–2 to find the critical value of *Z*.

Method 2 (if you are hypothesizing that $p_a = p_b$, that is, $D = 0$):

1. Calculate $\hat{p}$, $\hat{p}_a$, and $\hat{p}_b$:

$$p = \frac{X_a + X_b}{n_a + n_b}, \quad \hat{p}_a = \frac{X_a}{n_a}, \quad \text{and} \quad \hat{p}_b = \frac{X_b}{n_b}$$

2. Calculate Z:

$$Z = \frac{\hat{p}_a - \hat{p}_b}{\sqrt{\hat{p}(1 - \hat{p})(1/n_a + 1/n_b)}}$$

3. If you want to test the hypothesis at the 5 percent significance level, then accept the hypothesis if Z is between -1.96 and 1.96; otherwise reject the hypothesis.

4. If you want to test the hypothesis at another significance level, then look in Table A3–2 to find the critical value of Z.

KNOW THE CONCEPTS

DO YOU KNOW THE BASICS?

Test your understanding of Chapter 13 by answering the following questions:

1. If you decide to accept the null hypothesis, can you be sure that it is really true?

2. If you decide to reject the null hypothesis, can you be sure that it is really false?

3. Why is it necessary to choose a test statistic whose distribution is known if the null hypothesis is true?

4. When is a one-tailed test appropriate? When is a two-tailed test appropriate?

5. Suppose you have found statistical evidence to reject the hypothesis that the population mean μ is equal to 7. Is it possible that the true value of the mean may still be close to 7?

6. Suppose you see a car with license plate JXN 492 ahead of you and are astonished when you realize the probability of seeing this particular license plate is 1 in $26^3 \times 10^3 = 17{,}576{,}000$. You reject the hypothesis that this could have happened randomly. What is the problem with this thinking?

TERMS FOR STUDY

alternative hypothesis   test statistic
critical region   two-tailed test
critical value   Type I error
level of significance   Type II error
null hypothesis   zone of acceptance
one-tailed test

PRACTICAL APPLICATION

COMPUTATIONAL PROBLEMS

Given the following samples, test the hypothesis that the mean is as given:

1. 1, 5, 17, 9, 23, 17, 4, 3, 8, 8, 7, 8, 6, 0, −1: mean 7
2. 4, 30, −17, −29, 8, 7, −5, 4, 3, −6: mean −2
3. 15, 22, −19, 0, 1, 2, 4, 3, −3, 7: mean 14
4. 17, −9, −8, −10, 8, 5, 4, −7, 3, 4, −5, −7, −3, 2, 3: mean 0
5. Estimate the mean of the scores of your favorite football team last year. Test the hypothesis that the mean score is greater than 14.
6. Test the hypothesis that the mean number of pages in your favorite daily newspaper is greater than 50.
7. Estimate the mean price of a gallon of milk in your city over the past month. Test the hypothesis that the price this month is significantly greater than the price last month.
8. Consider a random variable with a binomial distribution with p unknown. How big does n have to be for you to be able to tell the difference (at the 5 percent significance level) between the hypothesis $p = .5$ and the hypothesis $p = .51$?
9. Make a list of the first letters of the last names of 20 people you know and assign each letter a number ($A = 1$, $B = 2$, etc.) Test the hypothesis that the resulting numbers come from a distribution with mean 13.
10. Repeat the same procedure as in Exercise 15, only this time use the first names, and assume that the variance of the distribution is 25.

For Exercises 11–40, you are given values for $\bar{x}$ and s calculated from a sample of size n. Test the hypothesis that the true mean equals 60.

	$\bar{x}$	s	n
11.	62	5	10
12.	63	5	10
13.	64	5	10
14.	65	5	10
15.	72	5	10
16.	62	5	20
17.	63	5	20
18.	64	5	20
19.	65	5	20
20.	72	5	20
21.	62	5	100
22.	63	5	100
23.	64	5	100
24.	65	5	100
25.	72	5	100
26.	62	10	10
27.	63	10	10
28.	64	10	10
29.	65	10	10
30.	72	10	10
31.	62	10	20
32.	63	10	20
33.	64	10	20
34.	65	10	20
35.	72	10	20
36.	62	10	100
37.	63	10	100
38.	64	10	100
39.	65	10	100
40.	72	10	100

For Exercises 41–70, you are given values for $\bar{x}$ and s calculated from a sample of size n. Test the hypothesis that the true mean is greater than 25.

	$\bar{x}$	s	n
41.	25	5	10
42.	26	5	10
43.	27.5	5	10
44.	28	5	10
45.	30	5	10
46.	25.5	5	20
47.	26	5	20
48.	27.5	5	20
49.	28	5	20
50.	30	5	20
51.	25.5	5	100
52.	26	5	100
53.	27.5	5	100
54.	28	5	100
55.	30	5	100
56.	25.5	10	10
57.	26	10	10
58.	27.5	10	10
59.	28	10	10
60.	30	10	10
61.	25.5	10	20
62.	26	10	20
63.	27.5	10	20
64.	28	10	20
65.	30	10	20
66.	25.5	10	100
67.	26	10	100
68.	27.5	10	100
69.	28	10	100
70.	30	10	100

For Exercises 71–86, you are given values of $\bar{x}_a$, $\bar{x}_b$, n_a, n_b, s_a, s_b for two independent samples. Test the hypothesis that the difference in the means is equal to the given value of D.

	$\bar{x}_a$	$\bar{x}_b$	n_a	n_b	s_a	s_b	D
71.	73	72	12	12	1.8	1.8	0
72.	74	72	12	12	1.8	1.8	0
73.	75	72	12	12	1.8	1.8	0
74.	76	72	12	12	1.8	1.8	0
75.	73	72	12	20	3.2	3.8	0
76.	74	72	12	20	3.2	3.8	0
77.	76	72	12	20	3.2	3.8	0
78.	78	72	12	20	3.2	3.8	0
79.	73	72	25	25	1.5	1.5	0
80.	74	72	25	25	1.5	1.5	0
81.	76	72	25	25	2.5	2.5	0
82.	78	72	25	25	3.9	3.9	0
83.	76	72	25	32	3.2	3.4	3
84.	77	72	25	32	3.2	3.4	3
85.	79	72	25	32	3.2	3.4	3
86.	82	72	25	32	5.2	5.4	3

For Exercises 87–90, there are observations from 12 days of sales figures from two different locations. These observations form a paired sample. Test the hypothesis that the means are the same.
87.

Date:	1	2	3	4	5	6	7	8	9	10	11	12
Location x:	78	67	72	75	73	83	78	81	85	82	79	81
Location y:	75	65	68	72	70	81	74	78	82	80	75	79

88.

Date:	1	2	3	4	5	6	7	8	9	10	11	12
Location x:	78	87	112	135	33	53	158	91	142	74	63	41
Location y:	75	85	98	132	30	51	154	88	142	75	62	42

89.

Date:	1	2	3	4	5	6	7	8	9	10	11	12
Location x:	98	67	112	75	83	133	68	89	125	62	89	91
Location y:	75	45	68	32	60	61	94	70	198	90	65	79

90.

Date:	1	2	3	4	5	6	7	8	9	10	11	12
Location x:	48	67	72	35	83	93	118	61	85	72	68	43
Location y:	50	68	72	37	85	91	117	62	82	75	70	43

For Exercises 91–94, you are given observations of the sample proportions $\hat{p}_a$ and $\hat{p}_b$ from two samples of size n_a and n_b, respectively. Test the hypothesis that the two proportions are the same.

	$\hat{p}_a$	$\hat{p}_b$	n_a	n_b
91.	0.54	0.56	10	10
92.	0.62	0.57	10	10
93.	0.73	0.78	4,900	4,800
94.	0.68	0.70	4,900	4,800

ANSWERS

KNOW THE CONCEPTS

1. No. There is always a possibility of committing a Type II error.

2. No. There is always a possibility of committing a Type I error.

3. You choose a test statistic of known distribution so that you can put an upper limit on the probability of a Type I error.

4. A one-tailed test is appropriate if the null hypothesis is to be rejected only if the test statistic has an extreme value in one direction, but not the other direction. A two-tailed test is appropriate if the null hypothesis is to be rejected if the test statistic is either too big or too small. For example, if you are testing a hypothesis about a population mean that uses an equality sign, you will generally use a two-tailed test.

5. Yes. You should always check the value of the sample average in addition to the value of the test statistic. For example, if the sample average is 7.01, you can be sure that the true value of the average is close to 7 even if your statistical evidence led you to reject the hypothesis that the true mean is exactly equal to 7.

6. The problem here is that you are testing a hypothesis using the same data that was used to form the hypothesis.

   It would have been truly remarkable if it had happened like this: In the morning you had been wondering to yourself, "what is the probability of seeing license plate JNX 492 today?" If you then saw that license plate (and it was on a car you had no connection with), then that would have been truly outstanding and you might think you were clairvoyant. (However, you would have to do this a few more times before you could convince anyone you have magic powers of foresight.)

   However, if you calculate the probability of an event happening *after* you have witnessed that event, then it's not very remarkable to note that you did observe an event that seemed improbable.

PRACTICAL APPLICATION

Calculations are shown for Exercises 1 and 5. The same methods can be applied to similar exercises.

1. Test statistic = $\sqrt{15}(7.667 - 7)/6.7365 = 0.383$; accept.

2. Test statistic = 0.380; accept.

3. Test statistic = -3.15; reject.

4. Test statistic = -0.101; accept.

For Exercises 11–40, use a two-tailed test.

	$\bar{x}$	s	n	Test Statistic	p Value	at 10% Level	at 5% Level	at 1% Level
11.	62	5	10	1.265	0.238	accept	accept	accept
12.	63	5	10	1.897	0.090	reject	accept	accept
13.	64	5	10	2.530	0.032	rejec	reject	accept
14.	65	5	10	3.162	0.012	reject	reject	accept
15.	72	5	10	7.589	3.36E−05	reject	reject	reject
16.	62	5	20	1.789	0.090	reject	accept	accept
17.	63	5	20	2.683	0.015	reject	reject	accept
18.	64	5	20	3.578	0.002	reject	reject	reject
19.	65	5	20	4.472	0.000	reject	reject	reject
20.	72	5	20	10.733	1.66E−09	reject	reject	reject
21.	62	5	100	4	0.000122	reject	reject	reject
22.	63	5	100	6	3.25E−08	reject	reject	reject
23.	64	5	100	8	2.4E−12	reject	reject	reject
24.	65	5	100	10	1.09E−16	reject	reject	reject
25.	72	5	100	24	4.68E−43	reject	reject	reject
26.	62	10	10	0.632	0.543	accept	accept	accept
27.	63	10	10	0.949	0.368	accept	accept	accept
28.	64	10	10	1.265	0.238	accept	accept	accept
29.	65	10	10	1.581	0.148	accept	accept	accept
30.	72	10	10	3.795	0.004	reject	reject	reject
31.	62	10	20	0.894	0.382	accept	accept	accept
32.	63	10	20	1.342	0.196	accept	accept	accept
33.	64	10	20	1.789	0.090	reject	accept	accept
34.	65	10	20	2.236	0.038	reject	reject	accept
35.	72	10	20	5.367	3.53E−05	reject	reject	reject
36.	62	10	100	2	0.048	reject	reject	accept
37.	63	10	100	3	0.003	reject	reject	reject
38.	64	10	100	4	0.000122	reject	reject	reject
39.	65	10	100	5	2.5E−06	reject	reject	reject
40.	72	10	100	12	5.13E−21	reject	reject	reject

For Exercises 41–70, use a one-tailed test.

	$\bar{x}$	s	n	Test Statistic	p Value	at 10% Level	at 5% Level	at 1% Level
41.	25	5	10	0	0.500	accept	accept	accept
42.	26	5	10	0.632	0.271	accept	accept	accept
43.	27.5	5	10	1.581	0.074	reject	accept	accept
44.	28	5	10	1.897	0.045	reject	reject	accept
45.	30	5	10	3.162	0.006	reject	reject	reject
46.	25.5	5	20	0.447	0.330	accept	accept	accept
47.	26	5	20	0.894	0.191	accept	accept	accept
48.	27.5	5	20	2.236	0.019	reject	reject	accept
49.	28	5	20	2.683	0.007	reject	reject	reject
50.	30	5	20	4.472	0.000	reject	reject	reject
51.	25.5	5	100	1	0.160	accept	accept	accept
52.	26	5	100	2	0.024	reject	reject	accept
53.	27.5	5	100	5	1.2407E–06	reject	reject	reject
54.	28	5	100	6	1.62296E–08	reject	reject	reject
55.	30	5	100	10	5.46988E–17	reject	reject	reject
56.	25.5	10	10	0.158	0.439	accept	accept	accept
57.	26	10	10	0.316	0.380	accept	accept	accept
58.	27.5	10	10	0.791	0.225	accept	accept	accept
59.	28	10	10	0.949	0.184	accept	accept	accept
60.	30	10	10	1.581	0.074	reject	accept	accept
61.	25.5	10	20	0.224	0.413	accept	accept	accept
62.	26	10	20	0.447	0.330	accept	accept	accept
63.	27.5	10	20	1.118	0.139	accept	accept	accept
64.	28	10	20	1.342	0.098	reject	accept	accept
65.	30	10	20	2.236	0.019	reject	reject	accept
66.	25.5	10	100	0.5	0.309	accept	accept	accept
67.	26	10	100	1	0.160	accept	accept	accept
68.	27.5	10	100	2.5	0.007	reject	reject	reject
69.	28	10	100	3	0.002	reject	reject	reject
70.	30	10	100	5	1.2407E–06	reject	reject	reject

	Degrees of Freedom	s_p^2	T	p Value	at 5 % Level
71.	22	3.2400	1.3608	0.187356	accept
72.	22	3.2400	2.7217	0.012456	reject
73.	22	3.2400	4.0825	0.000493	reject
74.	22	3.2400	5.4433	0.000018	reject
75.	30	12.9000	0.7625	0.451716	accept
76.	30	12.9000	1.5250	0.137733	accept
77.	30	12.9000	3.0500	0.004751	reject
78.	30	12.9000	4.5750	0.000077	reject
79.	48	2.2500	2.3570	0.022550	reject
80.	48	2.2500	4.7140	0.000021	reject
81.	48	6.2500	5.6569	0.000001	reject
82.	48	15.2100	5.4393	0.000002	reject
83.	55	10.9840	1.1304	0.263213	accept
84.	55	10.9840	2.2608	0.027749	reject
85.	55	10.9840	4.5215	0.000033	reject
86.	55	28.2349	4.9353	0.000008	reject

87. The differences are

$$3, 2, 4, 3, 3, 2, 4, 3, 3, 2, 4, 2$$

The t statistic is

$$t = \frac{\sqrt{n}(\overline{x_D})}{s_D} = \frac{\sqrt{12}(2.9167)}{0.7592} = 13.3082$$

p value: 3.99×10^{-8}; decisively reject the null hypothesis. Location X consistently has higher sales.

88. The differences are

$$3, 2, 14, 3, 3, 2, 4, 3, 0, -1, 1, -1$$

The t statistic is

$$t = \frac{\sqrt{n}(\overline{x_D})}{s_D} = \frac{\sqrt{12}(2.7500)}{3.7444} = 2.5441$$

p value $= 0.02728$. Reject the null hypothesis at the 5 percent level.

89. The differences are

$$23, 22, 44, 43, 23, 72, -26, 19, -73, -28, 24, 12$$

The t statistic is

$$t = \frac{\sqrt{n}(\overline{x}_D)}{s_D} = \frac{\sqrt{12}(12.9167)}{36.9447} = 1.2111$$

p value = .25; accept the null hypothesis.

90. The differences are

$$-2, -1, 0, -2, -2, 2, 1, -1, 3, -3, -2, 0$$

The t statistic is:

$$t = \frac{\sqrt{n}(\overline{x}_D)}{s_D} = \frac{\sqrt{12}(-0.5833)}{1.7540} = -1.1521$$

p value = .27; accept the null hypothesis.

For Exercises 91–94, the formula for the test statistic is

$$Z = \frac{\hat{p}_a - \hat{p}_b - 0}{\sqrt{\hat{p}_a(1 - \hat{p}_a)/n_a + \hat{p}_b(1 - \hat{p}_b)/n_b}}$$

Note that the larger sample makes us more likely to reject the null hypothesis that the two proportions are equal because we have more confidence that we can distinguish between them.

	$\hat{p}_a$	$\hat{p}_b$	n_a	n_b	Z
91.	0.54	0.56	10	10	−0.0899
92.	0.62	0.57	10	10	0.2281
93.	0.73	0.78	4,900	4,800	−5.7364
94.	0.68	0.70	4,900	4,800	−2.1301

14
THE CHI-SQUARE TEST

KEY TERMS

chi-square test a statistical method to test the hypothesis that two factors are independent

goodness-of-fit test a statistical procedure to test the hypothesis that a particular probability distribution fits an observed set of data

---

THE CONTINGENCY TABLE

Let's suppose that we are trying to test whether there is any difference between four competing cold-prevention medicines. None of the medicines is guaranteed to work—instead, each one just promises to reduce the chances of getting a cold. Therefore, the number of people who try each kind of medicine and then get colds can be regarded as a random variable. The null hypothesis is: there is no difference between the medicines. Another way of saying it: the condition of a person (whether they get sick or not) is independent of the medicine they took. Suppose we have checked with a sample of 495 people. We asked them what kind of medicine they used, and then whether or not they got colds. The results were as follows:

	Medicine 1	Medicine 2	Medicine 3	Medicine 4	Total
How many got colds	15	26	9	14	64
How many did not	111	107	96	117	431
total	126	133	105	131	495

(This type of table is a **contingency table**—in this case with two rows and four columns. Each location is a **cell**. This table has eight cells.)

We can see from the table that medicine 3 seemed to be the most effective; only 8.5 percent of the people who tried medicine 3 got colds. However, there are many other factors that could have determined whether those people got colds. Maybe the people who used medicine 3 just happened to be exposed to fewer cold germs; in that case, the fact that they got fewer colds is chance occurrence that has nothing to do with the fact that they used medicine 3.

Therefore, our null hypothesis will be as follows: There is basically no difference between the four medicines. In that case, the observed differences between the medicines arose solely by chance.

• *DEVELOPING A TEST STATISTIC*

Now we need to develop a test statistic to check this hypothesis. We can observe that in the total sample the fraction of people who got colds was .129 and the fraction who did not was .871. If there really was no difference between the medicines, then the fraction of people who got colds or did not get colds in each group should be close to these fractions. We can make a table comparing the actual and predicted values for the number of people in each group.

Enter the data into Excel:

	A	B	C	D	E	F
1	Actual	Med 1	Med 2	Med 3	Med 4	
2	w/cold	15	26	9	14	
3	w/o cold	111	107	96	117	

Next we need to calculate the totals in each row. Enter the formula = sum(B2:B3) into cell B4, and copy it to the right. Enter the fomula = sum(B2:E2) into cell F2 and copy it down:

	A	B	C	D	E	F
1	Actual	Med 1	Med 2	Med 3	Med 4	Total
2	w/cold	15	26	9	14	64
3	w/o cold	111	107	96	117	431
4	Total	126	133	105	131	495

Now we need to create a new table showing the expected values if the null hypothesis were true. Enter the formula =B$4*$F2/F4 into cell B7. (The dollar signs need to be entered exactly as shown so the cells will copy correctly.) Copy this formula down to cell B8 and then across to fill the range B7:E8.

	A	B	C	D	E	F
1	Actual	Med 1	Med 2	Med 3	Med 4	Total
2	w/cold	15	26	9	14	64
3	w/o cold	111	107	96	117	431
4	Total	126	133	105	131	495
5						
6	Expected	Med 1	Med 2	Med 3	Med 4	Total
7	w/cold	16.2909	17.1960	13.5758	16.9374	
8	w/o cold	109.7091	115.8040	91.4242	114.0626	

In cell A10 enter the formula = CHITEST(B2 : E3,B7 : E8). This will calculate the p value for the test, which for this example is 0.053811. Since this is slightly greater than .05, it means that we can accept the null hypothesis at the 5 percent significance level, but it is a close call so we should investigate further. To obtain the actual value of the chi-square statistic, enter the formula =CHIINV(A10,3). (In this example, A10 is the cell where we put the p value from the CHITEST function, and 3 is the number of degrees of freedom.) The resulting chi-square statistic is 7.65.

Here is the formula for the test statistic, which is based on the difference between the observed frequencies and the frequencies that are predicted if there is in fact no difference between the medicines. If this difference is small, we can reasonably accept the no-difference hypothesis. If this difference is large, then we should reject the hypothesis.

Let f_i represent the observed frequency in cell i, and let f_i^* represent the predicted frequency for cell i. Then, if there are N cells, we will use this test statistic:

$$S = \frac{(f_1 - f_1^*)^2}{f_1^*} + \frac{(f_2 - f_2^*)^2}{f_2^*} + \cdots + \frac{(f_N - f_N^*)^2}{f_N^*}$$

$$= \sum_{i=1}^{N} \frac{(f_i - f_i^*)^2}{f_i^*}$$

In our case we have eight cells, and the value of the test statistic is calculated to be 7.65.

As it turns out, if the null hypothesis is true this test statistic has approximately a chi-square distribution, so it is called the chi-square statistic. The number of degrees of freedom is given by

Degrees of freedom = (number of rows − 1) × (number of columns − 1)

In our case, we have two rows and four columns, so our chi-square statistic has $(2 − 1) × (4 − 1) = 3$ degrees of freedom.

Figure 14–1 illustrates a chi-square distribution with three degrees of freedom. From Table A3–3 in Appendix 3, we see that for this distribution, 95 percent of the area is below 7.81. The 5 percent of the area above this (shaded in the diagram) represents the rejection region. Our observed test statistic value is 7.65. We can see that this falls into the zone of acceptance, but just barely. Since this value is close to the borderline, these obervations indicate there is almost more variation between the medicines than would be expected to happen by pure chance. We should continue researching this question by collecting more data to see if we can establish that one of the medicines is more effective than the others.

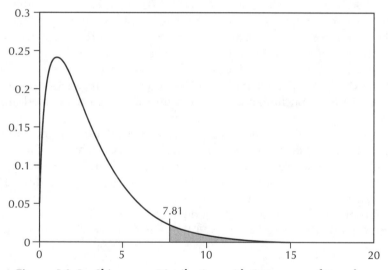

Figure 14–1. Chi-square Distribution with 3 Degrees of Freedom

The CHITEST function in Excel returns the p value, which is .0538 in this case. (Alternatively, if you know the test statistic value x, then CHIDIST (x, degrees of freedom) will also give you the p value.) The p value is above 5 percent, indicating we should accept the null hypothesis at the 5 percent level. However, since the p value is also below 10 percent, we would reject the null hypothesis at the 10 percent level (or any significance level greater than .0538).

Note that the chi-square test is a one-tailed test, because we reject the null hypothesis only if the calculated test statistic is too big.

General Procedure for Chi-square Test

Suppose you are given a contingency table with m rows (categories) and n columns (groups):

Category	Group 1	Group 2	Group 3	$\cdots$	Group n
Category a	a_1	a_2	a_3	$\cdots$	a_n
Category b	b_1	b_2	b_3	$\cdots$	b_n
Category c (and so on)	c_1	c_2	c_3	$\cdots$	c_n

The chi-square test is used to test the hypothesis that there is no significant difference between the groups. In other words, any observed difference in the proportion of each group belonging to a particular category arose solely by chance.

1. Calculate the total number of observations in each category:

$$a_{total} = a_1 + a_2 + \cdots + a_n$$
$$b_{total} = b_1 + b_2 + \cdots + b_n$$

and so on.

2. Calculate the total number of observations in each group:

$$t_1 = a_1 + b_1 + c_1 + \cdots$$
$$t_2 = a_2 + b_2 + c_2 + \cdots$$
$$\cdots\cdots\cdots\cdots\cdots\cdots\cdots$$
$$t_n = a_n + b_n + c_n + \cdots$$

3. Calculate the grand-total number of observations:

$$T = t_1 + t_2 + t_3 + \cdots + t_n$$

4. Calculate the proportion in each category:

$$P_a = \frac{a_{total}}{T}$$

$$P_b = \frac{b_{total}}{T}$$

and so on.

5. Calculate the predicted frequency of occurrence for each cell:

$$f_{a1} = p_a t_1 \quad f_{a2} = p_a t_2 \cdots f_{an} = p_a t_n$$
$$f_{b1} = p_b t_1 \quad f_{b2} = p_b t_2 \cdots f_{bn} = p_b t_n$$

6. Calculate the value of the chi-square statistic S:

$$S = \frac{(a_1 - f_{a1})^2}{f_{a1}} + \frac{(a_2 - f_{a2})^2}{f_{a2}} + \cdots + \frac{(a_n - f_{an})^2}{f_{an}}$$
$$+ \frac{(b_1 - f_{b1})^2}{f_{b1}} + \frac{(b_2 - f_{b2})^2}{f_{b2}} + \cdots + \frac{(b_n - f_{bn})^2}{f_{bn}} + \cdots$$

7. If the null hypothesis is true, the statistic S will have a chi-square distribution with $(m - 1) \times (n - 1)$ degrees of freedom. Look up the critical value in Table A3–3. If the observed value is greater than the critical value, then you should reject the hypothesis.

We can summarize the formula for the chi-square statistic with this expression:

$$\text{Chi-square statistic} = \sum \frac{(\text{observed} - \text{expected})^2}{\text{expected}}$$

where we calculate the observed entry for each cell in the contingency table and the expected frequency of occurrence for that cell, assuming the null hypothesis is true, and then take the summation over all of the cells.

• APPLICATION OF THE CHI-SQUARE TEST

In general, the **chi-square test** can be used to test whether two factors are independent. As we found in Chapter 5, two random events are independent if a knowledge that one of the events has occurred does not provide any information about whether the other event occurred. In our previous example we wanted to test whether knowledge of one factor (which medicine was taken) provided any information about the other factor (whether the person got a cold). In other words, we were trying to test whether or not the two factors were independent.

Here are two extreme examples. Suppose we run a factory, and we would like to test whether parts made on Mondays and Fridays are more likely to be defective than parts made in the middle of the week. Here is our table of observations:

Day	Defective Parts	Acceptable Parts
Monday	16	132
Tuesday	4	140
Wednesday	5	138
Thursday	2	149
Friday	13	126

It clearly looks as if there is a significantly higher proportion of defective parts on Mondays and Fridays. We will use a chi-square test to test the null hypothesis that the chance of a part being defective is independent of the day of the week when it was made. Here is a table comparing the observed frequencies to the expected frequencies:

Day	Defective Parts		Acceptable Parts	
	Actual	Predicted	Actual	Predicted
Monday	16	8.166	132	139.835
Tuesday	4	7.945	140	136.055
Wednesday	5	7.890	138	135.110
Thursday	2	8.331	149	142.669
Friday	13	7.669	126	131.331

The calculated value of the chi-square statistic is 20.16. There are $(5 - 1) \times (2 - 1) = 4$ degrees of freedom. The 95 percent critical value from the table is 9.48, so we can clearly reject the null hypothesis.

For another example, suppose that we are evaluating the effect of three worker training programs. Our null hypothesis is that the evaluation of a worker is not affected by which training program he or she took. Here are the data:

Program	Evaluation		
	Above Average	Average	Below Average
1	36	78	29
2	24	53	21
3	33	67	28

A casual glance at these numbers does not indicate much difference between the training programs. The calculated value of the chi-square statistic is 0.19, so this confirms our suspicion that we should accept the null hypothesis.

YOU SHOULD REMEMBER

1. The chi-square test is used to test whether there is any significant difference between several groups or whether the observed differences could have happened by chance.

2. The chi-square test is based on the difference between the observed frequencies in a contingency table and the expected frequencies that would occur if the null hypothesis were true.

3. The null hypothesis is rejected if the calculated value for the chi-square statistic is greater than the critical value.

GOODNESS-OF-FIT TESTS

The chi-square test can also be used to test whether a particular probability distribution fits the observed data very well. This type of test is called a **goodness-of-fit test**. Once again, we want to compare the observed frequencies f of a particular occurrence with the frequencies f^* that are predicted to occur if the alleged distribution really does fit the data well. Once again, we compute the statistic

$$\sum_{i=1}^{n} \frac{(f_i - f_i^*)^2}{f_i^*}$$

If the null hypothesis is true, this statistic will have approximately a chi-square distribution. If the value of the test statistic turns out to be too large, there is too much of a discrepancy between the actual results and the predicted results, so we can reject the hypothesis that the predicted distribution fits the data. The number of degrees of freedom for the chi-square statistic is

$$n - 1 - (\text{number of parameters that you have to}$$
$$\text{estimate using the sample})$$

For example, if you use the sample to estimate the mean of the distribution you are using, then the χ^2 statistic will have $n - 2$ degrees of freedom.

Let's perform a goodness-of-fit test to see if the Poisson distribution is appropriate for predicting the number of United States Supreme Court justices that will be appointed in a five-year period. Table 14–1 shows the number of court appointments that have been made during each five-year period in U.S. history.

Table 14-1. Appointments to United States Supreme Court

Period	Number of appointments	Period	Number of appointments
1790–94	3	1900–04	2
1795–99	4	1905–09	2
1800–04	2	1910–14	6
1805–09	2	1915–19	2
1810–14	2	1920–24	4
1815–19	0	1925–29	1
1820–24	1	1930–34	3
1825–29	2	1935–39	4
1830–34	1	1940–44	5
1835–39	5	1945–49	4
1840–44	1	1950–54	1
1845–49	3	1955–59	4
1950–54	2	1960–64	2
1855–59	1	1965–69	3
1860–64	5	1970–74	3
1865–69	0	1975–79	1
1870–74	4	1980–84	1
1875–79	1	1985–89	2
1880–84	4	1990–94	4
1885–89	3	1995–99	0
1890–94	4	2000–04	0
1895–99	2	2005–09	3

The mean is 2.477, so that on average 2.477 Supreme Court appointments are made in a five-year period. Here is the frequency distribution of these observations. The upper figure is the number of appointments; the lower figure, the number of periods in which there were that many appointments:

0	1	2	3	4	5	6
4	9	11	7	9	3	1

If the number of Supreme Court appointments is really given by a Poisson distribution with mean $\lambda = 2.477$, the predicted frequency is given by the formula $44 \times e^{-\lambda} \lambda^i / i!$ (since there are 44 five-year periods). Here are the values of the predicted frequencies:

0	1	2	3	4	5	6
3.695	9.153	11.337	9.362	5.798	2.873	1.186

We can now calculate the chi-square statistic:

$$\frac{(4 - 3.695)^2}{3.695} + \frac{(9 - 9.153)^2}{9.153} + \frac{(11 - 11.337)^2}{11.337} + \frac{(7 - 9.362)^2}{9.362} + \cdots$$

$$+ \frac{(9 - 5.798)^2}{5.798} + \frac{(3 - 2.873)^2}{2.873} + \frac{(1 - 1.186)^2}{1.186}$$

$$= 0.0252 + 0.0026 + 0.0100 + 0.5958 + 1.7685 + 0.0057 + 0.0292$$

$$= \text{test statistic} = 2.4369$$

It looks as though the observed frequencies match the predicted frequencies quite well. We have $n = 7$ categories, and we had to use the sample data to estimate the mean, so that leaves us with $7 - 1 - 1 = 5$ degrees of freedom. We can see from a chi-square table that a χ_5^2 random variable has a 95 percent chance of being less than 11.07, so the critical region occurs for values of the test statistic above 11.07. The observed value is well within this limit, so we will accept the hypothesis that the rate of Supreme Court appointments can be described by the Poisson distribution. (Note that this was a one-tailed test, since we only wanted to reject the hypothesis if the test statistic was larger than expected. If the test statistic is very small, that means that the predicted frequencies are very close to the observed frequencies.)

YOU SHOULD REMEMBER

1. The goodness-of-fit test using the chi-square statistic is used to test whether a particular distribution is appropriate for a given set of observations.

2. The chi-square statistic is based on the differences between the actual frequencies and the frequencies that would be expected to occur if the null hypothesis were true.

KNOW THE CONCEPTS

DO YOU KNOW THE BASICS?

Test your understanding of Chapter 14 by answering the following questions:

1. Is the chi-square test a one-tailed or a two-tailed test?

2. Can the value of a chi-square statistic ever be negative?

3. What does it mean if the value of a chi-square statistic is zero?

4. If the p value in a chi-square test is close to 0.05, what decision should you make?

5. If the p value in a chi-square test comes close to zero, what are the implications?

6. If you have developed a new medicine and you perform a chi-square test of that medicine, what do you hope is the result?

7. What if the people that took your medicine were sicker than the other people in the study? How does that affect your test? How can you avoid that?

8. How could you test whether or not a die is fair?

9. Suppose you observe that U.S. presidents elected in years ending in zero (such as 1960, 1940, 1920, and so on) are more likely to die in office than other presidents. Then you perform a chi-square test in which you reject the null hypothesis that the year of election has no effect on whether or not a president survives. What does this mean?

TERMS FOR STUDY

cell
chi-square test
contingency table
goodness-of-fit test

PRACTICAL APPLICATION

COMPUTATIONAL PROBLEMS

Given the following samples, test the hypothesis that the mean is as given:

1. Suppose that four new pesticides are being tested in a laboratory, with the following results:

Result	Type 1	Type 2	Type 3	Type 4	Total
Insects killed	139	100	73	98	410
Insects surviving	15	50	80	47	192
total tested	154	150	153	145	602

Is pesticide 1 significantly better than the rest?

2. Suppose five different meteorological theories are tested to see whether they predict the weather correctly. The results are as follows:

Result	Theory 1	Theory 2	Theory 3	Theory 4	Theory 5	Total
Reports correct	50	48	53	47	46	244
Reports incorrect	76	74	75	76	77	378
total reports	126	122	128	123	123	622

Is theory 3 significantly better than the rest?

3. Perform a goodness-of-fit test to see whether the normal distribution is appropriate for the heights of a sample of people you know.

4. Perform a goodness-of-fit test to see whether the Poisson distribution is appropriate for the number of phone calls that you receive at your house in a week.

5. Perform a goodness-of-fit test to see whether the uniform distribution is appropriate for the numbers that you roll on a die.

6. Test the hypothesis that there is no significant difference between groups *a*, *b*, *c*, and *d*:

	Group *a*	Group *b*	Group *c*	Group *d*
Number of successes	16	12	7	13
Number of failures	54	94	66	49

7. Divide your friends into categories by hair color and eye color. Perform a chi-square test to see whether there is a significant difference in eye color for people with different hair colors.

8. Perform a goodness-of-fit test to see whether the weights of a group of your friends fit the normal distribution.

In each exercise below you are given a table listing the results of a survey of some people in different occupational groups. Each exercise indicates the preferences of the people in the survey with regard to a particular item. For each exercise perform a chi-square test to see whether the preferences are independent of the groups.

9.

Favorite Color	Group 1	Group 2	Group 3
Red	16	8	20
Blue	48	21	54
Yellow	12	40	16

10.

Favorite Candidate	Group 1	Group 2	Group 3	Group 4
Smith	36	17	44	12
Jones	132	69	178	49

11.

Favorite Music	Group 1	Group 2	Group 3
Classical	26	16	13
Contemporary	58	91	30

12.

Favorite Fast Food	Group 1	Group 2	Group 3
Hamburger	30	16	17
Chicken	10	48	17

13.

Favorite Ice Cream	Group 1	Group 2	Group 3	Group 4
Vanilla	25	62	48	12
Strawberry	8	18	12	6
Chocolate	16	42	28	11

ANSWERS

KNOW THE CONCEPTS

1. It is a one-tailed test. The null hypothesis is rejected only if the test-statistic value is large.

2. No.

3. The predicted values always equal the actual values.

4. Reject the null hypothesis at the 5 percent significance level if the p value is less than 0.05. However, if it is close to that value, your test is not very decisive, so you should collect more observations.

5. If the p value is close to zero, you have high confidence that rejecting the null hypothesis is the right decision.

6. The null hypothesis states that the patients' conditions aren't affected by the medicine they take. If you developed the medicine, you will hope that the null hypothesis is rejected. However, don't let your hopes cloud your judgment as you perform the test.

7. The medicine would look less effective than it really is if the people that took it were sicker than the others in the study. If you use a random selection process to determine who takes what medicine, you can be guaranteed that your sample contains no systematic bias. You still might have bad luck with your random selection, but you can analyze the probability of that happening.

8. Perform a goodness-of-fit test to see if the numbers that appear fit the distribution, which has a 1/6 probability for taking on each number from 1 to 6.

9. There is a coincidental connection between the year of election and the probability of a president dying in office. However, if you state your hypothesis after you have observed this coincidence, it isn't very convincing that there is a real effect. To make sure you aren't mistaking coincidences for real effects, test your hypothesis with data that were collected after the hypothesis was stated, if possible.

PRACTICAL APPLICATION

1.
Type	Actual	Predicted
1		
Killed	139	104.8837
Survived	15	49.1163
2		
Killed	100	102.1595
Survived	50	47.8405
3		
Killed	73	104.2027
Survived	80	48.7973
4		
Killed	98	98.7542
Survived	47	46.2458

$$\text{Chi-square statistic} = \frac{(139 - 104.8837)^2}{104.8837} + \frac{(15 - 49.1163)^2}{49.1163}$$
$$+ \frac{(100 - 102.1595)^2}{102.1595} + \frac{(50 - 47.8405)^2}{47.8405}$$
$$+ \frac{(73 - 104.2027)^2}{104.2027} + \frac{(80 - 48.7973)^2}{48.7973}$$
$$+ \frac{(98 - 98.7542)^2}{98.7542} + \frac{(47 - 46.2458)^2}{46.2458}$$
$$= 64.251$$

Degrees of freedom = 3
Reject null hypothesis that there is no difference.

2.
Theory	Actual	Predicted
1		
Correct	50	51.9324
Incorrect	76	74.0676
2		
Correct	48	50.2838
Incorrect	74	71.7162

Theory	Actual	Predicted
3		
Correct	53	52.7568
Incorrect	75	75.2432
4		
Correct	47	38.3311
Incorrect	46	54.6689
5		
Correct	46	50.6959
Incorrect	77	72.3041

Chi-square statistic = 4.3759   Degrees of freedom = 4
Accept null hypothesis that there is no difference.

6.

Group	Actual	Predicted
A		
Success	16	10.8039
Failure	54	59.1961
B		
Success	12	16.3601
Failure	94	89.6399
C		
Success	7	11.2669
Failure	66	61.7331
D		
Success	13	9.5691
Failure	49	52.4309

Chi-square statistic = 7.6947   Degrees of freedom = 3
  The 95 percent critical value for a chi-square distribution with 3 degrees of freedom is 7.8, so at the 5 percent level we will accept the null hypothesis that there is no difference. However, note that the computed chi-square statistic is very close to the critical value.

9. Group	Actual	Predicted
1		
Red	16	14.2298
Blue	48	39.7787
Yellow	12	21.9915
2		
Red	8	12.9191
Blue	21	36.1149
Yellow	40	19.9660
3		
Red	20	16.8511
Blue	54	47.1064
Yellow	16	26.0426

Chi-square statistic = 40.2300   Degrees of freedom = 4
95 percent critical value = 9.48
Reject hypothesis that groups have same preferences.

10. Chi-square statistic = 0.1938   Degrees of freedom = 3
95 percent critical value = 7.8
Accept hypothesis that groups have same preferences.

11. Chi-square statistic = 8.0258   Degrees of freedom = 2
95 percent critical value = 5.99
Reject hypothesis that groups have same preferences.

12. Chi-square statistic = 25.1467   Degrees of freedom = 2
95 percent critical value = 5.99
Reject hypothesis that groups have same preferences.

13. Chi-square statistic = 1.7933   Degrees of freedom = 6
95 percent critical value = 12.59
Accept hypothesis that groups have same preferences.

15
ANALYSIS OF VARIANCE

KEY TERMS

analysis of variance a method for testing the hypothesis that several different groups all have the same mean

ANOVA table a table that summarizes the results of an analysis of variance calculation

two-way analysis of variance a test procedure that can be applied to a table of numbers in order to test two hypotheses: (1) there is no significant difference between the rows; and (2) there is no significant difference between the columns

---

TESTING FOR THE EQUALITY OF SEVERAL MEANS

Suppose that we have observed scores on a particular aptitude test for three different groups of 10 people each. The results were as follow:

Group *a*: 88, 92, 91, 89, 89, 86, 92, 86, 89, 89
Group *b*: 91, 92, 85, 94, 93, 87, 87, 92, 91, 89
Group *c*: 87, 88, 95, 88, 92, 87, 89, 88, 87, 88

The average scores for the three groups are close together. It seems reasonable to suppose that there is in fact no difference in aptitude between the groups, and that the observed difference in the average score has arisen solely by chance.

Suppose that we check the scores for three different groups and find these results:

Group *d*: 87, 94, 91, 89, 89, 84, 92, 86, 89, 89
Group *e*: 82, 76, 84, 79, 77, 84, 81, 69, 79, 74
Group *f*: 69, 79, 67, 64, 65, 69, 69, 64, 72, 66

In this case it seems clear that there is a real difference in aptitude between the three groups. In other words, we can reject the hypothesis that the observed differences between the groups arose solely by chance.

In both of these cases it was obvious whether or not there was a significant difference between the average scores for the three groups. However, in general it will be more difficult to tell if the observed difference in scores is significant or random. We need to develop a new method, called **analysis of variance**. For now, let's assume that we have $m = 3$ independent groups (call them group a, group b, and group c), and that there are n people in each group. Assume that we know that the aptitude scores for the people in each group are selected from a normal distribution, and assume that the variance of the distribution is the same for all three groups.

Let's say that μ_a is the unknown mean aptitude test score for group a, μ_b is the mean for group b, and μ_c is the mean for group c. Our mission is to test the null hypothesis:

$$\mu_a = \mu_b = \mu_c = \mu$$

In other words, the null hypothesis states that the mean score for each group is the same. The alternative hypothesis simply states that the means are not all the same.

First, one obvious thing to do is to calculate $\bar{a}$, $\bar{b}$, and $\bar{c}$ (the sample average for each sample). If $\bar{a}$, $\bar{b}$, and $\bar{c}$ are close to each other, we will be more willing to accept the hypothesis that μ_a, μ_b, and μ_c are all equal. We can calculate $\bar{x}$, the average for all the numbers:

$$\bar{x} = \frac{\bar{a} + \bar{b} + \bar{c}}{m} = \frac{\bar{a} + \bar{b} + \bar{c}}{3}$$

We can also calculate the sample variance for these three averages (we'll call that variance S^{*2}):

$$S^{*2} = \frac{(\bar{a} - \bar{x})^2 + (\bar{b} - \bar{x})^2 + (\bar{c} - \bar{x})^2}{m - 1}$$

The larger S^{*2} is, the *less* likely we will be to accept the no-difference null hypothesis.

We should also look at the sample variance for each individual sample:

$$S_a^2 = \sum_{i=1}^{n} \frac{(a_i - \bar{a})^2}{n - 1}, \quad S_b^2 = \sum_{i=1}^{n} \frac{(b_i - \bar{b})^2}{n - 1}, \quad S_c^2 = \sum_{i=1}^{n} \frac{(c_i - \bar{c})^2}{n - 1}$$

It will turn out to be useful to calculate the average of the three sample variances (call it S^2):

$$S^2 = \frac{s_a{}^2 + s_b{}^2 + s_c{}^2}{3}$$

The larger these three variances are, the more likely we are to see $\bar{a}$, $\bar{b}$, and $\bar{c}$ spread out, even if they really do come from distributions with the same mean. For example, suppose that the observed values of $\bar{a}$, $\bar{b}$, and $\bar{c}$ are 500, 400, and 450. If $s_a{}^2 = s_b{}^2 = s_c{}^2 = 1$, we know right away that it is extremely unlikely that $\bar{a}$, $\bar{b}$, and $\bar{c}$ could have the observed values if they really did come from distributions with the same mean. On the other hand, if $s_a{}^2 = s_b{}^2 = s_c{}^2 = 10,000$, we would be quite likely to see $\bar{a}$, $\bar{b}$, and $\bar{c}$ spread out by this much even if the null hypothesis is true. Therefore, the larger S^2 is, the *more* likely we will be to accept the null hypothesis.

We will calculate the following statistic (call it F):

$$F = \frac{nS^{*2}}{S^2}$$

Recall from the central limit theorem that the variance of $\bar{x}$ is σ^2/n, where σ^2 is the variance of the population. Thus the numerator of this fraction is an approximation for $n\sigma^2/n = \sigma^2$, and the denominator is also an approximation for σ^2. If the means are truly equal, then F should be close to 1. If it is much larger than 1 (it can be shown that it won't get much smaller), then we reject our null hypothesis.

This F statistic will have $m - 1$ degrees of freedom in the numerator (since we calculate a sample variance from m means for it) and $m(n - 1)$ degrees of freedom in the denominator (since we calculate a sample variance of n items in each of the m groups). The F distribution is described in Chapter 8 and Table A3–6 lists some values for the cumulative distribution function.

In the examples we discussed earlier, we had $m = 3$ and $n = 10$. Therefore, the F statistic will have 2 and 27 degrees of freedom. Table A3–6 shows that this type of F statistic has a 95 percent chance of being less than about 3.3. Therefore, if the observed F-statistic value is greater than 3.3, we will reject the null hypothesis; otherwise we will accept the null hypothesis.

In the first example, the F statistic is $4.133/6.693 = .6175$. Just as we suspected all along, we should accept the hypothesis. In the second example, the F value is $1,061/16.996 = 62.426$, so we should reject the hypothesis.

These calculations can be performed in Excel using the Data Analysis tool ANOVA procedure. All you need to do is identify the range containing the input data and tell Excel where to put the results.

General Procedure for an Analysis-of-Variance Test

(Assume that you have m groups, each with n members.)

1. Calculate the sample average for each group:

$$\bar{a} = \frac{a_1 + a_2 + \cdots + a_n}{n}$$

$$\bar{b} = \frac{b_1 + b_2 + \cdots + b_n}{n}$$

$$\bar{c} = \frac{c_1 + c_2 + \cdots + c_n}{n}$$

and so on.

2. Calculate the average of all the averages:

$$\bar{x} = \frac{\bar{a} + \bar{b} + \bar{c} + \cdots}{m}$$

3. Calculate the sample variance of the averages:

$$S^{*2} = \frac{(\bar{a} - \bar{x})^2 + (\bar{b} - \bar{x})^2 + (\bar{c} - \bar{x})^2 + \cdots}{m - 1}$$

4. Calculate the sample variance for each group:

$$s_a^{\,2} = \frac{(a_1 - \bar{a})^2 + (a_2 - \bar{a})^2 + \cdots + (a_n - \bar{a})^2}{n - 1}$$

$$s_b^{\,2} = \frac{(b_1 - \bar{b})^2 + (b_2 - \bar{b})^2 + \cdots + (b_n - \bar{b})^2}{n - 1}$$

$$s_c^{\,2} = \frac{(c_1 - \bar{c})^2 + (c_2 - \bar{c})^2 + \cdots + (c_n - \bar{c})^2}{n - 1}$$

and so on.

5. Calculate the average of all of the sample variances:

$$S^2 = \frac{s_a^2 + s_b^2 + s_c^2 + \cdots}{m}$$

6. Calculate the value of the F statistic:

$$F = \frac{nS^{*2}}{S^2}$$

7. Look in Table A3–6 to find the critical value for an F distribution with $m - 1$ and $m(n - 1)$ degrees of freedom.

8. If the observed value of the F statistic is greater than the critical value, reject the null hypothesis. Otherwise accept it.

YOU SHOULD REMEMBER

1. The analysis of variance procedure is used to test whether several groups of observations all come from distributions with the same mean.

2. In analysis of variance an F statistic is calculated.

3. If the null hypothesis is true and the means for all the groups really are the same, then the F statistic will have an F distribution.

4. If the calculated F-statistic value is larger than the critical value found in Table A3–6, then the null hypothesis (that the mean of each group is the same) is rejected.

SUM OF SQUARES

The analysis of variance approach can be further understood by looking at the sum of squared deviations (or the **sum of squares**). Again assume that we have m groups, each with n members. Each group has been treated differently in some manner, and our goal is to see if the treatments really made any difference. For example, we may have groups of people who were given different medicines. We will use x_{ij} to represent the ith item in the jth group. Note that we need two subscripts to identify each element uniquely. For example, if we have $m = 3$ groups with $n = 5$ members:

Group 1	Group 2	Group 3
16	38	19
13	21	14
36	36	17
29	39	15
18	26	12

we can represent each element like this:

$$
\begin{array}{lll}
x_{11} = 16 & x_{12} = 38 & x_{13} = 19 \\
x_{21} = 13 & x_{22} = 21 & x_{23} = 14 \\
x_{31} = 36 & x_{32} = 36 & x_{33} = 17 \\
x_{41} = 29 & x_{42} = 39 & x_{43} = 15 \\
x_{51} = 18 & x_{52} = 26 & x_{53} = 12
\end{array}
$$

To represent the sum of all of the items, we need to use two sigmas:

$$
T = \sum_{i=1}^{n} \sum_{j=1}^{m} x_{ij}
$$

This expression can be broken down like this:

$$
\begin{aligned}
T &= \sum_{i=1}^{n} (x_{i1} + x_{i2} + \cdots + x_{im}) \\
&= \quad x_{11} + x_{12} + \cdots + x_{1m} + \\
&\qquad x_{21} + x_{22} + \cdots + x_{2m} + \\
&\qquad \cdots \qquad\qquad + \\
&\qquad x_{n1} + x_{n2} + \cdots + x_{nm}
\end{aligned}
$$

For our example:

$$
\begin{aligned}
T &= 16 + 38 + 19 + \\
&\quad 13 + 21 + 14 + \\
&\quad 36 + 36 + 17 + \\
&\quad 29 + 39 + 15 + \\
&\quad 18 + 26 + 12 \\
&= 349
\end{aligned}
$$

We will use $\bar{\bar{x}}$ (x double bar) to represent the overall mean of all the elements (we could call it the **grand mean**):

$$\bar{\bar{x}} = \frac{T}{mn}$$

$$= \frac{\sum_{i=1}^{n}\sum_{j=1}^{m}x_{ij}}{mn}$$

$$= \frac{349}{15} = 23.267 \text{ for our example}$$

· TOTAL SUM OF SQUARES

For each element in the list we can calculate how far away it is from the grand mean $\bar{\bar{x}}$:

$$(\text{distance from } x_{ij} \text{ to } \bar{\bar{x}}) = |x_{ij} - \bar{\bar{x}}|$$

As you may have begun to suspect, we would like to square this distance:

$$(\text{squared distance from } x_{ij} \text{ to } \bar{\bar{x}}) = (x_{ij} - \bar{\bar{x}})^2$$

and then add all of the squared distances:

$$\text{TSS} = \sum_{i=1}^{n}\sum_{j=1}^{m}(x_{ij} - \bar{\bar{x}})^2$$

We will call this quantity the **total sum of squares**, or **TSS**. For our example we can calculate:

$$
\begin{aligned}
\text{TSS} = {} & (16 - 23.267)^2 + (38 - 23.267)^2 + (19 - 23.267)^2 + \\
& (13 - 23.267)^2 + (21 - 23.267)^2 + (14 - 23.267)^2 + \\
& (36 - 23.267)^2 + (36 - 23.267)^2 + (17 - 23.267)^2 + \\
& (29 - 23.267)^2 + (39 - 23.267)^2 + (15 - 23.267)^2 + \\
& (18 - 23.267)^2 + (26 - 23.267)^2 + (12 - 23.267)^2 \\
= {} & 1358.93
\end{aligned}
$$

We will look at several different sum of squares statistics. Note that a sum of squares is similar to a variance except that there is no division by n. The variance is calculated from the sum of squares about the mean, but we will see that there are several other types of sums of squares.

To analyze the total sum of squares, we need to break it into two parts. We know that, if the null hypothesis is true, the population mean is the same for each group and the deviation of any one element from the grand mean arises only by chance. On the other hand, if the population means are different, there are two reasons why an individual element may deviate from the grand mean: (1) because the mean of its own group is different from the overall population mean, and (2) because there is chance variation within its own group. Therefore, we will split the total sum of squares into two parts: the part arising from deviations of individual elements from their group mean, and the part arising from deviations of the group means from the grand mean. We can write the TSS formula like this:

$$\text{TSS} = \sum_{i=1}^{n} \sum_{j=1}^{m} (x_{ij} - \bar{\bar{x}})^2$$

$$= \sum_{i=1}^{n} \sum_{j=1}^{m} [(x_{ij} - \bar{x}_j) + (\bar{x}_j - \bar{\bar{x}})]^2$$

We will use $\bar{x}_j$ to stand for the sample average of group j. We have not done anything to our original expression but add and subtract $\bar{x}_j$. Now we have

$$\text{TSS} = \sum_{i=1}^{n} \sum_{j=1}^{m} [(x_{ij} - \bar{x}_j)^2 + (\bar{x}_j - \bar{\bar{x}})^2 + 2(x_{ij} - \bar{x}_j)(\bar{x}_j - \bar{\bar{x}})]$$

It turns out quite conveniently that, when the double summation is taken over the last term, the result is always zero. Hence we are left with:

$$\text{TSS} = \sum_{i=1}^{n} \sum_{j=1}^{m} [(x_{ij} - \bar{x}_j)^2 + (\bar{x}_j - \bar{\bar{x}})^2]$$

We can break that up into two double summations:

$$\text{TSS} = \sum_{i=1}^{n} \sum_{j=1}^{m} (x_{ij} - \bar{x}_j)^2 + \sum_{i=1}^{n} \sum_{j=1}^{m} (\bar{x}_j - \bar{\bar{x}})^2$$

Since the last term does not contain anything that depends on i, we can replace the summation $\sum_{i=1}^{n}$ by simply multiplying by n:

$$\text{TSS} = \sum_{i=1}^{n} \sum_{j=1}^{m} (x_{ij} - \bar{x}_j)^2 + n \sum_{j=1}^{m} (\bar{x}_j - \bar{\bar{x}})^2$$

• *ERROR SUM OF SQUARES*

We have now broken the total sum of squares into two components. The first part represents the deviation of each element from its group mean. Since we can think of these differences as arising because of unknown random factors (called statistical error), we will call this the **error sum of squares**, or **ERSS**. Then

$$\text{ERSS} = \sum_{i=1}^{n} \sum_{j=1}^{m} (x_{ij} - \bar{x}_j)^2$$

• *TREATMENT SUM OF SQUARES*

The second part of the total sum of squares represents the deviation of each group mean from the grand mean. We can think of these deviations as arising because the groups were given different treatments, so we will call this the **treatment sum of squares**, or **TRSS**. Then

$$TRSS = n \sum_{j=1}^{m} (\bar{x}_j - \bar{\bar{x}})^2$$

We can see that TSS = ERSS + TRSS. The larger the treatment sum of squares becomes, the less likely we will be to accept the null hypothesis that the treatments don't matter.

• *MEAN SQUARE VARIANCE*

Each sum-of-squares statistic has an associated quantity called its degrees of freedom. The degrees of freedom of TRSS is $m - 1$. The degrees of freedom of ERSS is $m(n - 1)$. (We are adding together m different sum of squares for each sample. Each individual sum of squares has $n - 1$ degrees of freedom.) When a sum of squares is divided by its degrees of freedom, the result is called a **mean square variance**:

$$(\text{treatment mean square variance}) = \frac{TRSS}{m - 1}$$

$$(\text{error mean square variance}) = \frac{ERSS}{m(n - 1)}$$

When we take the treatment mean square variance divided by the error mean square variance, then the result is exactly the same F statistic we used before:

$$F = \frac{\dfrac{TRSS}{m - 1}}{\dfrac{ERSS}{m(n - 1)}}$$

For our example, we have:

$$TRSS = 694.533, \quad m - 1 = 2$$
$$ERSS = 664.400, \quad m(n - 1) = 12$$
$$F = \frac{\dfrac{694.533}{2}}{\dfrac{664.400}{12}} = 6.272$$

If the null hypothesis is true and the treatments do not matter, then the F statistic will have an F distribution with 2 and 12 degrees of freedom. The critical value for a 5 percent test is 3.9, so in this case we can reject the null hypothesis.

• *ANOVA TABLE*

The information from the test can be summarized in a table known as an **ANOVA table**. (ANOVA is short for "analysis of variance.") The ANOVA table for our example looks like this:

Source of Variation	Sum of Squares	Degrees of Freedom	Mean Square Variance	F Ratio
Between means (treatment)	694.533	2	347.267	6.272
Within sample (error)	664.400	12	55.367	
total	1,358.933	14		

The table arranges the information about the sums of squares, their degrees of freedom, and the F statistic. Note that the total sum of squares has $mn - 1 = 14$ degrees of freedom, which is the sum of the degrees of freedom for the TRSS and ERSS.

The general formula for the ANOVA table looks like this:

ANOVA Table for m Different Groups Each with n Members

Source of Variation	Sum of Squares	Degrees of Freedom	Mean Square Variance	F Ratio
Between means (treatment)	$TRSS = n\sum_{j=1}^{m}(\bar{x}_j - \bar{\bar{x}})^2$	$m - 1$	$\dfrac{TRSS}{m-1}$	$\dfrac{TRSS/(m-1)}{ERSS/[m(n-1)]}$
Within samples (error)	$ERSS = \sum_{i=1}^{n}\sum_{j=1}^{m}(x_{ij} - \bar{x}_j)^2$	$m(n-1)$	$\dfrac{ERSS}{m(n-1)}$	
total	$TSS = TRSS + ERSS$	$mn - 1$		

We can use Excel to perform the analysis of variance test. Enter the data into three different columns. Put the labels "A," "B," and "C" at the top of the appropriate columns. Then call for the tools menu, then data analysis, then ANOVA. Highlight the range with your data (including the labels), and check the "labels in first row" box. Now click OK, and you'll see the results (The original data is not shown here to save space.):

Anova: Single Factor
SUMMARY

Groups	Count	Sum	Average	Variance
A	10	891	89.1	4.544444444
B	10	901	90.1	8.766666667
C	10	889	88.9	6.766666667

ANOVA

Source of Variation	SS	df	MS	F	P-value	F crit
Between Groups	8.266666667	2	4.133333333	0.617598229	0.546682068	3.354131195
Within Groups	180.7	27	6.692592593			
Total	188.9666667	29				

This example shows the results for the first example on page 349.

• TWO CONSIDERATIONS IN USING ANALYSIS OF VARIANCE TESTS

Here are two things to keep in mind when using analysis of variance tests. First, remember that the analysis of variance model assumes that the variance is the same for each group. If you observe that the sample variances of the different groups are markedly different, then the analysis of variance approach is not reliable.

Second, if you decide to reject the null hypothesis, then you are sure that the means of the groups are not all the same. However, you don't know whether all of the means are unequal, or whether they are all equal except for one particular mean that is different from the others, or whether there is perhaps some other pattern for the means. You will need to perform further investigations to determine exactly how the means differ.

• ANALYSIS OF VARIANCE WITH UNEQUAL SAMPLE SIZES

There may be times when the samples we have are not all the same size. In that case the analysis of variance formulas become more complicated, but we can still use our analysis of sums of squares to extend the applicability of the method. Suppose we have m different samples, with n_1 elements in sample

1, n_2 elements in sample 2, and so on, up to n_m elements in sample m. We will let x_{ij} represent the ith element in the jth sample. The total number of elements in all of the samples will be N:

$$N = n_1 + n_2 + \cdots + n_m = \sum_{j=1}^{m} n_j$$

We can calculate the mean for each group:

$$\bar{x}_j = \frac{\sum_{i=1}^{n_j} x_{ij}}{n_j}$$

and the grand mean:

$$\bar{\bar{x}} = \frac{\sum_{j=1}^{m} \sum_{i=1}^{n_j} x_{ij}}{N}$$

Note that the double summation is a bit more complicated now. We can calculate the total sum of squares:

$$\text{TSS} = \sum_{j=1}^{m} \sum_{i=1}^{n_j} (x_{ij} - \bar{\bar{x}})^2$$

and again we can partition the total sum of squares:

$$\text{TSS} = \sum_{j=1}^{m} \sum_{i=1}^{n_j} (x_{ij} - \bar{x}_j)^2 + \sum_{j=1}^{m} n_j (\bar{x}_j - \bar{\bar{x}})^2$$

The first part is the error sum of squares:

$$\text{ERSS} = \sum_{j=1}^{m} \sum_{i=1}^{n_j} (x_{ij} - \bar{x}_j)^2$$

which has $N - m$ degrees of freedom. The second part is the treatment sum of squares:

$$\text{TRSS} = \sum_{j=1}^{m} n_j (\bar{x}_j - \bar{\bar{x}})^2$$

which has $m - 1$ degrees of freedom. Now we can calculate the F statistic:

$$F = \frac{\dfrac{\text{TRSS}}{m-1}}{\dfrac{\text{ERSS}}{N-m}}$$

which has $m - 1$ degrees of freedom in the numerator and $N - m$ degrees of freedom in the denominator.

YOU SHOULD REMEMBER

1. The total sum of squares (TSS) for a group of numbers consists of the sum of the squares of the deviations of all the elements from the grand mean.

2. In analysis of variance the total sum of squares is divided into two parts: the treatment sum of squares (TRSS) and the error sum of squares (ERSS).

3. The treatment sum of squares indicates the effects of the differences between the groups.

4. The null hypothesis that there is no difference between the groups is more likely to be rejected when the treatment sum of squares is large relative to the error sum of squares.

5. The analysis of variance results can be summarized in an ANOVA table (see page 358).

TWO-WAY ANALYSIS OF VARIANCE

Consider a situation where we need to test the effectiveness of three different types of factory-air-pollution-control devices. To conduct a test we must install one of the devices on a factory smokestack for a test period of 1 week. Six different factories are available to conduct tests. The factories are all very similar, but we cannot be sure that they are exactly the same. Therefore, it would not be a good idea to design a test like this:

> Put device *a* on factories 1 and 2 during the test period.
> Put device *b* on factories 3 and 4 during the test period.
> Put device *c* on factories 5 and 6 during the test period.

Suppose that factories 1 and 2 happen to produce less pollution than the other factories. In that case this test procedure would tend to make device *a* look better than the other devices even if they were all the same. To be complete, therefore, we must install each device for a test period on each factory. Our table of measurements for the pollution looks like this:

Factory	Device a	Device b	Device c
1	50.8	53.0	49.7
2	49.5	49.2	49.1
3	51.5	51.7	49.6
4	48.3	49.8	49.3
5	48.8	48.1	47.1
6	48.4	52.2	47.9

We could start by assuming that all six factories are identical and that the output of pollution from each device follows a normal distribution as follows:

$$\text{device } a: \text{mean} = \mu_a, \quad \text{variance} = \sigma^2$$

$$\text{device } b: \text{mean} = \mu_b, \quad \text{variance} = \sigma^2$$

$$\text{device } c: \text{mean} = \mu_c, \quad \text{variance} = \sigma^2$$

Now we can employ the standard analysis of variance procedure to test the null hypothesis that there is no difference between the devices:

$$H_0: \mu_a = \mu_b = \mu_c$$

The ANOVA table is as follows:

Source of Variation	Sum of Squares	Degrees of Freedom	Mean Square Variance	F Ratio
Between means (treatment)	10.763	2	5.382	2.472
Within samples (error)	32.657	15	2.177	
total	43.420	17		

The 5 percent critical value for an F distribution with 2 and 15 degrees of freedom is 3.68. Since the observed value is less than the critical value, we can accept the null hypothesis that there is no difference between the devices.

However, we still should have some nagging doubts. What if the factories really are not identical? What if some of the observed variation in the pollution data came about because of differences in the factories? In our ANOVA table we have assumed that all of the variation not explained by differences in the control devices arises because of statistical error—that is, random, mysterious forces that we know nothing about. It would be very helpful if we could determine how much of the variation might be explainable by differences in the factories. That line of thought leads us to a new method: **two-way analysis of variance**. This new method provides an added bonus: it also allows us to test the hypothesis that the factories are identical.

In general, suppose we have m different levels of the first type of treatment and n different levels of the second type of treatment. In our case, the first type of treatment represents the difference in air-pollution-control devices (so $m = 3$) and the second type of treatment represents the different factories (so $n = 6$). We have a total of mn different possible levels of the combined treatments, and we will assume that we have one observation for each possibility. In our case, then, we have $3 \times 6 = 18$ observations. (In some cases you will have or will need more than one observation per treatment possibility, and in other cases you may not have observations for all of the possibilities. More advanced books can tell you what to do in these cases.) We will arrange the data in an array with m columns and n rows, using x_{ij} to represent the element in row i and column j:

m levels of first treatment

		1	2	$\cdots$	m
	1	x_{11}	x_{12}		x_{1m}
n levels	2	x_{21}	x_{22}		x_{2m}
of second	.				
treatment	.				
	.				
	n	x_{n1}	x_{n2}		x_{nm}

In theory we will assume that each observation consists of the sum of four different effects:

$$x_{ij} = \mu + \mu_{ri} + \mu_{cj} + e_{ij}$$

where μ represents the overall mean, and μ_{ri} represents the specific effect that row i has on all observations in that row. We put the r in the expression μ_{ri} to remind us that it represents row i. If the different levels of the second treatment have no effect, then all of these row effects μ_{r1} to μ_{rn} are zero. Suppose, however, that in our example factory 1 pollutes a little more than the average and factory 2 pollutes a little less than the average. The μ_{r1} will be a positive number and μ_{r2} will be a negative number.

Likewise, μ_{cj} represents the specific effect of column j. If the three pollution-control devices are the same, then $\mu_{c1} = \mu_{c2} = \mu_{c3} = 0$. On the other hand, if device 1 lets a higher than average level of pollution escape, then μ_{c1} will be positive.

There still will be mysterious factors (other than the device or the factory) that affect the level of pollution. Therefore we need to include the random error term e_{ij} to take all of these other factors into account.

We can calculate the grand mean of all the observations:

$$\bar{\bar{x}} = \frac{\sum_{i=1}^{n}\sum_{j=1}^{m} x_{ij}}{mn}$$

and once again we can calculate the total sum of squares:

$$\text{TSS} = \sum_{i=1}^{n}\sum_{j=1}^{m}(x_{ij} - \bar{\bar{x}})^2$$

• ROW, COLUMN, AND ERROR SUM OF SQUARES

Now we need to divide TSS into three parts: the part that can be explained by the effects of the columns, the part that can be explained by the effects of the rows, and the remaining part that can be explained only by error. We'll use ROWSS to represent the row sum of squares, COLSS to represent the column sum of squares, and ERSS to represent the error sum of squares. Then

$$\text{TSS} = \text{ROWSS} + \text{COLSS} + \text{ERSS}$$

The formula for the column sum of squares is basically the same as the formula for the treatment sum of squares with one-way analysis of variance:

$$\text{COLSS} = n\sum_{j=1}^{m}(\bar{x}_{cj} - \bar{\bar{x}})^2$$

In this formula $\bar{x}_{cj}$ represents the average of all the elements in column j. The formula for ROWSS looks very similar:

$$\text{ROWSS} = m\sum_{i=1}^{n}(\bar{x}_{ri} - \bar{\bar{x}})^2$$

where $\bar{x}_{ri}$ is the average of all the elements in row i. If the factories really are identical, then there is no reason for the row averages to be significantly different from $\bar{\bar{x}}$, so ROWSS will be small. COLSS has $m - 1$ degrees of freedom, and ROWSS has $n - 1$ degrees of freedom.

To get the error sum of squares, we need to subtract three parts from x_{ij}. We will use $\bar{\bar{x}}$ to estimate the overall population mean, $\bar{x}_{cj} - \bar{\bar{x}}$ to estimate the specific effect of column j, and $\bar{x}_{ri} - \bar{\bar{x}}$ to estimate the specific effect of row i. Then

$$\text{ERSS} = \sum_{i=1}^{n}\sum_{j=1}^{m}[x_{ij} - \bar{\bar{x}} - (\bar{x}_{cj} - \bar{\bar{x}}) - (\bar{x}_{ri} - \bar{\bar{x}})]^2$$

ERSS has $(m - 1)(n - 1)$ degrees of freedom.

Now we can perform the calculations for our example. We need to calculate the average of each row and column:

Factory	Device a	Device b	Device c	Average
1	50.8	53.0	49.7	51.167
2	49.5	49.2	49.1	49.267
3	51.5	51.7	49.6	50.933
4	48.3	49.8	49.3	49.133
5	48.8	48.1	47.1	48.000
6	48.4	52.2	47.9	49.500
overage	49.55	50.667	48.783	49.667

The grand mean is $\overline{\overline{x}} = 49.667$. Now we can calculate:

$$\begin{aligned}
\text{TSS} = &(50.8 - 49.667)^2 + (53.0 - 49.667)^2 + (49.7 - 49.667)^2 \\
&+ (49.5 - 49.667)^2 + (49.2 - 49.667)^2 + (49.1 - 49.667)^2 \\
&+ (51.5 - 49.667)^2 + (51.7 - 49.667)^2 + (49.6 - 49.667)^2 \\
&+ (48.3 - 49.667)^2 + (49.8 - 49.667)^2 + (49.3 - 49.667)^2 \\
&+ (48.8 - 49.667)^2 + (48.1 - 49.667)^2 + (47.1 - 49.667)^2 \\
&+ (48.4 - 49.667)^2 + (52.2 - 49.667)^2 + (47.9 - 49.667)^2 \\
= &\ 43.4
\end{aligned}$$

$$\begin{aligned}
\text{COLSS} &= 6 \times [(49.55 - 49.667)^2 + (50.667 - 49.667)^2 + (48.783 - 49.667)^2] \\
&= 10.8
\end{aligned}$$

$$\begin{aligned}
\text{ROWSS} &= 3 \times [(51.167 - 49.667)^2 + (49.267 - 49.667)^2 + (50.933 - 49.667)^2 \\
&\quad + (49.133 - 49.667)^2 + (48 - 49.667)^2 + (49.5 - 49.667)^2] \\
&= 21.3
\end{aligned}$$

$$\text{ERSS} = 43.4 - 10.8 - 21.3 = 11.3$$

• *TWO-FACTOR ANOVA TABLE*

Now we can construct an ANOVA table. The two-factor ANOVA table is very similar to the one-factor table. The only difference is that we now have another source of variation. We will include the sum of squares for the row along with the degrees of freedom and the mean square variance.

Two-factor ANOVA Table

Source of Variation	Sum of Squares	Degrees of Freedom	Mean Square Variance	F Ratio
Treatment 1 effect: columns (control devices)	10.763	2	5.382	4.746
Treatment 2 effect: rows (factories)	21.313	5	4.263	3.758
Error	11.343	10	1.134	
total	43.420	17		

Note that the total sum of squares and the sum of squares resulting from the different control devices are the same here, as they were in the one-way ANOVA table presented earlier. The difference is that now the error sum of squares is much smaller because a large part of the sum of squares previously attributed to error is now attributed to the effects of the different factories. We now have two F-statistic values. The first F statistic tests the null hypothesis that there is no difference between the columns. It is equal to

$(F$ statistic for columns$)$

$$= \frac{(\text{column sum of squares})/(\text{column SS degrees of freedom})}{(\text{error sum of squares})/(\text{error SS degrees of freedom})}$$

$$= \frac{\dfrac{\text{COLSS}}{m-1}}{\dfrac{\text{ERSS}}{(m-1)(n-1)}}$$

The second F statistic tests the hypothesis that there is no difference between the rows:

$(F$ statistic for rows$)$

$$= \frac{(\text{row sum of squares})/(\text{row SS degrees of freedom})}{(\text{error sum of squares})/(\text{error SS degrees of freedom})}$$

$$= \frac{\dfrac{\text{ROWSS}}{n-1}}{\dfrac{\text{ERSS}}{(m-1)(n-1)}}$$

Remember that our one-factor ANOVA table indicated that there was no difference between the three devices. Now the two-factor table gives us a clearer story. The F statistic for the columns has 2 and 10 degrees of freedom, and the 5 percent critical value from the F table is 4.1. The calculated value is greater than the critical value, so we can reject the null hypothesis that all columns are the same. Likewise, the F statistic for the rows has 5 and 10 degrees of freedom, for which the critical value is 3.3. Hence we can also reject the second null hypothesis, and we can conclude that there is a difference between the factories.

The problem with the one-factor test arose because the factories themselves added much variability. At that time we viewed all that variability as being random. There was so much random variability that it obscured the fact that the devices really were different. With the two-factor table we can separate the effects of the different factories from the effects of the different devices.

We can find alternative formulas for the sums of squares that are sometimes more convenient for calculation purposes.

Two-way Analysis of Variance

1. Let $N = mn$ be the number of values for x, T_x be the sum of all values of x, T_{x^2} be the sum of the squares of all values of x, T_{ri} be the sum of row i, and T_{cj} be the sum of column j:

$$T_x = \sum_{i=1}^{n}\sum_{j=1}^{m} x_{ij}, \quad T_{x^2} = \sum_{i=1}^{n}\sum_{j=1}^{m} x_{ij}^{2},$$

$$T_{ri} = \sum_{j=1}^{m} x_{ij}, \quad T_{cj} = \sum_{j=1}^{n} x_{ij}$$

2. Then calculate:

$$T_r^2 = \sum_{i=1}^{n} T_{ri}^2 \quad \text{(sum of squares of row totals)}$$

$$T_c^2 = \sum_{j=1}^{m} T_{cj}^2 \quad \text{(sum of squares of column totals)}$$

3. Now use these formulas:

$$TSS = T_{x^2} - \frac{(T_x)^2}{N}$$

$$COLSS = \frac{T_c^2}{n} - \frac{(T_x)^2}{N}$$

$$ROWSS = \frac{T_r^2}{m} - \frac{(T_x)^2}{N}$$

$$ERSS = T_{x^2} - \frac{T_c^2}{n} - \frac{T_r^2}{m} + \frac{(T_x)^2}{N}$$

Here is an example of the summary formulas. Our data matrix is as follows:

		First Treatment (3 levels)		
		1	2	3
	1	18	14	16
Second	2	56	59	53
treatment	3	46	48	50
(5 levels)	4	100	90	95
	5	28	31	25

We can clearly see from this table that there is much more variability between the rows than there is between the columns, so we can guess in advance how the ANOVA result will come out. We need to calculate these totals:

	1	2	3	Total
1	18	14	16	48
2	56	59	53	168
3	46	48	50	144
4	100	90	95	285
5	28	31	25	84
Total	248	242	239	729

Therefore, $T_x = 729$.
Now we can calculate:

$$T_c^2 = 248^2 + 242^2 + 239^2 = 177,189$$
$$T_r^2 = 48^2 + 168^2 + 144^2 + 285^2 + 84^2 = 139,545$$

We also need to calculate T_{x^2}:

$$T_{x^2} = 18^2 + 14^2 + 16^2 + 56^2 + 59^2 + 53^2$$
$$+ 46^2 + 48^2 + 50^2 + 100^2 + 90^2 + 95^2$$
$$+ 28^2 + 31^2 + 25^2$$
$$= 46,617$$

Now we can use the formulas:

$$TSS = 46,617 - \frac{729^2}{15} = 11,187.6$$

$$COLSS = \frac{177,189}{5} - \frac{729^2}{15} = 8.4$$

$$ROWSS = \frac{139,545}{3} - \frac{729^2}{15} = 11,085.6$$

$$ERSS = 46.617 - \frac{177,189}{5} - \frac{139,545}{3} + \frac{729^2}{15} = 93.6$$

Here is the ANOVA table. (Use Excel/Data Analysis/Anova Two-Factor Without Replication.)

Source of Variation	Sum of Squares	Degrees of Freedom	Mean Square Variance	F Ratio
Columns	8.4	2	4.2	0.359
Rows	11,085.6	4	2,771.4	236.872
Error	93.6	8	11.7	
total	11,187.6	14		

We can clearly see that the variation between the rows is significant while the variation between the columns is not.

YOU SHOULD REMEMBER

The two-way analysis of variance procedure is used to test these two hypotheses about an array of numbers;

null hypothesis 1: there is no significant difference between the columns in the array

null hypothesis 2: there is no significant difference between the rows in the array

KNOW THE CONCEPTS

DO YOU KNOW THE BASICS?

Test your understanding of Chapter 15 by answering the following questions:
For questions 1–5, consider normal (one-way) analysis of variance.

1. Explain intuitively why your likelihood of accepting the null hypothesis depends on the relation between the sample averages for all the groups involved.

2. Explain intuitively why your likelihood of accepting the null hypothesis depends on the degree of dispersion within each group.

3. If you decide to reject the null hypothesis, what conclusion can you reach about the population means?

4. What assumption does the analysis of variance procedure make about the variance of each population?

5. How would the analysis of variance results be affected if you doubled the size of each sample?

6. When do you apply the two-way analysis of variance procedure?

7. Could you apply two-way analysis of variance to the test score example presented in the chapter?

8. Suppose a situation really calls for two-way analysis of variance, but you use regular one-way analysis of variance instead. How will your results be affected?

TERMS FOR STUDY

analysis of variance	sum of squares
ANOVA table	total sum of squares (TSS)
error sum of squares (ERSS)	treatment sum of squares (TRSS)
grand mean	two-way analysis of variance
mean square variance	

PRACTICAL APPLICATION

COMPUTATIONAL PROBLEMS

Here are two simple problems for you to perform an analysis of variance test. See the book's web page for more examples of problems with data that you can paste into Excel.

1. A1	B1	C1	D1
4	8	12	16
6	6	10	18
5	9	15	20
3	7	11	15

2. A2	B2	C2	D2
9	10	5	7
6	5	3	10
8	7	9	12
4	4	8	6

ANSWERS

KNOW THE CONCEPTS

1. If the sample averages are close together, you will be more likely to accept the null hypothesis that the means are all the same.

2. If there is greater spread within each group, you will be more likely to accept the null hypothesis, because the observed difference between the sample averages is more likely to have occurred randomly even if the means are all the same.

3. You can conclude that the means of the different groups are not all the same, but you need to investigate further to determine the exact relation between the different means.

4. It assumes the variances are all the same.

5. If you have larger samples, you can say with more confidence that the observed differences (if any) among the sample averages arose because the population means are different, not because of random factors.

6. The two-way analysis of variance procedure is applied when there are two separate factors that affect each observation and you generally have one observation for each possible combination of the two factors.

7. No. The two-way analysis of variance procedure would be appropriate only if there was some treatment common to the first student in each sample, some other treatment common to the second student in each sample, and so on.

8. The error sum of squares will be larger because you are not recognizing the effect of the second factor. There is a greater chance that you will accept the null hypothesis even if there really is a difference between the populations.

PRACTICAL APPLICATION

1. Variable	Average	Variance	Stand. Dev.
A1	4.5000	1.6667	1.2910
B1	7.5000	1.6667	1.2910
C1	12.0000	4.6667	2.1602
D1	17.2500	4.9167	2.2174

Overall average: 10.3125
Var. of averages: 30.8906
Average of vars.:   3.2292
F statistic: 38.2645
Degrees of freedom: 3, 12

ANOVA table

Source of Variation	Sum of Squares	Degrees of Freedom	Mean Square Variance	F Ratio
Treatment	370.687	3	123.562	38.265
Error	38.750	12	3.229	
Total	409.437	15		

Reject the null hypothesis.

2. Variable	Average	Variance	Stand. Dev.
A2	6.7500	4.9167	2.2174
B2	6.5000	7.0000	2.6458
C2	6.2500	7.5833	2.7538
D2	8.7500	7.5833	2.7538

Overall average: 7.0625
Var. of averages: 1.3073
Average of vars.:   6.7708
F statistic: 0.7723
Degrees of freedom: 3, 12

ANOVA table

Source of Variation	Sum of Squares	Degrees of Freedom	Mean Square Variance	F Ratio
Treatment	15.687	3	5.229	0.772
Error	81.250	12	6.771	
Total	96.937	15		

Accept the null hypothesis.

16
SIMPLE
REGRESSION

KEY TERMS

r^2 a measure of how well the independent variable in a simple linear regression can explain changes in the dependent variable; its value is between 0 (meaning poor fit) and 1 (meaning perfect fit)

regression line a line calculated in regression analysis that is used to estimate the relation between two quantities (the independent variable and the dependent variable)

simple regression a method for analyzing the relation between one independent variable and one dependent variable

---

Often in statistics we want to investigate questions such as these: Is there a relation between two quantities? Do changes in one quantity cause changes in the other quantity? For example, do changes in interest rates affect the demand for houses? Other times we will want to know if we can use one variable to predict the value of another variable. For example, suppose you want to guess next year's value of consumption spending. Consumption spending may be difficult to predict directly; it may be easier to predict next year's value of disposable income. If you can find a relation between income and consumption, you're in business. You can use that relation plus the knowledge of income to predict the value of consumption.

THE REGRESSION LINE

In economics it is assumed that the level of income affects the quantity that will be demanded of a particular good. For most goods, higher income leads to higher demand. This is not always the case, though. There are some goods (called **inferior goods**) that people buy less often when their incomes increase. (Presumably they buy something better when they can afford it. For example, hamburgers might be inferior goods if people would rather buy steaks when their incomes rise.) The only way to tell whether a particular good is an inferior good is to collect some data.

Suppose we have observations of average income and total pizza sales for a 1-month period for eight different towns:

Town	Income (in thousands of dollars)	Pizza Sales (in thousands)
1	5	27
2	10	46
3	20	73
4	8	40
5	4	30
6	6	28
7	12	46
8	15	59

When faced with a real problem it would be better to have more observations, but this sample of eight observations will work well to illustrate the calculations.

One good way to determine whether there is a relation between income and pizza sales is to draw a picture. We will draw a diagram with income measured along the horizontal axis, pizza sales along the vertical axis, and a dot marking each observation. This type of graph is called a **scatter diagram** or **scatterplot**. (See Figure 16–1.)

From the diagram we can see clearly that there is a relationship between income and pizza sales, and we can see also that an increase in income leads to an increase in pizza sales. Therefore, pizzas are not an inferior good.

As the saying goes, "One picture is worth a thousand words," and we should not underestimate the value of a diagram for illustrating and clarifying the nature of a relationship. However, it would help to develop a more precise way of characterizing this type of relationship. The tool we will use is called *regression analysis*. In this chapter we will investigate **simple regression**, which applies when there is only one independent variable that affects the value of the dependent variable. In the next chapter we will look at situations with more than one independent variable, for which we use *multiple regression*.

The goal of simple regression analysis is to approximate a pattern of dots by a straight line. In the pizza case we cannot draw a line that passes through all the points, but we can find a line that comes close to most of them (See Figure 16–2). This type of line is called a **regression line**. It is possible to determine a regression line by visual inspection, but we will develop an easier method.

In some cases it is possible to find a line that fits a pattern of dots very well. For example, economic models sometimes assume that personal consumption is determined by disposable income. Here is a list of observations

Income (x)			
x	y	x	y
5	27	4	30
10	46	6	28
20	73	12	46
8	40	15	59

Figure 16–1

Figure 16–2

for total national consumption spending and disposable income for several recent years:

Year	Disposable Personal Income	Personal Consumption Expenditures
1959	350.5	317.6
1960	365.4	331.7
1961	381.8	342.1
1962	405.1	363.3
1963	425.1	382.7
1964	462.5	411.4
1965	498.1	443.8
1966	537.5	480.9
1967	575.3	507.8
1968	625.0	558.0
1969	674.0	605.2
1970	735.7	648.5
1971	801.8	701.9
1972	869.1	770.6
1973	978.3	852.4
1974	1,071.6	933.4
1975	1,187.4	1,034.4
1976	1,302.5	1,151.9
1977	1,435.7	1,278.6
1978	1,608.3	1,428.5
1979	1,793.5	1,592.2
1980	2,009.0	1,757.1
1981	2,246.1	1,941.1
1982	2,421.2	2,077.3
1983	2,608.4	2,290.6
1984	2,912.0	2,503.3
1985	3,109.3	2,720.3
1986	3,285.1	2,899.7
1987	3,458.3	3,100.2
1988	3,748.7	3,353.6
1989	4,021.7	3,598.5
1990	4,285.8	3,839.9
1991	4,464.3	3,986.1
1992	4,751.4	4,235.3
1993	4,911.9	4,477.9
1994	5,151.8	4,743.3
1995	5,408.2	4,975.8
1996	5,688.5	5,256.8
1997	5,988.8	5,547.4
1998	6,395.9	5,879.5

Year	Disposable Personal Income	Personal Consumption Expenditures
1999	6,695.0	6,282.5
2000	7,194.0	6,739.4
2001	7,486.8	7,055.0
2002	7,830.1	7,350.7
2003	8,162.5	7,703.6
2004	8,680.9	8,195.9
2005	9,062.0	8,694.1
2006	9,640.7	9,207.2
2007	10,170.5	9,710.2

www.gpoaccess.gov/eop/tables.09.html

We can draw a scatter diagram (Figure 16–3), that shows we could draw a line that closely matches this pattern of dots.

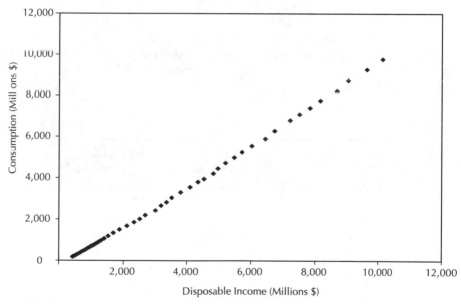

Figure 16–3

Figure 16–4 shows the scatter graph and regression line for the height and weight of the baseball players from Chapter 2. The line illustrates the trend but does not fit perfectly.

Figure 16–4

In other cases the pattern of dots will not look at all like a line. For example, suppose we wished to investigate whether more people live in states that have higher elevations. Here is a table comparing population with highest elevation for the 50 states:

State	Highest Elevation (feet)	Year 2000 Population (thousands)
Alabama	2,407	4,461
Alaska	20,320	629
Arizona	12,633	5,141
Arkansas	2,753	2,680
California	14,494	33,931
Colorado	14,433	4,312
Connecticut	2,380	3,410
Delaware	442	785
Florida	345	16,029
Georgia	4,784	8,207
Hawaii	13,796	1,217
Idaho	12,662	1,297

State	Highest Elevation (feet)	Year 2000 Population (thousands)
Illinois	1,235	12,439
Indiana	1,257	6,091
Iowa	1,670	2,932
Kansas	4,039	2,694
Kentucky	4,145	4,049
Lousiana	535	4,480
Maine	5,268	1,278
Maryland	3,360	5,308
Massachusetts	3,491	6,356
Michigan	1,980	9,956
Minnesota	2,301	4,926
Mississippi	806	2,853
Missouri	1,772	5,606
Montana	12,799	905
Nebraska	5,426	1,715
Nevada	13,143	2,002
New Hampshire	6,288	1,238
New Jersey	1,803	8,424
New Mexico	13,161	1,824
New York	5,344	19,005
North Carolina	6,684	8,068
North Dakota	3,506	644
Ohio	1,550	11,375
Oklahoma	4,973	3,459
Oregon	11,239	3,429
Pennsylvania	3,213	12,301
Rhode Island	812	1,050
South Carolina	3,560	4,025
South Dakota	7,242	757
Tennessee	6,643	5,700
Texas	8,749	20,904
Utah	13,528	2,237
Vermont	4,393	610
Virginia	5,729	7,101
Washington	14,410	5,909
West Virginia	4,863	1,813
Wisconsin	1,951	5,371
Wyoming	13,804	495

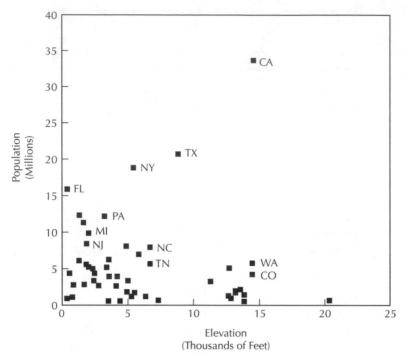

Figure 16–5

The scatter diagram is shown in Figure 16–5. We can try to draw a line that best fits these dots, but we can see that the line does not follow the pattern of dots very closely (Figure 16–6).

It is not good enough just to find the best line. We must also find a way to measure how well the line fits the points.

CALCULATING A REGRESSION LINE

Figure 16–7 illustrates the general situation. We will use x to represent the independent variable, which will be measured along the horizontal axis. We will use y to represent the dependent variable—that is, the variable that depends on x. In the pizza example, income is the independent variable and pizza sales are the dependent variable. We will measure the dependent variable along the vertical axis. Suppose we have four observations. Then the scatter diagram contains four points, which we will call (x_1, y_1), (x_2, y_2), (x_3, y_3), and (x_4, y_4).

Figure 16–6. Regression line

Figure 16–7

Any line can be described by specifying two numbers: the **slope** and the **vertical intercept**. We will use $\hat{b}$ to represent the slope and $\hat{a}$ to represent the intercept. (We will explain later why we put the hats on the letters.) The equation of the line can be written as

$$y = \hat{a} + \hat{b}x$$

Suppose we guess that the best regression line is the line shown in Figure 16–8. This line looks like a good choice, but it doesn't fit the data points perfectly. For each point there is a certain amount of vertical distance between the point and the line. We'll call that distance the **error** or **residual** of the line relative to that point. A larger value for the error means that the line does a worse job of representing the points. Each point has its own error. (We'll call these error$_1$, error$_2$, error$_3$, and error$_4$.) We'd like to choose the line so that the total error is as small as possible. The normal procedure in statistics is to minimize the sum of the *squares* of all the errors. The square of the error for the point (x_i, y_i) is

$$(\text{error}_i)^2 = \left[y_i - (\hat{a} + \hat{b}x_i)\right]^2$$

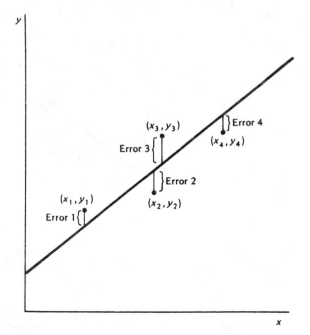

Figure 16–8

We will call the sum of the squares of all of the errors SE_{line} (short for "squared error about the line"):

$$SE_{line} = \left[y_1 - (\hat{a} + \hat{b}x_1)\right]^2 + \left[y_2 - (\hat{a} + \hat{b}x_2)\right]^2$$
$$+ \left[y_3 - (\hat{a} + \hat{b}x_3)\right]^2 + \left[y_4 - (\hat{a} + \hat{b}x_4)\right]^2$$

We originally looked at the question, Is there a relation between x and y? Here is another way of looking at this question: Does knowing the value of x help you predict the value of y? Suppose you have discovered that there is a very clear relation between x and y that can be represented by this line:

$$y = 2x + 15$$

Then, if you know that next year's value of x will be 10, you can predict that next year's value of y will be $2 \times 10 + 15 = 35$. If next year's value of x will be 30, you can predict that next year's value of y will be 75.

In general, if the variable x has the value x_i, we will use the symbol $\hat{y}_{x_i}$ to represent the **predicted value** of y for that given value of x. In general:

$$\hat{y}_{x_i} = \hat{a} + \hat{b}x_i$$

Note that there will be a different value of $\hat{y}_{x_i}$ for each different value of x_i. (The predicted value of y is also called the **fitted value**.)

We can write our expression for the first error like this:

$$Error_1 = y_1 - \hat{y}_{x1}$$

In general, we will use n to represent the number of data points, so we can write the expression for SE_{line} with summation notation:

$$SE_{line} = \Sigma\left[y_i - (\hat{a} + \hat{b}x_i)\right]^2$$
$$= \Sigma(y_i - \hat{y}_{x_i})^2$$

All through this chapter we will be taking summations from $i = 1$ to n. For convenience we will leave out the little numbers above and below the sigma. Whenever you see a capital sigma (Σ) in the chapter remember that it means $\Sigma_{i=1}^{n}$.

We have n observations for x and y, so the only unknowns in the expression for SE_{line} are $\hat{a}$ and $\hat{b}$. Somehow we need to find the values of $\hat{a}$ and $\hat{b}$ that will result in SE_{line} being as small as possible. Remember that we can choose the values of $\hat{a}$ and $\hat{b}$, but we can't change the values of the x's and the y's because we found these values when we conducted our observations. It requires calculus to find the optimum values of $\hat{a}$ and $\hat{b}$. The result is that $\hat{a}$ and $\hat{b}$ must satisfy these two equations:

$$\hat{b} = \frac{\overline{xy} - \bar{x}\bar{y}}{\overline{x^2} - \bar{x}^2}$$

$$\hat{a} = \bar{y} - \hat{b}\bar{x}$$

(See the appendix to Chapter 17 to learn how these formulas are derived. See page 419 to see an example of performing regression calculations in Excel.)

Now we can calculate the slope and the intercept for the pizza example. We will assume that pizza sales depend on income, so we will call income the independent variable (x) and pizza sales the dependent variable (y). We need to calculate $\bar{x}$, $\bar{y}$, $\overline{x^2}$, and $\overline{xy}$.

	x	y	x^2	xy	y^2
	5	27	25	135	729
	10	46	100	460	2,116
	20	73	400	1,460	5,329
	8	40	64	320	1,600
	4	30	16	120	900
	6	28	36	168	784
	12	46	144	552	2,116
	15	59	225	885	3,481
total	80	349	1,010	4,100	17,055
average	10.000	43.625	126.250	512.500	2,131.875

Therefore, $\bar{x} = 10$, $\bar{y} = 43.625$, $\overline{x^2} = 126.25$, and $\overline{xy} = 512.5$. Note that we also calculated $\overline{y^2} = 2,131.88$ because it will be useful later.

We can use the formulas for $\hat{a}$ and $\hat{b}$:

$$\hat{b} = \frac{512.5 - (10 \times 43.625)}{126.25 - 10^2} = 2.905$$

$$\hat{a} = \bar{y} - \hat{b}\bar{x} = 43.625 - 2.905 \times 10 = 14.577$$

Therefore, the equation of the regression line can be written as

$$y = 2.905x + 14.577$$

There are other ways to construct a regression line. One way is to pick a line that minimizes the sum of the absolute values of the errors instead of the sum of the squares of the errors. This method is not as seriously affected by points that are far from the main body of the data. Another method is the median-median line: the sample data is divided into three parts (according to the x values), and a **median point** found for each part (a median point having the median of that part's x values for its x coordinate and the median of that part's y values for its y coordinate). A line is then constructed, parallel to the two outside median points, moved a third of the way toward the middle point. For small samples, the median-median line is easier to construct by hand than the least-squares line.

Both of these methods become very difficult with large sample sizes and are difficult to analyze mathematically. The least-squares line is much more commonly used.

YOU SHOULD REMEMBER

1. If you have a scatter diagram with values of x along the horizontal axis and values of y along the vertical axis, then the slope and vertical intercept of the line that best fits these points can be found from these formulas:

$$\text{slope} = \hat{b} = \frac{\overline{xy} - \overline{x}\overline{y}}{\overline{x^2} - \overline{x}^2}$$

$$\text{intercept} = \hat{a} = \overline{y} - \hat{b}\overline{x}$$

The bars over the letters represent average values.

2. This line minimizes the sum of the squares of the errors (the vertical distance from each point to the line).

ACCURACY OF THE REGRESSION LINE

As we pointed out earlier, knowing the slope and the intercept of the regression line doesn't tell us anything about how well the line fits the data. Therefore, we need to develop another measure to tell how well the line fits. Our first inclination is just to use SE_{line}, since that formula measures how much discrepancy there is between the points on the line and the actual data points:

$$SE_{\text{line}} = \Sigma(y_i - \hat{y}_{x_i})^2$$

If SE_{line} is zero, then the line fits the data points perfectly. However, if the numerical value of SE_{line} is greater than zero, then we need something to compare this number with so that we can tell whether the fit of the line is any good.

We can compare the predictions of our regression line with those of a very simple-minded predictions plan: We could always predict that the value of y will be $\bar{y}$. For example, suppose you need to predict the total rainfall in your city next year. If you know nothing about what the weather conditions will be next year, but you do know the average rainfall in your city over the last several years, then your best prediction will be to guess that the rainfall next year will be the same as the average.

Let's have a contest between ourselves (using the regression line) and the simple-minded person who always will predict that the value of y will be equal to $\bar{y}$. We can calculate the total squared error of the simple-minded method (call it SE_{av}, since it is the total squared error of y about its average):

$$SE_{av} = \Sigma(y_i - \bar{y})^2$$

[We could also write: $SE_{av} = n\text{Var}(y)$.]

If y really does depend on x, and our regression line describes that relation accurately, then the contest will not even be close. We will do a much better job predicting the value of y using our regression line than our simple-minded opponent will be able to do without using the line. In that case our squared error (SE_{line}) will be much less than the simple-minded squared error (SE_{av}). However, suppose that y really does not depend on x. In that case knowing the regression line will not help us. The simple-minded prediction plan will work almost as well, and SE_{line} will be almost as big as SE_{av}. Therefore, we'll define our measure of the accuracy of the regression line as follows:

$$r^2 = 1 - \frac{SE_{line}}{SE_{av}}$$

The quantity r^2 is called the **coefficient of determination**. This measure has two features that our fitness measure should have:

1. If $SE_{line} = 0$, then $r^2 = 1$, and the line fits perfectly.
2. If $SE_{line} = SE_{av}$, then $r^2 = 0$, and the line fits very poorly.

The value of r^2 will always be between 0 and 1. The higher the value of r^2, the better the line fits. Here is another interpretation: the value of r^2 is the fraction of the variation in y that can be explained by variations in x. For example, an r^2 value of .75 means that 75 percent of the variations in y can be explained by variations in x. (The symbol r^2 is used because it is the square of the sample correlation coefficient between these two variables. The correlation coefficient was introduced on page 42.)

We can calculate the r^2 value for the pizza example by finding the sum of the squares of all of the residuals. For each value of x we can calculate the predicted value of y from the formula

$$\hat{y}_{x_i} = \hat{a} + \hat{b}x_i = 2.905x_i + 14.577$$

Then we can calculate the residual by subtracting the actual value of y from the predicted value. Here is a table of the results:

x	Actual Value y	Predicted Value $\hat{y}_{xi} = \hat{a} + \hat{b}x_i$	Residual $y_i - \hat{y}_{xi}$	Squared Residual $(y_i - \hat{y}_{xi})^2$
5	27	29.102	−2.102	4.418
10	46	43.627	2.373	5.631
20	73	72.677	0.323	0.104
8	40	37.817	2.183	4.765
4	30	26.197	3.803	14.463
6	28	32.007	−4.007	16.056
12	46	49.437	−3.437	11.813
15	59	58.152	0.848	0.719
total	80	349	349	0	57.970

This table illustrates two interesting properties of a regression line: (1) the sum of the residuals is always zero, and (2) the sum of the predicted values of y is always the same as the sum of the actual values of y.

We can calculate the variance of the y values from the formula

$$\mathrm{Var}(y) = \overline{y^2} - \bar{y}^2 = 2131.875 - 43.625^2 = 228.734$$

Since $\mathrm{Var}(y) = \mathrm{SE}_{\mathrm{av}}/n$, we can calculate:

$$\mathrm{SE}_{\mathrm{av}} = n\,\mathrm{Var}(y) = 8 \times 228.734 = 1829.875$$

Therefore:

$$r^2 = 1 - \frac{57.970}{1829.875} = .968$$

Just as we suspected, the regression line fits the data points very well; 96.8 percent of the variation in pizza sales can be explained by variations in income.

The value of r^2 can also be calculated from either of these formulas:

$$r^2 = \frac{(\overline{xy} - \overline{x}\,\overline{y})^2}{(\overline{x^2} - \overline{x}^2)(\overline{y^2} - \overline{y}^2)}$$

or

$$r^2 = \frac{(nT_{xy} - T_x T_y)^2}{(nT_{x^2} - T_x^2)(nT_{y^2} - T_y^2)}$$

where $T_x = \Sigma x$, $T_y = \Sigma y$, $T_{xy} = \Sigma xy$, $T_{x^2} = \Sigma x^2$, and $T_{y^2} = \Sigma y^2$.

Note that we cannot calculate r^2 if all of the y values are the same, because then $SE_{av} = 0$. If y is always constant, we don't really need the regression line to predict its value anyway.

In Chapter 2 we introduced the **correlation** (or correlation coefficient), which also measures the extent of the linear relation between two variables. The correlation (represented by r) is always between -1 and 1. The r^2 value for a regression is equal to the square of the correlation between the two regression variables. If the slope of the regression line is positive, then r is positive; if the slope is negative, then r is negative. The correlation is zero if the regression line has zero slope. A correlation near zero means that there is not much of a linear relation between the two variables. (There could perhaps be a nonlinear relation between the two variables even if the correlation is near zero. We will discuss that possibility later.) A correlation value near 1 or -1 indicates that there is a very strong linear relation between the two variables.

YOU SHOULD REMEMBER

1. The r^2 value is a number between 0 and 1 that indicates whether or not knowledge of the values of x helps you to estimate the values of y.

2. An r^2 value close to 1 indicates that the regression line fits the dots well.

3. The r^2 value can be calculated from one of these formulas:

$$r^2 = \frac{(\overline{xy} - \overline{x}\,\overline{y})^2}{(\overline{x^2} - \overline{x}^2)(\overline{y^2} - \overline{y}^2)}$$

or

$$r^2 = 1 - \frac{SE_{line}}{SE_{av}}$$

where $SE_{line} = \Sigma(y_i - \hat{y}_{xi})^2$ and $SE_{av} = \Sigma(y_i - \overline{y})^2$.

STATISTICAL ANALYSIS OF REGRESSIONS

Now we would like to perform statistical tests on our regression results. To do this we need to make some assumptions about the process relating x and y. In the standard regression model we assume that the true nature of the relation between x and y can be described by this equation:

$$y_i = a + bx_i + e_i$$

where x_i is the ith observation for the variable x, y_i is the ith observation for the variable y, and e_i is known as the random error term. We are assuming that x is the dominant influence on y, and the relationship can be represented by a straight line with y-intercept a and slope b. (Thus, each e_i should be independent of each x_i. This can always be checked by plotting e_i against x_i to see if there is any pattern.) Unfortunately the true values of a and b are unknown, but as you have probably guessed, we will use statistical procedures to estimate their values.

If the true equation was $y = a + bx$, then x would be the only factor that affected the value of y. Every single increase or decrease in y could be explained by an increase or a decrease in x. However, there are almost always some other factors that affect the value of the dependent variable. If the regression line represents the relationship well, these other factors will not be very important. Because all these other factors are mysterious and unknown, we will call them random error. In the equation given above e is a random variable that represents all of these other factors. (When we discuss multiple regression, we will see how it is possible to include some of these other factors in the regression model; but even so there will always be some remaining unexplained factors that make up the random error term.)

If we have n observations, then there will be n different random errors. We will let e_1 represent the random error effect on the first observation. In general, e_i is a random variable representing the random error effect on the ith observation. We know that the expected value of each random error is zero $[E(e_1) = 0]$ because of the fact that we have included the intercept term a in the equation. We will let $\text{Var}(e_1)$ be equal to σ^2, but unfortunately we don't know the true value of σ^2. If x is a very good predictor of y, then σ^2 will tend to be small. If σ^2 is large, then there are other important factors that affect y and we should try to include them in our model. We will also assume that each random error term has a normal distribution, that the variance σ^2 is the same for each random error, and that each random error is independent of all of the other random errors.

To summarize the situation:

$$y = a + bx + e$$

Here x is known and not random. We have a list of n observations for x. Also, y is known and random. We also have a list of n observations of y, with each observation being paired with one of the observations of x. The presence of the e term means that y is a random variable with a normal distribution.

$$E(y_i) = a + bx_i \quad \text{and} \quad \text{Var}(y_i) = \sigma^2$$

Here a and b are not random, but their true values are unknown; e is both random and unknown. We know that $E(e) = 0$, but $\text{Var}(e) = \sigma^2$ is unknown. We assume that e has a normal distribution.

Even though the true values of a and b are unknown, we can calculate the slope and the intercept of the regression line:

$$\hat{a} = \bar{y} - \hat{b}\bar{x}$$

$$\hat{b} = \frac{\overline{xy} - \bar{x}\bar{y}}{\overline{x^2} - \bar{x}^2}$$

Now you see why we included the hats. In statistical inference we often put a hat over a calculated statistic that is being used to estimate the value of an unknown parameter. The regression line is called the *least-squares* line, so $\hat{a}$ and $\hat{b}$ can be called the **least-squares estimators** of the parameters a and b.

Fortunately, it turns out that $\hat{a}$ and $\hat{b}$ have some very desirable statistical properties. For one thing, $\hat{a}$ and $\hat{b}$ are the maximum likelihood estimators of a and b. It can be shown that $\hat{b}$ has a normal distribution with $E(\hat{b}) = b$ and

$$\text{Var}(\hat{b}) = \frac{\sigma^2}{\Sigma(x_i - \bar{x})^2}$$

We can write the expression for $\hat{b}$ like this:

$$\hat{b} = \frac{\Sigma(x_i - \bar{x})(y_i - \bar{y})}{\Sigma(x_i - \bar{x})^2}$$

which can also be written as

$$\hat{b} = \frac{1}{\Sigma(x_i - \bar{x})^2} \Sigma(x_i - \bar{x})y_i$$

Remember that the x's are constants and the y's are random variables with a normal distribution. From the expression given above we can see that $\hat{b}$ is found by adding together a bunch of normal random variables multiplied by different constants, so we know from the properties of normal distributions that $\hat{b}$ will also have a normal distribution.

The fact that $E(\hat{b}) = b$ is important. It means that $\hat{b}$ is an unbiased estimator of the slope. It can also be shown that $\hat{b}$ is the best estimator (because it has the smallest variance) among a certain general class of all unbiased estimators.

The expression for the variance of $\hat{b}$ tells us that the variance of $\hat{b}$ is larger if σ^2 is larger. This seems reasonable, since a larger value of σ^2 means that we can expect more scatter about the true regression line, and the increased scatter will make it more difficult to pin down the true value of b. The expression $\Sigma(x_i - \bar{x})^2$ represents the squared error about the average of the x's, or we could write

$$\Sigma(x_i - \bar{x})^2 = n \, \text{Var}(x)$$

We can see that, when there is a greater spread among the x values, then the variance of $\hat{b}$ will be less and it will be easier to pin down the true value of b. Figure 16–9 illustrates two different situations. In each case the number of observations is the same. However, in example (a) there is not very much spread among the x values. In that case there will be much more uncertainty about the true value of slope than there will be in example (b).

Figure 16–9

Since $\hat{b}$ has a normal distribution with mean b and variance $\sigma^2/\Sigma(x_i - \bar{x})^2$, we know that this random variable.

$$\frac{\hat{b} - b}{\sqrt{\dfrac{\sigma^2}{\Sigma(x_i - \bar{x})^2}}}$$

will have a standard normal distribution. Therefore, we can determine a 95 percent confidence interval for b:

$$\hat{b} \pm \frac{1.96\sigma}{\sqrt{\Sigma(x_i - \bar{x})^2}}$$

(See Chapter 11.) However, there is one obvious problem with calculating the confidence interval in this way: we don't know the value of σ. We need a way to estimate it. If we knew the true values of a and b, then we would have n observations of the random variable e:

$$e_i = y_i - (a + bx_i)$$

and so on. Since $E(e) = 0$, we could write

$$\sigma^2 = \mathrm{Var}(e) = E(e^2) - [E(e)]^2 = E(e^2)$$

and we could estimate σ^2 by the average of the squares of the e's. Since we don't know a and b, we can use the residuals from our calculated regression line:

$$[y_1 - (\hat{a} + \hat{b}x_1)], \quad [y_2 - (\hat{a} + \hat{b}x_2)], \quad \text{and so on}$$

The sum of the squares of all these residuals is what we called SE_{line}. Here we run into a conflict between the different criteria for estimators. The maximum likelihood estimator of σ^2 is equal to SE_{line}/n. However, in order to have an unbiased estimator of σ^2, we must use $SE_{line}/(n-2)$. (Here $n-2$ is the degrees of freedom of the squared error about the line, since we started with n points but lost two degrees of freedom when we had to use our observations to estimate the values of the slope and the intercept.) The quantity $SE_{line}/(n-2)$ is called the **mean square error** (MSE for short):

$$\text{MSE} = \frac{SE_{line}}{n-2} = \frac{\Sigma(y_i - \hat{y}_{x_i})^2}{n-2} = \frac{\Sigma[y_i - (\hat{a} + \hat{b}x_i)]^2}{n-2}$$

The expected value of MSE is σ^2, which makes it an unbiased estimator of σ^2.

As you recall, we had established that this random variable:

$$\frac{\hat{b} - b}{\sqrt{\dfrac{\sigma^2}{\Sigma(x_1 - \bar{x})^2}}}$$

has a standard normal distribution. In similar situations in Chapter 11, we substituted an estimator for σ^2 in place of the unknown value of σ', and we ended up with something that had a t distribution. In this case, the random variable

$$\frac{\hat{b} - b}{\sqrt{\dfrac{\text{MSE}}{\Sigma(x_i - \bar{x})^2}}}$$

has a t distribution with $n-2$ degrees of freedom. Then the confidence interval is

$$\hat{b} \pm A \sqrt{\frac{\text{MSE}}{\Sigma(x_i - \bar{x})^2}}$$

Here A is a number found from Table A3–5 such that

$$\Pr(-A < t < A) = \text{CL}$$

where t is a random variable having a t distribution with $n-2$ degrees of freedom and CL is the confidence level.

For the pizza sales example we have MSE $= 57.97/6 = 9.662$ and $\Sigma(x_i - \bar{x})^2 = 210$. Since $n = 8$, we will have a t distribution with $8 - 2 = 6$ degrees of freedom. If we choose a 95 percent confidence interval, we can see from Table A3–5 that the value of A is 2.447. We already found that $b = 2.905$, so the confidence interval is

$$2.905 \pm 2.447 \sqrt{\frac{9.662}{210}}$$

which is from 2.38 to 3.43.

We can also perform hypothesis tests on our model. Here is one important null hypothesis: "The values of x do not have any relationship to the values of y." Obviously, if we think our regression is any good, we would like to collect enough statistical evidence to be able to prove this hypothesis wrong. From the equation $y = a + bx + e$, we can see that there will be no relation between x and y if the true value of the slope is zero. Since

$$\frac{(\hat{b} - b)}{\sqrt{\dfrac{MSE}{\Sigma(x_i - \bar{x})^2}}}$$

has a t distribution with $n - 2$ degrees of freedom, it follows that *if $b = 0$* then the statistic

$$\frac{\hat{b}}{\sqrt{\dfrac{MSE}{\Sigma(x_i - \bar{x})^2}}}$$

will have a t distribution with $n - 2$ degrees of freedom. We can calculate the value of that statistic. If it seems plausible that the calculated value could have come from the t distribution, then we will accept the null hypothesis; otherwise we will reject it. For the pizza sales the calculated t statistic is

$$2.905 \sqrt{\frac{210}{9.662}} = 13.542$$

For a two-tailed test at the 5 percent significance level the critical value for a t distribution with 6 degrees of freedom is 2.447. Since 13.542 is in the rejection region, well above the critical value, we can safely reject the null hypothesis that the true value of the slope is zero. The p value is 1.0×10^{-5}, from Excel TDIST (13.542, 6, 2). As we will see on page 419, Excel will automatically calculate the t statistic and p value for a regression coefficient.

YOU SHOULD REMEMBER

1. Assume that the true relation between x and y is given by this formula:

$$y = a + bx + e$$

where e is a normal random variable with mean 0 and unknown variance σ^2.

2. Then the least-squares estimators $\hat{a}$ and $\hat{b}$ are the maximum likelihood estimators of a and b, and they are also unbiased estimators.

3. The mean square error:

$$MSE = \frac{\Sigma\left[y_i - (\hat{a} + \hat{b}x_i)\right]^2}{n-2}$$

is an unbiased estimator of the unknown value of σ^2.

4. To test the hypothesis that the true value of the slope is zero, calculate this statistic:

$$\frac{\hat{b}}{\sqrt{\dfrac{MSE}{\Sigma(x_i - \bar{x})^2}}}$$

If the true value of the slope is zero, then this statistic will have a t distribution with $n - 2$ degrees of freedom.

PREDICTING VALUES OF y

• *FOUR WARNINGS ABOUT PREDICTING VALUES*

Now we will discuss how to use our regression model to predict values of the dependent variable. Before we get carried away making predictions with a regression model, however, we must heed several important warnings.

- Any prediction based on a regression model is a conditional prediction, since the prediction for the dependent variable depends on the value of the independent variable. Suppose you have found a

regression relationship that describes perfectly the relation between
y and x. In that case you can predict future values of y *if* (but only
if) you know the future value of x. If pizza sales do depend on
income as predicted by our regression relation, then we can predict
next year's pizza sales if we know next year's income. If we cannot
predict next year's income, then we cannot predict the actual value
of next year's pizza sales (although it still may be very useful to have
a regression model that tells us how much income affects demand
for pizza).

- The regression line has been estimated using past data. This line will
  not be able to predict the future if the relationship between x and
  y changes. A sudden change in people's pizza preferences will ruin
  the ability of the regression line to predict future values of pizza
  sales.

- Many regression predictions try to predict values of y in situations
  where the value of x falls outside the range of values previously
  observed for x. These predictions, known as **extrapolations**, are
  much less reliable than predictions based on values of the independent variable that fall within the range of previously observed
  values.

  For example, part (a) of Figure 16–10 shows a number of observations for pizza sales as a function of income in a new set of towns.
  It seems reasonable to represent the data with a straight line. Suppose
  that next year we expect income will be 25. Based on the regression
  line, it seems logical to predict that pizza sales next year will be 200.
  However, this prediction is an extrapolation. The regression analysis
  gives us good evidence that the relation between income and sales

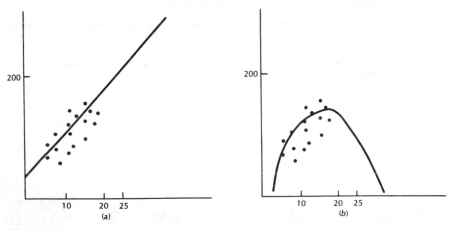

Figure 16–10

can be well represented by a straight line when income is in the range from 10 to 20, but we have no way of knowing for sure whether this linear relationship holds for other levels of income. It is quite possible that, unbeknownst to us, the true relation between income and pizza sales is given by the curve shown in part (b) of Figure 16–10. This curve suggests that pizza sales do not continue to increase as income increases. Instead, it appears that people start going to fancier restaurants and consume less pizza once income rises past a certain point. This curve fits the original data points as well as the regression line does, but it predicts a far different value for pizza sales if income is 25. As long as our observations cover only values of income within the narrow range shown, we have no way of distinguishing between these two situations, and extrapolations based on the regression line may be quite erroneous.

- The mere fact that there is a strong association between two variables does not indicate there is a cause and effect relationship between them. If you find a regression line that fits the relationship between y and x very well, then there are four possibilities:

1. The values of y may really depend on the values of x, as we have assumed so far.

2. The observed relation may have occurred completely by chance. If we have many observations, this is extremely unlikely, but we have seen that in statistics we cannot rule out the possibility that an event that looks significant may have occurred randomly

3. There may be a third variable that affects both x and y. This is the most likely explanation for situations where two variables are closely correlated but there does not seem to be a causal relationship between them. For example, many unrelated variables tend to increase with time.

4. There may indeed be a causal link between x and y, but it may be that y is causing x. We may have incorrectly determined which was the dependent variable and which was the independent variable. For example, we assumed that higher incomes cause people to buy more pizza. However, it may work this way: when people buy more pizzas, they   create more income for all the people who work in pizza places, and this leads to a multiplier effect that increases the income of the whole community. Therefore it could be that higher pizza sales cause higher incomes. Here is another example. You may have found a regression result that seems to indicate that higher advertising levels cause higher sales. However, suppose that firms allocate their advertising budgets on the basis of sales. Then it is quite likely that higher sales cause higher advertising budgets.

• PREDICTING VALUES OF THE DEPENDENT VARIABLE

Now that we have heeded all of these warnings, let's see how we can use our regression model to predict values of y. Assume that we have determined that x really does cause y, that this relationship will still apply in the future, and that it can be accurately described by the regression line $y = 2.905x + 14.577$. If we know that the value of income next year will be 16, then naturally we will predict that next year's value of y will be $2.905 \times 16 + 14.577 = 61.06$.

The next question is: How precise is this prediction? We would like to construct an interval such that there is a 95 percent chance that the value of y will be contained in that interval (given that $x = 16$). This type of interval is called a **prediction interval**. Note that it is similar to the confidence intervals we developed for unknown parameters. Suppose for the moment that we know the true values of a, b, and σ. Then, if $x = x_{new}$, we know that y will have a normal distribution with mean $\hat{y}_{x_{new}} = a + bx_{new}$ and variance σ^2. Therefore, there is a 95 percent chance that the value of y will be between $[(a + bx_{new}) - 1.96\sigma]$ and $[(a + bx_{new}) + 1.96\sigma]$.

Unfortunately, matters become much worse because we don't know the true values of a, b, and σ. Now there are two sources of uncertainty involved with predicting values of y: we don't know the true regression line, and the predicted value of y will deviate randomly about the line. The formula for the estimated variance of y for a given value of x is

$$\text{Var}(y) = \text{MSE}\left[1 + \frac{1}{n} + \frac{(x_{new} - \bar{x})^2}{\Sigma(x_i - \bar{x})^2}\right]$$

Note that the variance becomes larger when the value of x_{new} becomes farther from $\bar{x}$. When x_{new} is closer to $\bar{x}$, we have greater confidence that our estimated regression line is close to the true regression line. However, if our estimate for the slope of the line is slightly different from the true value, then this difference will cause our estimated regression line to depart farther and farther from the true line when we move farther from $\bar{x}$.

When x has the value x_{new} and we have calculated $\hat{y}_{x_{new}} = \hat{a} + \hat{b}x_{new}$ and Var(y) using the formula above, then the prediction interval for y is

$$\hat{y}_{new} \pm A\sqrt{\text{Var}(y)}$$

where

$$\Pr(-A < t < A) = \text{CL}$$

t is a random variable having a t distribution with
   $n - 2$ degrees of freedom
CL is the confidence level (such as .95)

Here are some sample calculations:

Value of x	Predicted Value of $y = \hat{a} + \hat{b}x$	95 Percent Prediction Interval for y
2	20.39	11.29–29.48
6	32.01	23.67–40.34
10	43.63	35.56–51.69
14	55.25	46.91–63.58
18	66.87	57.77–75.96
20	72.68	63.05–82.30

Figure 16–11 illustrates the prediction intervals compared to the regression line. You can see how the intervals become wider as the value of x is farther from $\bar{x}$.

Figure 16–11

ANALYSIS OF RESIDUALS

Another way to gain valuable information about a regression model is to make a graph of the residuals. For each data point (x_i, y_i) we can calculate the residual:

$$(i\text{th residual}) = y_i - \hat{y}_{x_i} = y_i - (\hat{a} + \hat{b}x_i)$$

Let's make a scatter diagram that measures values of x along the horizontal axis and the residual along the vertical axis. Excel will automatically prepare such a diagram if you wish. In the pizza example we have these values:

x	Residual
5	−2.102
10	2.373
20	0.323
8	2.183
4	3.803
6	−4.007
12	−3.437
15	0.848

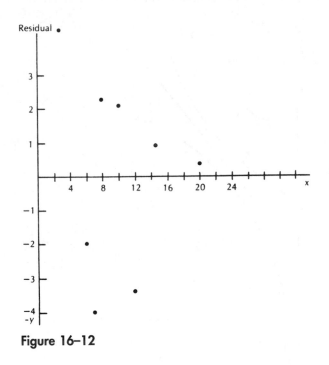

Figure 16–12

Figure 16–12 shows the scatter diagram.

If the assumptions of the regression model are met, the plot of the residuals should look like a random array of dots. There should be no apparent pattern. Because the error term in the model is assumed to have a normal distribution, there should be more values near zero than far from zero. In particular, here are some things to look for in a residual plot:

- Outliers. An **outlier** is a residual much larger (or much more negative) than the others. On the original scatter diagram an outlier will show up as a point that is far from the estimated regression line. When you have identified which observation corresponds to the outlier point, then you should check to make sure that the observation is correct. An outlier may have occurred because you made a typographical error in entering the data for that observation, in which case you can correct the error and run the regression again. If you are convinced that the outlier observation is indeed correct, then you should investigate to see whether there is some special circumstance that caused that observation to depart so far from the others. Perhaps you can identify a rare natural disaster that corresponds with the observation involved. If you are convinced that the circumstance that caused the outlier will not recur, you may drop that observation and then perform the regression again with the remaining points. If, on the other hand, you can identify the cause of the outlier with a variable that should be included in the model, you should set up a multiple regression model. (See the next chapter.) If you cannot identify any cause for the outlier, then you must leave the outlier in the regression and treat it as a random error.

- Nonnormal errors. The original regression model assumed that the error terms had normal distributions, but the plot of the residuals may indicate that this is not the case. The least-squares estimators $\hat{a}$ and $\hat{b}$ are unbiased estimators of the true values of a and b whether or not the errors are normally distributed, but the statistical tests we performed were all based on the assumption of normal errors.

- Nonconstant variances. We assumed that the variances of the error terms associated with the observations were all the same. If the residual diagram shows that the residuals are systematically bigger in one area of the diagram, however, this condition may not be met. The pizza regression residual plot indicates that the residuals tend to be greater for smaller values of x, so perhaps there is a situation of nonconstant variance here. (More observations would be needed to make this conclusion definite.) The impressive technical term for the situation with nonconstant variances among the error terms is **heteroscedasticity**. In situations of nonconstant variance it is sometimes possible to transform the model into an equivalent model with constant variances.

- Omitted variables. It may be worthwhile to make a plot of the residuals compared with another independent variable that seems significant but has not been included in the model. If there is an association between the residuals and the new variable, you should set up a multiple regression model including that variable.

- Nonlinearity. If the true relationship is not a straight line, the residual plot will usually reveal the situation immediately. For example, here are observations for two variables x and y:

x	y	Residual
1	10.000	0.786
2	10.800	0.386
3	11.664	0.050
4	12.597	−0.217
5	13.605	−0.409
6	14.693	−0.521
7	15.869	−0.546
8	17.138	−0.476
9	18.509	−0.305
10	19.990	−0.024
11	21.589	0.375
12	23.316	0.902

The simple linear regression calculation for these observations gives a slope of 1.2, an intercept of 8.014, and an r^2 value of .986. The scatter diagram is shown in Figure 16–13.

However, the residual plot shown in Figure 16–14 clearly is not random. When the residuals follow a definite curve like this one, there is strong

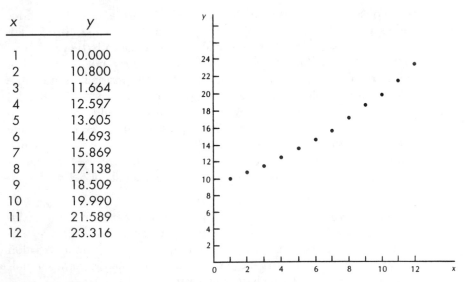

x	y
1	10.000
2	10.800
3	11.664
4	12.597
5	13.605
6	14.693
7	15.869
8	17.138
9	18.509
10	19.990
11	21.589
12	23.316

Figure 16–13

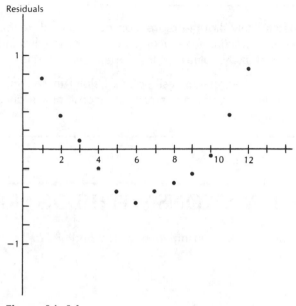

Figure 16–14

evidence either that the underlying model is not a linear model, or one of the other problems mentioned above has arisen. In this case we can see that for small or large values of x the residual is always positive, but for medium values of x the residual is always negative. This pattern indicates that the relationship between x and y can be better represented by a curve than by a line.

We will now turn our attention to transformations that can turn a model with a curve into an equivalent model with a straight line.

YOU SHOULD REMEMBER

1. There are four important points to keep in mind when using a regression equation to predict the value of the dependent variable:

a. Before the dependent variable can be predicted, it is necessary to make a prediction for the independent variable.

b. The regression line based on past observations will not reliably predict the future if the relation between the dependent variable and the independent variable changes.

c. An extrapolation prediction may not be reliable.

d. There may not be a causal connection between the two variables even if the regression equation indicates there is a strong relation.

> **2.** If it appears likely that the regression equation will reliably predict the future, a *prediction interval* may be constructed that indicates the range of most likely values for the dependent variable.
>
> **3.** Analysis of the regression residuals is helpful in spotting problems such as outliers, nonnormal errors, nonconstant variance, omitted variables, and nonlinearity.

TRANSFORMATIONS WITH LOGARITHMS

Suppose that the true relationship between x and y can be given by this equation:

$$y = ck^x$$

where c and k are two unknown constants. We cannot use simple linear regression to find the values for c and k. To handle this situation we must dig back into memory to find the concept called **logarithm**. You should have studied logarithms sometime previously, but we will review the basic ideas here.

Consider this question: What number will we get if we raise 2 to the 7th power? (Remember that raising a number to the power n means writing down that number n different times and then multiplying all of those n numbers together.) Here is a table of powers of 2:

$$2^0 = 1, \quad 2^1 = 2, \quad 2^2 = 4, \quad 2^3 = 8, \quad 2^4 = 16,$$
$$2^5 = 32, \quad 2^6 = 64, \quad 2^7 = 128, \quad 2^8 = 256, \quad 2^9 = 512$$

We can see that 128 is the result if we raise 2 to the 7th power. Now let's ask the opposite question: To what power should we raise 2 in order to get 128 as the result? The result is called the logarithm to the base 2 of 128. In this case we happen to know already that the answer is 7. In logarithm notation this is written as $\log_2 128 = 7$. We could also write

$$\log_2 1 = 0, \quad \log_2 2 = 1, \quad \log_2 4 = 2, \quad \log_2 8 = 3,$$
$$\log_2 16 = 4, \quad \log_2 32 = 5, \quad \text{and so on}$$

There are many different logarithm functions. Any positive number except 1 can act as the base for a logarithm function. In general, if a is the base of the logarithm function, then

$$\log_a x = n \quad \text{means} \quad a^n = x$$

The two most common bases for logarithms are 10 and a special number called e, which is about 2.71828. The expression $\log x$, where no base is specified, usually refers to logarithms to the base 10, which are called **common logarithms**. For example, $\log 10 = 1$, $\log 100 = 2$, $\log 1{,}000 = 3$, and so on. The expression $1n\ x$ usually refers to logarithms to the base e, which are called **natural logarithms**. Natural logarithms are especially important in calculus. Calculating logarithms is easy if the number you are interested in happens to be a whole-number power of the base. Otherwise the best thing to do is use a calculator or a computer with a built-in logarithm function to calculate the values. If you cannot do that, the next best thing is to look in a book that contains a table of logarithms.

Logarithms are very useful for our purposes because they satisfy these properties:

$$\log(ab) = \log a + \log b$$

$$\log\left(\frac{a}{b}\right) = \log a - \log b$$

$$\log a^n = n \log a$$

These properties are true for logarithms of any base, and a and b can be any positive, real numbers. For example, if the true relation between y and x is given by this formula:

$$y - ck^x$$

we can take the logarithm of both sides:

$$\log y = \log(ck^x)$$

Using the properties of logarithms, we can rewrite as follows:

$$\log y = \log c + \log k^x$$
$$= \log c + x \log k$$

Let's make these definitions:

$$\text{let } a = \log c, \quad \text{let } b = \log k$$

Then

$$\log y = a + bx$$

That looks very familiar: we have transformed our model into a situation where the linear regression model is appropriate. All we have to is use the values of $\log y$ as the dependent variable instead of the original values of y. (See Figure 16–15.)

y	log y	y	log y
10.000	1.000	15.869	1.201
10.800	1.033	17.138	1.234
11.664	1.067	18.509	1.267
12.597	1.100	19.990	1.301
13.605	1.134	21.589	1.334
14.693	1.167	23.316	1.368

Figure 16–15

Now we can perform the simple linear regression calculations, using x as the independent variable and $\log y$ as the dependent variable. The result is

$$\text{slope} = b = 0.0334, \quad \text{intercept} = a = 0.966$$

Since the original model is $y = ck^x$ with $a = \log c$ and $b = \log k$, we can calculate that

$$c = 10^{0.966} = 9.3 \quad \text{and} \quad k = 10^{0.0334} = 1.08$$

Therefore, our estimate for the true model is

$$y = 9.3 \times (1.08)^x$$

Note that we used common logarithms for our calculations, but you may use natural logarithms if you wish. This function is an example of a situation called *exponential growth* because the independent variable x appears as an exponent.

Here is another situation where a logarithmic transformation is useful. Suppose we have determined that the quantity demanded of a particular good is given by a formula like this:

$$Q = Q_0 P^{-e}$$

where P is the price of the good and Q_0 and e are unknown parameters. (In this formula e is the *elasticity* of demand for this product. We'll call it e because e stands for elasticity. This is not the same e that equals 2.718. . . . When the formula is written like this, it is assumed that the elasticity is constant.) Once again we need to take the logarithm of both sides:

$$\log Q = \log(Q_0 P^{-e})$$
$$= \log Q_0 - e \log P$$

Now let $a = \log Q_0$ and $b = -e$. Then

$$\log Q = a + b \log P$$

Now we can estimate a and b by performing a simple linear regression calculation using $\log P$ as the independent variable and $\log Q$ as the dependent variable.

YOU SHOULD REMEMBER

1. If $k^n = x$, then $\log_k x = n$ (n is the logarithm to the base k of x).

2. Logarithms are particularly useful with regression models because they can be used in transformations that convert curved relations into straight-line relations.

3. If the true relation between x and y is $y = ck^x$, then the transformed equation is

$$\log y = \log c + x \log k$$

4. If the true relation between x and y is $y = cx^n$, then the transformed equation is

$$\log y = \log c + n \log x$$

APPLICATION: PORTFOLIO ANALYSIS

Investing in the stock market is risky. Two kinds of risk apply to an individual stock: systematic risk, which applies to all stocks in the market, and specific risk, which is related to factors that affect only that individual stock. By holding a diverse portfolio, you can eliminate the specific risks since the specific risks would cause some stocks in your portfolio to go up while others were going down. However, you cannot eliminate the systematic risk by diversification because that affects all of the stocks in the market.

Regression analysis can be used to estimate these risks for a particular stock. Collect data in the recent past on stock prices. Then perform a regression calculation with the return on a broad, diversified portfolio (call it the market portfolio) as the independent variable and the return on a particular stock as the dependent variable. The value $1 - r^2$ for this regression is an indicator of the specific risk for this stock. The regression slope coefficient is known as the β (beta) for that particular stock. We can also calculate β from either of these formulas:

$$\beta_i = \frac{\text{Cov}_{i,m}}{\sigma_m^2} = \frac{r_{i,m}\sigma_i}{\sigma_m}$$

where β_i is the beta value for stock i, $\text{Cov}_{i,m}$ is the covariance between the returns on stock i and the market average, σ_m is the standard deviation of the return on the diversified market portolio, $r_{i,m}$ is the correlation between the returns of stock i and the market, and σ_i is the standard deviation of the return for stock i. These formulas are alternate forms of the formula for the slope of the regression line (see page 386).

A value of $\beta = 1$ means that the stock moves up and down with the market. A value greater than 1 means the stock will have greater volatility. (However, note that β values estimated with regression depend on past values, and they may change in the future if market conditions change.)

The β values are used in a model of financial markets known as the capital asset pricing model (CAPM), which predicts that the expected return $E(R_i)$ on stock i depends on its β according to the formula:

$$E(R_i) = R_F + [E(R_M) - R_F]\beta_i$$

where R_F is the return on a risk free asset and $E(R_M)$ is the expected return on the market portfolio. If $\beta_i = 1$, then stock i will have the same expected return as the market. If $\beta_i = 0$, there is no risk and the return on stock i would equal the risk-free rate. This model predicts that stocks with a higher β would have to offer a higher expected rate of return to compensate investors for the higher risk of holding them. (Note that in the theory, the return depends on β, not on the level of specific risk for that stock, because investors should be able to eliminate the specific risks in their portfolio by diversification. However, they cannot eliminate the risk of a stock with a higher β by diversification.)

KNOW THE CONCEPTS

DO YOU KNOW THE BASICS?

Test your understanding of Chapter 16 by answering the following questions:

1. If the r^2 value for a simple regression is .80, does this mean that 80 percent of the changes in the dependent variable are caused by changes in the independent variable?

2. List three ways to make regression estimates more precise.

3. What do you learn from a regression calculation if the estimated slope is zero?

4. What are two sources of uncertainty when you are using a regression equation to predict a value of the dependent variable?

5. What do you use the t statistic for?

6. Why are extrapolation predictions especially difficult?

7. Suppose you perform a regression calculation based on time series data, and it indicates that the demand for a particular good goes up when the price goes up. Can you think of an explanation why this might happen?

8. Does a correlation of zero indicate that there is no relation between two quantities?

9. Suppose someone reported a correlation between the diameters of the eight planets in the solar system and the crime rates in eight large cities. What does this analysis show?

10. If you have only two observations, will you be able to get a high r^2 value? Will you be able to obtain precise estimates of the slope and intercept?

11. In what situations will you take the logarithm of the dependent variable and then perform the regression calculation? In what situations will you take the logarithms of both the independent and the dependent variable?

TERMS FOR STUDY

coefficient of determination
common logarithm
correlation
error
extrapolation
fitted value

natural logarithm
outlier
predicted value
prediction interval
r^2
regression line

heteroscedasticity
inferior good
least-squares estimators
logarithm
mean square error (MSE)

residual
scatter diagram
simple linear regression
slope
vertical intercept

PRACTICAL APPLICATION

COMPUTATIONAL PROBLEMS

The following two exercises are small-scale examples of a simple regression where you can perform the calculations by hand. See the book's web page for more examples where you can paste the data into Excel and use Excel for the calculations.

1. independent variable:

   x: 2, 6, 10, 20

   dependent variable:

   y: 16, 28, 40, 70

2. independent variable:

   x: 2, 10, 2, 10

   dependent variable:

   y: 6, 6, 20, 20

ANSWERS

KNOW THE CONCEPTS

1. No. You can say that 80 percent of the changes in the dependent variable are associated with changes in the independent variable, but regression calculations do not indicate causation.

2. Obtain more observations; obtain observations with a greater spread; investigate a situation with a smaller value of σ.

3. There is no linear relation between the quantities.

4. One source of uncertainty arises because you do not know the true values of the slope and the intercept, and another source because any particular value of the dependent variable will deviate randomly from the line.

5. The t statistic is used to test the null hypothesis that the true value of the slope is 0.

6. You cannot be sure that the observed past relation between the variables applies in a new situation that you have never observed before.

7. Economic theory predicts that the quantity demanded will go down when the price goes up, provided that all else remains the same. It is possible, however, that other factors have been changing which have been causing the demand for the good to go up despite the price rise. In Chapter 16 we will discuss multiple regression, which makes it possible to take some of these other factors into account.

8. There could be a nonlinear relation.

9. This is a nonsensical calculation. Regression analysis can be applied only to pairs of observations. There must be some connection between the dependent variable and the independent variable in each pair; for example, both may be for the same week or the same town.

10. You will be able to obtain an r^2 value of 1, because you can always draw a line that fits any two points perfectly. However, your estimates of the slope and intercept will not be very reliable. It is important to remember that the r^2 value alone does not tell you whether the regression results are reliable.

11. Lex x be the independent variable, and let y be the dependent variable. You will take the logarithms of both x and y if you suspect that the true relation is of the form $y = ax^b$. You will take only the logarithm of y if you suspect that the true relation is of the form $y = ab^x$.

PRACTICAL APPLICATION

1. $\bar{x} = \dfrac{2+6+10+20}{4} = \dfrac{38}{4} = 9.500$

$\bar{y} = \dfrac{16+28+40+70}{4} = \dfrac{154}{4} = 38.500$

$\overline{x^2} = \dfrac{2^2+6^2+10^2+20^2}{4} = \dfrac{540}{4} = 135$

$\overline{y^2} = \dfrac{16^2+28^2+40^2+70^2}{4} = \dfrac{7,540}{4} = 1,885$

$\sigma_x = \sqrt{135 - 9.500^2} = 6.690$

$\sigma_y = \sqrt{1,885 - 38.500^2} = 20.069$

$\overline{x \times y} = \dfrac{(2 \times 13) + (6 \times 28) + (10 \times 40) + (20 \times 70)}{4} = \dfrac{2,000}{4} = 500$

$\text{slope} = \dfrac{500 - (9.5 \times 38.5)}{135 - 9.5^2} = 3$

intercept $= 38.5 - (3 \times 9.5) = 10$

$$\text{correlation} = r = \frac{500 - (9.500 \times 38.500)}{6.690 \times 20.069} = 1$$

$r^2 = 1^2 = 1$

2. $\bar{x} = \dfrac{2 + 10 + 2 + 10}{4} = \dfrac{24}{4} = 6$

$\bar{y} = \dfrac{6 + 6 + 20 + 20}{4} = \dfrac{52}{4} = 13$

$\overline{x^2} = \dfrac{2^2 + 10^2 + 2^2 + 10^2}{4} = \dfrac{280}{4} = 52$

$\overline{y^2} = \dfrac{6^2 + 6^2 + 20^2 + 20^2}{4} = \dfrac{872}{4} = 218$

$\sigma_x = \sqrt{52 - 6^2} = 4$

$\sigma_y = \sqrt{218 - 13^2} = 7$

$\overline{x \times y} = \dfrac{(2 \times 6) + (10 \times 6) + (2 \times 20) + (10 \times 20)}{4} = \dfrac{312}{4} = 78$

$\text{slope} = \dfrac{78 - (6 \times 13)}{52 - 6^2} = 0$

intercept $= 13 - (0 \times 6) = 13$

$$\text{correlation} = r = \frac{78 - (6 \times 13)}{4 \times 7} = 0$$

$r^2 = 0^2 = 0$

17

MULTIPLE REGRESSION

KEY TERMS

***F* statistic** a statistic used to test the hypothesis that the true value of each coefficient in a regression equation is 0

multiple regression a statistical method for analyzing the relation between several independent variables and one dependent variable

***t* statistic** a statistic used to test the hypothesis that the true value of one specific coefficient is 0

SEVERAL INDEPENDENT VARIABLES

Usually there is more than one independent variable that can affect the dependent variable we are trying to forecast. In that case simple regression is inadequate. Instead, we turn to multiple regression. We'll need to make a list of which independent variables might be useful for forecasting our dependent variable. Here are some examples where multiple regression analysis might be used:

- The price of houses in a neighborhood will be a function of variables such as the age of the house, the number of bedrooms, the size of the yard, the area of the house in square feet, the presence or absence of a garage, the presence or absence of a basement, or the distance to a school.

- The total cost of producing a product can be estimated as a function of the quantity produced and the cost of inputs.

- The shipping time for an order will depend on the distance being shipped and the shipping method used.

- The probability that a loan applicant will repay his or her loan can be estimated based on factors such as income, outstanding credit, and previous repayment history.

- The Federal Reserve needs to estimate the demand for money based on factors such as interest rates and the national income.

- The yields of agriculture crops depend on factors such as the amount of fertilizer used, the amount of rainfall or irrigation, and the number of hours of labor applied.

- The health of people can be affected by the amount they eat of a particular food. However, in order to study this effect, you need to take into account many other variables, such as the other foods they eat, the amount of exercise they get, and the medicines they take.

- A marketing survey will collect data on many variables about the respondents, and multiple regression analysis can be used to indicate the connection between these variables and the demand for the product you're studying.

- The amount of fuel used by a vehicle will be a function of the size of the engine, the weight of the vehicle, and the speed at which it is driven, among others.

- A psychological study on the effects of television on children would need to measure other characteristics of the children in addition to the amount of television watched.

- Some statisticians try to predict what factors affect the success of sports teams (for example, see the Society for American Baseball Research at *www.sabr.org*).

• AN EXAMPLE OF THE USE OF MULTIPLE REGRESSION

Suppose we have observations on the number of statistics books sold, the price of statistics books, and the per capita income in 15 different towns for a specified period. We will let y represent the independent variable, which is the quantity of statistics books sold. We have two independent variables: x_1 will represent price and x_2 will represent income.

We will assume that the relation between y, x_1, and x_2 is given by this equation:

$$y_i = B_1 x_{i1} + B_2 x_{i2} + B_3 + e_i$$

where y_i represents the ith value of the dependent variable, and x_{ij} represents the ith observation of the jth independent variable. We need two subscripts now because we must use one subscript to keep track of the observation number and another subscript to keep track of the variable number. For the observations listed below, x_{11} is 10, x_{21} is 9, x_{12} is 20, x_{22} is 21, and so on.

The true values of B_1, B_2, and B_3 are unknown, but we will try to estimate them. B_1 represents the effect that x_1 has on y, assuming that x_2 remains

Town	y (Books Demanded)	x_1 (Price)	x_2 (Income)
1	166	10	20
2	180	9	21
3	73	10	12
4	81	14	16
5	229	8	24
6	182	15	24
7	233	6	23
8	102	10	15
9	190	7	20
10	150	10	19
11	221	11	25
12	137	15	21
13	173	8	19
14	150	12	20
15	92	10	14

constant. Likewise, B_2 represents the effect that x_2 has on y when x_1 remains constant. If x_1 increases by 1 and everything else remains constant, then y will increase by B_1. When we design the model this way, we are assuming that the effects of x_1 and x_2 on y are additive. This means that the amount that x_1 affects y does not depend on the level of x_2, and vice versa. We expect that B_2 will be positive, since more books will be bought when income is higher, but that B_1 will be negative, since fewer books will be demanded when the price is higher. B_3 is called the constant term in the model. It is analogous to the y-intercept term in the simple linear regression model.

Again, e is a random variable called the *error term* that represents the effects of all possible factors other than price and income that might affect the demand for statistics books. Thus, e should be independent of x_1 and x_2. This can always be checked by plotting e against x_1 and e against x_2 to see if there is any pattern. The expectation of e is 0 and the variance of e is σ^2, which is unknown. We will assume that e has a normal distribution.

• TWO DIFFERENCES BETWEEN SIMPLE REGRESSION AND MULTIPLE REGRESSION

In principle, we will proceed exactly as we did with simple linear regression, when there was only one independent variable. We will calculate the values of B_1, B_2, and B_3 that minimize the sum of the squares of the errors between the values predicted by the equation and the actual values. There are two main differences between simple regression and multiple regression:

- We can't draw a picture of the relationship. Actually, if there are only two independent variables, we can attempt to draw a three-dimensional perspective drawing with x_1 and x_2 on the horizontal axes, y on the vertical axis, and one dot corresponding to each observation. Then the goal is to identify the plane that minimizes the sum of the squares of the vertical deviations between each observation and the plane. Drawing this type of diagram is very difficult, though. If there are more than two independent variables, it is impossible to draw a diagram. (Mathematicians still think of each observation as defining a point in multidimensional space, and the goal of multiple regression in that case is to find something called a *hyperplane* that best fits all the observations.)

- The calculation process is harder for multiple regression than it is for simple regression. But that won't worry us—we'll have the calculations done by a computer. In this book we will not attempt to explain how the multiple regression calculations are performed. Understanding those calculations requires a knowledge of matrix multiplication and matrix inversion. In a practical situation where you need to perform a multiple regression calculation, you will work with a computer.

In the rest of this chapter we will discuss how to interpret the results of a regression analysis.

YOU SHOULD REMEMBER

1. In multiple regression it is assumed that the true relation between the dependent variable y and the $m - 1$ independent variables x_1, $x_2, \cdots, x_{m-1}$ is given by the equation

$$y = B_1 x_1 + B_2 x_2 + \cdots + B_{m-1} x_{m-1} + B_m + e$$

where e is a normal random variable with mean 0 and unknown variance σ^2.

2. If you have a list of observations for each of these variables, then a computer regression program will calculate estimated values for each of the coefficients $B_1, B_2, \cdots, B_m$.

MULTIPLE REGRESSION OUTPUT

We'll use Excel to perform the multiple regression calculations for the statistics book data (page 417). (The appendix to this chapter shows how to derive the formula that the computer uses to find the regression results.)

Enter the data into the spreadsheet, with the labels "y," "$x1$," and "$x2$" at the top of the appropriate columns. From the menu, choose "data analysis," then choose "regression." A dialog box will appear where you need to enter the y range (for the dependent variable) and the x range (for the independent variables). (The independent variables should be in adjacent columns so you can enter one range that includes all of them.) Include the labels at the top of each column when you highlight the ranges, and then click the "labels" button in the dialog box. (When you do this, it allows Excel to include the labels in the regression output.) Now click "OK," and the regression results will appear.

SUMMARY OUTPUT					
Regression Statistics					
Multiple R	0.997851613				
R Square	0.995707842				
Adjusted R Square	0.994992483				
Standard Error	3.697121906				
Observations	15				
ANOVA					
	df	SS	MS	F	Significance F
Regression	2	38050.90881	19025.4544	1391.898274	6.25251E-15
Residual	12	164.0245247	13.66871039		
Total	14	38214.93333			
	Coefficients	Standard Error	t Stat	P-value	
Intercept	−2.76478812	6.390625329	−0.43263186	0.672955377	
x1	−7.737778054	0.363760467	−21.27162996	6.78343E-11	
x2	12.28610041	0.256556265	47.88852235	4.49774E-15	

Now we'll investigate the meaning of this information. From the coefficient column, we can write the regression equation:

$$y = -7.738x_1 + 12.286x_2 - 2.765$$

This equation lists the estimated values for the coefficients. The first thing we can learn from this result confirms what we expected: the coefficient for x_1 is negative, meaning that a higher price leads to lower sales. The coefficient of x_2 is positive, meaning that higher incomes lead to higher sales. We can use the estimated values of the coefficients to make predictions about the value of y (subject to all of the warnings discussed in Chapter 16). For example, if we knew of a town where average income was 20 and the price of statistics books was 6, then we would predict that the quantity of statistics books demanded would be

$$(-7.738 \times 6) + (12.286 \times 20) - 2.765 = 196.5$$

In general, we will use $\hat{b}_1$ to represent the computer's estimate of the coefficient B_1, $\hat{b}_2$ to represent the computer's estimate of the coefficient B_2, and so on. We'll consider a general situation where there are $m - 1$ independent variables. In that case we will have m coefficients to estimate (counting the constant term). Then the computer's regression output will look like this:

$$y = \hat{b}_1 x_1 + \hat{b}_2 x_2 + \cdots + \hat{b}_{m-1} x_{m-1} + \hat{b}_m$$

where $\hat{b}_m$ is the computer's estimate of the constant term.

• THE R^2 VALUE

The computer will also give an R^2 value for the regression. R^2 is called the **coefficient of multiple determination**. In this case the R^2 value is .9957. The interpretation of the R^2 value is similar to the interpretation of the r^2 value for a simple linear regression: R^2 measures the percent of variation in the dependent variable that can be explained by the regression. The value of R^2 will always be between 0 and 1.

To calculate R^2 we will first calculate several different sum of squares statistics. (See Chapter 15, where we calculated sum of squares statistics as part of analysis of variance.) The **total sum of squares (TSS)** is the sum of squares of the y values about $\bar{y}$:

$$\text{TSS} = \Sigma(y_i - \bar{y})^2$$

Again we will use Σ to mean $\Sigma_{i=1}^n$. Note that TSS is the same as the quantity we called SE_{av} in the simple linear regression case. We will use $\hat{y}_i$ to represent the regression's predicted value of y for the ith observation:

$$\hat{y}_i = \hat{b}_1 x_{i1} + \hat{b}_2 x_{i2} + \cdots + \hat{b}_{m-1} x_{i,m-1} + \hat{b}_m$$

For each observation we can calculate the difference between the value of y predicted by the regression line and the average value of y. Next we can sum the squares of all of those deviations and call it the **regression sum of squares (RGRSS)**:

$$\text{RGRSS} = \Sigma(\hat{y}_i - \bar{y})^2$$

Then we can calculate the residual for each observation, which is the difference between the actual value of y and the fitted value from the regression line:

$$(\text{residual}_i) = y_i - \hat{y}_i$$

The sum of the squares of all the residuals will be called the **error sum of squares (ERSS)**:

$$\text{ERSS} = \Sigma(y_i - \hat{y}_i)^2$$

This quantity is analogous to the quantity we called SE_{line} in the simple linear regression situation.

By performing the same type of calculation that we performed in Chapter 15, we can show that

$$TSS = RGRSS + ERSS$$

We can think of TSS as representing the total variation in the values of y. RGRSS is the amount of this variation that can be explained by the regression, and ERSS is the amount of remaining variation that cannot be explained by the regression. If the regression fits the data very well, then the value of RGRSS will be much bigger than the value of ERSS. We can calculate R^2 from either of these two formulas:

$$R^2 = 1 - \frac{ERSS}{TSS}$$
$$= \frac{RGRSS}{TSS}$$

For the statistics book example we have the following:

Town	y_i	x_1	x_2	$\hat{y}_i$	$(y_i - \hat{y}_i)$	$(y_i - \hat{y}_i)^2$	$y_i - \bar{y}$	$(y_1 - \bar{y})^2$
1	166	10	20	165.579	0.421	0.177	8.733	76.265
2	180	9	21	185.603	−5.603	31.397	22.733	516.789
3	73	10	12	67.291	5.709	32.597	−84.267	7,100.927
4	81	14	16	85.484	−4.484	20.106	−76.267	5,816.655
5	229	8	24	230.199	−1.199	1.439	71.733	5,145.623
6	182	15	24	176.035	5.965	35.582	24.733	611.721
7	233	6	23	233.389	−0.389	0.151	75.733	5,735.487
8	102	10	15	104.149	−2.149	4.618	−55.267	3,054.441
9	190	7	20	188.793	1.207	1.457	32.733	1,071.449
10	150	10	19	153.293	−3.293	10.846	− 7.267	52.809
11	221	11	25	219.272	1.728	2.985	63.733	4,061.895
12	137	15	21	139.177	−2.177	4.738	−20.267	410.751
13	173	8	19	168.769	4.231	17.902	15.733	247.527
14	150	12	20	150.104	−0.104	0.011	−7.267	52.809
15	92	10	14	91.863	0.137	0.019	−65.267	4,259.781
	total					164.025		38,214.933

From this table we can see the ERSS = 164.025 and TSS = 38,214.933. Then we can calculate

$$RGRSS = TSS - ERSS = 38,050.909$$

(Note: There will be slight discrepancies in some of these regression calculations because some intermediate results have been rounded.) Then we can calculate:

$$R^2 = \frac{38,050.909}{38,214.933} = .996$$

The estimated regression equation fits these points very well. However, there is an important caution you must keep in mind when interpreting the R^2 value of a multiple regression. It is always possible to increase the value of R^2 by adding more independent variables to the regression, whether or not they have anything to do with the dependent variable. For the regression results to be reliable the number of observations must be significantly greater than the number of coefficients you are estimating. Therefore, it is sometimes recommended to calculate the *adjusted R^2*:

$$(\text{adjusted } R^2) = 1 - \frac{(1 - R^2)(n - 1)}{n - m}$$

The adjusted R^2 will not necessarily go up if you add another variable because that will increase the value of m.

• *THE* F *STATISTIC*

Suppose some doubters tell you that they don't believe there is any connection between the dependent variable and the independent variables in your regression. They are making the following null hypothesis:

$$H_0: B_1 = B_2 = \cdots B_{m-1} = 0$$

In words, the person thinks that the true value of the coefficients for all $m - 1$ of the independent variables is zero. To test that hypothesis you may calculate this statistic:

$$F = \frac{\dfrac{\text{RGRSS}}{m - 1}}{\dfrac{\text{ERSS}}{n - m}}$$

This statistic is called the *F* **statistic** for the regression. If the null hypothesis is true, then it will have an *F* distribution with $m - 1$ degrees of freedom in the numerator and $n - m$ degrees of freedom in the denominator. (Remember that n is the number of observations and $m - 1$ is the number of independent variables.) If the null hypothesis is false, then we would expect RGRSS to be larger than ERSS, so the *F* statistic will be bigger than it would be if the null hypothesis was true. In our case the calculated value of the

F statistic is 1392, which is much larger than 3.9 (the 95 percent critical value for an F distribution with 2 and 12 degrees of freedom). Therefore we can unquestionably reject the null hypothesis.

These results can be summarized in an analysis of variance (ANOVA) table (see Chapter 15). (Note that Excel calculated this table on page 419.)

Source of Variation	Sum of Squares	Degrees of Freedom	Mean Square	F Ratio
Regression	38,050.909	2	19,025.455	1,391.89
Error	164.025	12	13.669	
total	38,214.933	14		

We will call ERSS/$(n - m)$ the mean square error (MSE), and we will use it as an estimator of the unknown variance σ^2. In this case MSE = 13.669.

TESTING INDIVIDUAL COEFFICIENTS

Now we will proceed with the statistical analysis of the individual coefficients. Our procedure will be very similar to our simple regression procedure. In Chapter 16 we said that b (the least squares estimator of the slope of the regression line) had a normal distribution whose mean was equal to the true value of the slope and whose variance was equal to σ^2 divided by a complicated expression that depends on the x's. We can find exactly analogous results in the multiple regression case.

Let B_i represent the unknown true value of the ith coefficient, and let $\hat{b}_i$ represent the least squares estimator of that coefficient. Then $\hat{b}_i$ has a normal distribution whose mean is equal to the true value B_i and whose variance is equal to σ^2 divided by a complicated expression that depends on the x's. Once again we will use MSE to estimate σ^2, but we will not describe the nature of the complicated expression that depends on the x's in this book. Fortunately, a computer regression program will always include with its output the estimated value of the standard deviation for each coefficient. We'll call that standard error $s(\hat{b}_i)$:

$$s(\hat{b}_i) = \sqrt{\text{Var}(\hat{b}_i)}$$

The values of the standard errors are often presented in parentheses below the coefficients:

$$y = -7.738x_1 + 12.286x_2 - 2.765$$
$$(0.364) \quad (0.257) \quad (6.39)$$

A smaller value of the standard error means that the coefficient estimate is more reliable.

As you might have expected, the quantity $(\hat{b}_i - B_i)/s(\hat{b}_i)$ has a t distribution with $n - m$ degrees of freedom. Therefore, we can calculate a confidence interval for B_i.

$$b_i \pm as(b_i)$$

where $\Pr(-a < t < a) = \text{CL}$

CL is the confidence level

t is a random variable having a t distribution with $n - m$ degrees of freedom

We can also test the null hypothesis that $B_i = 0$. If $B_i = 0$, then x_i does not have an effect on y. If the hypothesis is true, then the quantity $\hat{b}_i/s(\hat{b}_i)$ will have a t distribution with $n - m$ degrees of freedom. This quantity is called the *t* **statistic** for the ith coefficient. The values of the t statistics are often calculated by a computer regression program. (If they are not, you can calculate them very easily once you know $\hat{b}_i$ and $s(\hat{b}_i)$.) For the statistics book example we have:

Variable	Coefficient	Standard Error	*t* Statistic
Price	− 7.738	0.364	−21.3
Income	12.286	0.257	47.8
Constant term	− 2.765	6.39	−0.43

The 95 percent critical value for a t distribution with $15 - 3 = 12$ degrees of freedom is 2.179. The t statistics for both price and income are well outside this value, so we can safely reject the hypotheses that either the price or the income coefficient is zero. However, we cannot reject the hypothesis that the true value of the constant term is equal to zero.

YOU SHOULD REMEMBER

The computer will calculate, in addition to estimated values of B_1, $B_2, \cdots, B_m$, the following:

- the R^2 value for the regression (a value close to 1 means that the values estimated by the regression equation are close to the actual values of y)

- the *F* statistic for the regression (used to test the hypothesis that the coefficients of all the independent variables are zero)

- the standard error for each coefficient

- the *t* statistic for each coefficient (used to test the hypothesis that the true value of that coefficient is 0)

FURTHER ANALYSIS OF REGRESSION MODELS

We will mention a few more topics that apply to the analysis of regression. Some of these topics are the same for multiple regression and simple regression, but there are some special issues that arise only with multiple regression.

- Residuals. Once you have calculated the regression residuals, you may perform visual analysis just as we did in the last chapter. You may make several scatter diagrams comparing the residuals to the dependent variable and to each of the independent variables. In each case there should be no apparent pattern. If you have time series data, it also helps to make a plot of the residuals with time. It may also help to plot the residuals against another independent variable that you have not included in the model. If the residuals seem to be related to that variable, then you should include it in the model.

- Transformations. Again, a model that is not linear to begin with can often be transformed into a linear model by using logarithms or some other type of transformation. For example, if the true relation is

$$y = b_0 x_1^{b_1} x_2^{b_2} x_3^{b_3}$$

then you may take the logarithm of both sides:

$$\log y = \log b_0 + b_1 \log x_1 + b_2 \log x_2 + b_3 \log x_3$$

and you may estimate the values of b_0, b_1, b_2, and b_3 by ordinary linear regression.

- Multiple regression analysis can be applied to other types of curves. Figure 17–1 illustrates a total cost function, showing how the cost of producing the product increases as the quantity increases. Initially the

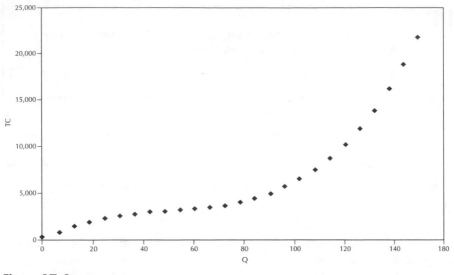

Figure 17–1

curve increases steeply, indicating that the production facility is not being efficiently used at very low levels of output. Then the curve becomes flatter, indicating that near the optimal range output can be increased with only a modest increase in cost. Then the curve becomes steeper again for larger quantities as capacity limits are reached. This type of curve (steeper, then flatter, then steeper again) can often be represented as a cubic, or third-degree polynomial. Create a multiple regression using Q, Q^2, and Q^3 as independent variables. The resulting regression equation is

$$TC = 207.464 + 144.538Q - 2.495Q^2 + 0.0166Q^3$$

- Figure 17–2 illustrates another curved relationship where multiple regression can be used. X represents the amount of fertilizer applied, and Y represents plant growth. Applying more fertilizer leads to more growth up to a point, but then applying still more fertilizer starts hurting the plant and growth declines. This relationship clearly cannot be represented by a line, but it can be represented by a quadratic, or second-degree polynomial. Set up a multiple regression using X and X^2 as two independent variables, and the result is

$$Y = -1790 + 27.6X - 0.092X^2$$

- You can download the data for these examples from the book's web page to perform these calculations for yourself.

Figure 17–2

- Serial correlation. In the regression model we have assumed that all of the errors are independent. Suppose we have a set of time series observations where a positive value for the error for one period is more likely to be followed by a positive value for the next period. In that case the errors are not independent. This situation is called **serial correlation** or **autocorrelation**. The least squares estimators are less reliable in this situation. A computer regression program will normally calculate the value of a statistic called the **Durbin-Watson statistic**. A small value of this statistic indicates the presence of one specific type of serial correlation. (How small is small? If the computer does not tell you, you will need to look in a Durbin-Watson table). In the case of serial correlation the regression results can be made more reliable by trying to find another independent variable to add to the model or by performing a transformation involving the differences between successive values of the variables.

- Multicollinearity. When two or more of the independent variables are closely correlated, then the problem of **multicollinearity** arises. If all of the independent variables are uncorrelated, then your regression model will still be able to accurately estimate the coefficients for the variables in the model even if some of the independent variables have been left out. However, the coefficient estimates become less reliable if some of the independent variables are highly correlated. In the extreme case where two of the independent variables are perfectly correlated, it is not even possible to calculate the least squares estimators. Also, the *t* statistics for the individual coefficients are not reliable when there is multicollinearity.

When two independent variables are highly correlated, it is not possible to accurately separate out their independent effects. For example, suppose you are trying to investigate the effects of income and education on demand for your product. You have collected information from a large sample of households. However, you are likely to find that the people with more income tend to be the people that have more education, so these two variables are highly correlated. A practical rule states that the problem of multicollinearity arises if the correlation coefficient between two variables is greater than .7. If you observe that people with higher income tend to buy your product more often, you do not know whether they do so because they have higher incomes or because they have more education.

Here is a similar type of example. Suppose you have observed that a particular chemical reaction occurs much more rapidly in warm, light environments than it does in cold, dark environments. However, you cannot tell whether it is the warmth or the light that speeds the reaction, since the two independent variables (temperature and amount of light) are correlated in your observations. The best way to solve the problem would be to obtain observations of the reaction in hot dark situations and cold light situations.

By analogy, the best solution in the income/education situation would be to obtain observations of people with high incomes/low educations and high educations/low incomes. However, it may be difficult to find these people. You may have no better alternative than removing either the education or the income variable from the regression and then remembering that the coefficient of the remaining variable represents the combined effect of the two variables.

• Dummy variables. Often some of the factors that affect the dependent variable are not quantitative factors that can be given by numbers. For example, suppose you are investigating consumption behavior with time series data for the period 1930 to 1950. You would expect that consumption behavior would have been significantly different during the years of World War II than it was before and after the war. To take this effect into account, you can create an artificial variable that will take the value 1 during each of the war years and the value 0 during each of the other years. This type of variable is called a **dummy variable** or an **indicator variable**. The coefficient of the World War II dummy variable indicates how much effect the war had on the constant term in the regression. Dummy variables can be used in many different situations with regressions. For example, in the house price regression you can use a dummy variable that will be 1 if the house has a garage and 0 if it does not.

- Simultaneous equations. Regression analysis is used to construct the economic models that try to predict economic activity. The branch of economics involved with this analysis is called **econometrics**. Econometric models require that regression analysis be applied to many different equations. The technique for applying regression in this situation is called *simultaneous equation analysis*.

YOU SHOULD REMEMBER

1. Analyzing the regression residuals is helpful in determining whether a particular multiple regression equation is appropriate.

2. Logarithms can often be used to transform a nonlinear model into a linear form.

3. The problem of *serial correlation* arises when the error terms are not independent for all observations.

4. The problem of *multicollinearity* arises when two or more of the inde pendent variables are correlated with each other.

5. The use of *dummy variables*, which always have the value 0 or 1, makes it possible to include nonquantitative factors in regression equations.

6. The development of *econometric models* requires the application of regression methods to several equations that must be true simultaneously.

APPENDIX: REGRESSION FORMULAS

This appendix derives the formulas that minimize the total squared error for a multiple regression calculation. Be warned that you need to understand calculus and matrix algebra to understand this appendix. Arrange your n observations of the independent variable y in a matrix y with n rows and 1 column:

$$
\mathbf{y} = \begin{pmatrix} y_1 \\ y_2 \\ \vdots \\ y_n \end{pmatrix}
$$

If you have $m - 1$ independent variables, then arrange those observations in a matrix $\mathbf{X}$ with n rows and m columns:

$$\mathbf{X} = \begin{pmatrix} X_{11} & X_{12} & \cdots & X_{1m} \\ X_{21} & X_{22} & \cdots & X_{2m} \\ & & \vdots & \\ X_{n1} & X_{n2} & \cdots & X_{nm} \end{pmatrix}$$

The final column of the matrix $\mathbf{X}$ consists of all 1s. This way we can think of the constant term in the regression B_m as the coefficient of an independent variable that always happens to have the value 1.

Arrange the regression coefficients in a matrix $\mathbf{B}$ with m rows and 1 column:

$$\mathbf{B} = \begin{pmatrix} B_1 \\ B_2 \\ \vdots \\ B_m \end{pmatrix}$$

The ith squared error term is:

$$e_i^2 = \left(\sum_{j=1}^{m} X_{ij} B_j - y_i \right)^2$$

The total squared error is found by summing the above expression from 1 to n:

$$TSE = \sum_{i=1}^{n} \left(\sum_{j=1}^{m} X_{ij} B_j - y_i \right)^2$$

$$TSE = \sum_{i=1}^{n} \left(\left(\sum_{j=1}^{m} X_{ij} B_j \right)^2 - 2 \sum_{j=1}^{m} X_{ij} B_j y_i + y_i^2 \right)$$

We want to minimize this expression. The Xs and ys are constants (because they represent the data we observe). The values we choose are the Bs. We need to find the partial derivatives of TSE with respect to each B:

$$\frac{\partial TSE}{\partial B_k} = \sum_{i=1}^{n} \left(\frac{\partial}{\partial B_k} \left(\sum_{j=1}^{m} X_{ij} B_j \right)^2 - \frac{\partial}{\partial B_k} 2 \sum_{j=1}^{m} X_{ij} B_j y_i + \frac{\partial}{\partial B_k} y_i^2 \right)$$

Since the last term does not depend on B_k, its partial derivative is zero. The partial derivative of the middle term is $2X_{ik}y_i$ since that is the coefficient of B_k. The most complicated derivative is the first term, which comes from this general rule: if $z = u^2$, then

$$\frac{dz}{dv} = 2u\,\frac{du}{dv}$$

Therefore:

$$\frac{\partial TSE}{\partial B_k} = \sum_{i=1}^{n}\left(2\left(\sum_{j=1}^{m}X_{ij}B_j\right)\left(\frac{\partial}{\partial B_k}\sum_{j=1}^{m}X_{ij}B_j\right) - 2X_{ik}y_i\right)$$

The partial derivative $\dfrac{\partial}{\partial B_k}\sum_{j=1}^{m}X_{ij}B_j$ is simply X_{ik} since that is the coefficient of B_k.

$$\frac{\partial TSE}{\partial B_k} = \sum_{i=1}^{n}\left(2\left(\sum_{j=1}^{m}X_{ij}B_j\right)(X_{ik}) - 2X_{ik}y_i\right)$$

There will be m partial derivatives of this form $\dfrac{\partial TSE}{\partial B_1},\ \dfrac{\partial TSE}{\partial B_2},\ \dots,\ \dfrac{\partial TSE}{\partial B_m}$.

Setting all of these partial derivatives equal to zero will give m equations of this form:

$$0 = \sum_{i=1}^{n}\left(2\left(\sum_{j=1}^{m}X_{ij}B_j\right)(X_{ik}) - 2X_{ik}y_i\right)$$

$$\sum_{i=1}^{n}\left(\left(\sum_{j=1}^{m}X_{ij}B_j\right)(X_{ik})\right) = \sum_{i=1}^{n}X_{ik}y_i$$

$$\sum_{j=1}^{m}\left(\sum_{i=1}^{n}X_{ji}X_{ik}\right)B_j = \sum_{i=1}^{n}X_{ik}y_i$$

The expression $\sum_{i=1}^{n}X_{ji}X_{ik}$ represents the element in row j, column k of the matrix formed by multiplying the transpose of matrix X (represented by X') by the matrix X. Represent this element by $X'X_{jk}$.

$$\sum_{j=1}^{m}X'X_{jk}B_j = \sum_{i=1}^{n}X_{ki}y_i$$

The expression $\sum_{j=1}^{m}X'X_{jk}B_j$ represents element k of the matrix product $X'XB$:

$$X'XB_k = \sum_{i=1}^{n}X_{ki}y_i$$

The right-hand side expression represents element k of the matrix product $\mathbf{X'y}$:

$$\mathbf{X'XB}_k = \mathbf{X'y}_k$$

Since we have k of these equations, we can write the complete equation system in matrix notation:

$$\mathbf{X'XB} = \mathbf{X'y}$$

Now multiply both sides of this equation by the inverse matrix $(\mathbf{X'X})^{-1}$:

$$(\mathbf{X'X})^{-1}\mathbf{X'XB} = (\mathbf{X'X})^{-1}\mathbf{X'y}$$
$$\mathbf{IB} = (\mathbf{X'X})^{-1}\mathbf{X'y}$$
$$\mathbf{B} = (\mathbf{X'X})^{-1}\mathbf{X'y}$$

The final matrix equation gives the formula for how to find the least squares regression coefficients. Since performing the matrix inversion is very cumbersome, this calculation is best left to the computer.

In the case of simple regression, the formula is simpler. The matrix $\mathbf{B}$ has two rows and one column. B_1 represents the slope of the regression line, and B_2 represents the constant (intercept) term. The matrix $\mathbf{X}$ has n rows but only 2 columns, and the second column is all 1s:

$$\mathbf{X} = \begin{pmatrix} x_1 & 1 \\ x_2 & 1 \\ \vdots & \\ x_n & 1 \end{pmatrix}$$

The transposed matrix $\mathbf{X'}$ becomes:

$$\mathbf{X'} = \begin{pmatrix} x_1 & x_2 & \cdots & x_n \\ 1 & 1 & \cdots & 1 \end{pmatrix}$$

$$\mathbf{X'X} = \begin{pmatrix} \sum_{i=1}^{n} x_i^2 & \sum_{i=1}^{n} x_i \\ \sum_{i=1}^{n} x_i & 1 \end{pmatrix}$$

$$\mathbf{X'y} = \begin{pmatrix} \sum_{i=1}^{n} x_i y_i \\ \sum_{i=1}^{n} y_i \end{pmatrix}$$

The equation system $\mathbf{X'XB = X'y}$ becomes:

$$\begin{pmatrix} \sum_{i=1}^{n}x_i^2 & \sum_{i=1}^{n}x_i \\ \sum_{i=1}^{n}x_i & 1 \end{pmatrix}\begin{pmatrix} B_1 \\ B_2 \end{pmatrix} = \begin{pmatrix} \sum_{i=1}^{n}x_iy_i \\ \sum_{i=1}^{n}y_i \end{pmatrix}$$

Write this expression as these two equations:

$$\sum_{i=1}^{n}x_i^2B_1 + \sum_{i=1}^{n}x_iB_2 = \sum_{i=1}^{n}x_iy_i$$

$$\sum_{i=1}^{n}x_iB_1 + B_2 = \sum_{i=1}^{n}y_i$$

Divide both sides of these equations by n, and use a bar over a quantity to represent its average:

$$\overline{x^2}B_1 + \bar{x}B_2 = \overline{xy}$$
$$\bar{x}B_1 + B_2 = \bar{y}$$

The second equation states that the regression line must pass through the point $(\bar{x}, \bar{y})$. Solve the second equation for B_2:

$$B_2 = \bar{y} - \bar{x}B_1$$

and plug this equation into the first equation:

$$\overline{x^2}B_1 + \bar{x}(\bar{y} - \bar{x}B_1) = \overline{xy}$$
$$\overline{x^2}B_1 + (\bar{x} \times \bar{y}) - (\bar{x} \times \bar{x}B_1) = \overline{xy}$$
$$B_1(\overline{x^2} - \bar{x}^2) = \overline{xy} - (\bar{x} \times \bar{y})$$
$$\text{regression slope} = B_1 = \frac{\overline{xy} - (\bar{x} \times \bar{y})}{\overline{x^2} - \bar{x}^2}$$

This equation can also be written in this form:

$$\text{regression slope} = B_1 = \frac{n\sum_{i=1}^{n}x_iy_i - (\sum_{i=1}^{n}x_i)(\sum_{i=1}^{n}y_i)}{n\sum_{i=1}^{n}x_i^2 - (\sum_{i=1}^{n}x)^2}$$

Once the slope B_1 is found, the constant term B_2 can be found from the equation:

$$B_2 = \bar{y} - \bar{x}B_1$$

KNOW THE CONCEPTS

DO YOU KNOW THE BASICS?

Test your understanding of Chapter 17 by answering the following questions:

1. Is it correct to say that in a multiple regression the independent variable with the largest coefficient has the greatest effect on the dependent variable?

2. What hypothesis do you test with the F statistic?

3. When you perform hypothesis tests with the t statistics and the F statistic from a multiple regression, are they one-tailed tests or two-tailed tests?

4. What happens to regression calculations if an important independent variable is left out?

5. Suppose two of the independent variables in your regression analysis are perfectly correlated. Explain intuitively why this creates problems for the regression calculation.

6. Will adding another independent variable make the R^2 value for the regression go up or down?

7. Suppose someone reports a regression result for ten observations and nine independent variables with an R^2 value of 1. Do you think this regression calculation is reliable?

8. What does the graph of a regression equation with two independent variables look like?

9. Is a regression more reliable if the data is collected before or after the regression equation is stated?

10. If a researcher reports that a particular independent variable has a "statistically significant" effect on the dependent variable, does this necessarily mean that this variable has an important effect? What other information should you see?

11. If you use daily observations of sales, instead of monthly observations, you will have many more observations for a given time period. In general this will be helpful, but which of the problems mentioned in the chapter might arise in this case?

12. If you try to do a multiple regression with a long list of independent variables, which of the problems mentioned in the chapter might arise?

13. If you reported a multiple regression result estimating demand for music CDs in the year 2000, what problem would you have encountered in trying to use that equation for forecasting?

14. If you performed a multiple regression calculation trying to forecast shipping volume at a port by using total employment and the gross domestic product as measures of the national economy, what problem would you have?

15. How could you use multiple regression analysis to determine whether another product is a substitute or a complement for your product?

16. During fall of 2008 gasoline prices fell rapidly from record high values that summer. At the same time the economy was falling into a severe recession. Does this mean that falling gas prices were bad for the economy?

17. If the true equation for sales of your product is

$$Q = B_{s0} + B_1 P$$

in spring and summer, and

$$Q = B_{w0} + B_1 P$$

during fall and winter, how could you estimate these coefficients with one multiple regression calculation? Do you expect B_1 is negative or positive?

TERMS FOR STUDY

coefficient of multiple determination
dummy variable
Durbin-Watson statistic
econometrics
error sum of squares (ERSS)
F statistic
multicollinearity

multiple regression
R^2
regression sum of squares (RGRSS)
serial correlation
standard error for coefficient
t statistic
total sum of squares (TSS)

PRACTICAL APPLICATION

COMPUTATIONAL PROBLEMS

See the book's web page for more examples of multiple regression calculations, with data you can paste into Excel.

1. The following table shows the results of a multiple regression calculation with 44 observations that attempts to forecast the value of sales of copper, using three independent variables: X1 = price of copper; X2 = price of aluminum; X3 = GDP growth.

X1	Coefficient:	−16.0
	Standard error:	3.0
X2	Coefficient	9.0
	Standard error	2.7
X3	Coefficient	15.0
	Standard error	9.0
	Constant	82,400

(a) For each coefficient, test the hypothesis that the true coefficient is zero.

(b) What level of sales would you predict if X1 = 42, X2 = 23, and X3 = 3.8?

ANSWERS

KNOW THE CONCEPTS

1. In general, a larger coefficient value indicates a greater effect. However, remember that the numerical value of a coefficient depends on the unit that is used to measure the variable. For example, the coefficient value will increase if a variable is measured in feet instead of inches. You must examine the situation carefully before you make judgments based on the numerical values of the coefficients.

2. The hypothesis tested is that the true values of all coefficients are zero.

3. The t test is a two-tailed test; the F test is a one-tailed test.

4. The random error will be larger; the coefficient estimates may be biased.

5. If two independent variables are perfectly correlated, then you have no observations that allow you to distinguish the separate effects of each variable.

6. The R^2 value will go up.

7. This result is meaningless, since a regression equation with a perfect fit can always be found if there are as many coefficients as observations. Note that in this case the number of degrees of freedom becomes 0, which makes no sense.

8. It is a plane in three-dimensional space.

9. The data will be more reliable if the data is collected after the regression equation is stated. That way you can be sure that the equation was not manipulated just to fit the observed data. Of course, you often need to revise your equations after viewing the data, but you will have more confidence in the reliability of your equation if you subsequently test the equation with new data. See discussion on page 325, number 6.

10. If they report that the coefficient of an independent variable is "statistically significant," most likely this means that the observed t statistic value causes one to reject the null hypothesis that this variable has no effect on the dependent variable, using the 5 percent significance level. This may or may not mean that there is an important effect. (See discussion on page 313.) First, you would like to see the p value. If the p value is 0.0498, it means that the null hypothesis is just barely rejected. A small p value would strengthen the case that the true coefficient is different from zero. However, even if the true coefficient is not exactly zero, this independent variable won't have an important effect if the coefficient is close to zero. Testing this effect is more complicated because the numerical value of the coefficient depends on the units being used. It would be helpful to know what would be the percentage change in the dependent variable for a 1 percent change in this independent variable, if all the other independent variables remained constant at their mean values.

11. With high-frequency data, such as daily sales figures, there is a greater chance that the factors that effect sales on one day will effect sales on the following day. This means that there could be the problem of serial correlation.

12. With a long list of independent variables, there is a greater chance that two or more of them will be highly correlated, which creates the multicollinearity problem.

13. The introduction of digital music players led to such a significant change in the music industry that any regression analysis based on data before that time would not be very reliable for subsequent times.

14. Since these two independent variables tend to be correlated, the multicollinearity problem would arise.

15. If you could obtain a collection of observations where the only significant change was the price of your product and the price of the other product, you can perform a multiple regression using your sales as the independent variable and the two prices as the independent variables. You would expect that the coefficient of your price would be negative, indicating that if you raise your price your sales would decline (other things being equal). If the coefficient of the price of the other product is positive, it means that when they raise their price it leads to more sales for you, which would indicate that people view your product as a substitute for the other product. If the coefficient of the price of the other product is negative, it means that when they raise their price it leads to less sales for you, which would indicate that people use the two products together, so they are complements.

16. Most likely the fall in the economy led to a fall in demand for gasoline, leading to a lower price for gasoline. This means you have to be careful when interpreting the coefficients in regression analysis. It may not be clear which variable is causing the change in the other variable. (Also note that a fall in the price of gasoline is not good for those in the gasoline business, even if it is good for gasoline buyers.)

17. You expect B_1 to be negative. When you raise your price, sales fall, but the effect is different in different seasons. Set up a multiple regression equation with two independent variables: price (P) and a dummy variable for the season S_D, equal to 1 in spring and summer, and 0 in fall and winter.

$$Q = B_0 + B_1 P + B_2 S_D$$

The B_0 you estimate from this equation will be B_{u0} (the intercept term that applies in fall and winter), and the value $B_0 + B_2$ will be B_{s0}, the intercept term that applies in spring and summer. (Note: Don't include two dummy variables, one for spring and summer and another for fall and winter, because those two would have a perfect negative correlation—whenever one is 0, the other would be 1.)

PRACTICAL APPLICATION

1. (a) Calculate the t statistic for each coefficient:

$$-16.0/3.0 = -5.3$$
$$9.0/2.7 = 3.3$$
$$15.0/9.0 = 1.7$$

The number of degrees of freedom is $44 - 4 = 40$. If the t statistic is outside the range -2.021 to 2.021, then reject the null hypothesis that the true coefficient is zero, indicating that this variable does belong in the regression

(b) $82,400 + (-16 \times 42) + (9 \times 23) + (15 \times 3.8000) = 81,992$

18

NONPARAMETRIC METHODS

You may have noticed a common thread running through the last few chapters. When testing hypotheses or generating confidence intervals, we've assumed that the population(s) we were sampling had a given distribution, usually normal. Although we may not have known what the parameters (that is, the mean and variance) were, we could estimate them from the samples and go on from there.

Often, we've assumed also that the data were continuous—that is, someone's height in centimeters could be 180.1, or 180.11, or 180.109, etc. What should we do if the data consist of people's ratings of a given product or service on a scale from 1 to 10? How do we allow for the fact that numerical ratings are subjective, that a product that is given an 8 is not necessarily "twice as good" as a product that is given a 4 by the same person?

In these instances we don't have the usual distributions and parameters to fall back on, and they call for different procedures, called **nonparametric methods**.

YOU SHOULD REMEMBER

1. Most of the statistical methods we discussed in preceding chapters involve estimating values for unknown parameters when a particular form of distribution is assumed to apply.

> **2.** Other statistical methods, called *nonparametric* methods, can be applied to situations where it is not necessary to make an assumption about the form of the distribution.

SIGN TEST

One of the simplest nonparametric methods is called the **sign test**. It is useful when evaluating a survey that tests which option the surveyee prefers, but not by how much. For example, suppose Jones Cola Company conducts a blind taste test matching its brand against that of its rival, Smith Cola Company. We will test the null hypothesis that among the population as a whole there is no difference in preferences between the two colas. If each person in the survey provided an accurate estimate of his or her liking for each cola on a scale of 1 to 10, we could use the statistical methods employed before with the *t* statistic. However, we might not have these rankings available; moreover, we might doubt the accuracy of interpersonal rating comparisons even if they were available. Therefore, we will use the sign test. We will simply ask 20 people in the survey which cola they prefer, using a plus sign to indicate people who prefer Jones cola and a minus sign to indicate the people who prefer Smith cola. Suppose the results are as follows:

$$+, -, +, +, +, +, -, +, +, -, +, +, +, -, +, +, -, +, +, +$$

Of the 20 people in the survey, 15 favored Jones Cola and 5 favored Smith Cola. If the null hypothesis is true, then each individual had a 50 percent chance of selecting Jones Cola and a 50 percent chance of selecting Smith Cola. Therefore, the number of plus signs would come from a binomial distribution with $n = 20$ and $p = .5$. We will use n_+ to stand for the number of plus signs. Then

$$E(n_+) = np = 10 \quad \text{and} \quad \text{Var}(n_+) = np(1-p) = \frac{20}{4} = 5$$

We can use the normal distribution as an approximation for the binomial distribution. (For the sign test this approximation will generally be valid when $n > 10$.) Therefore, we'll use a test statistic Z:

$$Z = \frac{n_+ - np}{\sqrt{np(1-p)}} = \frac{n_+ - n/2}{\sqrt{n}/2} = \frac{2n_+ - n}{\sqrt{n}}$$

which will have a standard normal distribution if the null hypothesis is true. In our case $n_+ = 15$ and $n = 20$, so we can calculate $Z = 2.236$. We can reject the null hypothesis at the 5 percent level, since 2.236 is outside 1.96.

One important advantage of the sign test is that you need not make restrictive assumptions about the nature of the population. For example, you do not need to assume that preferences are distributed according to the normal distribution. The disadvantage of the sign test is that it ignores some information that you may have in certain cases. If, as in the cola examples, the only information available tells you which brand was preferred, then you will have to use the sign test. If you also have available information that indicates the strength of each person's preferences, then the sign test is not as effective because it ignores that information.

FRIEDMAN F_r TEST

Above, where we were testing only two options, we cared only about which one people liked better. Given three or more options, we might also want to know which option people like second best, third best, and so on. Thus, given n options, we would ask people to rank their preferences. This would rule out a null hypothesis assuming a multinomial distribution (a straightforward generalization of the two-option case), which would take into account only which option a person liked best.

We therefore use the **Friedman F_r test** and construct a new test statistic:

$$F_r = \left[\frac{12}{bk(k+1)} \right] \left(\sum_{j=1}^{k} R_j^2 \right) - 3b(k+1)$$

where b is the sample size
  k is the number of options
  R_j is the rank sum of the jth option (that is, for the jth option, the sum of the ratings given by those surveyed)

Given the null hypothesis that there is no preference among the k options, and either $k > 5$ or $b > 5$, then F_r has approximately a chi-square distribution with $k - 1$ degrees of freedom, which can be used to test the null hypothesis.

Example: Application of the Friedman F_r Test

PROBLEM   Suppose 10 salesmen for a company compare their sales (working independently) in four cities. Test to see whether they do better or worse than average in any of the cities. Here is the data table:

Salesman	City No. 1	Rank No. 1	City No. 2	Rank No. 2	City No. 3	Rank No. 3	City No. 4	Rank No. 4
1	15	3	18	4	9	1	11	2
2	19	3	20	4	13	2	6	1
3	27	4	7	1	15	3	8	2
4	43	4	9	1	19	2	29	3
5	18	4	17	3	16	2	11	1
6	12	4	10	2	11	3	9	1
7	20	4	13	1	16	2	18	3
8	14	1	22	2	23	3	31	4
9	40	4	14	2	25	3	13	1
10	9	1	14	2	26	3	19	4
	$R_1 = 32$		$R_2 = 22$		$R_3 = 24$		$R_4 = 22$	

SOLUTION   Then $b = 10$, $k = 4$, $F_r = 4.08$; and, by checking Table A3–3, we see that we can accept the null hypothesis at the 5 percent level.

Our general procedure, given survey results ranking preferences of choices (either because numerical data are not available, or because they don't fit a known distribution), is to test the null hypothesis that there is no preference among the choices, when either the size of the sample (b) or the number of options (k) is greater than 5.

Procedure for the Friedman F_r Test

1. Calculate the rank sums R_j.

2. Calculate

$$F_r = \left[\frac{12}{bk(k+1)} \right] \left(\sum_{j=1}^{k} R_j^2 \right) - 3b(k+1)$$

3. F_r has approximately a chi-square distribution with $k - 1$ degrees of freedom. Check Table A3–3 for $k - 1$ degrees of freedom. Accept or reject the null hypothesis at a chosen significance level.

Note: Ties may occur when ranking numerical data. If there are only a few ties, average the rankings among those tied; for example, 10, 20, 10, 15 would be ranked 1.5, 4, 1.5, 3 since there is a tie for first and second rankings. If there are many ties, your data may be unreliable.

YOU SHOULD REMEMBER

1. The sign test is used to test the hypothesis that there is no difference between two quantities when you have rankings instead of numerical values.

2. The Friedman F_r test is used to test the hypothesis that there is no difference between preferences when there are more than two possibilities.

WILCOXON RANK SUM TEST

Suppose now that you have samples (not necessarily the same size) from two populations that you think have the same (unknown) distribution. One way of testing whether they really do come from the same distribution is to pool the samples and see how they mix. If all the values of one sample are smaller than all the values of the other, then you should probably reject the null hypothesis (that the two populations have the same distribution). On the other hand, if they are well mixed, then you have no cause to reject the hypothesis.

A way of measuring how well the pooled samples are mixed is the **Wilcoxon rank sum test**. It consists of pooling the samples A and B, ranking them, and adding the ranks given to A to form the rank sum T. If the size of each sample is at least 8, then T has an approximately normal distribution with parameters

$$\mu_T = \frac{n_A(n_A + n_B + 1)}{2} \quad \text{and}$$

$$\sigma_r^2 = \frac{n_A n_B(n_A + n_B + 1)}{12}$$

where n_A = the size of sample A and n_B = the size of sample B. Then, by comparing $(T - \mu_T)/\sigma_T$ with Table A3–2, we can determine whether to accept the hypothesis.

Example: Application of the Wilcoxon Rank Sum Test

PROBLEM   Suppose nine Harvard and eight Yale economics professors make the following predictions for inflation for the coming year:

Harvard	Inflation Prediction (in percent)	Rank	Yale	Inflation Prediction (in percent)	Rank
1	8.6	1	1	15.8	15
2	9.7	3	2	13.4	11
3	11.8	6	3	12.2	7
4	17.1	16	4	17.3	17
5	12.9	10	5	12.6	9
6	11.7	5	6	14.3	14
7	12.4	8	7	14.2	13
8	10.3	4	8	13.5	12
9	8.9	2			

Test the null hypothesis that the professors' predictions have the same distributions.

SOLUTION   Here

$$T = 55, \qquad \mu_T = \frac{(18)}{2} = 81,$$

$$\sigma_T{}^2 = \frac{(9)(8)(18)}{12} = 108, \qquad \frac{T - \mu_T}{\sigma_T} = -2.5$$

and, by comparing with Table A3–2, we see that we can reject the hypothesis at the 95 percent level.

Thus we have the procedure shown below to test the null hypothesis that samples come from two populations with the same distribution.

Procedure for the Wilcoxon Rank Sum Test

1. Pool the samples.

2. Rank them (again, if there are relatively few ties, average their ranks).

3. Compute the rank sum T for sample A,

$$\mu_T = \frac{n_A(n_A + n_B + 1)}{2} \qquad \text{and} \qquad \sigma_T{}^2 = \frac{n_A n_B(n_A + n_B + 1)}{12}$$

4. Compare the standard normal random variable $(T - \mu_T)/\sigma_T$ with Table A3–2 at a given level to determine whether to accept the hypothesis.

KRUSKAL-WALLIS *H* TEST

The **Kruskal-Wallis *H* test** is a generalization of the Wilcoxon rank sum test to more than two populations.

Example: Application of the Kruskal-Wallis H *Test*

PROBLEM Suppose that we have samples of k populations, and we want to test the hypothesis that the populations have the same distributions.

SOLUTION Again we pool the samples and rank them. Our test statistic is a bit more complicated, however:

$$H = \left[\frac{12}{n(n+1)}\right]\left[\sum_{j=1}^{k}\left(\frac{R_j^2}{n_j}\right)\right] - 3(n+1)$$

where

$$n = \sum_{j=1}^{k} n_j$$

n_j = the size of the sample of the jth population, and R_j = the jth rank sum. H has approximately a chi-square distribution with $k - 1$ degrees of freedom, if each of the n_j is larger than 5.

Thus, given a significance level and samples of k different populations (with every sample size larger than 5), calculate H, and check Table A3–3 under $k - 1$ degrees of freedom to decide whether to accept the null hypothesis (that the populations have the same distributions).

WILCOXON SIGNED RANK TEST

As you might guess, the **Wilcoxon signed rank test** is similar in some ways to the Wilcoxon rank sum test. It is applicable to situations similar to those discussed for the sign test. The null hypothesis states that there is no difference between the two populations.

Suppose we have a survey asking people to evaluate two options A and B. This time, rather than just stating which they prefer, they rate each on a scale (for example, from 1 to 10 or 100). We then rank the absolute values of the differences between the ratings for A and B, and sum the ranks for the positive differences and negative differences, giving T_+ and T_-. If we let T be the smaller of T_+ and T_-, and the sample size N is large, then T is a normal random variable with parameters

$$\mu_T = \frac{N(N+1)}{4} \quad \text{and} \quad \sigma_T = \frac{N(N+1)(2N+1)}{24}$$

if the null hypothesis is correct. We then have a standard normal random variable $(T - \mu_T)/\sigma_T$ that we can compare with Table A3–2 to decide whether to accept our hypothesis.

Example: Application of the Wilcoxon Signed Rank Test

PROBLEM   Suppose we take a random sample of 10 people who have rented cars from both Able Rental Cars and Baker Rental Cars, and ask them to rate both rental services on a scale of 1 to 10. We then have the following table:

Person	A	B	A − B	|A − B|	Rank	+	−
1	4	7	−3	3	9		9
2	5	6	−1	1	3		3
3	9	6	3	3	9	9	
4	5	7	−2	2	6.5		6.5
5	4	5	−1	1	3		3
6	9	8	1	1	3	3	
7	5	4	1	1	3	3	
8	7	6	1	1	3	3	
9	3	5	−2	2	6.5		6.5
10	3	6	−3	3	9		9
				totals		18	37

Test the hypothesis that there is no difference between the two companies.

SOLUTION   Then $T_+ = 18$, $T_- = 37$. Also,

$$T = T_+ = 18, \qquad \mu_T = \frac{10(11)}{4} = 27.5,$$

$$\sigma_T^2 = \frac{10(11)(21)}{24} = 96.25.$$

Thus $(T - \mu_T)/\sigma_T = -0.97$, and we can accept the hypothesis at the 95 percent level.

Again in case of ties, average the ranks involved. If persons give the same rating to A and B (that is, $A - B = 0$), perform the test twice, first counting 0 as a positive difference, the second time counting 0 as a negative difference. If the results agree, fine. If not, your data may be unreliable.

We then have the procedure shown below, given ratings of two options by N people (companies, departments, etc.).

Procedure for the Wilcoxon Signed Rank Test

1. Rank the absolute values of the differences of the ratings.

2. Calculate the rank sums T_+ and T_-.

3. Let T be the smaller of T_+ and T_-,

$$\mu_T = \frac{N(N+1)}{4}, \quad \text{and} \quad \sigma_T^2 = \frac{N(N+1)(2N+1)}{24}$$

4. Compare $(T - \mu_T)/\sigma_T$ with Table A3–2 to determine whether to accept the null hypothesis at a given significance level.

YOU SHOULD REMEMBER

1. The Wilcoxon rank sum test is used to test the hypothesis that there is no difference between the means of populations.

2. The Kruskal-Wallis H test is a generalization of the Wilcoxon rank sum test, used when there are more than two populations.

3. The Wilcoxon signed rank test is used to test the hypothesis that there is no difference between the means of populations.

KNOW THE CONCEPTS

DO YOU KNOW THE BASICS?

Test your understanding of Chapter 18 by answering the following questions:

1. In general, what is one of the main advantages of nonparametric statistical methods? What is one of the main disadvantages?

2. Can you explain intuitively why the sign test works?

3. Is the sign test a two-tailed test or a one-tailed test?

4. Which test makes more use of the available information: the sign test or the Wilcoxon signed rank test?

5. Why would the presence of too many ties in the rankings make the Friedman F_r test unreliable?

TERMS FOR STUDY

Friedman F_r test
Kruskal-Wallis H test
nonparametric method

sign test
Wilcoxon rank sum test
Wilcoxon signed rank test

PRACTICAL APPLICATION

COMPUTATIONAL PROBLEMS

1. Of 25 rental car users surveyed, 9 preferred Arthur's Rental Cars to Beaumont's Rental Cars, the other 16 preferring Beaumont's. Test the null hypothesis that rental car users have no preference between Arthur's Rental Cars and Beaumont's Rental Cars.

2. On a certain uneven piece of ground, Route 13 splits into two roads that eventually merge, one going over some mountains and the other down through a valley. If a random sampling of 30 drivers showed that 8 drivers took the high road and 22 drivers took the low road, test the null hypothesis that Route 13 drivers have no preference between the two roads.

3. In a taste test, 13 out of 18 people preferred spaghetti sauce made with ground oregano to sauce made with crushed oregano leaves, the other 5 people preferring the crushed leaves. Test the null hypothesis that people are indifferent to which form of oregano is used in their spaghetti sauce.

4. Fifteen frequent fliers are asked to rate in order of preference three airlines: Aircat (*A*) Bluebird (*B*), and Condor (*C*) Airlines. The results are as follows:

A	B	C	A	B	C	A	B	C
1	3	2	3	1	2	1	3	2
1	3	2	3	2	1	3	2	1
1	3	2	2	3	1	2	3	1
1	2	3	1	3	2	3	1	2
2	1	3	1	2	3	1	3	2

Test the null hypothesis that there is no preference among fliers between the three airlines.

5. Four people (A, B, C, D) are asked to rate in order of preference the 12 months of the year. The results are as follows:

	J	F	M	A	M	J	J	A	S	O	N	D
A	12	11	5	3	4	6	7	8	1	2	9	10
B	12	1	2	9	4	3	5	6	7	8	10	11
C	1	2	4	5	6	9	3	7	8	10	11	12
D	1	4	3	12	10	5	9	11	8	7	6	2

Use these data to test the null hypothesis that people have no preference between the months of the year.

6. Six companies show the following profits (in thousands of dollars) from sales in four different cities (A, B, C, D):

A	B	C	D
22	11	16	14
20	19	18	14
19	24	16	13
15	18	17	19
18	17	13	15
17	16	19	12

Use the Friedman F_r statistic to test the null hypothesis that the four cities are equally profitable for the companies.

7. Thirteen voters surveyed showed the following preferences between three presidential candidates (A, B, C):

A	B	C	A	B	C
3	2	1	1	2	3
2	3	1	3	1	2
3	1	2	3	2	1
1	2	3	2	1	3
1	2	3	2	1	3
3	2	1	1	2	3
1	2	3			

Test the null hypothesis that voters have no preference between the candidates.

8. Here are the sales figures (in hundreds) for a company in 10 towns in Arizona and 15 towns in Michigan:

   AZ: 16, 8, 7, 14, 22, 27, 19, 23, 18, 30

   MI: 13, 28, 17, 26, 12, 11, 33, 35, 5, 40, 39, 10, 6, 32, 31

   Test the null hypothesis that the distribution of sales in Arizona is the same as that in Michigan.

9. Here are the defense budgets (in millions of dollars, adjusted for inflation) of two countries (A, B) over a decade:

   A: 10, 12, 15, 16, 18, 22, 26, 28, 30, 29

   B: 9, 8, 17, 14, 13, 19, 24, 25, 27, 31

   Test the null hypothesis that the budgets have the same distribution.

10. Twelve light bulbs of brand X and fifteen of brand Y were tested to see how long they would last, with the following results (in hundreds of hours):

    X: 15, 19, 23, 25, 26, 28, 30, 29, 32, 31, 20, 14

    Y: 20, 18, 16, 19, 22, 24, 17, 21, 10, 11, 32, 27, 12, 14, 9

    Test the null hypothesis that the lifetimes of the two brands of light bulbs have the same distribution.

11. Here are the incomes (in thousands of dollars) of 15 plumbers in California and 13 plumbers in Maine:

    CA: 22, 19, 17, 24, 25, 30, 29, 31, 28, 37, 15, 40, 38, 39, 17

    ME: 21, 20, 18, 17, 23, 26, 28, 29, 32, 35, 19, 27, 16

    Test the null hypothesis that plumbers' incomes are distributed equally in both states.

12. Here are the benefits (in thousands of dollars) paid to employees of three yo-yo manufacturers (A, B, C) over a decade:

A	B	C	A	B	C
10	25	16	23	19	28
26	12	24	30	14	18
29	20	13	31	38	35
21	11	22	39	32	37
17	27	15	33	36	34

Test the hypothesis that the benefits expenditures of the three companies have the same distribution.

13. Four experimental precision scales (A, B, C, D) are tested on a fixed weight, with the following results:

     A: 103, 121, 106, 120, 114, 128, 116

     B: 112, 105, 132, 136, 109, 138, 135, 126, 124, 117

     C: 131, 104, 130, 108, 123, 119, 113, 133, 127, 134, 125, 115

     D: 129, 111, 122, 137, 107, 110, 139, 118

Test the null hypothesis that the distributions of values given by the four scales are the same.

14. Fifteen people are asked to rate on a scale of 1–100 two different stereo systems (A, B), with the following results:

A	B	A	B	A	B
85	78	95	70	65	83
60	99	99	65	85	72
70	85	93	62	89	95
75	99	75	80	90	60
88	90	60	78	95	50

Test the null hypothesis that people have no preference between the two kinds of stereos.

15. Twenty people rate on a scale of 1–10 two political candidates (A, B), with the following results:

A	B	A	B	A	B	A	B
2	8	8	4	6	5	9	7
5	6	9	8	7	4	8	9
3	5	8	9	8	5	4	6
7	8	7	8	8	6	10	7
4	5	5	6	9	6	8	5

Test the null hypothesis that people have no preference between the candidates.

16. Eighteen people rate on a scale of 1–20 two different brands (A, B) of water pistols, with the following results:

A	B	A	B	A	B
18	15	17	13	11	17
14	12	12	15	13	12
17	19	13	17	14	16
16	12	18	15	12	13
18	15	19	16	11	10
11	9	12	16	16	12

Test the null hypothesis that people have no preference between the pistols.

17. Twenty-five people rate on a scale of 1–10 two car models (A, B), with the following results:

A	B	A	B	A	B
4	6	6	4	8	2
8	7	8	7	9	8
5	4	5	8	8	6
4	2	7	6	7	8
3	7	4	8	6	7
6	5	5	9	3	6
9	8	6	3	5	6
7	8	7	3	4	2
2	5				

Test the null hypothesis that people have no preference between the car models.

ANSWERS

KNOW THE CONCEPTS

1. The main advantage of nonparametric methods is that it is not necessary to make assumptions about the specific form of the distributions you are dealing with. The main disadvantage is that nonparametric tests do not use all of the data you may have available.

2. If the null hypothesis is true, then the number of pluses will have a binomial distribution with $p = .5$.

3. The sign test is a two-tailed test.

4. The Wilcoxon signed rank test makes more use of the information.

5. If there were too many ties in the rankings for the Friedman F_r test, the data points that were not part of the ties would have too great an effect on the result. The situation would be similar to using too small a sample.

PRACTICAL APPLICATION

1. $n = 25$, $n_+ = 16$, $Z = 1.4$; accept the null hypothesis.
2. $n = 30$, $n_+ = 22$, $Z = 2.56$; reject the null hypothesis.
3. $n = 18$, $n_+ = 13$, $Z = 1.89$; accept the null hypothesis.
4. $R_A = 26$, $R_B = 35$, $R_C = 29$,

$$F_r = \left(\frac{12}{(15)(3)(4)}\right)(26^2 + 35^2 + 29^2) - 3(15)(4) = 2.8$$

and you would accept the null hypothesis at the 90 percent level.

5. $R_1 = 26$, $R_2 = 18$, $R_3 = 14$, $R_4 = 29$, $R_5 = 24$, $R_6 = 23$, $R_7 = 24$, $R_8 = 32$, $R_9 = 24$, $R_{10} = 27$, $R_{11} = 36$, $R_{12} = 35$,

$$F_r = \left(\frac{12}{(4)(12)(13)}\right)(26^2 + 18^2 + 14^2 + 29^2 + 24^2 + 23^2 + 24^2$$
$$+ 32^2 + 24^2 + 27^2 + 36^2 + 35^2) - 3(4)(13) = 8.77$$

and you would accept the null hypothesis at the 90 percent level.

6. $R_A = 19$, $R_B = 16$, $R_C = 14$, $R_D = 11$,

$$F_r = \left(\frac{12}{(6)(4)(5)}\right)(19^2 + 16^2 + 14^2 + 11^2) - 3(6)(5) = 3.4$$

and you would accept the hypothesis at the 90 percent level.

7. $R_A = 26$, $R_B = 23$, $R_C = 29$

$$F_r = \left(\frac{12}{(13)(3)(4)}\right)(26^2 + 23^2 + 29^2) - 3(13)(4) = 1.38$$

and you would accept the null hypothesis at the 90 percent level.

8. $T = 116$, $\mu_T = 10(26)/2 = 130$, $\sigma_T^2 = (10)(15)(26)/12 = 325$, $(T - \mu_T)/\sigma_T = -0.776$, and you would accept the null hypothesis at the 90 percent level.

9. $T = 113$, $\mu_T = 10(21)/2 = 105$, $\sigma_T^2 = (10)(10)(21)/12 = 175$, $(T - \mu_T)/\sigma_T = 0.605$, and you would accept the null hypothesis at the 90 percent level.

10. $T = 214$, $\mu_T = 12(28)/2 = 168$, $\sigma_T^2 = (12)(15)(28)/12 = 420$, $(T - \mu_T)/\sigma_T = 2.25$, and you would reject the null hypothesis at the 95 percent level.

11. $T = 240.5$, $\mu_T = 15(29)/2 = 217.5$, $\sigma_T^2 = (15)(13)(29)/12 = 471.25$, $(T - \mu_T)/\sigma_T = 1.06$, and you would accept the null hypothesis at the 90 percent level.

12. $R_A = 169$, $R_B = 144$, $R_C = 152$,

$$H = \left(\frac{12}{30(31)}\right)\left(\frac{169^2}{10} + \frac{144^2}{10} + \frac{152^2}{10}\right) - 3(31) = 0.421$$

and you would accept the null hypothesis at the 90 percent level.

13. $R_A = 94$, $R_B = 214$, $R_C = 238$, $R_D = 157$,

$$H = \left(\frac{12}{37(38)}\right)\left(\frac{94^2}{7} + \frac{214^2}{10} + \frac{238^2}{12} + \frac{157^2}{8}\right) - 3(38) = 2.44$$

and you would accept the null hypothesis at the 90 percent level.

14. $T_+ = 70$, $T_- = 50$, $T = 50$, $\mu_T = 15(16)/4 = 60$, $\sigma_T^2 = (15)(16)(31)/24 = 310$, $(T - \mu_T)/\sigma_T = -0.568$, and you would accept the null hypothesis at the 90 percent level.

15. $T_+ = 132$, $T_- = 78$, $T = 78$, $\mu_T = 20(21)/4 = 105$, $\sigma_T^2 = (20)(21)(41)/24 = 717.5$, $(T - \mu_T)/\sigma_T = -1.007$, and you would accept the null hypothesis at the 90 percent level. Note: In view of the large number of ties in this sample, the data may not be reliable.

16. $T_+ = 100$, $T_- = 71$, $T = 71$, $\mu_T = 18(19)/4 = 85.5$, $\sigma_T^2 = (18)(19)(37)/24 = 527.25$, $(T - \mu_T)/\sigma_T = -0.630$, and you would accept the null hypothesis at the 90 percent level.

17. $T_+ = 164$, $T_- = 161$, $T = 161$, $\mu_T = 25(26)/4 = 162.5$, $\sigma_T^2 = (25)(26)(51)/24 = 1,381.25$, $(T - \mu_T)/\sigma_T = -0.040$, and you would accept the null hypothesis at the 90 percent level. Note: In view of the large number of ties in this sample, the data may not be reliable.

19

ECONOMIC DATA
AND BUSINESS
FORECASTING

KEY TERMS

gross domestic product (GDP) a measure of the total value of all goods and services produced in the country.

price index a measure of the price level

price level the average level of all prices in the country; can be measured by the GDP deflator, consumer price index, or producer price index

seasonal adjustment a procedure for adjusting time series data to compensate for seasonal variation in order to make nonseasonal changes in the data more apparent

time series data data that consist of several observations of a quantity at different points in time; can often be broken down into four components: a trend component, a cyclical component, a seasonal component, and an irregular component

Many times it is helpful to know about the current state of the economy. In this chapter we will discuss some of the most important statistical measures that describe the economy, as well as some general techniques for analyzing different types of business data.

GROSS DOMESTIC PRODUCT

The most common statistic for measuring the overall level of production in the entire economy is called the **gross domestic product** (**GDP** for short). It measures the total value of all goods and services produced in the country

455

in a given year. The job of collecting the statistics used to compile GDP is handled by the Department of Commerce, and the results are available from the Commerce Department's Bureau of Economic Analysis at *www.bea.gov.* Estimates of GDP are calculated for each quarter of the year. Measuring GDP requires an immense data collection effort. The process of analyzing these data is called *national income accounting.*

In reality, of course, the Department of Commerce cannot observe every single good or service produced, so it needs to use statistical procedures to estimate GDP based on the data it collects from surveys of businesses. Suppose that we could compile a list of all goods and services produced in the economy. To simplify our discussion, let's assume that our economy produces only three goods: pizza, ice cream cones, and statistics books.

Good	Quantity Produced This Year
Pizzas	500
Ice cream cones	615
Books	90

(We are assuming that all pizzas are identical, all ice cream cones are identical, and so on. In reality we would need separate measures for each type of pizza, each type of ice cream cone, and each type of every other good.) Now we must add up the total production. We cannot simply add the quantities, because then we would (literally) have the problem of adding up apples and oranges. Instead, what we will do is add up the total *value* of each type of good produced. Therefore, we also need a list of the price of each good:

Good	Quantity	Price
Pizzas	500	$5.00
Ice cream cones	615	2.00
Books	90	7.00

To get the total value of each good we must multiply the price times the quantity:

Good	Quantity	Price	Value
Pizzas	500	$5.00	$2,500
Ice cream cones	615	2.00	1,230
Books	90	7.00	630
	GDP:		$4,360

This quantity is called the *nominal GDP*; later we will see how the *real GDP* corrects for inflation.

• *SOME CAUTIONS IN MEASURING GDP*

The GDP is found by adding up the total value. There are some complications that must be kept in mind while measuring GDP.

1. Intermediate goods cannot be counted. An intermediate good is a good produced by one firm and then sold to another firm for use in producing some other good. If intermediate goods were directly included in GDP, then they would be double counted, because they are counted as part of the final goods in which they are used.

   Here is an example. Suppose that our economy consists of a peanut farmer who produces $50 worth of peanuts. She sells $30 worth of peanuts to consumers and $20 worth to a peanut butter factory, which uses the peanuts to produce $60 worth of peanut butter. Here is the wrong way to calculate GDP.

   $$\text{Value of peanuts} = 50$$

   $$\text{Value of peanut butter} = \underline{60}$$

   $$\text{Total GDP} = 110 \ (wrong)$$

   The peanuts that were sold to the peanut butter firm were counted twice in this calculation.

   There are two correct ways to calculate GDP. One way is to count only the final goods (sold to consumers) produced by each supplier:

   $$\text{Value of peanuts sold to consumers} = 30$$

   $$\text{Value of peanut butter sold to consumers} = \underline{60}$$

   $$\text{Total GDP} = 90 \ (right)$$

   The other way is to subtract the value of the intermediate goods used by each firm from its output. (The value of a firm's output minus the value of its intermediate goods is called the *value added*.)

   $$\text{Value added by peanut farmer} = 50 - 0 = 50$$

   $$\text{Value added by peanut butter firm} = 60 - 20 = \underline{40}$$

   $$\text{Total GDP} = 90 \ (right)$$

   (We have assumed that the farmer does not use any intermediate goods. In reality the farmer probably buys some fertilizer and other goods to use in the peanut farming process.)

2. Purely financial transactions are not included in GDP. If you put some money in the bank or buy shares of stock, you are buying a financial asset, not a currently produced good or service. However, if you pay a fee to a broker to handle the transaction, that fee is included in GDP because you are paying for broker service.

3. Transactions in old objects are not included in GDP. Suppose you buy a 2005 model used car. The value of the car cannot be counted as part of this year's GDP because it was already counted as part of GDP in 2005, and the same car cannot be counted twice. However, the profit that your used car dealer makes on the sale counts as part of the GDP because he is providing used car dealing service. (If you don't want to pay for his service, you can try on your own to find someone willing to sell the kind of car you want to buy.)

   If a good is produced this year but not sold until next year, it counts as part of GDP this year. It is counted as part of a category called "increase in inventory." If you are bothered by the question "How do we calculate the value of the good if it has not been sold yet?" we suggest you study accounting.

4. Government services are usually valued at their cost of production. Since most government services are not sold, it is harder to attach values to them. For example, if a U.S. Air Force pilot is paid $50,000, then it is assumed that the pilot is adding $50,000 to GDP. The salary of a commercial airline pilot, on the other hand, is not directly added to GDP; instead the value of the tickets sold by his airline is included. This procedure can sometimes lead to strange results. When the government pays $5,000 for a wrench, that wrench is counted as adding $5,000 to GDP.

It is important to remember that GDP is not intended to measure national welfare. For one thing, GDP leaves out some important parts of national production: nonmarket activities. All the work performed by do-it-your-selfers and housekeepers really should be counted as part of national production, but their work cannot be counted in GDP (unless they are paid) because it would be too difficult to measure the value of their services. The GDP does not include the value of leisure time, nor does it take into account the effects of harmful phenomena such as pollution. Also, if you are interested in the average goods and services available to each person in the country, you should look at per capita GDP rather than total GDP.

In the 1990s, the Commerce Department changed the way it reports these statistics. Previously, the main focus was on a figure called gross national product (GNP). GNP measures the total value of all production by factors (inputs) owned by U.S. citizens, whether or not the production occurs in the

United States. The GDP and GNP will usually have similar values. Here is the difference between them in 2008:

gross domestic product:	$14.265 trillion
add receipts of factor income from the rest of the world:	$0.798 trillion
subtract payment of factor income to rest of world:	$0.665 trillion
equals gross national product	$14.398 trillion

Part of the gross national product is used to replace capital goods that have worn out, so another statistic, the **net national product (NNP)**, is calculated which subtracts out the value of capital goods that have worn out. (This amount is called depreciation, or capital consumption.) For 2008:

gross national product:	$14.398 trillion
subtract consumption of fixed capital:	$1.832 trillion
equals net national product (NNP)	$12.566 trillion

Another closely related concept is the **national income**. Every time a good is purchased, it shows up as part of national production, but it also generates income (wages or profits) for someone. Therefore, if we added up the value of all of the income in the country, we would get a figure close to net national product. The difference between NNP and national income arises because of incomplete measurements, known as the statistical discrepancy. For 2008, national income was $12.427 trillion.

PRICE INDEXES

If production in the country remained the same but all prices went up, then the value of GDP would go up. However, since GDP is supposed to measure national production, we need to find a way to separate the effects of a price increase from the effects of a production increase. There are many other reasons why we need to measure the average size of prices (called the **price level**) or the rate of change in the price level (called the **inflation rate**). Determining the price level is very difficult, but we can estimate it with a quantity called a **price index**. We will discuss three different price indexes: the **GDP deflator**, the **consumer price index**, and the **producer price index**.

Let's return to our pizza/ice cream/books economy. Suppose these are the figures for production in 2011.

	2011		
	Quantity	Price	Value
Pizza	500	5.00	2,500
Ice cream cones	615	2.00	1,230
Books	90	7.00	630
	GDP:		4,360

The value of GDP calculated this way, using the current year's prices and quantities, is called the **nominal GDP**. Compare these with the figures for 2012:

	2012		
	Quantity	Price	Value
Pizza	800	5.50	4,400
Ice cream cones	650	3.00	1,950
Books	100	8.00	800
	GDP:		7,150

The nominal GDP is higher than it was in 2011 for two reasons: the production of each good has gone up, but so has the price of each good. The **real GDP** is designed so that it increases only when production goes up, not when prices go up. If the production of each good went up by 10 percent, then we would say that the real GDP increased by 10 percent. However, since the percent increase varies for different products, it is more difficult to determine the increase in real GDP. Let's ask this hypothetical question: how much would the GDP have gone up in 2012 if the prices had all stayed the same as they were in 2011?

	Quantity (in 2012)	Price (in 2011)	Value
Pizza	800	5.00	4,000
Ice cream cones	650	2.00	1,300
Books	100	7.00	700
	GDP:		6,000

Because we are using 2011 prices, we say that 2011 is the **base year**. We can determine the growth factor for real GDP:

real GDP growth factor from 2011 to 2012 with 2011 as base =

$$\frac{\Sigma Q_{2012}P_{2011}}{\Sigma Q_{2011}P_{2011}} = \frac{6,000}{4,360} = 1.37615$$

The expression $\Sigma Q_i P_j$ means to multiply the quantity of each good in year i by the price of the good in year j, and then add up the total value for all goods. This growth factor means that real GDP grew about 37.6 percent from 2011 to 2012.

Prior to 1996, the Department of Commerce estimated growth in real GDP by arbitrarily calling one year the base year, and then evaluating the real GDP for all other years by using the prices from that base year. In the early 1990s, 1987 was the base year. However, this method has a big disadvantage. A few years after the base year the economy will have changed significantly, but the real GDP will be distorted since it keeps using prices from the base year. Therefore, in 1996 the department began using the **chain-weight** approach. Unfortunately, this approach is more complicated than simply sticking with a fixed base year, but it will give an improved picture of the economy.

Here is how to calculate the chain-weight real GDP growth for our example. We have already seen that growth from 2011 to 2012 was 37.6 percent, using 2011 prices as the base year. However, the choice of 2011 was arbitrary; we could also use 2012 prices as the base. To do this, we have to go back and recalculate what the 2011 GDP would have been if the prices had taken on their 2012 values:

	Quantity (in 2011)	Price (in 2012)	Value
Pizza	500	5.50	2,750
Ice cream cones	615	3.00	1,845
Books	90	8.00	720
	GDP:		5,315

Therefore, using 2012 prices, we estimate real GDP grew from 5,315 in 2011 to 7,150 in 2012, giving a growth factor of:

real GDP growth factor from 2011 to 2012 with 2012 as base =

$$\frac{\Sigma Q_{2012}P_{2012}}{\Sigma Q_{2011}P_{2012}} = \frac{7,150}{5,315} = 1.34525$$

Using 2012 as the base, we estimate real GDP grew only by 34.5 percent. Which estimate is better? you might wonder. There is no way that one is necessarily better than the other, so the solution is to compromise. We will combine the estimates by multiplying them together and taking the square root:

$$\text{estimated growth factor} = \sqrt{1.37615 \times 1.34525} = 1.36061$$

Therefore, according to the chain-weight approach, we estimate real GDP grew by about 36 percent from 2011 to 2012. Note that the production of some goods increased by more than 36 percent, and the production of other goods increased by less.

	Quantity (in 2011)	Quantity (in 2012)	Percent Increase
Pizza	500	800	60.0
Ice cream cones	615	650	5.7
Books	90	100	11.1

In general, the percentage growth in real GDP from year t to year $t + 1$ is given by this formula:

$$100 \times \left(\sqrt{\frac{\Sigma Q_{t+1} P_t}{\Sigma Q_t P_t} \times \frac{\Sigma Q_{t+1} P_{t+1}}{\Sigma Q_t P_{t+1}}} - 1 \right)$$

Each year, the Department of Commerce will estimate the growth in real GDP from the previous year, using the chain-weight method. For convenience, they still express real GDP in terms of a base year. However, this no longer means that real GDP is calculated by assuming that all prices stayed the same as in the base year; instead, it tells the value that GDP would have had if, starting from the base year, there was no inflation and instead the GDP grew each year at the rate given by the chain-weight index.

Currently, the base year is 2000. In the base year, the real GDP is always the same as the nominal GDP. This value is 9,817 billion dollars for 2000.

In 2008, the nominal GDP (that is, the GDP using 2008 prices and 2008 quantities) was 14,264.6 billion dollars. If we divide the nominal GDP by the real GDP, we find a quantity called the **GDP deflator**:

$$\text{GDP deflator} = \frac{\text{nominal GDP}}{\text{real GDP}} = \frac{14,264.6}{11,652.0} = 1.2241$$

In the base year the GDP deflator is always 1. The GDP deflator is a measure of the average level of prices. Since the GDP deflator in 2008 is 1.2241, it means that, on average, prices in 2008 were 22.41 percent higher than they were in 2000.

• THE CONSUMER PRICE INDEX

The GDP deflator doesn't necessarily measure how much inflation affects you personally. You would be much more interested in a measure that told you how much the average prices of the things you buy had gone up. The Bureau of Labor Statistics calculates a quantity called the consumer price index that measures how much increases in the price level affect the average consumer. The percent change in the consumer price index is the most widely publicized measure of inflation. It usually makes the news when its value is reported each month.

Let's suppose that you are an average consumer and you always buy exactly the same goods each year: 30 pizzas, 25 ice creams, and 2 books. Then it is easy to calculate how price changes will affect you. Your cost of living is simply the amount of money it costs to buy that particular bundle of goods you consume each year.

Cost of Living—2011			
	Quantity	Price	Cost
Pizzas	30	$5.00	$150
Ice cream cones	25	2.00	50
Books	2	7.00	14
		total cost of living:	$214

Cost of Living—2012			
	Quantity	Price	Cost
Pizzas	30	$5.50	$165.00
Ice cream cones	25	2.10	52.50
Books	2	8.00	16.00
		total cost of living:	$233.50

It cost you $233.50 to maintain your standard of living in 2012 or 1.091 times as much as it did in 2011. Therefore, according to the consumer price index, the rate of inflation was 9.1 percent from 2011 to 2012.

The consumer price index is currently calculated so that the average level of prices in 1982 to 1984 is set equal to 100. In 2008, the value of the index was 215.3. For comparison, in 1950 the index was 24.1, meaning that on average consumer prices in 1950 were only one-quarter of what they became by 1982 to 1984.

The consumer price index is based on the cost of a bundle of specific consumer goods that represent the expenditures of an average consumer. The contents of this bundle were determined by a survey called the Consumer Expenditure Survey that checked with a sample of over 40,000 families to find out what they bought. This table lists the relative importance of the items in the CPI:

Good	Percent of Expenditures
Food and beverages	15.8
Housing	43.4
Apparel	3.7
Transportation	15.3
Medical care	6.4
Recreation	5.7
Education and communication	6.3
Other goods and services	3.4

(Source: Bureau of Labor Statistics, web page *www.bls.gov/cpi*)

If you happen to buy exactly the same mix of goods, then the consumer price index will exactly reflect how price increases affect you. If you happen to spend relatively more on goods whose prices increase faster than average, then you will suffer from price increases more than the CPI indicates. On the other hand, if you tend to buy more goods with slower price increases, then you will not feel the effects of inflation as much.

An even more difficult problem arises because the expenditure patterns for the average consumer change with time. The Bureau of Labor Statistics (BLS) periodically conducts new expenditure surveys and revises the bundle of goods used to calculate the CPI. However, the BLS cannot do this too frequently because then it becomes difficult to compare CPI values from different years.

• *THE PRODUCER PRICE INDEX*

The BLS calculates another price index called the producer price index that measures changes in the prices of a basket of commodities used by firms in the production process. Values for the price indexes are released during the third week of each month for the preceding month.

See the book's web page *myhome.spu.edu/ddowning/bstat.html* for links to sources of other key indicators of the state of the economy.

YOU SHOULD REMEMBER

1. Other important measures of the national economy are price indexes, which measure the average price level.

2. Three commonly used price indexes are the following:
   GDP deflator: a price index based on all goods that are part of the GDP
   consumer price index: a price index based on the cost of a specific market basket of consumer goods.
   producer price index: a price index based on the cost of a specific market basket of goods used by firms in the production process.

3. The *real gross domestic product* is a measure of GDP that corrects for inflation.

TIME SERIES DATA

When you have measurements for the same quantity for several consecutive time periods, you have **time series data**. Many interesting economic variables are in the form of time series. The GDP figures are calculated every quarter. Many other figures, such as the CPI and the unemployment rate, are calculated every month. Some statistics, such as the money supply, are calculated every week, and other time series, such as the Dow Jones industrial average closing level, have daily values. When analyzing time series data you often have two goals: to describe the patterns of the series in the past and to predict future values of a particular quantity. We will describe briefly some of the analytic techniques that are used to investigate time series data.

Many times series show definite trends up or down if you follow their values over long periods of time. For example, the value of real GDP in the

United States has been increasing fairly steadily for the last few decades. Here are some figures:

Year	Real GDP	Year	Real GDP
1971	3,898.6	1990	7,112.5
1972	4,105.0	1991	7,100.5
1973	4,341.5	1992	7,336.6
1974	4,319.6	1993	7,532.7
1975	4,311.2	1994	7,835.5
1976	4,540.9	1995	8,031.7
1977	4,750.5	1996	8,328.9
1978	5,015.0	1997	8,703.5
1979	5,173.4	1998	9,066.9
1980	5,161.7	1999	9,470.3
1981	5,291.7	2000	9,817.0
1982	5,189.3	2001	9,890.7
1983	5,423.8	2002	10,048.8
1984	5,813.6	2003	10,301.0
1985	6,053.7	2004	10,675.8
1986	6,263.6	2005	10,989.5
1987	6,475.1	2006	11,294.8
1988	6,742.7	2007	11,523.9
1989	6,981.4	2008	11,652.0

Source: www.bea.gov

The table shows annual data from 1971 to 2008. Figure 19–1 shows the trend in real GDP using quarterly data from 1947 to early 2009.

If you had to predict the value of next year's real GDP, you probably would guess that it would continue to rise. In that case you are assuming that the value of real GDP will continue to follow the same upward trend that it has been following. For the past few decades real GDP has been growing at a rate averaging about 3 percent per year. However, your prediction for next year would not necessarily be correct. Some year's real GDP grows faster than its trend, and other years it does not grow as fast, or perhaps it even declines. In the period from 1929 to 1933 there was a major decline in the value of real GDP as the Great Depression hit. When the economy slows down, it is said that a **recession** has started. The United States suffered deep recessions in 1975, 1982, and 2008–2009, and smaller recessions in 1970, 1980, 1991, and 2001.

The deepest time in a recession is called the *trough*. After the trough has been passed, the economy starts of grow more quickly. This phase is called

Figure 19–1. Real GDP

the *expansion* or *recovery*. The economy continues to expand until it reaches the *peak*. These variations are called *cyclical variations* in the economy, because they seem to come in cycles of recession followed by expansion followed by recession. However, the cycles are not at all like the regular cycles in a clock or in the movements of the planets. You cannot use the lengths of past cycles to predict future cycles, but it is clear that these cyclical effects play a very important role in determining the level of business activity. At some times the economy is booming and there is a lot of spending, but at other times the economy is in a slump and unemployment is higher than usual.

One particularly interesting time series is the **index of leading indicators**. The index consists of a weighted average of several economic variables, such as construction permits issued, that tend to turn up before the whole economy turns up and tend to turn down before the whole economy turns down. The index can be used to forecast future upturns and downturns in the economy.

• COMPONENTS OF TIME SERIES DATA
We will view time series data as consisting of three components:

- the **trend component**
- the **cyclical component**
- the **irregular component**

The irregular component is included because there will always be some movements up to down in a time series that cannot be explained by a trend or by cyclical variations.

There is one other important part of many time series: the **seasonal component**. There is no seasonal component when you are looking at yearly data because in that case you have averaged over all seasons of the year, and the averaging process hides the seasonal variation. The seasonal component, however, is a very important part of quarterly, monthly, or weekly time series. We will discuss methods of analyzing seasonal variation in a later section of this chapter.

We will look at two methods for determining the trend of a set of data.

YOU SHOULD REMEMBER

1. Many important economic statistics are available in the form of *time series data*, consisting of observations of a variable for several consecutive time periods (such as every year or every week).

2. It is often possible to observe a *trend component*, a *cyclical component*, and a *seasonal component* in time series data.

3. The level of economic activity undergoes cyclical variations. A slowdown in the overall level of economic activity is called a *recession*.

4. The *index of leading indicators* is a time series consisting of a weighted average of several economic variables that tend to turn up or down before the whole economy changes direction. This index can sometimes be used to forecast future movement in the economy.

• *DETERMINING THE TREND BY CALCULATING MOVING AVERAGES*

The first method for calculating the trend component is the moving average method. Suppose we're trying to see whether the value of real GDP in a particular year was higher or lower than the trend value. Calculate the average real GDP for the 5 years closest to that year (2 before, 2 after, and that year itself). This type of calculation is called a **moving average** (because the periods you average together "move" when you move your attention to a new period).

For example, the table shows that the value of real GDP in 1982 was below its trend value. This was a year when the economy was in a severe recession.

Year	Actual Real GDP	5-Year Moving Average	Ratio
1971	3898.6	—	—
1972	4105.0	—	—
1973	4341.5	4195.2	1.0349
1974	4319.6	4323.6	0.9991
1975	4311.2	4452.7	0.9682
1976	4540.9	4587.4	0.9899
1977	4750.5	4758.2	0.9984
1978	5015.0	4928.3	1.0176
1979	5173.4	5078.5	1.0187
1980	5161.7	5166.2	0.9991
1981	5291.7	5248.0	1.0083
1982	5189.3	5376.0	0.9653
1983	5423.8	5554.4	0.9765
1984	5813.6	5748.8	1.0113
1985	6053.7	6006.0	1.0079
1986	6263.6	6269.7	0.9990
1987	6475.1	6503.3	0.9957
1988	6742.7	6715.1	1.0041
1989	6981.4	6882.4	1.0144
1990	7112.5	7054.7	1.0082
1991	7100.5	7212.7	0.9844
1992	7336.6	7383.6	0.9936
1993	7532.7	7567.4	0.9954
1994	7835.5	7813.1	1.0029
1995	8031.7	8086.5	0.9932
1996	8328.9	8393.3	0.9923
1997	8703.5	8720.3	0.9981
1998	9066.9	9077.3	0.9989
1999	9470.3	9389.7	1.0086
2000	9817.0	9658.7	1.0164
2001	9890.7	9905.6	0.9985
2002	10048.8	10146.7	0.9904
2003	10301.0	10381.2	0.9923
2004	10675.8	10662.0	1.0013
2005	10989.5	10957.0	1.0030
2006	11294.8	11227.2	1.0060
2007	11523.9	—	—
2008	11652.0	—	—

Note that we cannot calculate the moving average for the first 2 years or the last 2 years. You may be wondering how many observations you should put in each moving average. We chose five observations. If you choose too short a period, then the moving average itself will be affected by the cyclical and irregular variations and it will be harder to identify these components. If you choose too long a period, then you lose too many data points at the beginning and end of the series.

To investigate the cyclical component we would like to observe the deviations of the actual values from the trend values. There are two ways to do this.

We might think we have an *additive* model, in which case the actual value of real GDP is determined by a formula like this:

GDP = trend value + cyclical component + irregular component

Then we calculate the deviation from the trend by subtracting the trend value from the actual value.

We would use the other method if we think we have a multiplicative model, in which case the actual value is determined by a formula like this:

GDP = trend value × cyclical component × irrregular component

In this case the cyclical and irregular components are represented by numbers whose average value is 1, and we calculate the deviation by dividing the actual value by the trend value: (See the previous table).

We can plot these ratios on a graph. (See Figure 19–2.) We can clearly see that the recessions in 1982 and 1975 caused the value of real GDP to be below

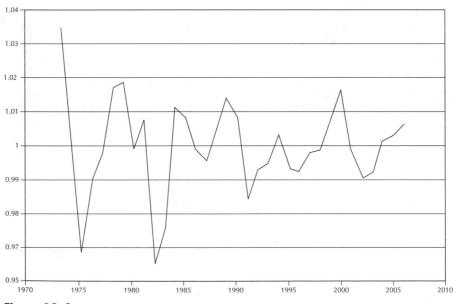

Figure 19–2

its trend value. (The 2008 downturn is too recent to show up on this graph.) All of the movement in Figure 19–2 is attributed to either cyclical factors or irregular factors. There are more advanced techniques (known as *Fourier analysis*) that make it possible to analyze the cyclical components in a time series, but we will not discuss them in this book.

• *DETERMINING THE TREND BY REGRESSION*

It is also possible to use regression to determine the trend component in a time series. Consider this time series of yearly pizza sales in a small town:

50, 66, 81, 90, 98,
106, 115, 130, 146, 162,
177, 186, 194, 202, 211,
226, 242, 258, 273, 282,
290, 298, 307, 322, 338

Figure 19–3 shows a graph of these sales. There is a clear upward trend, and there also is a clear cyclical component. Apparently people in this town go on pizza binges that last about 4 years, but then they become tired of

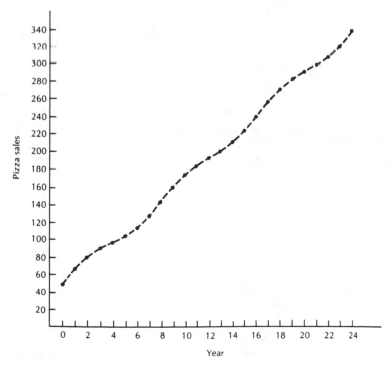

Figure 19–3

pizza and the growth of pizza consumption slows for the next 4 years. We can determine the trend by fitting a line through all of the data points (see Figure 19–4), and we can find the slope and intercept of the line by simple regression:

Trend line:

slope = 11.862

intercept = 51.662

Note that on Figures 19–3 and 19–4 we call the first year "year 0," instead of using the actual year number, in order to make the regression calculations easier. We can now make a graph of the residuals to illustrate the cyclical variation (Figure 19–5):

Year	Actual Sales	Trend Value	Residual
0	50.0	51.7	−1.7
1	66.0	63.5	2.5
2	81.0	75.4	5.6
3	90.0	87.2	2.8
4	98.0	99.1	−1.1
5	106.0	111.0	−5.0
6	115.0	122.8	−7.8
7	130.0	134.7	−4.7
8	146.0	146.6	−0.6
9	162.0	158.4	3.6
10	177.0	170.3	6.7
11	186.0	182.1	3.9
12	194.0	194.0	0.0
13	202.0	205.9	−3.9
14	211.0	217.7	−6.7
15	226.0	229.6	−3.6
16	242.0	241.5	0.6
17	258.0	253.3	4.7
18	273.0	265.2	7.8
19	282.0	277.0	5.0
20	290.0	288.9	1.1
21	298.0	300.8	−2.8
22	307.0	312.6	−5.6
23	322.0	324.5	−2.5
24	338.0	336.3	1.7

Figure 19–4

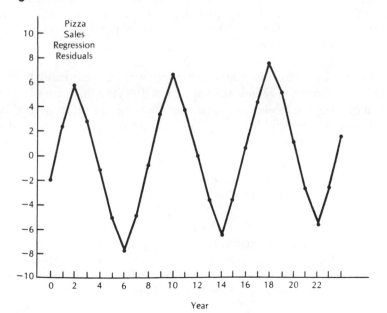

Figure 19–5

EXPONENTIAL SMOOTHING

We will look at one more technique for forecasting time series values: **exponential smoothing**. For our example we will look at information on the saving rate (the percent of personal disposable income that is saved):

Year	Saving	Year	Saving
1990	7.0	2000	2.3
1991	7.3	2001	1.8
1992	7.7	2002	2.4
1993	5.8	2003	2.1
1994	4.8	2004	2.1
1995	4.6	2005	0.4
1996	4.0	2006	0.7
1997	3.6	2007	0.6
1998	4.3	2008	1.8
1999	2.0		

Source: *www.bea.gov*

Our goal is to forecast next year's saving rate by using the known past values of the saving rate. Suppose that we observe that this year's saving rate is higher than the rate we had forecasted for this year. There are two ways we could proceed:

1. We could assume that this year's saving rate was an abnormally high value. Perhaps something very unusual happened this year that caused people to save more, but we expect that next year they will return to normal behavior. In that case we should ignore the value for this year when we develop the forecast for next year.
2. We could assume that there has been a permanent change in people's behavior. In that case we will ignore all of the past values and our forecast for next year will be exactly the same as the actual value for this year.

In reality we do not know whether an increase in the saving rate in any one year is the result of a temporary aberration or is the start of a permanent change. Therefore, we will compromise between the two extreme plans. Our forecast of next year's value of the saving rate will depend both on this year's actual value and on this year's forecasted value:

$$F_{t+1} = aX_t + (1-a)F_t$$

Where X_t represents the actual value of the variable in
time period t (this year)
F_t represents our forecasted value in time period t
F_{t+1} represents our forecasted value for
period $t + 1$ (next year)
a is a number between 0 and 1

We can choose the value of a. Obviously we want to choose the value that will lead to the best forecasts. Setting a equal to 1 means that our forecasted value will always be equal to last period's actual value. This means that we are ignoring all past values except the most recent value. Setting a equal to 0 means that our forecasted value will always be equal to last year's forecasted value. In other words, we will never change our forecast, no matter what happens in the real world. We will regard each deviation from our forecasted value as being a temporary random deviation.

Setting a value of a between 0 and 1 allows us to compromise between these two extremes. For example, here are the results for the savings example, using a value of $a = .5$:

Year	Actual	Forecast
1990	7.0	7.00
1991	7.3	7.00
1992	7.7	7.15
1993	5.8	7.42
1994	4.8	6.61
1995	4.6	5.71
1996	4.0	5.15
1997	3.6	4.58
1998	4.3	4.09
1999	2.0	4.19
2000	2.3	3.10
2001	1.8	2.70
2002	2.4	2.25
2003	2.1	2.32
2004	2.1	2.21
2005	0.4	2.16
2006	0.7	1.28
2007	0.6	0.99
2008	1.8	0.79

For the first year of the process (1990) we do not have any past forecasted value, so we set the forecast for that year equal to the actual value. Note that so far we have not really "forecasted" anything, since all we have done is generate forecasted values for past years. However, we can now carry the process forward 1 year at a time. Every year we can learn the new actual value of the saving rate, and then we can calculate the new forecasted value for the following year.

With a little mathematical manipulation we can show that the forecasted value can also be found from this equation:

$$F_{t+1} = aX_t + a(1-a)X_{t-1} + a(1-a)^2 X_{t-2}$$
$$+ a(1-a)^3 X_{t-3} + \cdots$$

This year's forecasted value is equal to a weighted average of the past values. The weight attached to values in the recent past is greater than the weight attached to values from farther back.

One question remains: How do we choose the value of a? If our time series exhibits many random year-to-year fluctuations, then we should choose a relatively small value of a. In that case we don't want our forecasts to be too dependent on transitory swings in the variable. If long-term changes are more important, then we should choose a larger value of a so that the forecasted value will react more quickly to observed changes. In practice we can test several different values of a. Look at the past data and determine the error for each year. Then square all of the errors and add up all of the squares. Choose the value of a that leads to the smallest total squared error.

YOU SHOULD REMEMBER

1. The *trend component* in a time series is the component that increases or decreases smoothly with time. This component can be identified by using exponential smoothing, the moving average method, or regression analysis with time as the independent variable.

2. The *moving average* is the average value of the observations in a time series that are closest to one particular value. For example, a three-term moving average can be calculated that consists of the average value of one observation, its predecessor, and its successor.

SEASONAL ADJUSTMENT

• *THE NEED FOR SEASONAL ADJUSTMENT*
Suppose you are analyzing monthly time series data for retail toy sales. You will find that every year there is a big surge in toy sales in December.

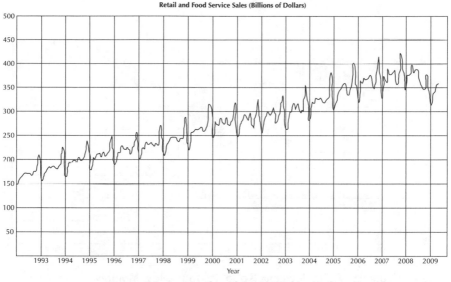

Figure 19–6. Retail and Food Service Sales

Or, if you are analyzing time series for construction, you will probably find that construction tends to be higher in the summer. Many other economic variables, such as employment, labor force participation, money demand, and heating oil demand, exhibit significant seasonal variation. For example, Figure 19–6 shows monthly data for U.S. retail sales. Note that every year, sales significantly increase in December. Figure 19–7 shows monthly data for the employment of 16 to 19 year olds. Note that teenage employment significantly increases in the summer, and there also is a noticeable increase in December. It is not hard to understand why these variations occur, but they do make it more difficult to analyze time series data. If you observe that toy sales have increased in December, you need to investigate to determine whether there has been a real increase in demand for toys or whether sales have gone up just because they always go up in December. It is also possible that the toy business is in a slump. Sales may have gone up relative to what they were in November, but they may have risen less than you normally would have expected them to in December.

When time series data are used to analyze trends in the economy, it is necessary to separate out the seasonal variations. This process is known as **seasonal adjustment**. Many of the widely published economic statistics, such as the unemployment rate, are seasonally adjusted before they are published.

The actual (unadjusted) employment figures are highest in the summer. So the adjusted figure is lower because it compensates for this seasonal effect. During the early months of the year, actual employment tends to be less than it is the rest of the year, so the adjusted figure is higher than the actual figure.

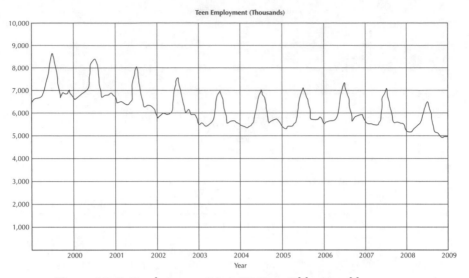

Figure 19–7. Employment, 16 to 19 Year Olds, Monthly

• *THE RATIO TO MOVING AVERAGE METHOD*

Calculating the seasonal adjustment factors is difficult, and the actual procedure used by the Bureau of Labor Statistics is very complicated. We will look at a relatively simple method of analyzing seasonal variation called the **ratio to moving average method**. Here is a table for 5 years of monthly observations for teenage employment:

	Employment, Ages 16 to 19 (millions)				
	2004	2005	2006	2007	2008
Jan	5503	5460	5620	5656	5277
Feb	5475	5395	5700	5592	5242
Mar	5402	5570	5757	5611	5347
Apr	5522	5524	5760	5549	5544
May	5690	5707	5990	5611	5660
Jun	6517	6714	7023	6725	6343
July	7114	7260	7494	7184	6698
Aug	6621	6775	6801	6274	6142
Sep	5645	5789	5783	5649	5317
Oct	5775	5801	5978	5749	5239
Nov	5816	5803	5989	5652	5008
Dec	5800	5934	6052	5679	5058

Source: www.bls.gov/data

To estimate the effect of the seasonal variations we will first calculate a 12-period moving average for each figure. It is trickier to calculate a moving average with an even number of periods. For each entry we will calculate two moving averages:

- The average of the six preceding elements and the five following elements

- The average of the five preceding elements and the six following elements

For example, for July 2004 we first average all values from January 2004 to December 2004; then we average all values from February 2004 to January 2005. The value for the moving average for July is the average of these two values.

Here is a table of the moving averages for the employment data:

	2004	2005	2006	2007	2008
Jan	x	5934.50	6110.75	6057.17	5779.75
Feb	x	5947.00	6121.58	6022.29	5754.00
Mar	x	5959.42	6122.42	5994.75	5734.67
Apr	x	5966.50	6129.54	5979.62	5699.58
May	x	5967.04	6144.67	5956.04	5651.50
Jun	x	5972.08	6157.33	5926.46	5598.79
July	5904.87	5984.33	6163.75	5895.12	x
Aug	5899.75	6003.71	6160.75	5864.75	x
Sep	5903.42	6024.21	6150.17	5839.17	x
Oct	5910.50	6041.83	6135.29	5827.96	x
Nov	5911.29	6063.46	6110.71	5829.79	x
Dec	5920.21	6088.12	6082.50	5815.92	x

Note that we cannot calculate a moving average for the first six values or the last six values.

Now we can calculate the ratio between each actual value and the corresponding moving average value. In this way we can see which months are lower or higher than the average for the 12-month period surrounding the month in question. We can call this ratio the **monthly trend ratio**.

	2004	2005	2006	2007	2008	Avg	St. Avg
Jan	x	0.9200	0.9197	0.9338	0.9130	0.9216	0.9198
Feb	x	0.9072	0.9311	0.9286	0.9110	0.9195	0.9176
Mar	x	0.9347	0.9403	0.9360	0.9324	0.9358	0.9339
Apr	x	0.9258	0.9397	0.9280	0.9727	0.9416	0.9397
May	x	0.9564	0.9748	0.9421	1.0015	0.9687	0.9667
Jun	x	1.1242	1.1406	1.1347	1.1329	1.1331	1.1308
July	1.2048	1.2132	1.2158	1.2186	x	1.2131	1.2106
Aug	1.1223	1.1285	1.1039	1.0698	x	1.1061	1.1039
Sep	0.9562	0.9610	0.9403	0.9674	x	0.9562	0.9543
Oct	0.9771	0.9601	0.9744	0.9865	x	0.9745	0.9725
Nov	0.9839	0.9570	0.9801	0.9695	x	0.9726	0.9707
Dec	0.9797	0.9747	0.9950	0.9765	x	0.9815	0.9795
					Sum:	12.0423	12

If there is a regular seasonal variation, then a month that is below its moving average value one year will tend to be lower than its moving average value every year. For example, the monthly trend ratios for January are all below 1, and the monthly trend ratios for July are all above 1.

Therefore, we will calculate the average monthly trend ratio for each month. These figures, shown in the column headed Average, will form the basis for our seasonal adjustment factor. If we add up the total of these figures, we obtain 12.0423. It would be convenient to have our seasonal factors add up to 12, so we will multiply each value by 12/12.0423. The final results, in the column headed Standardized Average, are the seasonal adjustment factors we will use. For example, the actual figure for December 2008 is 5058. The seasonal adjustment factor for December is .9795, so the seasonally adjusted value for December 2008 is 5058/.9795 = 5164. Here is a complete table of the seasonally adjusted values:

	2004	2005	2006	2007	2008
Jan	5983	5936	6110	6149	5737
Feb	5967	5879	6212	6094	5713
Mar	5784	5964	6164	6008	5725
Apr	5877	5879	6130	5905	5900
May	5886	5903	6196	5804	5855
Jun	5763	5937	6210	5947	5609
July	5876	5997	6190	5934	5533
Aug	5998	6138	6161	5684	5564

	2004	2005	2006	2007	2008
Sep	5915	6066	6060	5920	5572
Oct	5938	5965	6147	5911	5387
Nov	5992	5978	6170	5823	5159
Dec	5922	6058	6179	5798	5164

Figure 19–8 compares the seasonally adjusted data with the original data. The bottom part of the figure clearly shows how the actual employment peaks every summer and falls every January. The seasonally adjusted data averages out the peaks and valleys in the actual data.

YOU SHOULD REMEMBER

1. The *seasonal component* in a time series is the component that varies on a regular basis throughout the seasons of the year. The seasonal adjustment process is used to compensate for the regular seasonal variations in the observations to make nonseasonal changes more clearly apparent.

2. The *ratio to moving average method* is one possible seasonal adjustment method.

Figure 19–8. Employment, Aged 16 to 19, Millions.
(SA (seasonally adjusted); NSA (not seasonally adjusted))

KNOW THE CONCEPTS

DO YOU KNOW THE BASICS?

Test your understanding of Chapter 19 by answering the following questions:

1. Why is the gross domestic product calculated by looking at the value added instead of the total value produced by each firm?

2. When a used car dealer sells a car, is the cost of that car included in GDP?

3. How is real GDP calculated?

4. Will the inflation rate be higher if it is measured by the GDP deflator or if it is measured by the consumer price index?

5. How are the values of government services measured when GDP is being calculated?

6. What is the purpose of seasonal adjustment?

7. If the actual value of a statistic for January is higher than the seasonally adjusted value, would we expect this statistic normally to be higher in January than it is the rest of the year?

8. When you analyze a trend with the moving average method, how many periods should you include in each moving average?

9. How do you choose the value of a, the constant used in exponential smoothing?

10. If the temperature on July 1 is different from the temperature on January 1, does this provide evidence of climate change?

11. If the temperature on July 1 this year is different from the temperature on July 1 last year, does this provide evidence of climate change?

12. If you have these observations for housing prices in a city, can you forecast their trend?

Year	Average Price
2000	$150,000
2001	$190,000
2002	$230,000
2003	$270,000
2004	$310,000
2005	$350,000
2006	$390,000

13. Suppose you were in the music business in 1985 and had developed a reliable regression model to forecast the trend and seasonal pattern for traditional 33rpm records. How accurate would this model work in the future?

14. If your sales have been growing at a constant percent per year, what transformation should you perform before using regression analysis to determine the trend?

TERMS FOR STUDY

base year

chain weight

consumer price index (CPI)

cyclical component

depreciation

exponential smoothing

GDP deflator

gross domestic product (GDP)

index of leading indicators

inflation rate

irregular component

monthly trend ratio

moving average

national income

net national product (NNP)

nominal gross domestic product

price index

price level

producer price index (PPI)

ratio to moving average method

real gross domestic product

recession

seasonal adjustment

time series data

trend component

PRACTICAL APPLICATION

COMPUTATIONAL PROBLEMS

See the book's web page for computational problems with data you can paste into your spreadsheet.

ANSWERS

KNOW THE CONCEPTS

1. The value added is used to avoid double-counting intermediate goods.

2. The value of the car itself is not included, because that value was included in GDP in the year the car was produced. The profit of the car dealer is included, however, because that is a payment for a current service.

3. Real GDP is calculated with the chain-weight method; it indicates the amount of output produced after removing the effect of inflation.

4. In general, it is impossible to say.

5. Government services are valued at their costs of production.

6. The purpose of seasonal adjustment is to make changes arising from nonseasonal factors more apparent.

7. This statistic is usually higher in January than it is the rest of the year; its seasonal adjustment factor is greater than 1.

8. There is a trade-off. If you include too few periods, then the trend will not be clear. If you include too many periods, then the average will be less sensitive to each individual item and you will lose too many observations at the beginning and end.

9. You choose the value that seems to have provided the best forecasts in the past. A smaller value is appropriate if there are many random yearly fluctuations.

10. No. Temperature data obviously needs to be seasonally adjusted if you are trying to determine trends.

11. No. Temperature data is subject to many random variations. Many observations over a very long time period would be needed to determine trends.

12. Trying to forecast requires making an extrapolation, which may not be accurate. In reality, the rising trend in home prices came to an end, and home prices in many cities declined starting in 2007.

13. The increasing popularity of music CDs in the late 1980s would have meant any model of sales of traditional records would become obsolete. (Also, after 2000 the increasing popularity of digital music players would have made an estimate of CD sales obsolete.) The important lesson is that no forecast model, no matter how carefully constructed, will be accurate if there is a sudden major change in an industry.

14. Take the logarithm of the sales figures. If $Q = Q_0(1 + g)^t$, then sales (Q) will grow at a constant rate of $100g$ percent each year, where Q_0 is the level of sales in year 0. Taking the logarithm:

$$\log Q = \log Q_0 + t\log(1 + g)$$

and you can see that $(1 + g)$ will be coefficient of time (t) in the logarithmic regression equation.

20
DECISION THEORY

KEY TERMS

decision theory the study of making decisions designed to achieve some objective, often under conditions of uncertainty

decision tree a diagram that illustrates all possible consequences of different decisions in different states of nature

expected payoff the expected value of the payoff resulting from a decision

Every day of our lives, we are faced with many decisions. Many of them involve outcomes where the difference between the possible results is inconsequential. If I use the "wrong" toothpaste, my teeth may not be as white. If I put my shoes on before my socks in the morning, I waste several minutes in correcting my error, and risk stretching my socks. In business, decisions usually have more important consequences. A company choosing one manufacturing process over another may go bankrupt if the choice was wrong. Thus it is important to come up with some rules, based on **decision theory**, that will help us to make the best decision possible, given the information that we have.

Statisticians distinguish between three different kinds of decisions:

1. Decisions under certainty. These are decisions where you have all the information you need and can calculate precisely the outcome of every choice you make. This doesn't necessarily mean that you know exactly what to do: there may be more data than a person can comprehend. For example, you may wish to maximize the production of a certain chemical while simultaneously satisfying 531 related Environmental Protection Agency regulations. In cases like this, it is usually best to use an appropriate algorithm, such as linear programming to evaluate the data and select the best outcome. You will often need a computer program to perform the calculations for you. We shall not deal with this category of decision here.

2. Decisions under uncertainty. These are decisions where you have to take chance into account, without worrying about what a competitor may be

doing, just you and Nature. Here, intuition about what random chance may be up to comes into play. A farmer may have to choose what crops to grow on the basis of what he thinks the weather will be like. He will probably base his decision on past weather and long-range forecasting.

3. Decisions under conflict. These are decisions where you have to take into account what a competitor may do. A company has to consider what its competitors may charge for an item when deciding its price. This category of decisions is dealt with by game theory and will not be discussed here.

DECISION TREE

Before making an intelligent decision, it is a good idea to have all of the possible choices and their outcomes charted for you. One way of doing this is to use a **decision tree**.

Suppose that you want to manufacture an item and have k different processes, $A_1, \ldots, A_k$, to choose from. Then you start out going from left to right with k branches (see Figure 20–1).

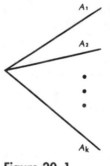

Figure 20–1

For each of the processes, there are different possible outcomes that we call **states of nature**. A state of nature is a chance result, usually unpredictable beforehand, such as the number rolled on a die or a particular day's weather. We'll call the states of nature $B_1, \ldots, B_t$. For example B_1 might be the outcome where the item came out perfect, B_2 the outcome where the item came out flawed, B_3 the outcome where the plant blew up, and so on. These are depicted as additional branches (see Figure 20–2).

Now you may have further decisions, $C_1, \ldots, C_m$, to make as a result of these outcomes, for example, to improve the process, rebuild the factory, or declare bankruptcy. These can be shown as more branches (see Figure 20–3).

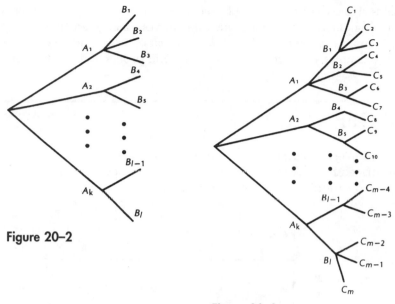

Figure 20–2

Figure 20–3

The branching can be carried out as far as you wish, depending on how many levels you wish to analyze. The branches alternate between your choices and states of nature.

YOU SHOULD REMEMBER

1. Many business decisions must be made in environments of uncertainty. The field of decision theory provides guidance in such cases.

2. A decision tree is a diagram listing all possible outcomes for each possible decision and each possible state of nature.

OBJECTIVE VARIABLES

We need to have some way of deciding which outcomes are better than others. A yo-yo manufacturer may think it best to make blue yo-yos because they sell better than yo-yos of other colors, or because blue is her favorite color.

Sales figures are examples of **objective variables**. They provide a way of comparing outcomes that mean the same to you, me, or anybody else. If item A sells more than item B, this is true no matter who reads the sales report. Other examples of objective variables include profits and production.

PAYOFF TABLE

In the simplest of decision trees, we have one level of choices, one level of states of nature, and, for each choice, the same states of nature to consider. Then we can form a table (see Figure 20–4).

Figure 20–4

Of course, it looks a little empty now. If we have an objective variable X, then we can enter its values (see Figure 20–5). Here X_{ij} is the value of the objective variable corresponding to the ith choice and the jth state of nature. This array is then called the **payoff table**.

The payoff table may be huge, and it would be helpful if we could simplify it. One way is to reject *dominated* or *inadmissible actions*. These are choices that should not be made because there are other choices that are always better. More accurately, A_i is dominated by A_j if, for all k, X_{ik} is less than or equal to X_{jk}, and there is at least one value of k such that $X_{ik} < X_{jk}$. Thus we would never choose A_i because A_j would always be better for us. For example, see Figure 20–6, where A_4 is dominated by A_2 and A_3 and thus is inadmissible.

Once we've eliminated any inadmissible actions, we've done just about all we can do with complete certainty.

Figure 20–5

	B_1	B_2	B_3	B_4	B_5
A_1	1	2	5	8	3
A_2	2	2	5	2	7
A_3	3	9	8	7	6
A_4	0	1	3	2	4

Figure 20–6

YOU SHOULD REMEMBER

1. An objective variable is a variable that you are trying to maximize or minimize in making a decision.

2. A payoff table lists the payoff (the value of the objective variable) that would result for each possible decision and each possible state of nature.

EXPECTED PAYOFF

Even though we are uncertain about what state of nature will occur, we can often estimate the probability of one particular state occurring. A farmer can check past weather history, a company can survey consumer tastes, and so on. Then to each state of nature B_j we can associate a probability p_j. For the above example (Figure 20–6) we might have the probabilities given in Figure 20–7. Naturally we require that the p_j's add up to 1.

State	B_1	B_2	B_3	B_4	B_5
Probability	.30	.05	.50	.05	.10

Figure 20–7

Even though the probabilities are at best estimates, we can still take the expected values of the objective variable for a given choice. Thus, for A_1,

$$E(X_{1j}) = 1(.3) + 2(.05) + 5(.5) + 8(.05) + 3(.1) = 3.6.$$

Similarly, $E(X_{2j}) = 4.0$, $E(X_{3j}) = 6.3$, and we don't bother to check choice A_4 since it is inadmissible.

The expected value of the objective variable for a given choice is called the **expected payoff**. If we compare expected payoffs, we see that A_3 has the highest, and we might want to choose it over A_1 and A_2 (again, A_4 is out of the running). Such a decision is said to be based on the *maximum expected payoff criterion*. This is not the criterion for making a decision, but it is usually helpful.

Example: Using the Maximum Expected Payoff Criterion

PROBLEM   Suppose you have the following payoff table for a board game, where your choices are options available to you on your present turn, and the states of nature are the numbers your opponent may roll with two six-sided dice (see Figure 20–8). Which option should you choose, according to the maximum expected payoff criterion?

SOLUTION   It's reasonable to assume that the dice are fair, and we have the following probabilities for the states of nature (see Figure 20–9). Then

$$E(X_{1j}) = 10.14, \quad E(X_{2j}) = 8.56,$$

$$E(X_{3j}) = 12.86, \quad \text{and} \quad E(X_{4j}) = 6.44$$

State Choice	2	3	4	5	6	7	8	9	10	11	12
A₁	5	7	26	9	29	−6	8	15	4	−6	23
A₂	12	8	5	7	13	3	11	14	7	8	6
A₃	9	23	15	24	9	22	13	13	−5	−6	0
A₄	22	−3	−7	5	4	15	9	12	4	−2	6

Figure 20–8

State	2	3	4	5	6	7	8	9	10	11	12
Probability	1/36	2/36	3/36	4/36	5/36	6/36	5/36	4/36	3/36	2/36	1/36

Figure 20–9

Thus, using the maximum expected payoff criterion, you would choose option A_3.

YOU SHOULD REMEMBER

1. The expected payoff is the expected value of the payoff resulting from a decision. You can calculate it if you know the probability of occurrence for each state of nature.

2. The maximum expected payoff criterion is a helpful, but not the only, criterion for making a decision.

Here is an example where you are considering what size factory to build. If you build a larger factory, you will be better able to serve your customers if demand is high, but you will have greater expenses and so will lose money if demand is low. Here is the payoff table:

Choice	State of Nature		
	Low Demand 0.35	Medium Demand 0.40	High Demand 0.25
Giant	–10,000	–2,000	40,000
Big	–1,000	1,000	12,000
Medium	3,000	8,000	7,000
Small	6,000	5,000	4,000

We can calculate the expected payoff from each choice. Giant factory expected payoff:

$$(0.35 \times -10,000) + (0.40 \times -2,000) + (0.25 \times 40,000)$$
$$= -3,500 - 800 + 10,000 = 5,700$$

Big factory expected payoff:

$$(0.35 \times -1,000) + (0.40 \times 1,000) + (0.25 \times 12,000)$$
$$= -350 + 400 + 3,000 = 3,050$$

Medium factory expected payoff:

$$(0.35 \times 3,000) + (0.40 \times 8,000) + (0.25 \times 7,000)$$
$$= 1,050 + 3,200 + 1,750 = 6,000$$

Small factory expected payoff:

$$(0.35 \times 6,000) + (0.40 \times 5,000) + (0.25 \times 4,000)$$
$$= 2,100 + 2,000 + 1,000 = 5,100$$

Therefore, the medium factory has the greatest expected payoff.

UTILITY AND RISK

If you were given a choice between a certain $5,000 and a ticket that has a 50 percent chance of being worth zero and a 50 percent chance of being worth $10,000, which would you choose? Note that the expected value of the payoff would be the same in each case. Some people would prefer the risky choice, but most people would likely choose the certain $5,000 in this situation. These people are said to be risk averse. This means that given a choice between two alternatives with the same expected payoff, they would choose the alternative with less risk.

What choice would you make if your alternatives were a certain $5,000 or a ticket that has a 25 percent chance of being worth zero and a 75 percent chance of being worth $10,000? You might be indifferent between these choices since the higher expected value of the risky choice offsets the higher risk.

A Neumann-Morgenstern utility function is a function that determines the choices that people will make under conditions of risk if they satisfy some reasonable behavioral assumptions that seem to apply to many (but not all) people. Suppose we have made the arbitrary assumption that the worst possible situation will be worth $W = 1$ utility point and the best possible situation will be worth $B = 100$ utility points. Establish a lottery ticket that has a probability p of awarding the best situation and a probability $1 - p$ of awarding the worst situation. Then we can determine the utility of a situation A by adjusting p so that the person is indifferent between A and this lottery. Then the utility of situation A (call it $U(A)$) is:

$$U(A) = pB + (1 - p)W = 100p + (1 - p)$$

For example, if $p = .7$, then $U(A) = 70 + .3 = 70.3$.

Once you've determined the utility of each payoff, you can determine how a person will make decisions in a risky situation. The person will make the choice with the highest expected value of the utility. For example, suppose you are considering a decision (call it X) with these payoffs and probabilities:

State of Nature	Probability	Payoff (dollars)	Probability × Payoff
State 1	0.12	0	0.00
State 2	0.24	250	60.00
State 3	0.28	500	140.00
State 4	0.24	750	180.00
State 5	0.12	1,000	120.00
		Sum:	500.00

By summing the last column, we can see that the expected payoff of X is $500. Therefore, if someone made decisions only on the basis of expected payoff, this person would consider decision X to be just as good as another decision that offered a certain payoff of $500.

However, if you were risk averse and make decisions on the basis of expected utility, your decision would be different. Suppose that we've determined these utilities for the different states:

State of Nature	Payoff	Utility
State 1	0	1
State 2	250	50
State 3	500	75
State 4	750	87
State 5	1,000	93

The utilities are determined by adjusting the value of p in the best/worst lottery described earlier. These utilities display a property called diminishing marginal utility, meaning that additional dollars do increase your utility but at a decreasing rate. For example, if you have $250, then gaining $250 will cause your utility to increase from 50 to 75 (a gain of 25), However, if you have $500, then gaining $250 will cause your utility to increase only from 75 to 87 (a gain of 12).

Now we can calculate the expected utility of decision X:

State of Nature	Probability	Utility	Probability × Payoff
State 1	0.12	1	0.12
State 2	0.24	50	12.00
State 3	0.28	75	21.00
State 4	0.24	87	20.88
State 5	0.12	93	11.16
		Sum:	65.16

Note that a certain $500 has a utility of 75, which is greater than 65.16. Therefore, this person would prefer a certain $500 rather than decision X even though decision X also has an expected payoff of $500. In general, a person whose preferences follow diminishing marginal utility and who makes decisions involving risk according to a Neumann-Morgenstern utility function will act in a risk-averse manner.

KNOW THE CONCEPTS

DO YOU KNOW THE BASICS?

Test your understanding of Chapter 20 by answering the following questions:

1. How do you determine the probabilities used when evaluating business decisions?
2. Why are inadmissible choices ruled out?
3. What is the value of a decision tree?
4. If two decisions provide the same expected return, how do you think you would choose between them?
5. Consider two stocks, one which is very safe and one which is very risky. Which do you think will provide the greater expected return?

TERMS FOR STUDY

decision theory	objective variable
decision tree	payoff table
expected payoff	states of nature

PRACTICAL APPLICATION

COMPUTATIONAL PROBLEMS

1. In the following payoff table, which of the choices are inadmissible?

		State				
		I	II	III	IV	V
	A	4	3	6	9	7
choice	B	1	5	7	6	8
	C	0	2	-2	6	3
	D	1	5	4	6	8

2. If you estimate that the probabilities of the states in Exercise 1 are as follows:

I	II	III	IV	V
.2	.3	.1	.2	.2

what is the expected payoff for each choice?

3. Draw a decision tree relating the weather to the way you dress. How many outcomes can you list?

4. Your are playing blackjack alone with the dealer, who has two 10's, and you have been dealt a queen and a 6. Draw a decision tree for your response.

5. Construct a payoff table for the first level of Exercise 4, with the state of nature being the next card to be dealt, using the following objective variables: −1 if you lose, 0 if your turn continues, and 1 if you win. (Remember that the dealer wins all ties and cannot draw another card on 20.)

6. Which is (are) the inadmissible choice(s)? in Exercise 4?

7. Assuming that the two 10's, the queen, and the 6 (Exercise 4) are the only cards drawn from a regular 52-card deck, calculate the probabilities for the states of nature (Exercise 5), and calculate the expected payoffs for the choices.

8. Suppose that you play the following game: you pick a number from 2 to 12 and roll two six-sided dice. If the number you pick is bigger than the number you roll, you lose in points the number you picked. If the number you pick is smaller than the number you roll, you gain in points the number you picked. If you pick the number you roll, you get 10 points. Construct a payoff table for this game.

9. Calculate the expected payoffs for the game described in Exercise 8.

10. List five objective variables.

ANSWERS

KNOW THE CONCEPTS

1. Often these probabilities are subjective estimates.

2. There is one choice that is better in all circumstances.

3. A decision tree illustrates the consequences of many different types of actions in different states of nature.

4. If you are like most people, you would probably choose the one with the least risk.

5. If they provided the same expected return, few people would want to buy the risky stock. Therefore, the risky stock must promise a higher expected return.

PRACTICAL APPLICATION

1. *C* and *D*.

2. 5.5 for *A*, 5.2 for *B*, 2.2 for *C*, 4.9 for *D*

3.

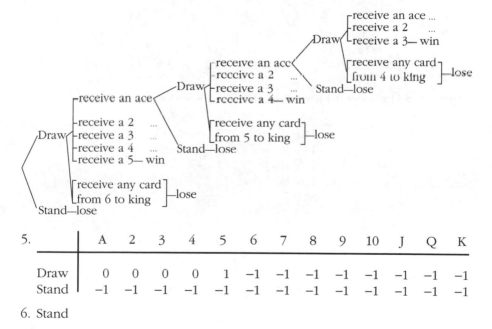

Weather	Dress

Rain —
- Wear a raincoat.
- Carry an umbrella.
- Wear rubber boots.

Cold, dry —
- Wear a heavy coat.
- Wear thermal underwear.

Windy, mild, dry —
- Wear a windbreaker.
- Wear long sleeves.

Hot, dry — Wear short sleeves.

(Feel free to add more branches to this tree. There is no limit to the number of possibilities.)

4. Here is part of the tree:

5.

	A	2	3	4	5	6	7	8	9	10	J	Q	K
Draw	0	0	0	0	1	−1	−1	−1	−1	−1	−1	−1	−1
Stand	−1	−1	−1	−1	−1	−1	−1	−1	−1	−1	−1	−1	−1

6. Stand

7. The probabilities of the states of nature are as follows:

A	4/48	6	3/48	J	4/48
2	4/48	7	4/48	Q	3/48
3	4/48	8	4/48	K	4/48
4	4/48	9	4/48		
5	4/48	10	2/48		

The expected value for draw is −1/2, and that for stand is −1.

8.

						Roll					
	2	3	4	5	6	7	8	9	10	11	12
2	10	2	2	2	2	2	2	2	2	2	2
3	−3	10	3	3	3	3	3	3	3	3	3
4	−4	−4	10	4	4	4	4	4	4	4	4
5	−5	−5	−5	10	5	5	5	5	5	5	5
6	−6	−6	−6	−6	10	6	6	6	6	6	6
7	−7	−7	−7	−7	−7	10	7	7	7	7	7
8	−8	−8	−8	−8	−8	−8	10	8	8	8	8
9	−9	−9	−9	−9	−9	−9	−9	10	9	9	9
10	−10	−10	−10	−10	−10	−10	−10	−10	10	10	10
11	−11	−11	−11	−11	−11	−11	−11	−11	−11	10	11
12	−12	−12	−12	−12	−12	−12	−12	−12	−12	−12	10

9. The expected payoff for each choice is as follows:

2	80/36	8	−38/36
3	116/36	9	−140/36
4	138/36	10	−240/36
5	140/36	11	−332/36
6	116/36	12	−410/36
7	60/36		

APPENDIX 1
GLOSSARY

alternative hypothesis the hypothesis that states, "The null hypothesis is false"

analysis of variance a method for testing the hypothesis that several different groups all have the same mean

ANOVA table a table that summarizes the results of an analysis of variance calculation

autocorrelation see **serial correlation**

average see **mean**

base year an arbitrary year relative to which a price index measures the average level of prices

Bayesian approach an approach to statistics where the researcher starts with a prior distribution and then uses results from observations to calculate an updated distribution

Bayes's rule a rule that tells how to calculate the conditional probability $Pr(B|A)$ provided that $Pr(A|B)$ and $Pr(A|B^c)$ are known

Bernoulli trial an experiment that has only two possible results: one called "success" and one called "failure"

bimodal (a distribution) having two modes

binomial distribution the discrete probability distribution that applies when an experiment is conducted n times with each trial having a probability p of success and each trial being independent of every other trial

cell one of the locations in a contingency table

central limit theorem a theorem that states: the average of a large number of independent, identically distributed random variables will have a normal distribution

central tendency a measure that indicates the typical medium value of a distribution; the mean and median are examples of measures of central tendency

Chebyshev's theorem a theorem that states: for any group of numbers, the fraction that will be within k standard deviations of the mean will be at least $1 - 1/k^2$; also spelled **Tchebysheff's theorem**

chi-square distribution a continuous probability distribution related to the normal distribution; used in the chi-square test

chi-square test a statistical method to test the hypothesis that two factors are independent

class limits the two boundaries of a class used to group data

class mark the midpoint of a class

classical approach to probability an approach to probability based on defining a probability space consisting of all possible outcomes of an experiment where it is assumed that each outcome is equally likely

cluster sampling a sampling method where the population is divided into clusters; some clusters are selected at random, and then some members of the chosen clusters are selected at random to make up the sample

coefficient of determination a value between 0 and 1 that indicates how well variations in the independent variable in a regression explain variations in the dependent variable (symbolized by r^2)

coefficient of variation the standard deviation divided by the mean; this value indicates how big the dispersion is compared to the mean

combinations the number of different ways of selecting j objects from a group of n objects when the order in which the objects are chosen does not matter

common logarithm a logarithm to the base 10

complement for an event, all outcomes that are not part of that event

conditional density function the density function for one random variable when it is given that another random variable has a specified value; it can be calculated from the joint density function for the two random variables

conditional probability the probability that a particular event will occur when it is given that another event has occurred

confidence interval an interval based on observations of a sample and so constructed that there is a specified probability that the interval contains the unknown true value of a parameter (for example, it is common to calculate confidence intervals that have a 95 percent chance of containing the true value)

confidence level the degree of confidence associated with a confidence interval; the probability that the interval contains the true value of the parameter

consistent estimator an estimator that tends to converge toward the true value as the sample size becomes larger

consumer price index (CPI) a measure of the average price level at a particular time based on the cost of purchasing a fixed market basket of consumer goods

contingency table a table that shows how many observations fall within each cell, where the cells represent all of the possible combinations of two factors; a contingency table is used in the chi-square test to determine whether two factors are independent

continuous random variable a random variable that can take on any real-number value within a certain range; it is characterized by a density function curve such that the area under the curve between two numbers represents the probability that the random variable will be between those two numbers (for contrast, see **discrete random variable**)

control group in a statistical test, the control group is not given the treatment, so a comparison can be made with the treatment group

convenience sampling a method of sampling where the items that are most conveniently available are selected as part of the sample; it is not appropriate to apply statistical analysis to samples selected in this manner

correction factor see **finite population correction factor**

correlation an indication of the degree of association between two quantities; its value is always between −1 and 1

covariance an indication of the degree of association between two quantities; it is related to the correlation but is not constrained to be between −1 and 1

critical region if the calculated value of the test statistic falls within the critical region, the null hypothesis is rejected (same as **rejection region**)

critical value the value (or values) at the boundary of the critical region

cumulative distribution function the function that gives the probability that a random variable will be less than or equal to a specific value

Current Population Survey a monthly survey of over 100,000 people conducted by the Census Bureau

cyclical component the component of a time series that moves up or down with the overall level of business activity in the economy

decision theory the study of making decisions designed to achieve some objective, often under conditions of uncertainty

decision tree a diagram that illustrates all possible consequences of different decisions in different states of nature

degrees of freedom the nature of a chi-square or a t-distribution is character-ized by its degrees of freedom; the F distribution is characterized by the degrees of freedom in the numerator and the degrees of freedom in the denominator

density function see **probability density function**

dependent variable the variable in a regression that is assumed to be caused by the independent variable

depreciation the loss in value of capital goods as they wear out

descriptive statistics the study of ways of summarizing data

discrete random variable a random variable for which it is possible to make a list of all possible values (for contrast, see **continuous random variable**)

disjoint events two events that cannot both happen

dispersion the degree to which a distribution is spread out (same as *spread*)

dummy variable an independent variable used in regression analysis that has the value 1 when a specified condition is met and otherwise has the value 0 (same as *indicator variable*)

Durbin-Watson statistic a statistic used in regression analysis to test for the presence of serial correlation

econometrics the branch of economics that uses statistical analysis to analyze and forecast the economy

error a random term included in regression and analysis of variance that rep-resents the effects of all factors other than those that have been specifi-cally included in the analysis

error sum of squares a quantity that indicates the degree of random error in analysis of variance or regression

estimate the value of an estimator in a particular circumstance

estimator a quantity based on observations of a sample whose value is taken as an indicator of the value of an unknown population parameter (for example, the sample average $\bar{x}$ is often used as an estimator of the unknown population mean μ)

expectation the average value that would appear if a random variable was observed many times; also called the *expected value* or *mean* and sym-bolized by μ

expected payoff the expected value of the payoff resulting from a decision

expected value see **expectation**

experimental group in a statistical test, the experimental group is given the treatment, so a comparison can be made with the control group

exponential smoothing a method for analyzing the trend in a time series

extrapolation a forecast that attempts to predict what will happen in a situation that is outside the range of previously observed data

F **distribution** a continuous random variable distribution related to the chi-square distribution; it is used in the analysis of variance procedure and in regression analysis

F **statistic** in analysis of variance, a statistic to test the null hypothesis that all the groups come from populations with the same mean; in regression analysis, a statistic to test the null hypothesis that there is no connection between the independent variables and the dependent variable

factorial for a particular whole number, the product of all the whole numbers from 1 up to that number

finite population correction factor when sampling without replacement, the formulas for the standard deviation of the sample mean and sample proportion need to be multiplied by $\sqrt{(N - n)/(N - 1)}$, where N is the population size and n is the sample size; this is not necessary if the population is much larger than the sample

fitted value for a given set of values of the independent variables, the value of the dependent variable that is predicted by the regression equation

frequency diagram a bar diagram that illustrates how many observations fall within each category

frequency polygon a diagram that illustrates a frequency distribution with the use of line segments instead of bars

frequency table a table showing how many observations fall within each category

Friedman F_r **test** a procedure to test the hypothesis that there is no difference between preferences when there are more than two possibilities

GDP deflator a measure of the average price level

goodness-of-fit test a statistical procedure to test the hypothesis that a particular probability distribution fits an observed set of data

grand mean the mean of all elements in an analysis of variance test

gross domestic product (GDP) a measure of the total value of all goods and services produced in the country

gross national product measure of national output related to gross domestic product; it includes production by inputs owned by U.S. citizens but not production from domestic inputs that are foreign owned

grouped data a way of arranging data where, instead of listing each individual value, a table is made that shows how many values fall within certain categories

heteroscedasticity a situation in regression analysis where the error terms do not all have the same variance

histogram a bar diagram that illustrates a frequency distribution; each bar is drawn so that its area is proportional to the number of items in the interval it represents

hypergeometric distribution the discrete probability distribution that applies when a group of items is sampled without replacement

hypothesis testing a statistical procedure that involves collecting evidence and then making a decision as to whether a particular hypothesis should be accepted or rejected

independent events two or more events that do not affect each other

independent random variables two random variables that do not affect each other; knowing the value of one of the random variables does not provide any information about the other variable

independent variable a variable in a regression that affects the dependent variable, but is assumed not to be affected by the other variables in the regression

index of leading indicators an index consisting of 12 different economic time series that tend to turn up or down before the whole economy shows the same trend

indicator variable see **dummy variable**

inferior good a good that people buy less of as their income increases

inflation rate the rate of change in the average price level

interquartile range the value of the third quartile minus the value of the first quartile; half of the items in a list fall within the interquartile range

intersection for two sets, the set that consists of all elements that are in both of these sets

interval estimate an estimate for a parameter that gives a range of likely estimates for the parameter, instead of just a single value (see also **confidence interval**)

irregular component the component of a time series that moves up or down with no apparent pattern

joint probability density function if $f_{x,y}(x,y)$ is the joint probability density function for two random variables X and Y, then $f_{x,y}(x,y) = \Pr[(X = x)$ and $(Y = y)]$

Kruskal-Wallis *H* test a generalization of the Wilcoxon rank sum test to the situation where there are more than two populations

law of large numbers a law stating that, if a random variable is observed many times, the average of those observations will tend toward the mean of that random variable

least-squares estimators the estimates for the coefficients found from regression analysis; these estimates are calculated because they minimize the square of the error between the actual values of the dependent variable and the values predicted by the regression equation

level of significance for a hypothesis-testing procedure, the probability of committing a Type I error

logarithm if $a^x = y$, then x is the logarithm to the base a of y

marginal probability function the probability function for one particular random variable that is calculated from a joint probability function

maximum likelihood estimator an estimator with the following property: if the true value of the unknown parameter has this value, then the probability of obtaining the sample that was actually observed is maximized

mean the value that is equal to the sum of a list of numbers divided by the number of numbers (same as *average*); the mean of a random variable is the average value that would appear if you observed the random variable many times (same as *expectation*); it is symbolized by the Greek letter μ (mu)

mean absolute deviation the average value of the absolute values of the distances from all numbers in a list to their mean

mean square a quantity, used in analysis of variance, that is equal to a sum of squares divided by its degrees of freedom

mean square error (MSE) a quantity used in regression to estimate the unknown value of the variance of the error term

mean square variance see **mean square**

median the value such that half of the numbers in a list are above it and half are below it

mode the value that occurs most frequently in a list of numbers

moving average the average value of the observations in a time series that are closest to one particular value

multicollinearity a problem that arises in regression analysis when two or more of the independent variables are closely correlated

multiple regression a statistical method for analyzing the relation between several independent variables and one dependent variable

multiplication principle a principle that states: if there are m possible outcomes of the first experiment and n possible outcomes of the second experiment, then there are mn possible combined outcomes of both experiments (if the two experiments are independent)

national income the sum of all income earned in a country; equal to the gross national product minus depreciation and indirect taxes

natural logarithm a logarithm to the base e, where $e = 2.71828\ldots$

negatively correlated (two quantities) related so that one tends to be large when the other tends to be small

net national product (NNP) a measure of the national economy that is equal to gross national product minus depreciation

nominal gross domestic product the gross domestic product measured in current dollars, not corrected for inflation (for contrast, see **real gross domestic product**)

nonparametric method a statistical method that does not make assumptions about the specific forms of distributions and therefore does not focus on estimating unknown parameter values

normal distribution the most important continuous random variable distribution; its density function is bell-shaped; many real populations are distributed according to the normal distribution

null hypothesis the hypothesis that is being tested in a hypothesis-testing situation; often the null hypothesis is of the form, "There is no relation between two quantities"

objective variable a variable that the researcher is trying to maximize or minimize in decision theory

ogive a graph showing cumulative distribution

one-tailed test a hypothesis test where the critical region consists of only one tail of a distribution; the null hypothesis is rejected only if the test statistic has an extreme value in one direction

open-ended class a class for grouping data with no upper class limit or no lower class limit

outcome one of the possible results of a probability experiment

outlier an observation that is significantly different from the other observations

p value in hypothesis testing, the probability of getting the observed test statistic, or one more extreme, if the null hypothesis is true. A smaller p value provides stronger evidence that the null hypothesis should be rejected

parameter a quantity (usually unknown) that characterizes a population (for example, the population mean and population standard deviation are parameters)

payoff table a table showing payoffs in different states of nature in decision theory

percentile the pth percentile of a list is the number such that p percent of the elements in the list are less than that number

perfectly correlated two quantities X and Y are perfectly correlated if there is a relation between them of the form $Y = aX + b$, where a and b are two constants; their correlation will be 1 if a is positive and -1 if a is negative

permutations the number of different ways of selecting j objects from a group of n objects when each distinct way of ordering the chosen objects counts separately

pie chart a graph where a circle represents the whole amount and wedge-shaped sectors indicate the fraction in each category

point estimate a single value used as an estimator for an unknown parameter (for contrast, see **interval estimate**)

Poisson distribution the discrete probability distribution that gives the frequency of occurrence of certain types of random events; it can be used as an approximation for the binomial distribution

population the set of all items of interest

population standard deviation the standard deviation calculated when the values of all items in the population are known (for contrast, see **sample standard deviation**)

population variance the variance calculated when the values of all items in the population are known (for contrast, see **sample variance**)

positively correlated two quantities are positively correlated if they are related so that, if one quantity is large, the other tends to be large; their correlation is greater than 0

predicted value a value of a dependent variable that is calculated from a regression equation and values of the independent variables

prediction interval an interval so constructed that there is a specified probability that a certain random variable will be within that interval

price index a measure of the price level

price level the average level of all prices in the country; it can be measured by the GNP deflator, consumer price index, or producer price index

probability the study of chance phenomena

probability density function for a discrete random variable, the probability density function at a specific value is the probability that the random variable will have that value; for a continuous random variable, the probability density function is represented by a curve such that the area under the curve between two numbers is the probability that the random variable will be between those two numbers

probability function for a discrete random variable, the probability function at a specific value is the probability that the random variable will have that value

probability of an event the number of outcomes that corresponds to that event divided by the total number of possible outcomes

probability space the set of all possible outcomes from a random experiment (same as *sample space*)

producer price index (PPI) a measure of the price level based on a fixed market basket of goods used by producers

quartile the first quartile of a list is the number such that one quarter of the numbers in the list are below it; the third quartile is the number such that three quarters of the numbers are below it; the second quartile is the same as the median

r^2 a measure of how well the independent variable in a simple linear regression can explain changes in the dependent variable; its value is between 0 (meaning poor fit) and 1 (meaning perfect fit)

R^2 a measure of how well a multiple regression equation is able to explain changes in the dependent variable

random sample a sample chosen by a method such that each possible sample had an equal chance of being selected; also, a collection of independent random variables all chosen from the same distribution

random variable a variable whose value depends on the outcome of a random experiment

range the largest value in a list minus the smallest value

ratio to moving average method a method for seasonally adjusting the values in a time series

raw data the initial data the researcher starts with before beginning analysis

real gross domestic product a measure of the GDP that corrects for inflation; it only increases when there is an increase in the goods and services produced in a nation

recession a time when there is a slowdown in business activity in the country

regression line a line calculated in regression analysis that is used to estimate the relation between two quantities (the independent variable and the dependent variable)

regression sum of squares a quantity that indicates the degree to which a regression equation can explain the variations in the dependent variable

rejection region the set of values of the test statistic for which the hypothesis will be rejected

relative frequency view of probability a view that regards the probability of an event as being the fraction of times the event would occur if an experiment was repeated many times

residual the difference between the actual value of the dependent variable and the value predicted by the regression equation

sample a group of items chosen from the population and used to estimate the properties of the population

sample space see **probability space**

sample standard deviation the standard deviation calculated from the values in a sample; it is used to estimate the value of the population standard deviation

sample variance the variance calculated from the values in a sample; it is used to estimate the value of the population variance

sampling distribution the probability distribution of a statistic, such as the sample average $\bar{x}$

sampling with replacement a method for choosing a sample where an item that has been selected is put back in the population and therefore has a chance of being selected again

sampling without replacement a method for choosing a sample where an item that has been selected is not put back in the population and therefore cannot be selected again

scatter diagram a diagram showing the relation between two quantities; one quantity is measured on the vertical axis, the other quantity is measured on the horizontal axis, and each observation is represented by a dot

seasonal adjustment a procedure for adjusting time series data to compensate for seasonal variation in order to make nonseasonal changes in the data more apparent

serial correlation a problem that arises in regression analysis involving time series data when successive values of the random error term are not independent (same as *autocorrelation*)

set a well-defined collection of objects

sign test a procedure to test the hypothesis that there is no difference between two quantities for which there are rankings instead of numerical values

simple linear regression a method for analyzing the relation between one independent variable and one dependent variable

skewed not symmetrical

slope a number that describes the orientation of a line; a horizontal line has zero slope and a vertical line has infinite slope; the slope can be found by calculating the vertical distance between any two points on the line and dividing by the horizontal distance between those two points

spread see **dispersion**

standard deviation the square root of the variance

standard error the estimated standard deviation for a sample statistic

standard error for coefficient in regression analysis, the estimated standard deviation of the estimated coefficient; a small value of the standard error means that the estimated coefficient is a more precise estimate of the true coefficient

standard normal distribution the normal distribution with mean 0 and variance 1

state of nature in decision theory, an unpredictable outcome

statistic a quantity calculated from the items in a sample, such as the sample average $\bar{x}$; a statistic is often used as an estimator of an unknown population parameter

statistical inference the process of using observations of a sample to estimate the properties of the population

statistics the study of ways to analyze data; it consists of *descriptive statistics* and *statistical inference*

stratified sampling a sampling method where the population is divided into strata that are as much alike as possible

subjective view of probability a view that regards the probability of an event as being an individual's estimate of the likelihood of occurrence of that event

subscript a small number or letter written next to and slightly below another character

subset set A is a subset of set B if all elements in A are also in B

sum of squares the sum of the squared deviations of the elements in a list about a specified quantity; several sum of squares statistics are used in analysis of variance and regression

summation notation a notation that uses the Greek capital letter sigma (Σ) to mean "add up the values"; for example, ΣX means "add up all values of X"

symmetrical a distribution is symmetrical about a particular line if the halves of the distribution on either side of that line are mirror images of each other; for example, a normal distribution is symmetrical about its mean

t **distribution** a continuous random variable distribution related to the normal and chi-square distributions; it is used for confidence interval calculations and hypothesis testing for small samples

t **statistic** a statistic used to test the null hypothesis that the true value of a coefficient in regression analysis is zero

tail the extreme upper or lower end of a distribution

test statistic a quantity calculated from observed quantities used to test a null hypothesis; the test statistic is constructed so that it will come from a known distribution if the null hypothesis is true; therefore the null hypothesis is rejected if it seems implausible that the observed value of the test statistic could have come from that distribution

time series data data that consist of several observations of a quantity at different points in time

total sum of squares the sum of the squares of the deviations of all numbers in a list from the mean; used in analysis of variance and regression

treatment group in a statistical test, the treatment group is given the treatment, so a comparison can be made with the control group

treatment sum of squares in analysis of variance, a quantity that indicates the degree to which differences in the observations can be explained by the fact that the observations come from different groups

trend component the component in a time series that increases or decreases smoothly with time

two-tailed test a hypothesis test where the critical region consists of both tails of the distribution, so that the null hypothesis is rejected if the test statistic value is either too large or too small

two-way analysis of variance a test procedure that can be applied to a table of numbers in order to test two hypotheses: (1) there is no significant difference between the rows; and (2) there is no significant difference between the columns

Type I error an error that occurs in hypothesis testing when the null hypothesis is rejected when it is really true

Type II error an error that occurs in hypothesis testing when the null hypothesis is accepted when it is really false

unbiased estimator an estimator whose expected value is equal to the true value of the parameter it is trying to estimate

union for set A and set B, the set consisting of all elements that are in A or B or both

variance a measure of dispersion for a random variable or a list of numbers; it is symbolized by σ^2, where σ is the Greek lower case letter sigma; the standard deviation is the square root of the variance

vertical intercept the point where a line crosses the vertical axis

Wilcoxon rank sum test a procedure to test the hypothesis that there is no difference between the means of populations

Wilcoxon signed rank test a procedure to test the hypothesis that there is no difference between the means of populations

zone of acceptance if the calculated value of the test statistic falls within the zone of acceptance, the null hypothesis is accepted (for contrast, see **critical region**)

APPENDIX 2
CALCULATIONS

STATISTICAL CALCULATIONS ON A CALCULATOR

• *INTRODUCTION*

Many calculators perform statistical computations for you. This chapter will discuss *Texas Instrument*'s TI-83 calculator for a couple of reasons. It is used by a lot of statistics students, and it is designed to perform a large amount of statistical work compared with most calculators.

Anytime that you are using a machine to perform statistical computations, you have at least two issues to deal with:

- Getting the data into the machine

- Choosing the right command

If you are trying to draw a graph, there is a third concern:

- Choosing what xs and ys to display

The following sections will deal with each of these concerns.

• *ENTERING DATA*

LISTS

Measurements like height or weight, which consist of a sequence of numbers, are stored as *lists* on the TI-83. You can type in a simple list on the keyboard by surrounding the numbers by set braces (in yellow above the parentheses keys) and separating the numbers by commas:

$$\{2, 3, 5, 7\}$$

Such a list has no name. In order to do anything interesting with lists, you need to store the list under a name. Then, when a command needs to know what list you want to use, you can type in the list's name.

There are six built-in lists named L1, L2, L3, L4, L5, and L6. Their names are on the keyboard in yellow above the keys 1, 2, 3, 4, 5, and 6. You can store a list under one of these (or any other) names by using the STORE key (above the ON key, written as STO = ¿). When you press the STORE key, you will only see a right arrow → on the screen. You can store the list above as L1:

$$\{2, 3, 5, 7\} \rightarrow L1$$

After you press ENTER, you will see the list again to confirm that it has been stored. If you now type L1, you can see the list whenever you need it.

The six built-in lists are great for quick calculations. However, if you think that you will need a list later on, you should give it a name that you can remember. A list name can be any combination of 1–5 letters. To type letters use the green ALPHA key (one letter at a time) or above it in yellow the A-LOCK key (which acts as if you are pressing the ALPHA key before each letter until you hit ALPHA again). For example, to store the same list as before under the name PRAC (for practice), type:

$$\{2, 3, 5, 7\} \rightarrow PRAC$$

If you need to get the name of a list or to see what lists are already named in your calculator, press the LIST key (in yellow above the third key in the third row). You can also find a lot of list operations in that menu that we won't go into here.

Using lists is how the TI-83 works with data. Since you will need to work with data a lot in statistics, the TI-83 has provided an easier way to work with data using the *Statistics Editor*.

STATISTICS EDITOR

The statistics editor is the easiest way to enter, revise, and review lists on the TI-83. Press STAT (third key, third row), and then choose option 1 (Edit) from the menu to enter the editor.

The editor displays a number of lists as columns, with the names of the lists at the top above the data. To create a list or review an existing list, use the arrow keys to highlight the top left name in the editor, and press INS (in yellow above the third key, second row) for insert. At the bottom of the screen you will be prompted for the name of the list. The flashing A lets you know that the ALPHA key has already been "pressed" for you. Type in the name of your list and press ENTER. (If you want to work with one of the built-in lists, type the appropriate key for it.) If it is a new list, use the down arrow key to get to the first blank in the list and start typing your numbers, hitting ENTER after each number. If you make a mistake, use the arrow keys to get back to the wrong number and retype it.

If you no longer want to work with a list in the editor, use the arrow keys to highlight its name, and then press the DEL (third key, second row) for delete. You aren't deleting the list itself, but rather, you are deleting it from the editor. You can still work with the list later.

SORTING LISTS

You can sort lists in ascending or descending order. If several lists are related, you should rearrange them simultaneously when sorting one of them. Otherwise, the lists will be out of synchronization.

For example, suppose that you have two lists, HT and WT, for the heights and weights of 10 people. The first person's height is the first number in HT and that person's weight is the first number in WT. If we sort HT without also paying attention to WT, then the first number in HT will probably belong to a different person, while the first number in WT will still be the weight of the first person. The lists will no longer be synchronized.

To sort a list in ascending order on the TI-83, press STAT and then choose **Sort A(** from the menu. Use the LIST menu to enter the name of the list that you want sorted, and then enter (separated by commas) the names of the lists that you want to rearrange with your first list. Finish with a right parenthesis, and then press ENTER. To sort a list in descending order, use **SortD(** instead.

In our example, you would sort the heights and weights by height by typing the following:

SortA(HT, WT)

TRANSFERRING LISTS BETWEEN CALCULATORS

Sometimes with a large list you may want to copy the list to another calculator, either to share it with a friend or colleague or just to have a back-up copy in case something happens to your first calculator. The TI-83 comes with a data cord that plugs into a jack at the bottom of the calculator. It can be used to copy lists and other things from one calculator to another.

To copy one or more lists:

1. Plug the cord into the jack at the bottom of both calculators. Make sure the pin is pushed in all the way.

2. Turn on both calculators. On both calculators press LINK, which is in yellow on the second button in the third row.

3. On the calculator that will be sending the data:
   (a) Choose 4: List.
   (b) Use the up and down arrow keys to get to your selection, then press ENTER to mark it. When you use the arrow keys, you should see a solid square by anything that you have selected. If you want to undo a selection, press the ENTER key a second time.
   (c) Use the right arrow key and go to TRANSMIT.

4. On the receiving calculator, press the right arrow key to go to RECEIVE.

5. When both calculators are ready, press ENTER on the receiving calculator and then press ENTER on the sending calculator. You will receive confir-

mation that the transmission is successful or an error message if there is a problem.

The order is important: receive, then send.

DELETING LISTS

If you use your calculator a lot, you may eventually start to run short of memory. Alternatively, you may like to clean house from time to time and want to remove lists that you'll never use again.

We've already seen how to delete a list from the editor. However, that doesn't actually erase the list, it just removes it from the editor. To delete a list (or anything else), go into MEM (in yellow above the + key) and choose the delete menu option. (The menu option will vary depending whether you have the TI-83 or the TI-83 Plus calculator. This is one of the few menu differences between these versions.)

• *STATISTICAL COMMANDS*

The statistical commands are listed under two sets of menus, found by pressing the STAT key. The first set, under CALC, involves calculations of statistics and regression models. The commands in this set place you in the "Home" screen, and you enter the list name(s) afterward separated by commas. The second set, under TEST, involves hypothesis tests and confidence intervals. The commands in this set place you in menus prompting you for the name of the list and other input.

For all of these commands, when you need to enter the name of a list use the keyboard for the built-in lists' names, and use the LIST menu for the named lists' names.

STATISTICS FOR A SINGLE VARIABLE

The command 1-Var Stats under the CALC menu is followed by the name of the list of data. It lists the following statistics:

- Mean

- Sum

- Sum of squares

- Sample standard deviation

- Population standard deviation

- Sample size

- Minimum

- First quartile

- Median

- Third quartile

- Maximum

REGRESSION

The TI-83 will find the following regression models:

- Median-median

- Linear

- Quadratic

- Cubic

- Quartic

- Logarithmic

- Exponential

- Power

- Logistic

- Sinusoidal

In each case, type **RegressionCommand XList, YList**. If you would like to store the regression formula for later use, type **RegressionCommand XList, YList, Y1** where Y1 is found by pressing VARS (fourth key, fourth row), Y-VARS, Function, Y1. The formula is then stored under the function name Y1 and can be used in graphing or evaluating at a given input.

HYPOTHESIS TESTS

The TI-83 will compute p values for the following hypothesis tests under the TEST menu:

- Z-Test: test on the population mean given a value for the population standard deviation

- T-Test: test on the population mean without a given value for the population standard deviation

- 2-SampZTest: test on two population means given the two population standard deviations

- 2-SampTTest: test on two population means without given values for the population standard deviations

- 1-PropZTest: test on one population proportion

- 2-PropZTest: test on two population proportions

- X^2-Test: goodness of fit test

- 2-SampFTest: test on two population standard deviations

- LinRegTTest: test on coefficients of linear regression model

- ANOVA: analysis of variance

Most of these tests are in a similar menu format. You are prompted as to whether you have data sets or summary statistics. If you have the data sets, you are prompted for their names; if not, you are prompted for the summary statistics. You are prompted for the constant value for the population parameter when working with one population as well as the form of the alternative hypothesis. When you are done entering information, highlight **Calculate** and press ENTER.

CONFIDENCE INTERVALS

The TI-83 will compute the following confidence intervals under the TEST menu:

- Z-Interval: confidence interval for the population mean given a value for the population standard deviation

- T-Interval: confidence interval for the population mean without a given value for the population standard deviation

- 2-SampZInt: confidence interval for the difference between two population means given the two population standard deviations

- 2-SampTInt: confidence interval for the difference between two population means without given values for the population standard deviations

- 1-PropZInt: confidence interval for one population proportion

- 2-PropZInt: confidence interval for the difference between two population proportions

Most of these confidence intervals are in a similar menu format. You are prompted as to whether you have data sets or summary statistics. If you have the data sets, you are prompted for their names; if not, you are prompted for the summary statistics. You are prompted for the confidence level. When you are done entering information, highlight **Calculate** and press ENTER.

• STATISTICAL GRAPHS

The statistical graphs on the TI-83 are all found under the menu STAT PLOT (in yellow above the first key, first row). You can draw up to three graphs simultaneously, although usually you would want to draw only one at a time.

The six types of graphs are:

- Scatterplot: plots data from two lists as points
- Trend line: same as scatterplot, with line segments connecting the points
- Histogram: bar chart
- Modified boxplot: display of quartiles and outliers
- Boxplot: display of quartiles
- Normal plot: display of list versus expected z score if data came from a normal distribution

For each of these types of graph, you will be prompted for the names of your lists. When you are ready to draw your graph, press ZOOM (third key, first row), and choose **ZoomStat**, which will automatically select the best window for your graph.

If you find in graphing that you have extra lines or curves appearing, check that

- you don't have any STAT PLOT items turned on that you don't want turned on and
- you don't have any curves under Y= being plotted that you don't want plotted

STATISTICAL CALCULATIONS USING A COMPUTER SOFTWARE PACKAGE

For most practical applications of statistics, it is best to use a computer software package such as SAS, Minitab, SPSS, etc. Why?

- A computer software package can handle much more in the way of arithmetic calculations than you can by hand or with a calculator.
- A computer software package can offer a much wider array of statistical calculations and types of data displays than a calculator can.
- It is possible to insert the results of your work directly into a word-processing document.
- It is easier to transmit your data and/or analysis to someone else, either by disk or via electronic mail.

• Computer displays can show more information in their screens at a given time than a calculator can, making data review and display much easier.

Statistical software packages are sold for a variety of operating systems (DOS, Macintosh, Windows, UNIX, VMS, etc.), but all follow the same sort of basic operations:

1. Entering data. Data can be entered at the keyboard (which can involve a substantial amount of work for large data sets) or loaded from an existing data file. Data can be entered or stored outside of the statistical software package in an ASCII file, but it is usually easier to enter the data from within the package itself. Typically the data will be displayed in a spreadsheet format; you may then use the arrow keys to move around to review or edit data.

2. Saving data. One of the basic principles in working with calculators and computers is that you should never have to type in the same set of numbers twice. If there is any chance that you will want to analyze your data set further at a later date, it would be a good idea to save your data. Software packages will always prompt you before you exit them to save your data first into a data file; even so, it is best to save your data as soon as you have entered it in case of a systems crash.

3. Transferring data and results to a word-processing document. Within the Windows and Macintosh operating systems, it is possible to save your data and/or results onto a clipboard and then insert them into your document. You can also dynamically link the document to your data file so that if you change your data file at a later date the document will automatically be updated.

4. Statistical calculations. Statistical software packages will perform for you every calculation described in this book. The functions will typically be grouped together into menus. For example, descriptive statistics such as the mean, variance, standard deviation, etc., will typically be contained in a menu item called "One-variable statistics," regression models in a menu item called "Regression," etc.

5. Graphs. Statistical software packages will create for you every display discussed in this book. The different kinds of graphs will typically be contained in a menu item called "Plot."

If you are working from a DOS, VMS, or UNIX operating system, you will start your program by typing a command at the command prompt. If you are working from a Windows or Macintosh environment, you will start your program by clicking with your mouse on the program's icon. Once the program is running, you should be able to get specific advice on any topic from the program's Help feature (usually listed as a menu item).

STATISTICAL FUNCTIONS IN THE MICROSOFT EXCEL SPREADSHEET

A third possible choice of tools for statistical calculations is a general purpose spreadsheet, such as Microsoft Excel. If you use a spreadsheet for other purposes anyway, then learning the spreadsheet commands would be a good way to do statistical calculations.

The following table lists some examples of the statistical functions included with newer versions of Microsoft Excel.

Description of Function	Example	Result
BINOMDIST(k, n, p, FALSE) calculates the probability that $X = k$, where X has a binomial distribution with parameters n and p.	= BINOMDIST(6,10,0.75,FALSE)	0.14600
BINOMDIST(k, n, p, TRUE) calculates the cumulative probability that X is less than or equal to k; in other words, it sums the probabilities from $X = 0$ up to $X = k$.	= BINOMDIST(6,10,0.75,TRUE)	0.22412
CHIDIST(a, df) gives the probability that a chi square random variable with df degrees of freedom will be greater than a.	= CHIDIST(11.07,5)	0.05001
CHINV(p, df) gives the value of a such that $Pr(\chi_{df}^2 > a) = p$, where χ_{df}^2 is a chi square random variable with df degrees of freedom. This function is the inverse of the previous one.	= CHINV(0.05,5)	11.07048
COMBIN(n, j) gives the number of combinations when j objects are selected from n objects.	= COMBIN(52,5)	2,598,960
FACT(n) gives $n!$ (n factorial).	= FACT(9)	362,880
FDIST(a, df_{num}, df_{den}) gives the probability that an F random variable with df_{num} and df_{den} degrees of freedom will be greater than a.	= FDIST(5.96,10,4)	0.05006
FINV(p, df_{num}, df_{den}) gives the value of a such that $Pr(F > a) = p$, where F is an F random variable with df_{num} and df_{den} degrees of freedom. This function is the inverse of the previous one.	= FINV(0.05,10,4)	5.96435

Description of Function	Example	Result
HYPGEOMDIST(*k, ns, M, N*) gives Pr(*X* = *k*), where *X* has a hypergeometric distribution with population size *N*, sample size *ns*, and *M* objects in the population of type *M*, and *k* objects in the sample of type *M*.	= HYPGEOMDIST(3,10,13,52)	0.27806
NORMDIST(*x, mu, sigma*, TRUE) gives the probability that a normal random variable (with mean *mu* and standard deviation *sigma*) will be less than *x*.	= NORMDIST(12,10,2,TRUE)	0.84134
NORMINV(*p, mu, sigma*) gives the value of *a* such that Pr(*X* < *a*) = *p* where *X* has a normal distribution. This function is the inverse of the previous one.	= NORMINV(0.841345,10,2)	12.00000
NORMSDIST(*a*) gives Pr(*Z* < *a*), where *Z* has a standard normal distribution.	= NORMSDIST(1.96)	0.97500
NORMSINV(*p*) gives the value of *a* such that Pr(*Z* < *a*) = *p*, where *Z* has a standard normal distribution. This function is the inverse of the previous one.	= NORMSINV(0.975)	1.95996
TDIST(*a, df*, 1) gives the one-tail probability for a *t* distribution: Pr(*T* > *a*), where *T* is a random variable with the *T* distribution with *df* degrees of freedom.	= TDIST(2.365,7,1)	0.02499
TDIST(*a, df*, 2) gives the two-tail probability for a *t* distribution: Pr(*T* > *a*) + Pr(*T* < −*a*), or 2Pr(*T* > *a*).	= TDIST(2.365,7,2)	0.04997
TINV(*p, df*) gives the value *a* such that Pr(*T* > *a*) = *p*, where *T* is a random variable with the *T* distribution with *df* degrees of freedom.	= TINV(0.05,7)	2.36462

Excel also provides several functions that calculate descriptive statistics for a range of data:

AVERAGE(*range*)	calculate average
STDEVP(*range*)	standard deviation of a population
STDEV(*range*)	standard deviation of a sample
MEDIAN(*range*)	calculate median
PERCENTRANK(*range, value*)	give the percentile rank of *value* within the list *range*

These functions can be used for simple regression and correlation:

SLOPE(*yrange, xrange*)	slope of simple regression line
INTERCEPT(*yrange, xrange*)	*y* intercept of simple regression line
RSQ(*yrange, xrange*)	r squared value of simple regression
CORREL(*yrange, xrange*)	correlation coefficient between two ranges

The Data Analysis toolpack will automatically perform regression, analysis of variance, correlation, and other statistical tasks. The HELP option provides information on how to enter the data.

APPENDIX 3
STATISTICAL
TABLES

STANDARD NORMAL (Z) TABLE

TABLE A3-2: TWO-TAILED STANDARD NORMAL (Z) TABLE: $p = \Pr(-a < Z < a)$

This table gives the probability p that a standard normal random variable Z (mean 0, standard deviation 1) will be between $-a$ and a.

a	p	a	p
0.100	0.0796	1.400	0.8384
0.200	0.1586	**1.439**	**0.8500**
0.300	0.2358	1.500	0.8664
0.400	0.3108	1.600	0.8904
0.500	0.3830	**1.645**	**0.9000**
0.600	0.4514	1.700	0.9108
0.700	0.5160	1.800	0.9282
0.800	0.5762	1.900	0.9426
0.900	0.6318	**1.960**	**0.9500**
1.000	0.6826	2.000	0.9544
1.100	0.7286	2.500	0.9876
1.200	0.7698	**2.576**	**0.9900**
1.282	**0.8000**	3.000	0.9974
1.300	0.8064	3.100	0.9980

The values in boldface are those commonly used for confidence intervals and hypothesis testing.

The table on the next two pages gives the probability p that a standard normal random variable Z will be less than the specified value a: $p = \Pr(Z < a)$. Also, it gives the area under the standard normal density function to the left of the specified value a.

Here is the connection between the two tables. If $p_2 = \Pr(-a < Z < a)$ (the value from the two-tailed table), and $p_1 = \Pr(Z < a)$ (the value from the one-tailed table), then $p_2 = 2p_1 - 1$.

TABLE A3–1: ONE-TAILED STANDARD NORMAL (Z) RANDOM VARIABLE TABLE: Pr(Z < a) = p

a	p	a	p	a	p	a	p	a	p	a	p
−2.99	.0014	−2.49	.0064	−1.99	.0233	−1.49	.0681	−0.99	.1611	−0.49	.3121
−2.98	.0014	−2.48	.0066	−1.98	.0239	−1.48	.0694	−0.98	.1635	−0.48	.3156
−2.97	.0015	−2.47	.0068	−1.97	.0244	−1.47	.0708	−0.97	.1660	−0.47	.3192
−2.96	.0015	−2.46	.0069	−1.96	.0250	−1.46	.0721	−0.96	.1685	−0.46	.3228
−2.95	.0016	−2.45	.0071	−1.95	.0256	−1.45	.0735	−0.95	.1711	−0.45	.3264
−2.94	.0016	−2.44	.0073	−1.94	.0262	−1.44	.0749	−0.94	.1736	−0.44	.3300
−2.93	.0017	−2.43	.0075	−1.93	.0268	−1.43	.0764	−0.93	.1762	−0.43	.3336
−2.92	.0018	−2.42	.0078	−1.92	.0274	−1.42	.0778	−0.92	.1788	−0.42	.3372
−2.91	.0018	−2.41	.0080	−1.91	.0281	−1.41	.0793	−0.91	.1814	−0.41	.3409
−2.90	.0019	−2.40	.0082	−1.90	.0287	−1.40	.0808	−0.90	.1841	−0.40	.3446
−2.89	.0019	−2.39	.0084	−1.89	.0294	−1.39	.0823	−0.89	.1867	−0.39	.3483
−2.88	.0020	−2.38	.0087	−1.88	.0301	−1.38	.0838	−0.88	.1894	−0.38	.3520
−2.87	.0021	−2.37	.0089	−1.87	.0307	−1.37	.0853	−0.87	.1922	−0.37	.3557
−2.86	.0021	−2.36	.0091	−1.86	.0314	−1.36	.0869	−0.86	.1949	−0.36	.3594
−2.85	.0022	−2.35	.0094	−1.85	.0322	−1.35	.0885	−0.85	.1977	−0.35	.3632
−2.84	.0023	−2.34	.0096	−1.84	.0329	−1.34	.0901	−0.84	.2005	−0.34	.3669
−2.83	.0023	−2.33	.0099	−1.83	.0336	−1.33	.0918	−0.83	.2033	−0.33	.3707
−2.82	.0024	−2.32	.0102	−1.82	.0344	−1.32	.0934	−0.82	.2061	−0.32	.3745
−2.81	.0025	−2.31	.0104	−1.81	.0351	−1.31	.0951	−0.81	.2090	−0.31	.3783
−2.80	.0026	−2.30	.0107	−1.80	.0359	−1.30	.0968	−0.80	.2119	−0.30	.3821
−2.79	.0026	−2.29	.0110	−1.79	.0367	−1.29	.0985	−0.79	.2148	−0.29	.3859
−2.78	.0027	−2.28	.0113	−1.78	.0375	−1.28	.1003	−0.78	.2177	−0.28	.3897
−2.77	.0028	−2.27	.0116	−1.77	.0384	−1.27	.1020	−0.77	.2206	−0.27	.3936
−2.76	.0029	−2.26	.0119	−1.76	.0392	−1.26	.1038	−0.76	.2236	−0.26	.3974
−2.75	.0030	−2.25	.0122	−1.75	.0401	−1.25	.1056	−0.75	.2266	−0.25	.4013
−2.74	.0031	−2.24	.0125	−1.74	.0409	−1.24	.1075	−0.74	.2296	−0.24	.4052
−2.73	.0032	−2.23	.0129	−1.73	.0418	−1.23	.1093	−0.73	.2327	−0.23	.4090
−2.72	.0033	−2.22	.0132	−1.72	.0427	−1.22	.1112	−0.72	.2358	−0.22	.4129
−2.71	.0034	−2.21	.0136	−1.71	.0436	−1.21	.1131	−0.71	.2389	−0.21	.4168
−2.70	.0035	−2.20	.0139	−1.70	.0446	−1.20	.1151	−0.70	.2420	−0.20	.4207
−2.69	.0036	−2.19	.0143	−1.69	.0455	−1.19	.1170	−0.69	.2451	−0.19	.4247
−2.68	.0037	−2.18	.0146	−1.68	.0465	−1.18	.1190	−0.68	.2483	−0.18	.4286
−2.67	.0038	−2.17	.0150	−1.67	.0475	−1.17	.1210	−0.67	.2514	−0.17	.4325
−2.66	.0039	−2.16	.0154	−1.66	.0485	−1.16	.1230	−0.66	.2546	−0.16	.4364
−2.65	.0040	−2.15	.0158	−1.65	.0495	−1.15	.1251	−0.65	.2578	−0.15	.4404
−2.64	.0041	−2.14	.0162	−1.64	.0505	−1.14	.1271	−0.64	.2611	−0.14	.4443
−2.63	.0043	−2.13	.0166	−1.63	.0516	−1.13	.1292	−0.63	.2643	−0.13	.4483
−2.62	.0044	−2.12	.0170	−1.62	.0526	−1.12	.1314	−0.62	.2676	−0.12	.4522
−2.61	.0045	−2.11	.0174	−1.61	.0537	−1.11	.1335	−0.61	.2709	−0.11	.4562
−2.60	.0047	−2.10	.0179	−1.60	.0548	−1.10	.1357	−0.60	.2743	−0.10	.4602
−2.59	.0048	−2.09	.0183	−1.59	.0559	−1.09	.1379	−0.59	.2776	−0.09	.4641
−2.58	.0049	−2.08	.0188	−1.58	.0570	−1.08	.1401	−0.58	.2810	−0.08	.4681
−2.57	.0051	−2.07	.0192	−1.57	.0582	−1.07	.1423	−0.57	.2843	−0.07	.4721
−2.56	.0052	−2.06	.0197	−1.56	.0594	−1.06	.1446	−0.56	.2877	−0.06	.4761
−2.55	.0054	−2.05	.0202	−1.55	.0605	−1.05	.1469	−0.55	.2912	−0.05	.4801
−2.54	.0055	−2.04	.0207	−1.54	.0618	−1.04	.1492	−0.54	.2946	−0.04	.4840
−2.53	.0057	−2.03	.0212	−1.53	.0630	−1.03	.1515	−0.53	.2981	−0.03	.4880
−2.52	.0059	−2.02	.0217	−1.52	.0642	−1.02	.1539	−0.52	.3015	−0.02	.4920
−2.51	.0060	−2.01	.0222	−1.51	.0655	−1.01	.1562	−0.51	.3050	−0.01	.4960
−2.50	.0062	−2.00	.0228	−1.50	.0668	−1.00	.1587	−0.50	.3085	0.00	.5000

TABLE A3–1: ONE-TAILED STANDARD NORMAL (Z) RANDOM VARIABLE TABLE: Pr(Z < a) = p

a	p	a	p	a	p	a	p	a	p	a	p
0.01	.5040	0.51	.6950	1.01	.8438	1.51	.9345	2.01	.9778	2.51	.9940
0.02	.5080	0.52	.6985	1.02	.8461	1.52	.9357	2.02	.9783	2.52	.9941
0.03	.5120	0.53	.7019	1.03	.8485	1.53	.9370	2.03	.9788	2.53	.9943
0.04	.5160	0.54	.7054	1.04	.8508	1.54	.9382	2.04	.9793	2.54	.9945
0.05	.5199	0.55	.7088	1.05	.8531	1.55	.9394	2.05	.9798	2.55	.9946
0.06	.5239	0.56	.7123	1.06	.8554	1.56	.9406	2.06	.9803	2.56	.9948
0.07	.5279	0.57	.7157	1.07	.8577	1.57	.9418	2.07	.9808	2.57	.9949
0.08	.5319	0.58	.7190	1.08	.8599	1.58	.9429	2.08	.9812	2.58	.9951
0.09	.5359	0.59	.7224	1.09	.8621	1.59	.9441	2.09	.9817	2.59	.9952
0.10	.5398	0.60	.7257	1.10	.8643	1.60	.9452	2.10	.9821	2.60	.9953
0.11	.5438	0.61	.7291	1.11	.8665	1.61	.9463	2.11	.9826	2.61	.9955
0.12	.5478	0.62	.7324	1.12	.8686	1.62	.9474	2.12	.9830	2.62	.9956
0.13	.5517	0.63	.7357	1.13	.8708	1.63	.9484	2.13	.9834	2.63	.9957
0.14	.5557	0.64	.7389	1.14	.8729	1.64	.9495	2.14	.9838	2.64	.9959
0.15	.5596	0.65	.7422	1.15	.8749	1.65	.9505	2.15	.9842	2.65	.9960
0.16	.5636	0.66	.7454	1.16	.8770	1.66	.9515	2.16	.9846	2.66	.9961
0.17	.5675	0.67	.7486	1.17	.8790	1.67	.9525	2.17	.9850	2.67	.9962
0.18	.5714	0.68	.7517	1.18	.8810	1.68	.9535	2.18	.9854	2.68	.9963
0.19	.5753	0.69	.7549	1.19	.8830	1.69	.9545	2.19	.9857	2.69	.9964
0.20	.5793	0.70	.7580	1.20	.8849	1.70	.9554	2.20	.9861	2.70	.9965
0.21	.5832	0.71	.7611	1.21	.8869	1.71	.9564	2.21	.9864	2.71	.9966
0.22	.5871	0.72	.7642	1.22	.8888	1.72	.9573	2.22	.9868	2.72	.9967
0.23	.5910	0.73	.7673	1.23	.8907	1.73	.9582	2.23	.9871	2.73	.9968
0.24	.5948	0.74	.7704	1.24	.8925	1.74	.9591	2.24	.9875	2.74	.9969
0.25	.5987	0.75	.7734	1.25	.8944	1.75	.9599	2.25	.9878	2.75	.9970
0.26	.6026	0.76	.7764	1.26	.8962	1.76	.9608	2.26	.9881	2.76	.9971
0.27	.6064	0.77	.7794	1.27	.8980	1.77	.9616	2.27	.9884	2.77	.9972
0.28	.6103	0.78	.7823	1.28	.8997	1.78	.9625	2.28	.9887	2.78	.9973
0.29	.6141	0.79	.7852	1.29	.9015	1.79	.9633	2.29	.9890	2.79	.9974
0.30	.6179	0.80	.7881	1.30	.9032	1.80	.9641	2.30	.9893	2.80	.9974
0.31	.6217	0.81	.7910	1.31	.9049	1.81	.9649	2.31	.9896	2.81	.9975
0.32	.6255	0.82	.7939	1.32	.9066	1.82	.9656	2.32	.9898	2.82	.9976
0.33	.6293	0.83	.7967	1.33	.9082	1.83	.9664	2.33	.9901	2.83	.9977
0.34	.6331	0.84	.7995	1.34	.9099	1.84	.9671	2.34	.9904	2.84	.9977
0.35	.6368	0.85	.8023	1.35	.9115	1.85	.9678	2.35	.9906	2.85	.9978
0.36	.6406	0.86	.8051	1.36	.9131	1.86	.9686	2.36	.9909	2.86	.9979
0.37	.6443	0.87	.8078	1.37	.9147	1.87	.9693	2.37	.9911	2.87	.9979
0.38	.6480	0.88	.8106	1.38	.9162	1.88	.9699	2.38	.9913	2.88	.9980
0.39	.6517	0.89	.8133	1.39	.9177	1.89	.9706	2.39	.9916	2.89	.9981
0.40	.6554	0.90	.8159	1.40	.9192	1.90	.9713	2.40	.9918	2.90	.9981
0.41	.6591	0.91	.8186	1.41	.9207	1.91	.9719	2.41	.9920	2.91	.9982
0.42	.6628	0.92	.8212	1.42	.9222	1.92	.9726	2.42	.9922	2.92	.9982
0.43	.6664	0.93	.8238	1.43	.9236	1.93	.9732	2.43	.9925	2.93	.9983
0.44	.6700	0.94	.8264	1.44	.9251	1.94	.9738	2.44	.9927	2.94	.9984
0.45	.6736	0.95	.8289	1.45	.9265	1.95	.9744	2.45	.9929	2.95	.9984
0.46	.6772	0.96	.8315	1.46	.9279	1.96	.9750	2.46	.9931	2.96	.9985
0.47	.6808	0.97	.8340	1.47	.9292	1.97	.9756	2.47	.9932	2.97	.9985
0.48	.6844	0.98	.8365	1.48	.9306	1.98	.9761	2.48	.9934	2.98	.9986
0.49	.6879	0.99	.8389	1.49	.9319	1.99	.9767	2.49	.9936	2.99	.9986
0.50	.6915	1.00	.8413	1.50	.9332	2.00	.9772	2.50	.9938	3.00	.9987

TABLE A3-3: CHI-SQUARE TABLE

The table gives the value of a such that $Pr(\chi_{DF}^2 < a) = p$, where χ_{DF}^2 is a chi-square random variable with DF degrees of freedom. For example, there is a probability of .95 that a chi-square random variable with 6 degrees of freedom will be less than 12.6.

DF	p = .005	.01	.025	.05	.25	.5	.75	.9	.95	.975	.99
1	.000	.000	.001	.004	.10	.45	1.32	2.71	3.84	5.02	6.64
2	.010	.020	.051	.10	.58	1.39	2.77	4.61	5.99	7.38	9.21
3	.072	.11	.22	.35	1.21	2.37	4.11	6.25	7.81	9.35	11.3
4	.21	.30	.48	.71	1.92	3.36	5.39	7.78	9.49	11.1	13.3
5	.41	.55	.83	1.15	2.67	4.35	6.63	9.24	11.1	12.8	15.1
6	.68	.87	1.24	1.64	3.45	5.35	7.84	10.6	12.6	14.4	16.8
7	.99	1.24	1.69	2.17	4.25	6.35	9.04	12.0	14.1	16.0	18.5
8	1.34	1.65	2.18	2.73	5.07	7.34	10.2	13.4	15.5	17.5	20.1
9	1.73	2.09	2.70	3.33	5.90	8.34	11.4	14.7	16.9	19.0	21.7
10	2.16	2.56	3.25	3.94	6.74	9.34	12.5	16.0	18.3	20.5	23.2
11	2.60	3.05	3.82	4.57	7.58	10.3	13.7	17.3	19.7	21.9	24.7
12	3.07	3.57	4.40	5.23	8.44	11.3	14.8	18.5	21.0	23.3	26.2
13	3.56	4.11	5.01	5.89	9.30	12.3	16.0	19.8	22.4	24.7	27.7
14	4.07	4.66	5.63	6.57	10.2	13.3	17.1	21.1	23.7	26.1	29.1
15	4.60	5.23	6.26	7.26	11.0	14.3	18.2	22.3	25.0	27.5	30.6
16	5.14	5.81	6.91	7.96	11.9	15.3	19.4	23.5	26.3	28.8	32.0
17	5.70	6.41	7.56	8.67	12.8	16.3	20.5	24.8	27.6	30.2	33.4
18	6.26	7.01	8.23	9.39	13.7	17.3	21.6	26.0	28.9	31.5	34.8
19	6.84	7.63	8.91	10.1	14.6	18.3	22.7	27.2	30.1	32.9	36.2
20	7.43	8.26	9.59	10.9	15.5	19.3	23.8	28.4	31.4	34.2	37.6
21	8.03	8.90	10.3	11.6	16.3	20.3	24.9	29.6	32.7	35.5	38.9
22	8.64	9.54	11.0	12.3	17.2	21.3	26.0	30.8	33.9	36.8	40.3
23	9.26	10.2	11.7	13.1	18.1	22.3	27.1	32.0	35.2	38.1	41.6
24	9.89	10.9	12.4	13.8	19.0	23.3	28.2	33.2	36.4	39.4	43.0
25	10.5	11.5	13.1	14.6	19.9	24.3	29.3	34.4	37.7	40.6	44.3
26	11.2	12.2	13.8	15.4	20.8	25.3	30.4	35.6	38.9	41.9	45.6
27	11.8	12.9	14.6	16.1	21.7	26.3	31.5	36.7	40.1	43.2	47.0
28	12.5	13.6	15.3	16.9	22.7	27.3	32.6	37.9	41.3	44.5	48.3
29	13.1	14.3	16.0	17.7	23.6	28.3	33.7	39.1	42.6	45.7	49.6
30	13.8	14.9	16.8	18.5	24.5	29.3	34.8	40.3	43.8	47.0	50.9
35	17.2	18.5	20.6	22.5	29.0	34.3	40.2	46.1	49.8	53.2	57.3
40	20.7	22.2	24.4	26.5	33.7	39.3	45.6	51.8	55.8	59.3	63.7
50	28.0	29.7	32.4	34.8	42.9	49.3	56.3	63.2	67.5	71.4	76.2
60	35.5	37.5	40.5	43.2	52.3	59.3	67.0	74.4	79.1	83.3	88.4
70	43.3	45.4	48.8	51.7	61.7	69.3	77.6	85.5	90.5	95.0	100.4
80	51.2	53.5	57.2	60.4	71.1	79.3	88.1	96.6	101.9	106.6	112.3
90	59.2	61.8	65.6	69.1	80.6	89.3	98.6	107.6	113.1	118.1	124.1
100	67.3	70.1	74.2	77.9	90.1	99.3	109.1	118.5	124.3	129.6	135.8

TABLE A3-4: ONE-TAILED *t* DISTRIBUTION TABLE

If T is a random variable with a t distribution with DF degrees of freedom, then the table gives the value of a such that $Pr(T < a) = p$. For example, there is a .975 probability that a T random variable with T degrees of freedom will be less than 2.365.

DF	p = .750	p = .900	p = .950	p = .975	p = .990	p = .995
1	1.000	3.078	6.314	12.706	31.821	63.657
2	0.816	1.886	2.920	4.303	6.965	9.925
3	0.765	1.638	2.353	3.182	4.541	5.841
4	0.741	1.533	2.132	2.776	3.747	4.604
5	0.727	1.476	2.015	2.571	3.365	4.032
6	0.718	1.440	1.943	2.447	3.143	3.707
7	0.711	1.415	1.895	2.365	2.998	3.499
8	0.706	1.397	1.860	2.306	2.896	3.355
9	0.703	1.383	1.833	2.262	2.821	3.250
10	0.700	1.372	1.812	2.228	2.764	3.169
11	0.697	1.363	1.796	2.201	2.718	3.106
12	0.695	1.356	1.782	2.179	2.681	3.055
13	0.694	1.350	1.771	2.160	2.650	3.012
14	0.692	1.345	1.761	2.145	2.624	2.977
15	0.691	1.341	1.753	2.131	2.602	2.947
16	0.690	1.337	1.746	2.120	2.583	2.921
17	0.689	1.333	1.740	2.110	2.567	2.898
18	0.688	1.330	1.734	2.101	2.552	2.878
19	0.688	1.328	1.729	2.093	2.539	2.861
20	0.687	1.325	1.725	2.086	2.528	2.845
21	0.686	1.323	1.721	2.080	2.518	2.831
22	0.686	1.321	1.717	2.074	2.508	2.819
23	0.685	1.319	1.714	2.069	2.500	2.807
24	0.685	1.318	1.711	2.064	2.492	2.797
25	0.684	1.316	1.708	2.060	2.485	2.787
26	0.684	1.315	1.706	2.056	2.479	2.779
27	0.684	1.314	1.703	2.052	2.473	2.771
28	0.683	1.313	1.701	2.048	2.467	2.763
29	0.683	1.311	1.699	2.045	2.462	2.756
30	0.683	1.310	1.697	2.042	2.457	2.750
35	0.682	1.306	1.690	2.030	2.438	2.724
40	0.681	1.303	1.684	2.021	2.423	2.704
45	0.680	1.301	1.679	2.014	2.412	2.690
50	0.679	1.299	1.676	2.009	2.403	2.678
55	0.679	1.297	1.673	2.004	2.396	2.668
60	0.679	1.296	1.671	2.000	2.390	2.660
80	0.678	1.292	1.664	1.990	2.374	2.639
100	0.677	1.290	1.660	1.984	2.364	2.626
120	0.677	1.289	1.658	1.980	2.358	2.617

TABLE A3-5: TWO-TAILED *t* DISTRIBUTION TABLE

If *T* is a random variable with a *t* distribution with *DF* degrees of freedom, then the table gives the value of *a* such that $\Pr(-a < T < a) = p$. For example, there is a 95 percent probability that a *T* random variable with 7 degrees of freedom will be between −2.365 and 2.365.

DF	p = .900	p = .950	p = .99
1	6.314	12.706	63.657
2	2.920	4.303	9.925
3	2.353	3.182	5.841
4	2.132	2.776	4.604
5	2.015	2.571	4.032
6	1.943	2.447	3.707
7	1.895	2.365	3.499
8	1.860	2.306	3.355
9	1.833	2.262	3.250
10	1.812	2.228	3.169
11	1.796	2.201	3.106
12	1.782	2.179	3.055
13	1.771	2.160	3.012
14	1.761	2.145	2.977
15	1.753	2.131	2.947
16	1.746	2.120	2.921
17	1.740	2.110	2.898
18	1.734	2.101	2.878
19	1.729	2.093	2.861
20	1.725	2.086	2.845
21	1.721	2.080	2.831
22	1.717	2.074	2.819
23	1.714	2.069	2.807
24	1.711	2.064	2.797
25	1.708	2.060	2.787
26	1.706	2.056	2.779
27	1.703	2.052	2.771
28	1.701	2.048	2.763
29	1.699	2.045	2.756
30	1.697	2.042	2.750
35	1.690	2.030	2.724
40	1.684	2.021	2.704
45	1.679	2.014	2.690
50	1.676	2.009	2.678
55	1.673	2.004	2.668
60	1.671	2.000	2.660
80	1.664	1.990	2.639
100	1.660	1.984	2.626
120	1.658	1.980	2.617

TABLE A3-6: *F* DISTRIBUTION TABLE

In each of the three tables below, the numerator degrees of freedom are read along the top, and the denominator degrees of freedom are read along the left side. The table gives the value of *a* such that $\Pr(F < a) = p$, where F is a random variable with an F distribution with DF_{num} numerator degrees of freedom and DF_{den} denominator degrees of freedom. Each table has a different value of p; first .99; then .95; then .90. These are values commonly used for hypothesis testing. Another way to describe the table is to give the value of $1 - p$, which is the right tail area (that is, the area to the right of the given value of a). For example, there is a .99 probability that an F random variable with 5 numerator degrees of freedom and 9 denominator degrees of freedom will be less than 6.06.

$\Pr(F < a) = .99$; right tail area = .01:

DF_{den}	$DF_{num} = 2$	3	4	5	10	15	20	30	60	120
2	99.00	99.16	99.25	99.30	99.40	99.43	99.45	99.47	99.48	99.49
3	30.82	29.46	28.71	28.24	27.23	26.87	26.69	26.50	26.32	26.22
4	18.00	16.69	15.98	15.52	14.55	14.20	14.02	13.84	13.65	13.56
5	13.27	12.06	11.39	10.97	10.05	9.72	9.55	9.38	9.20	9.11
6	10.92	9.78	9.15	8.75	7.87	7.56	7.40	7.23	7.06	6.97
7	9.55	8.45	7.85	7.46	6.62	6.31	6.16	5.99	5.82	5.74
8	8.65	7.59	7.01	6.63	5.81	5.52	5.36	5.20	5.03	4.95
9	8.02	6.99	6.42	6.06	5.26	4.96	4.81	4.65	4.48	4.40
10	7.56	6.55	5.99	5.64	4.85	4.56	4.41	4.25	4.08	4.00
15	6.36	5.42	4.89	4.56	3.80	3.52	3.37	3.21	3.05	2.96
20	5.85	4.94	4.43	4.10	3.37	3.09	2.94	2.78	2.61	2.52
30	5.39	4.51	4.02	3.70	2.98	2.70	2.55	2.39	2.21	2.11
60	4.98	4.13	3.65	3.34	2.63	2.35	2.20	2.03	1.84	1.73
120	4.79	3.95	3.48	3.17	2.47	2.19	2.03	1.86	1.66	1.53

$\Pr(F < a) = .95$; right tail area = .05:

DF_{den}	$DF_{num} = 2$	3	4	5	10	15	20	30	60	120
2	19.00	19.16	19.25	19.30	19.40	19.43	19.45	19.46	19.48	19.49
3	9.55	9.28	9.12	9.01	8.79	8.70	8.66	8.62	8.57	8.55
4	6.94	6.59	6.39	6.26	5.96	5.86	5.80	5.75	5.69	5.66
5	5.79	5.41	5.19	5.05	4.74	4.62	4.56	4.50	4.43	4.40
6	5.14	4.76	4.53	4.39	4.06	3.94	3.87	3.81	3.74	3.70
7	4.74	4.35	4.12	3.97	3.64	3.51	3.44	3.38	3.30	3.27
8	4.46	4.07	3.84	3.69	3.35	3.22	3.15	3.08	3.01	2.97
9	4.26	3.86	3.63	3.48	3.14	3.01	2.94	2.86	2.79	2.75
10	4.10	3.71	3.48	3.33	2.98	2.85	2.77	2.70	2.62	2.58
15	3.68	3.29	3.06	2.90	2.54	2.40	2.33	2.25	2.16	2.11
20	3.49	3.10	2.87	2.71	2.35	2.20	2.12	2.04	1.95	1.90
30	3.32	2.92	2.69	2.53	2.16	2.01	1.93	1.84	1.74	1.68
60	3.15	2.76	2.53	2.37	1.99	1.84	1.75	1.65	1.53	1.47
120	3.07	2.68	2.45	2.29	1.91	1.75	1.66	1.55	1.43	1.35

$$\Pr(F < a) = .90; \text{right tail area} = .10:$$

DF_{den}	$DF_{num} = 2$	3	4	5	10	15	20	30	60	120
2	9.00	9.16	9.24	9.29	9.39	9.42	9.44	9.46	9.47	9.48
3	5.46	5.39	5.34	5.31	5.23	5.20	5.18	5.17	5.15	5.14
4	4.32	4.19	4.11	4.05	3.92	3.87	3.84	3.82	3.79	3.78
5	3.78	3.62	3.52	3.45	3.30	3.24	3.21	3.17	3.14	3.12
6	3.46	3.29	3.18	3.11	2.94	2.87	2.84	2.80	2.76	2.74
7	3.26	3.07	2.96	2.88	2.70	2.63	2.59	2.56	2.51	2.49
8	3.11	2.92	2.81	2.73	2.54	2.46	2.42	2.38	2.34	2.32
9	3.01	2.81	2.69	2.61	2.42	2.34	2.30	2.25	2.21	2.18
10	2.92	2.73	2.61	2.52	2.32	2.24	2.20	2.16	2.11	2.08
15	2.70	2.49	2.36	2.27	2.06	1.97	1.92	1.87	1.82	1.79
20	2.59	2.38	2.25	2.16	1.94	1.84	1.79	1.74	1.68	1.64
30	2.49	2.28	2.14	2.05	1.82	1.72	1.67	1.61	1.54	1.50
60	2.39	2.18	2.04	1.95	1.71	1.60	1.54	1.48	1.40	1.35
120	2.35	2.13	1.99	1.90	1.65	1.55	1.48	1.41	1.32	1.26

INDEX